"In this book, Merton presents his finest and clearest statements on the monastic life . . . His concern was for the fullest and most complete contemplative life and, though his other writings discussed the results of that life, it is in the 21 essays of this book that we are asked to consider directly the contemplative life itself . . .

Six of the most interesting essays in this collection present a militant case for eremitism . . . The popular conception of a hermit is that he is one who withdraws from people because he hates them. Merton spoke the truth of the matter when he wrote, with characteristic simplicity, that 'some of us *have to be* alone to be ourselves.'

At a time in American society when new forms of living are being attempted by a significant number of youth, this collection of essays is especially important, even for those who find formal religion repugnant . . . [Merton] did not believe that the cenobitic life was the only way. It was merely his, and it afforded him certain answers to the personal and social problems that each of us must address."

—*New York Times Book Review*

"If there are those who judge that the monastic and eremitic life is either a quaint ecclesiastical trapping like the maniple that went out of style a few years ago, or a bucolic retreat where a group of men or women go because they cannot do anything else but pray and hoe a row or two of vegetables, then they have missed the whole point of the contemplative life of the monk and of contemplation in their own lives. According to the late Father Merton, 'what the monastic life should provide is a special awareness and perspective, an authentic understanding of God's presence in the world and His intention for man.' This theme Merton richly nuances in 21 essays that have to do with monastic renewal, the case for solitary hermits and the contemplative life."

—*America*

"[Merton's] whole book is a plea for the renewal of 'the primitive simplicity and authenticity of the monastic life' which, by the establishment of 'a certain distance from society' . . . will permit a fruitful 'contemplation in a world of action.' Merton describes in movingly serene prose his own way of living in his latter years."

—*Publishers Weekly*

Other works by Thomas Merton
available in Image Books

CONJECTURES OF A GUILTY BYSTANDER

CONTEMPLATIVE PRAYER

LIFE AND HOLINESS

NO MAN IS AN ISLAND

THE SECULAR JOURNAL OF THOMAS MERTON

THE SEVEN STOREY MOUNTAIN

THOUGHTS IN SOLITUDE

CONTEMPLATION IN A WORLD OF ACTION

Thomas Merton

INTRODUCTION BY JEAN LECLERCQ O.S.B.

IMAGE BOOKS

Garden City, New York
A Division of Doubleday & Company, Inc.

1973

Image Books edition 1973
by special arrangement with Doubleday & Company, Inc.
Image Books edition published February, 1973

CONTENTS

INTRODUCTION

I. *"Unless a grain of wheat falls into the ground and dies . . ."*

What was true of Christ is also true of his disciples: something in us, something of ourselves, must die for the fruit to be born; and the greater the degree of death, the greater will be the rebirth and the fruit. When Doubleday asked me to write this Foreword, I started rereading the letters that I had had from Thomas Merton. From the very first one of those I had kept, dated 1950, he expressed his hope of seeing formed in his country's monasteries men capable of "cultivating in their souls the grain that is the word of God" and of bearing fruit in the field of spiritual theology. He himself never ceased to work toward this goal. He never really saw the result of his efforts; but, for example, under the title of *Cistercian Publications,* a project is taking shape, with the general plan of which he was at least acquainted, and of which the first volume is a posthumously published book of his own.

I am writing this as I am about to leave for the first convention, in Korea, of the Union of Asiatic Monasteries. When Merton was taken from us, in December 1968, at the beginning of the Meeting of the Monks of Asia, at Bangkok, we all made a promise to God, in the presence of his body and in communion with his spirit, to carry on the work he loved and to which he had dedicated his efforts earlier than any one of us—the creation of an Asiatic Christian monasticism, beginning in the country where he died. He only saw the start of our work. Today, a small group of Christian monks who have chosen to become a part of the cultural and religious fabric of Asia has come into being in Thailand. And within a few days, representatives of monasticism from five Asian countries will remember Merton and his presence among them and try to find ways of becoming at the same time more truly Christian, more completely monks, more wholly Asiatic.

Throughout his life as a Trappist, Merton tried to overcome what he called, in one of his letters, an excess of "rigidity" in his own Order's structure. He wanted a spiritual and institutional renewal which he knew would meet with some resistance, and in his last days one felt that he was almost hoping against hope. But only a few months after his death, one of his students, and the man who succeeded him as Novice Master at Gethsemani, was entrusted with an important office which had to do with the renewal of the entire Trappist Order.

For fifteen years, he wrote and taught and worked in every way that he could to try to insure that monks in the communal life, when they reached maturity, would bear fruit in the solitary life. He was stunned by the lack of comprehension of those who thought that "the hermit's life was inhuman." By patience and obedience, yet always faithful to what he clearly recognized as a call from God, he won approval to live as a hermit himself, and it was easy to see that he became not only more a monk, but also more human: closer to men, to all men, more universal. Before he died, he saw his former Abbot become a hermit and his Community elect as successor a novice whom Merton himself had trained and who was living, as he did, in a hermitage not far from the monastery. And now, from the North to the South Pacific, from Oregon to Santiago de Chile, and elsewhere throughout the world, I have encountered Trappists who are living as hermits to everyone's satisfaction.

One could go on citing areas where Merton's fruitfulness was equal to his sacrifice. These few examples suffice to show that his work was linked to his experience: he wrote with his entire being, he lived and died for what he was teaching, he suffered for the truth of his message. The true value of this book can be grasped only if it is read in the context of how very much of a monk he was.

II. *The Mission*

There were in him, not two men—for few personalities have been as well-integrated as his—but two spheres of activity: that of the writer—what he called with self-deprecating irony, "being an author"—and that of the close friend. He excelled in making the reader feel that he was close to him, that he even identified with him. That was the whole secret of his appeal. I remember, one day in England, asking a young man who had become a Christian through reading *The Seven Storey Mountain* why this book moved him so much. "I felt," he answered, "that this story was my story: I followed Thomas Merton's path and I reached the end of it, just as he did." When one knew Merton personally, one realized that his friendship was far richer and deeper than would have appeared even from the warmth of his writing.

When his spiritual journey is traced in the light of all the texts and all the memories he left behind, it will be seen, I think, that the first years of his monastic life were used for an intense scrutiny of history. Not that he engaged in what he himself called, in the 1950 letter to which I have already referred, a "mass of futile research," but he read, studied, tried to understand the greatest possible number of witnesses to the spiritual life in which he himself was being formed, and which he believed himself called upon to teach. He knew he had a mission: he would speak of "the job Providence has given to me." He had a tremendous capacity for enjoying every sign of beauty, every spark of truth, but it was by no means for his own pleasure that he read the early writers: he believed he could understand tradition only through immersing himself in the knowledge of the past. His study of history was his preparation for the present.

Even before I met him at Gethsemani, I had been watching his development through his letters. I shared, at a distance, in his successive enthusiasms—which both stimulated and amused his fellow monks—for the Desert Fathers, the Greek Fathers and their vocabulary, for Clement, Origen, the

Alexandrians, for Diadochus of Photike, for Cassian, and in the Middle Ages for Grimlaic, Aelred, Adam de Perseigne, for St. Bernard in particular and then for Blessed Paul Giustiniani. He asked incessant questions about them. His intuition enabled him to go straight to the essence of a passage and to make it his own.

Yet, at the same time, he was acutely aware of everything which was gestating or was already happening within the Church: the first foundations of "simple monasteries" in France, following World War II; the changing pattern of several monastic Orders; the expansion of monasticism. When I began my first trips to Morocco, and then into Black Africa and later to Asia, he would always ask, not about details, but about basic problems, the direction in which things were moving, the hopes and the aims. He never refused to write a note or send a book to some unknown monk who owed his vocation to Merton's writing; to someone poor or sick whom I had met and who was too shy to write to him. Then came the Vatican Council and his close interest in the successive schemas of the Decree of the Renewal of Religious Life and particularly in how it was going to treat of monks.

The problem of eremitism arose very early in his correspondence. For him it was not just a topic for academic discussion: it was a matter of life and death. But the quality of his scholarship is clearly evident in the fact that as he pursued his vocation he never bypassed historical or theological points: he was rooted in the Church and in its tradition. Someday we shall learn of the struggles which arose from his longing for the life of solitude, until finally he was given the solution which brought him peace. When one realizes that he had also to contend with critics who would have preferred a less strident message, one can fully grasp the fact that his writing was supported and nourished by personal and often painful experience.

Only two years before his death, in a letter dated November 1966, in which he thanked me for having publicly defended him against those whom he described as "these nice 'defenders of the faith'", he described himself as someone "whom most people don't know what to make of." He added two things which sum up the two sides of his vocation: "That which is the basis of my solitude . . ." and "that which helps me evaluate my own life and my position in the Church."

Isolation, misunderstanding, but always the conviction of a mission, a sense of totality: always the two aspects of the same paradox. The position of a servant who is not above the Master: "If the grain of wheat does not die, it will bear no fruit."

III. *The Message*

If Merton was convinced that he had a mission it was because he knew that he had a message. A message is not necessarily a scholarly lecture—and when Merton spoke from a platform he was not at his best. He was not dealing, after all, with abstract knowledge, timeless science, a course which could be given again and again, unchanged, each year. According to its etymology, which is the same as that of mission, a message is always composed of truths sent (*missus*) to a person, a group, a period in time, to satisfy an expectation and sometimes to answer a call for help. Those who receive it may not even have understood their need, but even before they recognize it and are able to express it in words, they have been looking for that message and hoping that someone will come to help them and that God will send them a messenger. A message is, therefore, something prophetic, mobile, running, even flying—St. Bernard used the word *praevolare*—to fulfill man's hopes. They take it for granted that its author, or messenger, has had a glimpse of the solution of their problem; prophecy implies the gift of anticipation. But each time the pace quickens, each time that anyone sees farther than the "man of the actual moment," as Kierkegaard put it, there is bound to be opposition. A message is something for which one must suffer and occasionally die. Certainly a message cannot remain a personal possession: definitely it must be "delivered."

As I reread Merton's letters, remembering his other works,

his ideas about the message recur to me. He expressed his thoughts on so many subjects, from the arts to politics, and touched all aspects of religious life. Yet, at the heart of everything he said was his vocation, his monastic experience. He saw everything through a monk's eyes. This was both his limitation and his strength: a limitation because, after all, monastic life is not the totality of the Church or of society; other points of view are also valid. A strength, because he was a man of single purpose, a lone warrior. He persevered until the final moment, and now the message has been delivered, has been decoded and has begun to bear fruit.

What originally made Merton's message contemporary, and still keeps it so, is what might be called its dynamism, in the original meaning of the word, which conveys a force in motion. He was not concerned with a "definitive work," a scholarly tome, needing no further commentary, but with a number of "essays," trials, thrusts, breakthroughs moving beyond the fragile present, which others are now trying to consolidate in order to preserve the message and increase its life.

Thomas Merton was the man Christianity needed in a time of transition which began, not with Vatican II, but with World War II. Earlier than others, he had seen, he had known without a doubt that—in monasticism as well as in everything else—many things would change. One might even say everything—except the essential, except for Him who is not a thing, and the primordial encounter made with Him in love. Merton understood that it was necessary to reinforce the foundations if the whole structure were not to collapse. All the details, the outward observances, ideas even, all these "things," could change; but the union of man with God in Jesus Christ, through his Church, for the salvation of the world would continue to be a living reality. Faith need not be shaken, hope need not be disappointed, love need not be lessened.

It is the dual orientation which one sees throughout his monastic work and it is that which gives it its unity. On the one hand there is the protest against the exaggerated worth attributed to the historic observances of monasticism, its so-called traditional practices and ideas which in many cases go back no further than the nineteenth century, or at the very most to the seventeenth; and, on the other hand, there is an increased emphasis on spiritual experience which is reached in prayer and love: "union with God" is not the whole of the mystery, because the experience is at the same time communion with men. Solitude in which there is no other activity at all becomes, for Merton, the symbol of this absolute, ultimate and inexhaustible encounter with God and with humanity. More and more in his writing, the idea, too easily labeled ambiguous because of its appeal to "feelings," of "intimacy with God," gives way to the idea of objective, effective union with the Word manifested in and by Jesus Christ, far beyond all sensation, in the humble recognition of one's self as a sinner, in the mysterious allegiance to Him who identified Himself with our condition, in order to transform it. Nothing occurs, nothing happens, and yet everything is given, received, shared, given back by God to man in many ways, through the written word, through conversation, through the example of a smile, of joy, and the message becomes more and more specific, simple in its form, more and more direct and perhaps even shocking, but always more apt to leap over the barricades, to push back the frontiers.

A message presupposes a language which changes as the message evolves. From the serious, almost pedantic, tone of *The Ascent to Truth* to the all but goliardic irony of the notebooks of art and poetry, *Monk's Pond,* which Merton sent his friends in the late sixties, what progress there had been! In the crucible of patience and contradiction, all had been purified, simplified and calmed; yet everything is more vigorous and the vehemence has sometimes almost a note of violence. Some people even feared that he might go too far in his championship of freedom, which might explain how it was possible for someone to make the completely incredible remark I heard about his death: "It was really the Trappists who liquidated him . . ." But his abbot, his brother monks, his friends all are convinced that God called him back, and that in him patience and impatience are reconciled, thanks to a power which gives a peace far beyond our frail security.

IV. *Pushing Back the Frontiers*

I have not written thus far without emotion, in this Soviet jet flying swiftly over Siberia, carrying me to Asia. Except for the Table of Contents for this volume, which Merton used always to send to his friends before publication so that he could get their criticism and suggestions, I took along on this journey only two mimeographed texts of his: the prefaces he wrote for the Japanese editions of *The Seven Storey Mountain* and *Seeds of Contemplation*. Flying over this Marxist world which interested him so much—he was to draw parallels between it and monasticism in his last speech, on the very day of his death—and going to Japan where so many friends had waited for him, I cannot help thinking about the image he had of himself during these last years, about the way in which he saw his own development.

In his letters, his writings, the conferences he gave at Gethsemani on The Christian and the World, the talks he gave in the United States and in Asia on his last trip, he seemed to be more and more preoccupied with the relationship which the Church and Christians, monasticism and monks could and should have with the world. He meditated deeply on the major problems of contemporary culture: Marxism and Neo-Marxism, mass media and communication between men, technology and urbanization. He read and evaluated recent and contemporary writers such as Faulkner, Camus, Koestler, Garaudy, Hromodka. He was interested in the new sociology, saw its impact on the monasticism of the present-day society, in the encounter between East and West at every level. But his point of view remained essentially religious: he did not consider that any area could be indifferent or foreign to the affinity which exists between God and man.

In his later monastic writing, he often returned to Buddhism. In an essay in 1967 on *Marcel and Buddha* he chose to stress the idea that the emphasis on presence to the world was common to Buddhist teaching as well as to Marcel's. He took exception to the purely negative concept—all too popular in the West—of "nirvana," just as he spoke out against a Christian contemplation which was an escape or a vacuum. All must end in vitality, joy, love—and that is communion. At the same time, in the last talks he gave in India and Ceylon, he was careful always to stress and appreciate what was common to Christian and Far Eastern monasticism: this common factor, above and beyond doctrine and practices, he saw as an "experience" that was both a deeper enrichment and a transcendence. It is in the very center of himself where man encounters God that Merton saw the possibility of a religious communion between the disciples of Christ and the followers of other schools of spiritual thought. In his writings on the spiritual tradition of the Far East, especially on Zen Buddhism, Japanese and other scholars have a right to criticize him for excessive optimism. But for a Christian of the West to adopt this confident attitude was, really, in Merton's case, a manifestation of charity. For there was growing in him, more and more, a search for the essential which is love.

The final stage of his own growth was already apparent in what he revealed of himself to his Japanese readers, some of whom he imagined would not have been formed in Christian tradition. "Twenty years ago," he says, in the new preface to The Seven Storey Mountain, "I left the world. But since that time, I have learned—I believe—to look upon the world with more compassion . . ." He is very definite in saying that his separation from the world did not separate him from men: he found himself identifying more and more with all men. In the beautiful profession of faith in which he affirms his loyalty to what he was, to what he did and to what he wrote in his youth, the key words of his vocabulary—liberation, the beyond, All—could have been expressed by the religious of the Far East, but for Merton, in Christian terminology, those words mean "to live in Christ," and "in his Spirit." In order to be "in the All" he had to become, not nothing, not a zero, but "nothing," "no thing"; to become a person completely in communion with all others in Christ, and this state is not achieved without sacrifice.

The first thing he had to sacrifice was his reputation: Merton used to smile at the legends that were always going around, all of which tended to discredit him. He did not refute them, he did not complain, yet one felt that the seed had already died in him: soon it would bear fruit. He wanted to make his whole existence an affirmation of peace, of non-violence, a silent protest against any form of tyranny, against every compromise of Christianity with the secular world and, at the same time, to encourage everything good, beautiful, pure, free in the world and in man. And in doing so, he firmly intended to carry on the protest of the fourth-century monks against the temptation to dominate, to which even for men of faith, power—even Christian power—inevitably leads.

It is always the monk in Merton that has the last word. In 1965, in the Japanese preface of *Seeds of Contemplation,* he faces, in the very first lines, the problem of contemplation. But since Japan is fast becoming a leader in the field of technology, it is the reconciliation of technology and religious experience that claims his attention. How acquire this "inner peace," so little encouraged in the modern man's life by activism, science, machinery, the drive to acquire power and proficiency? In his answer, Merton makes use of a vocabulary that is perfectly acceptable to oriental contemplatives. He speaks of the "way" and the "wisdom" which help to reduce the divisiveness in us, and, thus, around us and in the world, and permits us to reach the experience of inner unity, which is the noblest effort man can make for his own good and for the good of all men.

In this connection, Merton offers a formula which gives us the key to his own spiritual progress, to his own "advancement" throughout his last years: "Thus, far from wishing to abandon this way, the author seeks only to travel further and further along it . . ." Always the same concern with pushing back frontiers, with throwing out anything that might cause disunity. He will come then, traveler as he is, to a meeting place with other pilgrims walking in other traditions and he will know that he is close to them: "The author of this book can say that he feels himself much closer to the Zen monks of ancient Japan than to the busy and impatient men of the West . . ." The mission of the contemplative, no matter what doctrine he professes, is to work for unity, for peace. Once Merton has stated this common ideal, he can emphasize the distinctive points of his program as a Christian: to become one in all in the Incarnate Word of whom St. John said, "The true light that enlightens every man was coming into the world . . . In him was life, and the life was the light of men. The light shines in the darkness . . ."

Perhaps one might question the usefulness of discussing here texts which are not included in the present volume, but it is impossible to grasp the whole of Merton's monastic thinking, as it appaars in this book, unless one realizes how far this line of thought would lead him and how far it is right for us, too, to be guided by him. Little by little, today, in the midst of great technological advances, churches and religions are rediscovering their contemplative values. Even before the Pan-Indian Synod of the Church, held in Bangalore in 1969, where the fact that Catholicism appeared to be merely a "way of works" was sharply contradicted, Merton, in his preface to the Japanese edition of *Seeds of Contemplation* pleaded for Catholicism in Asia to manifest "the hidden element of contemplation in Christianity." One sees that he is deeply influenced by his reading in Buddhist literature and, at the same time, faithful to the Cistercian tradition which he had studied so long. He comments on the "unity of spirit" of which St. Paul spoke, in a way that reminds one of St. Bernard's commentary; he seems to be inspired by a saying of William of St. Thierry—"love itself is knowledge" —to show the unity that exists between the two. He argues explicitly from "the tradition of early monasticism." And, at the end, since he had started out with the idea of "the way," he gives the biblical quotation: did not Christ say, "I am the way, the truth and the life?"

And here I would like to call attention to the construction, which in much of Merton's work is a great deal more disciplined than one would think at first glance from the apparent detours around the subtleties of a fine point, and a style that is poetic and paradoxical. He liked always to come back to the place from which he had started, to restate the theme upon which he had played his free variations. For always he was led back to the same central point: to the same Love, to the God he encountered in Jesus Christ through the gift of the spirit.

I am not giving in to an ingenuous, admiring expression of friendship when I rank Merton with the Fathers of the Early Church and those of the Middle Ages. Not only, as do all Christians, did he live the same mystery as they did, but he lives it and expresses it in the same way. His humanism explains why his message, as did theirs, has found so great an audience. Just as they drew from the culture of their own times in order to make it a part of their inner experience, so did Merton work in our times toward bringing "the good news" to the world, less by converting individuals than by christianizing cultures. Not that he always stated, any more than the great Fathers, definitive, irrefutable truths; not that he avoided all exaggeration, all error, or was always precise. Nothing would more offend his memory than to read his work uncritically or without personal opinions. But at least he has shown—especially to monks—in the chapters of this book, an orientation, a "way," given a direction for a renewal both free and profound. As he wrote in the letter in which he accepted the invitation to speak at the Congress in Bangkok where he was to die, the great problem for monasticism today "is not survival, but prophecy."

JEAN LECLERCQ O.S.B.
Between Moscow and Tokyo
Easter 1970

Translated from the French
by Catharine Misrahi

EDITORIAL NOTE

Most of the material in this book was put together by Thomas Merton before his death in December 1968. In his last letter to me, on September 6, 1968, he said that he felt that "the Monastic Essays" should be published (by Doubleday) after *My Argument with the Gestapo*. On September 10 the manuscript was sent to me from the Abbey of Gethsemani with a covering letter from Brother Patrick Hart O.C.S.O., who was taking care of Tom's literary correspondence.

I had recently received another manuscript from Tom and read it—one which he specifically asked to be held up for a time—so I did not do more than glance at the book until after his death. When I did so I found that there was work to be done. For instance, two chapters had such similar material that clearly one had to be dropped. This was nothing new in my experience. Tom would put together a collection of related pieces and say, "Here is a book," and often I would, as his agent or later editor, say, "Here it is back. How about a little editing to make it into a book?" But now that was no longer possible.

I have tried to do as little editing as possible, only removing words that too closely identify a chapter with a magazine article. I also removed one of the repetitive chapters, asking the advice of Brother Patrick Hart as to which would be of most value to the potential reader of this book.

At the suggestion of Brother Patrick, it was also decided to add to the original collection several chapters dealing with the hermit life, so that the reader would have in one place all of Thomas Merton's most important writing on monastic renewal as well as his thoughts about the life of deeper solitude which he himself had sought so long and been living since 1966.

I would only add that when I used so lightheartedly to say, "Tom, you must make this into a *book*," and he so good-naturedly did so, I did not realize how much I was asking.

NAOMI BURTON

ONE

MONASTIC RENEWAL

PROBLEMS AND PROSPECTS

Before the Second Vatican Council the monastic orders had begun to consider the question of renewal. Some efforts at renewal were already under way. But these efforts mostly presupposed that existing institutions would continue as they already were and had been for centuries. Changes in the horarium, in the liturgical celebration offices, in the formation and recruitment of new members, in the size and character of the community, in the understanding and observance of the vows would suffice to meet the requirements of aggiornamento. After the Council, even though the decree *Perfectae Caritatis* was very general and in no sense revolutionary, religious as a whole have begun to question the basic institutional structures of the religious life. Though this is not what the Council formally enjoined upon them, it has been an inevitable result of the investigations and self-questioning which the Council demanded.

The monastic Orders have hitherto proved themselves among the most conservative in the Church in the sense that they have tended more than the active institutes to preserve a traditional and somewhat archaic style of life. Before the Council, even those who were in favor of the most sweeping changes still seem to have thought of the monastic community as permanently established on medieval foundations. The renewal of the monastic life has seemed, to many monks and to General Chapters, to demand merely a modernization and adaptation of familiar medieval patterns, freeing them of all that was most obviously feudal and antique, but maintaining their structure, since that structure is conceived to be essential to the monastic way of life.

This is obviously not enough. The monks have been under fire from critics outside the monastic Orders. Many have openly questioned the right of the monastic Orders to continue in existence. It is a bit ironic to see that when Protestants themselves have begun to rediscover monastic values, the Lutheran arguments against monasticism have been adopted and turned against the monks by some Catholic publicists. Thus the very essence of the monastic life itself is attacked, as if the very nature of monasticism made all renewal and adaptation to the present needs of the Church impossible. This presupposes, however, that the monastic life is *essentially* medieval, and that if the medieval formalities, ritualism, observances and conceptions of the vowed life are discarded, there will be nothing left. What complicates matters is that the conservative element in monasticism does, to a great extent, accept this challenge on their critics' terms, assuming that the medieval forms are of the essence, and must therefore be preserved. This incites the younger and more radical element to side with those who demand that the monks leave the cloister, come out into the world, join in the labor of evangelization and justify their existence by active and secular lives. This sweeping attack takes for granted that "the contemplative life" is sterile, foolish, wasteful, selfish and that it serves no purpose but to keep monks immature, walled off from contemporary reality, in a state of self-delusion, dedicated to childish formalities.

Some monks are quite willing to accept this diagnosis, and they also maintain that the only remedy is active work in the world. In effect, however, this extreme solution does not differ from the anti-monastic view in any way. It amounts to an abandonment of the monastic vocation—a capitulation to the arguments of those who deny that there is any place left for a life which "leaves the world." Indeed, the vagaries of a theology and spirituality which overemphasized "contempt for the world" have all been blamed on the monks. Some critics even seem to think that all the aberrations in the theology and devotionalism of an entrenched and defensive Christianity, suspicious of the world and excessively clerical in its outlook, are to be traced to monasticism. It is true that medieval monasticism did exercise an enormous influence on post-medieval spirituality but, once again, must we assume that medieval monasticism is the *only* possible form?

Medieval monasticism was feudal, aristocratic, highly

ritualized, thoroughly organized. The medieval monk might indeed lead a personally austere life, and the atmosphere of the monasteries was often not only highly cultured and spiritual but often genuinely mystical. Contemplative *otium* (leisure) was paid for by hard sacrifice, but the monk (while no doubt seriously concerning himself with the Benedictine ladder of humility) found himself at the top of society in a privileged kind of existence. This air of aristocratic leisure, of privilege and of lordly isolation from the common run of men became more frankly questionable when monasteries were, in fact, places of easy and comfortable retirement from the responsibilities of secular existence. There is, then, plenty of historical warrant for the suspicion that the monastic life can become merely a refuge for the inadequate. On the other hand, the struggle to restore monasticism, after the French Revolution had almost swept it out of existence, certainly modified this. There are, it is true, a few highly aristocratic communities still in existence. No one seriously considers them ready for renewal. Everyone recognizes that these do indeed belong to the feudal past. Nevertheless this suspicion has caused many to question all large and manifestly prosperous monasteries as if they were as feudal as twelfth-century Cluny. This is by no means true. Nevertheless, it must be admitted that the nineteenth-century restorers of monasticism were not only traditionalists in theology and spirituality but even at times royalists and feudalists in politics. They deliberately attempted to restore the medieval structures of monasticism in Europe as models for a reformation of medieval society. Those who came from Europe to make new foundations in America were seldom tempted to question this concept until very recent years.

The fact that this "triumphalist" monasticism is seriously undermined today means that all the arguments which it advanced to justify its existence are now questionable.

Is it enough to wall the monk off in a little contemplative enclave, and there allow him to ignore the problems and crises of the world, should he forget the way other men have to struggle for a living, and simply let his existence be justified by the fact that he punctually recites the hours in choir, attends conventual Mass, strives for interior perfection and makes an honest effort to "live a life of prayer?" Do these innocuous occupations make him a "contemplative?" Or do they make of the monastery a dynamo which "generates spiritual power" for those who are too busy to pray? The famous argument of Pius XI in *Umbratilem* (praising the Carthusians) has been twisted out of shape by decades of routine monastic self-justification, and the sound, traditional theology of that document has been gradually distorted into a quaint superstition, a kind of magic prayer-wheel concept which has lost all power to convince anyone.

On the other hand, no one who is familiar with authentic monastic theology will be seriously disturbed by these arguments, which are all based on the false premise that monasticism is and can only be the sham gothic stereotype re-created a hundred and fifty years ago. The monastic community does not have to be a museum or a liturgical showplace with a college or brewery attached. There are other possibilities, and the monk can justify his existence without rushing back to join in the apostolic life which is, in fact, just as seriously questioned as the monastic life itself.

The essence of the monastic vocation is positive, not negative. It is more than a matter of turning one's back on the world and then doing something or other that can be effectively carried on behind walls—saying prayers, painting pictures, brewing beer, navel-gazing, or what have you.

The monk is (at least ideally) a man who has responded to an authentic call of God to a life of freedom and detachment, a "desert life" outside normal social structures. He is liberated from certain particular concerns in order that he may belong entirely to God. His life is one dedicated completely to love, the love of God and man, but a love that is not determined by the requirements of a special task. The monk is, or should be, a Christian who is mature enough and decided enough to live without the support and consolation of family, job, ambition, social position or even active mission in the apostolate. He is also mature enough and determined enough to use this freedom for one thing only: the love and praise of God and the love of other men. He is mature and free enough to exercise a love of other men that is not confined to this or that apostolic routine, this or that particular form of work.

The monk is not defined by his task, his usefulness. In a certain sense he is supposed to be "useless" because his mission is not to *do* this or that job but to *be* a man of God. He does not live in order to exercise a specific function: his business is life itself. This means that monasticism aims at the cultivation of a certain *quality* of life, a level of awareness, a depth of consciousness, an area of transcendence and of adoration which are not usually possible in an active secular existence. This does not imply that the secular level is entirely godless and reprobate, or that there can be no real awareness of God in the world. Nor does it mean that worldly life is to be considered wicked or even inferior. But it does mean that more immersion and total absorption in worldly business end by robbing one of a certain necessary perspective. The monk seeks to be free from what William Faulkner called "the same frantic steeplechase toward nothing" which is the essence of "worldliness" everywhere.

Teilhard de Chardin has developed a remarkable mystique of secularity which is certainly necessary for our time when the vast majority of men have no choice but to seek and find God in the busy world. But where did Teilhard acquire this perspective? In the deserts of Asia, in vast solitudes which were in many ways more "monastic" than the cloisters of our monastic institutions. So too Bonhoeffer, regarded as an opponent of all that monasticism stands for, himself realized the need for certain "monastic" conditions in order to maintain a true perspective in and on the world. He developed these ideas when he was awaiting his execution in a Nazi prison.

What the monastic life should provide, then, is a special awareness and perspective, an authentic understanding of God's presence in the world and His intentions for man. A merely fictitious and abstract isolation does not provide this awareness. The symbol of medieval monasticism is the wall and the cloister. Instead of merely being self-enclosed, the modern monk might perhaps emulate Teilhard in the desert of Mongolia or Bonhoeffer in prison. These are more primitive and more authentic examples of what a charismatic solitude can mean!

The need for a certain *distance* from the world does not make the monk love the world less. Nor does it imply that he never has any contact with the outside world. Certainly the monastic community has the right and duty to create a certain solitude for the monks: it is no sin to live a silent life. But at the same time the monastic community owes other men a share in that quiet and that solitude. Obviously the balance must be very delicate, for quiet and solitude are destroyed by the movement of crowds. But the fact remains all the more true: the monk has a quiet, relatively isolated existence in which it is possible to concentrate more on the *quality* of life and its mystery, and thus to escape in some measure from the senseless tyranny of quantity.

It is certainly true, then, that this special perspective necessarily implies that the monk will be in some sense critical of the world, of its routines, its confusions, and its sometimes tragic failures to provide other men with lives that are fully sane and human. The monk can and must be open to the world, but at the same time he must be able to get along without a naive and uncritical "secularity" which blandly assumes that everything in the world is at every moment getting better and better for everybody. This critical balance is no doubt difficult to achieve. But it is something which the monk *owes to the world*. For the monastic life has a certain prophetic character about it: not that the monk should be able to tell what is about to happen in the Kingdom of God, but in the sense that he is a living witness to the freedom of the sons of God and to the essential difference between that freedom and the spirit of the world. While admitting that God "so loved the world that he gave his only begotten Son" (John 3:16), the monk does not forget that when the Son of God came into the world it did not receive him because it *could* not. It was bound to oppose and reject him (John 1:10–11, 7:7, 15:18, 14:17, etc.).

The monastic life then must maintain this prophetic seriousness, this wilderness perspective, this mistrust of any shallow optimism which overlooks the ambiguity and the potential tragedy of "the world" in its response to the Word. And there is only one way for the monk to do this: to live as a man of God who has been manifestly "called out of the world" to an existence that differs radically from that of other men, however sincere, however Christian, however holy, who have remained "in the world."

In other words, the problem of monastic renewal is this: though it must obviously involve a radical reshaping of institutional structures, the renewal is by no means merely an institutional concern. It would be a great mistake to assume that renewal is nothing but *reorganization* or even juridical reform. What is needed is not only new rules but new structures and new life. The new life stirs, but faintly, incoherently. It does not know if it can exist without the old structures. What is also needed is a new outlook and a new faith in the capacities of modern men to be monks in a new way. Then the organization of monastic life can perhaps become less cramped, less obsessive, less narcissistic, and new life can develop with creative spontaneity. This spontaneity should be rooted in living tradition. But living tradition must not be confused with dead conventionalism and futile routine, as it so often has been. The situation of monasticism in America is now such that a genuine renewal, and not merely a few new rules, is imperative if American monasticism is to continue a fruitful existence.

Authentic renewal is going to demand a great deal of variety and originality in experimentation. Obviously, the mere issuing of decrees and ordinances from the top down, carried out mechanically on a massive scale, will simply stifle what life is left in monasticism. On the other hand the danger of irresponsibility and levity in ill-considered innovation remains real. But renewal must be bought at the price of risk. Undoubtedly a juncture obsession with novelty for its own sake will cause the ruin of some monastic communities. The winds are blowing and a lot of dead wood is going to fall. The true strength of monasticism is to be sought in its capacity for renunciation, silence, prayer, faith, and its realization of the cross in our life. All genuine renewal must seek life at the source of life: the cross and Resurrection of Jesus.

Fortunately there are signs that such a renewal, though perhaps still tentative and painful, is trying to get under way.

The monastic Orders came to America in the nineteenth century. On one hand the Cistercians (Trappists) brought with them a strictly enclosed penitential form of common life which disconcerted Americans more than it inspired them. The Benedictines brought missionary and apostolic abbeys which maintained schools, colleges, parishes, and seminaries on the frontier, thus fulfilling an urgent need, but tending to depart from the ancient contemplative tradition of monasticism.

One of the most curious phenomena in the life of the American Church after World War II was the sudden interest in the strict contemplative life of the Cistercians and the rush of vocations to the three Cistercian abbeys, which rapidly made foundations in all parts of North America and even in the Southern Hemisphere. Those of us who lived through this minor explosion took it more or less as it came, but now we look back on it aghast, realizing that we cannot really account for it, and soberly aware that it was not an unequivocal success. On the contrary, most of those who entered Cistercian monasteries by the scores and even by the hundreds (there were in all about two thousand postulants received into the Gethsemani community over a period of some ten years in the forties and fifties), later took their departure. Most of those who left, went during their novitiate. Others were dispensed from simple and even solemn vows.

It is perhaps too soon to decide what this commotion signified. But this much can certainly be said: there was a sincere interest in monastic ideals and a genuinely experienced *need* for what the monastic life offered. There were many authentic monastic vocations and they were *lost*. Men who clearly demonstrated their ability to live as excellent monks found themselves defeated and confused by a system that apparently frustrated their development. They discovered two things: first, that they wanted what the monastic life had to offer; second, that the monastic life was now built in such a way that what it offered remained, for many monks, a dream or an impossibility. In effect, one could live fruitfully enough as a novice, but after that one became caught in a complex and fatal machinery in which one was finally exhorted to renounce even what he had come to the monastery to find. This does not mean that the values of monasticism no longer existed, but that they were present in a form that made them morally, psychologically or spiritually inaccessible to many modern men and women. The Cistercians themselves recognized this, and already in the early fifties considerable changes began to be made in the daily schedule and in the various observances. These changes have continued to be made and the whole shape of the life has been significantly altered in the last fifteen years. But the problem of renewal remains just as real and just as perplexing as before, since changes in schedule and in details of observance do not seem to have got right down to the root of the matter. Nor will they ever do so as long as medieval or baroque attitudes prevail.

Meanwhile monastic foundations of a new type began to be made, in the fifties, more than ten years before the Council. Already the "Primitive Benedictine" monasteries like Mount Saviour and Weston felt that monasticism had to get off to a new start. Pioneering efforts were attempted, especially in the vernacular liturgy. The community structure of two classes, lay brothers and priests, was modified to create a community of simple monks in one class, only a few of whom were priests. At the same time the Primitive Benedictines applied themselves to a more serious study of monastic tradition and of the Bible, while experimenting in more flexible and simple formulas of monastic observance than those which had been imported from Europe by the big monasteries a century before. The keynote of the new monasticism was a simple, natural, more or less hard life in contact with nature, nourished by the Bible, the monastic fathers and the liturgy, and faithful to the ancient ideal of prayer, silence, and that "holy leisure" (*otium sanctum*) necessary for a pure and tranquil heart in which God could be experienced, tasted, in the silence and freedom of the monk's inner peace. It can be said that though the Primitive Benedictines were at first criticized (doubtless because they were envied), the older monasteries soon began in various ways to imitate them and attempt changes along lines which the Primitive Benedictine experiments had suggested. Thus even before the Council decree *Perfectae Caritatis* all the monks were working more or less at renewal.

The ferment produced by the Council resulted in increased and unexpected activity among the Cistercians. Monks of the larger abbeys or even of their small foundations began to question the existing formula as such, and to seek opportunities to make a new beginning of their own. Several small experimental foundations have therefore been made by Cistercians in various parts of the United States. These have generally not managed to get a high degree of official backing. Their state is still, at the time of writing,[1] too uncertain for any kind of comment, particularly since detailed information has not been readily available.

Finally, the question of a completely solitary life in hermitages has been admitted back into the full light of the monastic consciousness, after centuries of burial in the darkness of suppressed fantasies. This was made possible and even necessary by the fact that Dom Jacques Winandy, a retired Benedictine abbot from Luxembourg, who had lived as a hermit in Switzerland and then Martinique, formed a colony of hermits in British Columbia. This colony was recruited largely from Cistercian and Benedictine abbeys in the United States, where there have always been a few monks attracted to complete solitude. Taking stock of the situation, the Cistercians realized that a place might be made for hermit vocations within the Order itself. It is now possible for Cistercians to obtain permission to live as hermits in the woods near their monasteries—a solution which had also been arrived at ten years before the Primitive Benedictines. This in fact is nothing radically new: there exists a long tradition of Benedictine hermits going back to the time of Benedict himself. It is admittedly a good solution but it affects only a few

[1] [1967.]

individuals. These have the advantage of a solitary life and of freedom to develop according to their own needs and personal vocation. They have a minimum of concern about temporalities, and they are able to continue their monastic life as members of the community where they made profession. Normally, however, monks have neither the desire nor the grace to live this particular kind of life, and the real problems remain to be solved in the context of common living.

All that has been attempted so far is a provisional beginning, and we cannot yet safely predict what will happen to the monastic movement in this country. One thing is certain: the destinies of the big monasteries are not what they were thought to be a decade ago, and the large new buildings put up to accommodate the many who are no longer there may one day seem a bit bleak and void. But things are certainly a lot quieter—and more peaceful. Life in a big Cistercian monastery may be far from the perfect ideal, but monastically there is still a lot to be said for it, and many of the monks may grudgingly admit that they never had it so good. The admission is, however, no sign of complete satisfaction, because all eyes are on the future, and the present state of affairs is not accepted by anyone as final. How good do they expect to have it?

Speaking as one who has more or less retired to a marginal existence, I am inclined to think they are not yet quite sure themselves. Nor is anyone quite sure just what direction the monastic renewal will take. It may go in different directions in different places: one monastery may be concerned with more openness to the world, another with a return to the desert wilderness and solitude. There is room for variety and for original solutions, provided always that the essence of the monastic vocation is respected. But there is uncertainty because, even to the monks themselves, that essence has seemingly never been quite clear.

In order to understand monasticism, it is important to concentrate on the *charism of the monastic vocation* rather than on the *structure of monastic institutions or the patterns of monastic observance.*

Most of the ambiguities and distresses of the current renewal seem to come from the fact that there is too much concern with changing the observances or adapting the institution and not enough awareness of the charism which the institution is meant to serve and protect. Indeed, one sometimes feels that too many monks have got the cart before the horse, and assume that the vocation or charism exists for the sake of the institution, and that men who are called by God to the peace and inner freedom of the monastic life can be regarded as material to be exploited for the good of the monastic institution, its prestige, its money-making projects and so on.

Obviously, in a community life each monk will want to do an honest job of work and earn his share of the bread that is placed on the common table. But we must be fully aware of the fact that men do not come to a monastery today in order to live the routine busy life of an employee in a big business corporation. The mere fact that a busy life is lived in a monastic enclosure does not make it "contemplative." There are certain forms of exhausting and meaningless servitude which are characteristic of "the world." It is of the very essence of the monastic life to protest, by its simplicity and its liberty, against these servitudes. Of course there is obedience in the monastic life: it is the very heart of that life. Obedience is, paradoxically, the one guarantee of the monk's charismatic inner liberty. But obedience must always be consciously oriented to the fulfillment of the monastic vocation in the monk's own person and not *merely* to the impersonal success of some business project. Not only is there serious danger of monastic obedience being used today to frustrate the true purpose of monastic life, but the renewal may be carried out in such a way that this deformity is carefully protected and preserved. Indeed, one sometimes feels that all sorts of token changes are made on a superficial level, with care being taken to see that in no case the priority of the institution over the person will ever be threatened. In such conditions, "renewal" can never be anything but futile.

The whole question of monastic work, and of the support of the monastic community, is, today, an extremely vexed one. On the one hand there are monks who are claiming that the only honest way for a monk to earn his living is to go out and be a wage earner and then return at night to his community (in this case a small group) and his life of contemplation. Others are for a more complete return to nature and to primitive forms of farm work and handicrafts, etc. Still others think that a highly mechanized monastic "plant" will guarantee enough leisure for reading and contemplation. All these solutions have clear disadvantages, and they all seem to suffer from distorted perspectives and even from a kind of pragmatism that is concerned not with the essence of monasticism but with one or another aspect of it. The ones who want to go and work in factories are concerned with being and appearing poor and also with sharing the lot of the workman in the modern world. Poverty and work are, it is true, essential to the monastic life: but so too is a certain authentic solitude and isolation from the world, a certain protest against the organized and dehumanizing routines of a worldly life built around gain for its own sake. The danger is that the witness of monastic poverty will simply get lost in the mammoth machinery geared for one thing only: profit. The same thing happens when the monastery itself becomes a prosperous industrial unit with the monks working in offices and living on a comfortable income. As to the primitive and ideally agrarian setup: this tends to become a self-consciously arty-and-crafty venture in archaism which, in practice, has to be supported by benefactions from the mammon of iniquity.

When the concern for institutional adjustment is uppermost, then all monastic problems tend to fall into this kind of pattern. It becomes a struggle to adjust the institution in order to emphasize some one aspect, *some particular value*, which an individual or a group appreciates over all the others. When everything is centered on liturgy and on the harmonious, aesthetic decorum of traditional monasticity, then poverty and work may suffer. When everything is centered on poverty and labor, then the community may be over-

worked and lose interest in reading, prayer and contemplation. When everything is centered on "openness to the world"
the monks may become agitated and self-complacent gossips
and under the pretext of "charity" forget that love which
originally drew them to the monastery. In the past an excessive Trappist rigorism produced communities of well-meaning
and devout men who sometimes bordered on the boorish or
the fanatical.

Actually, the renewal of monasticism cannot have any real
meaning until it is seen as a renewal of the *wholeness* of
monasticism in its *charismatic* authenticity. Instead of con-
centrating on this or that means, we need first of all to look
more attentively at the end. And here, while we must certainly focus accurately on the traditional ideal, a little realism
and common sense will not be out of place. These were, after
all, characteristic of that Benedictine Rule on which, whatever may be our time and its problems, renewal will normally
be based.

The charism of the monastic life is the freedom and peace
of a wilderness existence, a return to the desert that is also a
recovery of (inner) paradise. This is the secret of monastic
"renunciation of the world." Not a *denunciation*, not a den-
igration, not a precipitous flight, a resentful withdrawal, but
a liberation, a kind of permanent "vacation" in the original
sense of "emptying." The monk simply discards the useless
and tedious baggage of vain concerns and devotes himself
henceforth to the one thing really necessary—the one thing
that he really wants: the quest for *meaning* and for *love,* the
quest for his own identity, his secret name promised him by
God (Apocalypse 2:17) and for the peace of Christ which
the world cannot give (John 14:27). In other words the monk
renounces a life of agitation and confusion for one of order
and clarity. But the order and clarity are not his own making; nor are they, so to speak, an institutional product, an
effect of exterior regularity. They are the fruit of the Spirit.
The monastic life is a response to the call of the Spirit
to espousals and to peace in the wilderness (Hosea 2:19–20).

The monastic charism is not, however, one of pure solitude
without any community. It is also a charism of brotherhood

in the wilderness: for the monk, even though he may eventually, in an exceptional case, live as a hermit, is prepared for solitude by living in close brotherly relationship with his fellow monks in the monastic community. This closeness is understood as being at least ideally a very human and warm relationship, and the charism of the monastic life is, and has been from the beginning, a grace of *communion* in a shared quest and a participated light. It is then a charism of special love and of mutual aid in the attainment of a difficult end, in the living of a hazardous and austere life. The monk is close to his brother in so far as he realizes him to be a fellow pilgrim in the spiritual "desert." Monastic work, obedience, poverty, chastity, are all in some way colored and tempered by the communal charism of brotherhood in pilgrimage and in hope.

Obviously the monastic life is not purely charismatic. Nothing could be more ruinous for monasticism than to turn a lot of inexperienced monks loose to live without any institutional structures and without organization—or to assume them capable of improvising new institutions overnight. Though the monastic life today is too rigidly institutionalized and too hidebound with senseless traditions, the basic lines of a monastic communal structure must be preserved and the authentic wisdom, drawn from the experience of ages in which monasticism was fully *lived,* must not be lost. The new monastic communities will need to be much more democratic than in the past. The abbot will have to be a spiritual father, not a prelate, a police chief and a corporation president rolled into one. The monks will have to have much more initiative in running their own lives, and the abbot will have to concern himself more with genuine spiritual guidance than with institutional control. The spiritual role of the superior presupposes a certain freedom and discretion in the subject. The superior can no longer arrogate to himself the right to do all his subjects' thinking for them and to make all their decisions for them. Obviously, in the period of transition, mistakes will be made. But with the grace of God these mistakes themselves will be more fruitful than the stifling inertia of overcontrol.

The monks will learn for themselves some lessons that they could never learn any other way.

The charism of the monastic vocation is one of simplicity and truth. The monk, whether as hermit or as cenobite, is one who abandons the routines, the clichés, the disguised idolatries and empty formalities of "the world" in order to seek the most authentic and essential meaning of the dedicated life on earth. Ideally speaking, then, the monastery should be a place of utter sincerity, without empty and deceptive formalities, without evasions, without pretenses.

Often, the rules and disciplines of community life have merely created an atmosphere of formalism and artificiality which, instead of helping the monks to live in close rapport as true brothers, served only to estrange them from one another. It is tragic that in the name of discipline and obedience monastic silence has been exploited as a means of keeping the monks out of touch with each other, indeed fearful and suspicious of one another. Monastic enclosure has at times become nothing more than a means of keeping the monks ignorant of the outside world in the hope that they would become indifferent to its tragic conflicts and not create any bother by having problems of conscience over things like war, poverty, race and revolution.

There is no question that one of the most disturbing things about the monastic institution for most of those moderns who have come seeking to give themselves to God in solitude, prayer and love, has been the current interpretation of religious vows, especially obedience. One who dedicates himself to God by vows today finds himself committed for life to a massively organized, rigidly formalistic institutional existence. Here everything is decided for him beforehand. Everything is provided for by rule and system. Initiative is not only discouraged, it becomes useless. Questions cease to have any point, for you already know the answers by heart in advance. But the trouble is that they are not answers, since they imply a firm decision to ignore your questions. Obedience then no longer consists in dedicating one's will and love to the service of God, but almost the renunciation of all human rights, needs and feelings in order to conform to the rigid demands of an institution. The institution is identified with God, and becomes an end in itself. And the monk is given to understand from the start that there is *no alternative* for him but to regard this institutional life in all its details, however arbitrary, however archaic, however meaningless to him, as the *only way* for him to be perfect in love and sincere in his quest for God. This has been impressed upon him not only as a most solemn religious duty but almost as an article of faith: indeed, the young monk who has serious problems with a life that may seem to him increasingly fruitless and even absurd, may be forcefully told that he is failing in Christian faith and verging on apostasy!

It is here that we see how far the perversion of the "spiritual dynamo" idea can sometimes be carried. The monastic institution, with its constant prayer, its regularity, its impeccable observance, its obedient and submissive monks, is implicitly regarded as a beautiful machine which, as long as it runs smoothly, obtains infallible results from God. The object of the monastic order, of the superiors, chapters and so on, is to make sure that the machine is well oiled and keeps running exactly as it should. Faith assures us that the monastic machine is exerting an irresistible influence on God who, it is assumed, takes a mysterious pleasure in the operation of this ingenious toy. The legal clockwork of monasticism has been specially devised by the Church to enchant the Almighty and to cunningly manipulate His power. For what? For the institutional benefit of the rest of the Church—its manifold projects, the conversion of infidels, the return of heretics and apostates to humble submission, the humiliation and destruction of the Church's enemies and so on. Obviously such a valuable machine must not be tampered with in any way. "Renewal" simply means a cleaning and oiling that will make the clock run more perfectly than before!

The most tragic misunderstandings have arisen from this attitude which, in some cases, one must frankly admit it, savors of gross superstition and arrogance. In any event, it has led to the ruin of many monastic vocations which seemed to be in every respect serious and genuine. One feels that if there had been a little flexibility, a little humaneness shown—if the monk, when he began to have trouble with the life, had been allowed a change of scene or a more genuinely human relationship with his brothers—he might have adjusted to the life after all. Unfortunately, there still exists such a grave fear of the austere institutional image being tarnished by concessions, that vocations are sacrificed in order to preserve a monastic façade.

As everywhere else in American life, there has been an enormous amount of neurotic anxiety in monasteries. The tendency has been, in each case, to blame the individual. Sometimes, however, one wonders if a certain neurotic pattern has not finally got built into the system itself. Indeed one might at times wonder if the system does not require and favor neurotic insecurity, both in subjects and in superiors, in order to continue functioning as it does. Certainly neurosis is not endemic in monasticism as such. But a particular concept of monastic regularity and obedience does seem to encourage neuroses while loudly deploring them and advocating therapy —which then becomes part of the process.

Monks are human in their needs, their frailties and also in their unconscious efforts to compensate for what they have given up by leaving the world. The man who has renounced family life and the love of children may, without realizing it himself, seek compensation in some other way—for instance by dominating other people. Men and women in the cloister have sometimes been notoriously aggressive, ambitious, given to a bitter and thoroughly worldly struggle for political power in their community. Those who lack the forcefulness required to exercise power themselves, are content to live as monastic Peter Pans, in passive dependence on those whom they flatter and try to manipulate. In the long run, they find that this passivity too implies a certain power, for by subservience and manipulation they can get their own will incorporated into the system and have their ideas imposed by a superior.

The man who loves power can, with most idealistic motives, seek to gratify this love not only by exercising his power over his contemporaries, but even by building his will into the structure of the institution so that later generations will go on being dominated by him long after his death. In the current effort at renewal, it may happen that this kind of underground power struggle is being carried on without the monks realizing it too clearly. Many of those who are most enthusiastic and active in the work of "renewal" seem to be going about it in such a way as to make sure that *their* ideas and plans will not be seriously contested, and that in the end it will be *their* reforms that will win out. It also unfortunately happens that the adjustment these people advocate is superficial only: and if they have their way, they will hand on the *status quo,* embellished with a few trimmings of their own, and it will be a monument to themselves. This "monumental," "massive" and basically static concept of the monastic life is certainly to blame for the institutional rigidities that prevent true adjustment today. But such monasticism as this cannot survive. It is doomed. The sense of outrage, protest and refusal is too evident in monastic communities. Unfortunately there is also a growing impatience, and those who allow themselves to become obsessed with the problem may forget that monastic renewal is God's work and not theirs, and they too may be tempted, in a basically selfish desperation, to abandon the effort that the Church asks of them.

The monastic movement needs leaders who must come from the new generation. These must have the patience to undergo the testing and formation without which their ability cannot be proved. No one will entrust himself to the guidance of men who have never had to suffer anything and have never really faced the problems of life in all their bitter seriousness. The young must not be too ready to give up in despair. They have work to do! Fortunately there are creative forces at work. There are communities and superiors who are fully aware of the real nature of the monastic vocation not simply as a summons to become a cog in an institutional machine, but as a charismatic breakthrough to liberation and love. It is more and more clearly realized that fidelity to monastic tradition no longer means simply dictating pre-formulated answers to all the questions of the young monk, and forcing him to look at his life through somebody else's glasses. Tradition is not passive submission to the obsessions of

former generations but a living assent to a current of unin-
terrupted vitality. What was once real in other times and
places becomes real in us today. And its reality is not an official parade of externals. It is a living spirit marked by freedom and by a certain *originality*. Fidelity to tradition does
not mean the renunciation of all initiative, but a new initiative that is faithful to a certain spirit of freedom and of vision
which demands to be incarnated in a new and unique situation. True monasticism is nothing if not creative.

The creativity in monastic life springs from pure love: the
natural desire of man for truth and for communion first of
all, and the supernatural gift of grace in the spirit of the Risen
Lord, calling man to the highest truth and most perfect communion in the Mystery of Christ. Love is not mere emotion
or sentiment. It is the lucid and ardent response of the whole
man to a value that is revealed to him as perfect, appropriate
and urgent in the providential context of his own life. Hence
there are innumerable ways in which man can be awakened
from the sleep of a mechanical existence and summoned to
give himself totally in the clarity of love. To restrict vocations to this or that narrow area, as if there were only one way
to love, is to stifle the spirit and fetter the freedom of the
Christian heart. Why are people so intent on refusing others
the right to see a special value in a life apart from the world,
a life dedicated to God in prayer "on the mountain alone"
when the New Testament itself repeatedly shows Christ retiring to the solitary prayer which he himself loved? Certainly
one can find God "in the world" and in an active life but this
is not the only way, any more than the monastic life is the
only way. There are varieties of graces and vocations in the
Church and these varieties must always be respected. The
specific value that draws a Christian into the "desert" and
"solitude" (whether or not he remains physically "in the
world") is a deep sense that *God alone suffices*. The need to
win the approval of society, to find a recognized place in the
world, to achieve a temporal ambition, to "be somebody"
even in the Church seems to them irrelevant. They realize
themselves to be called to a totally different mode of existence,
outside of secular categories and *outside of the religious es-*

tablishment. This is the very heart of monasticism; hence a firmly "established" monasticism is a self-contradiction.

The creative spirit of initiative in monasticism is bound to be killed by an exaggerated emphasis on a well-established monastic "presence," an undue concern with law and ritual and with the externals of observance. The true creative spirit must be fired with love and with *an authentic desire of God.* This means, in so many words, that the monastic vocation is one which implicitly, if not explicitly, seeks *the experience of union with God.* True, the humility and obedience which are essential to the monastic life are absolutely necessary to purge this desire from all elements of self-will and of spiritual ambition. But the need for spiritual liberation, the need for vision, the hunger and thirst for that perfect "justice" which is found in total surrender to God as love to the Beloved: these are the only real justifications for the monk's wilderness life and his desert pilgrimage. If these are systematically frustrated, and if institutional formalities are everywhere substituted for the inner desire of holiness and union, monks will not remain in the monastery. If they are true to themselves and to God they will be compelled to look elsewhere. This is the real problem of monastic renewal: not a surrender to the "secular city" but a recovery of the deep desire of God that draws a man to seek a *totally new way of being in the world.*

This is perhaps a better way of envisaging the monastic vocation. There is no longer any place for the idea that monasticism is mere *repudiation* of the world. It is not enough to "say no," to develop "contempt" for the world and to spend one's life in a walled-up existence which simply rejects all the pleasures, interests and struggles of the world as suspect or as sinful. This negative idea of monasticism has caused it to be completely misunderstood by its critics because it has so often been misunderstood by the monks themselves. And that is why, when the young monk in quest of renewal looks for something to say "yes" to, he comes up with the same "yes" as the world itself. In either case, there is no real awareness of what monasticism is all about.

The monastic life is neither worldly nor unworldly. It is

not artificially "otherworldly." It is merely intended to be liberated and simple. The purpose of monastic detachment—which demands genuine sacrifice—is simply to leave the monk unencumbered, free to move, in possession of his spiritual senses and of his right mind, capable of living a charismatic life in freedom of spirit. To love, one must be free, and while the apostolic life implies one mode of freedom in the world, the monastic life has its own freedom which is that of the wilderness. The two are not opposed or mutually exclusive. They are complementary and, on the highest level, they turn out to be one and the same: union with God in the mystery of total love, in the oneness of His Spirit.

In the solitude of the monastic life, the monk begins obscurely to sense that great depths are opened up within him, and that the charism of his monastic vocation demands an obedience that is carried out in an abyss too deep for him to understand. It is an obedience that permeates the very roots of his being. Such obedience is far more difficult than any compliance with the will of man, but it must be tested by rule, by discipline, and by submission to the wills of other men. Otherwise it is sheer illusion. Nevertheless, for rule and command to retain their worth in the monastic life, they must be seen in their right relation to the ultimate purpose of that life. Monastic obedience exists not to make yes-men and efficient bureaucrats who can be used in institutional politics, but to liberate the hearts and minds into the lucid and terrible darkness of a contemplation that no tongue can explain and no rationalization can account for. And it must always be remembered that this contemplative liberation is a gift of God, granted not necessarily to the perfect only, and certainly not as a prize for political collaboration with the schemes and ambitions of others.

It remains to speak one word to the monks themselves, that is to those who now, at this time, are persevering in monasteries and hermitages. That word is: *do not be impatient and do not be afraid.* Do not imagine that everything depends on some instant magic transformation of constitutions and of laws. You already have what you need right in your hands! You have the grace of your vocation and of your love. No earthly situation has ever been ideal. God does not need an ideal situation in order to carry out His work in our hearts. If we do what we can with the means and grace at our disposal, if we sincerely take advantage of our genuine opportunities, the Spirit will be there and His love will not fail us. Our liberation, our solitude, our vision, our understanding and our salvation do not depend on anything remote from us or beyond our reach. Grace has been given us along with our good desires. What is needed is the faith to accept it and the energy to put our faith to work in situations that may not seem to us to be promising. The Holy Spirit will do the rest. There will continue to be monasteries in the mountains and the forests of this continent. And they will be good monasteries, places of silence, of peace, of austerity, of simplicity, of prayer, and of love. They will house communities of men who love one another and share with the world the light they have received, though in a silent and obscure way. They will open out on to the desert solitude in which every monk, at one time or another, whether for a short time or for life, seeks to be alone in the silence and the mystery of his God, liberated from the images of Egypt and from the Babel of tongues.

Yet there is no such thing as a purely charismatic monasticism without any institution. There will always be laws and Rules. And Christ must always be especially present in the person of an abbot, a spiritual father. Indeed spiritual fatherhood itself is a charism and one of the greatest. Not only is it a signal blessing for any monastic community, but it is essential for the work of genuine renewal. Without experienced guides who are completely open to the full dimension—the mystical and prophetic dimension—of love in Christ, renewal will mean little more than the replacement of old rules by new ones and of old traditions by novel frenzies.

VOCATION AND
MODERN THOUGHT

To what extent are the vocation problems of novices and monks the result of a conflict between "modern thought" and "traditional monastic ideas?" To what extent is this inevitable conflict something we are able to understand and resolve? Obviously our novices are men (or at least "boys") of our time. This is a fact which is irreversible. Should we regard this as a misfortune? We would be very foolish if we did. Is "modern thought" an irreparable evil? Should we assume that the only way a postulant can adapt to our life is to submit to a total and ruthless process of disinfection so that he is completely cleansed of all twentieth-century ideas? This would be insult, at once presumptuous and absurd. It would mean the extinction of the monastic life. We must on the contrary try to understand how modern ideas can become relevant and acceptable, indeed useful, in helping us to meet our monastic problems.

And yet we must preserve our detachment and our sense of proportion. In opening our minds to modern thought (and after all this means recognizing that we too are "moderns") we must also realize its limitations and its own peculiar hazards. Above all we must be aware of its complexities, its variations, its confusions, since "modern thought" is not a harmonious unity. Modern man is not in agreement with himself. He has no one voice to listen to, but a thousand voices, a thousand ideologies, all competing for his attention in a Babel of tongues. Our responsibility to modern man goes far beyond playing games with him, learning some of his lingo in order to tell him what we imagine he wants to hear. Our responsibility to him begins within ourselves. We must recognize that his problems are also ours, and stop imagining that we live in a totally different world. We must recognize that our common problems are not to be solved merely by logical answers, still less by official pronouncements. Yet in taking the modern temper seriously we must not accept all its myths and illusions without question, or we will end up by echoing slogans without meaning, substituting sociology, psychoanalysis, existentialism and Marxism for the message of the Gospel. We must use the insights of modern thought, but without deceiving ourselves. The satisfaction that comes from being in tune with our times is certainly not a charism, still less a sign of supernatural life.

We must concern ourselves with the failure of vocations, not the failure of poor vocations or non-vocations, but the failure of apparently good vocations. It is not the fact that novices and young professed leave the monastery and return to secular life, but rather that some who seem very serious and well endowed, who have apparently adapted well at first, who have been good monks, undergo a vocation crisis (often after five or ten years in the monastery) and leave. The reason given is not so much an inability to accept the physical hardships of the life (no longer so great) but an incapacity to accept any longer the climate of thought, and certain attitudes prevalent in the monastery. This is not primarily a failure of faith, or a deep religious crisis, but a psychological incapacity to accept as authentic the climate of thought in which they think the monks are bound to live. Many ambiguities and misunderstandings are involved here on both sides.

To begin with, though this is not generally a purely religious crisis, it may well be so. The psychological temptation can quite easily become a failure of faith. Nevertheless we cannot understand it properly if we regard it merely as an intervention of the devil and a loss of faith. What happens is that communication tends to break down under certain pressures that arise when the young monk suddenly takes a critical and objective view of the monastery and of his fellow monks. Now, the fact that he does this relatively late in his monastic life (even after solemn profession) raises many serious questions. These questions seem to him to invalidate his supposed vocation, while his superiors tend to take the attitude *"Si non es vocatus, fac te vocatum,"* appealing naturally to his vow. This may seem to the young monk an incomprehensible attitude, an "infidelity" on some other level which he has newly discovered—or thinks he has discovered—but which he cannot clearly discern. He thinks he has found "the truth" about himself and that he must "obey" his new insights.

The great question is this: has he simply relinquished his commitment to a way of life and to a belief which now seems threatening to the very roots of his being? Is he "discovering" himself in a secular and psychological sense, and taking refuge in this discovery so as not to have to confront the severe demands of God's word spoken in mystery and apparent "absurdity?" Or is he on the contrary hearing that word clearly for the first time and obeying its demand to relinquish an inadequate and complacent security which he had embraced passively and without serious motives?

These questions should be anticipated before profession, indeed before the entrance of the postulant into the novitiate. But they cannot always be anticipated.

Hence, once the monk is professed, he must in some way learn to answer his questions in the monastery, in his vow of *conversatio morum*. The monastic commitment and consecration does remain the most deep and authentic solution. But how can he understand this? He must be formed with such a capacity to understand. The monastic ideal must consequently be presented in an understandable way, in all its depth, in its existential reality and its demands, not in formulas of words and slogans. What is called for today is not a crude modernizing of monastic tradition but a new and sharp perspective on the real values which are latent in the monastic life and tradition and which modern man can reasonably expect to find there. The values are certainly there, but they may be hidden through the lack of attention and sensitivity on the part of those who have hitherto been satisfied with old formulas and conceptions which need to be rethought and seen from a new angle, with greater and more serious concern. Need we add: the vows must no longer be regarded in a spirit of vain observance, magic or superstition?

There is no point in stressing modern moral confusion, broken homes, delinquency, alcoholism, pornography, drug addiction, teen-age riots, etc., etc., which are only *sympto-*

matic, not the real trouble. Rather than analyze the mentality of the (American) affluent and marketing society, we will simply note two essential aspects of this climate of thought.

Alexis Carrel remarked: "Technological progress has run wild, and in doing so has ceased to take serious account of man's real needs except as an afterthought." In other words the development of technology is not really geared to human needs. Carrel said: "The environment which science and technology have succeeded in developing for man does not suit him because it has been *constructed at random without regard for his true self.*"[1]

Also, though we still pay lip service to the old myth that what is good for the market is good for everybody, as a matter of fact the development of new products and the marketing of commodities has really little or nothing to do with man's real good and his real needs. The aim is not the good of man but higher profits. Instead of production being for the sake of man, man exists for the sake of production. Thus we live in a culture which, while proclaiming its humanism and pretending indeed to glorify man as never before, is really a systematic and almost cynical affront to man's humanity. Man is a consumer who exists in order to keep business going by consuming its products whether he wants them or not, needs them or not, likes them or not. But in order to fulfill his role he must come to believe in it. Hence his role as consumer takes the place of his identity (if any). He is then reduced to a state of permanent nonentity and tutelage in which his more or less abstract presence in society is tolerated only if he conforms, remains a smoothly functioning automaton, an uncomplaining and anonymous element in the great reality of the market.

It is characteristic of this affluent marketing society to generate at the same time unrealistic expectations and superficial optimism overlaying an undercurrent of suspicion, compounded of self-doubt, inferiority feelings, resentment, cynicism and despair. In all our young postulants, these two conflicting forces tend to be present, even where there is great

[1] From *Man the Unknown.*

simplicity and good will, and though the negative trend (doubt) may be rather thoroughly repressed. It soon comes out.

What is worse, since our society is one in which man is expected to sell himself and put himself across by flashing a favorable image of himself, and by having high expectations of himself, this too affects the mentality of our postulants. Those who are most glib and adroit in this matter may sell themselves as very earnest vocations, while others who are simpler and less aggressive may seem to "have nothing" that recommends them for monastic life.

However, it must be said that they are conscious of all this and all more or less deliberately come to the monastery to escape this system of false values and to find here values that are at once more honest and more in the human measure.

I would say that this manifests itself particularly in a very real concern for monastic simplicity and poverty and for complete honesty in monastic observance. This may at times express itself in ways that sound fanatical and neurotic, but in the main it seems to proceed from the Holy Spirit and is one of the more authentic signs of a true vocation. Yet it is precisely those who have this ideal who also tend to develop problems and dissatisfaction.

There is no question that most of our postulants are quite conscious of the confusion and disorder of the world and honestly intend to leave that all behind them. They come to us precisely because they are aware of the chaos of life outside. But the problem arises when, after a certain time, the kind of order and peace that they find here is finally rejected by them as unsatisfactory. Why?

They are products of a particular climate of thought and, in this connection, it may be useful to remind ourselves that "modern thought" is very complex and is in rapid evolution. It is not homogeneous, but is rather made up of many conflicting trends and new developments, and very often trends tend to develop side by side without much influence on each other. It is therefore extraordinarily difficult to say precisely what is going on in "the mind of modern man." We live in a world of chaotic and revolutionary change. The development of rapid communications and of mass media has insured a certain superficial uniformity in the thinking of "the common man" all over the world. And yet can we say precisely who is this "common man?" He has an enormous variety of ideas and influences acting upon him, and often his mentality is an extraordinary mixture of mental clichés that he has picked up at random without knowing where they come from or what they imply. Yet his mind often remains shallow, dissatisfied, frustrated—unless by chance it becomes simply complacent and passive, habitually reacting to mental stimuli without real thought and without mature response.

However, we can say that the man of our time who has been "educated," say on a level corresponding to American college, has been exposed to the ideas of those thinkers who have revolutionized thought and indeed society itself in the last hundred and fifty years. It is necessary therefore to cast a glance at some of these thinkers.

Who are they? Marx, Darwin, Kierkegaard, Nietzsche, and later Freud, Jung, Adler, etc., Lenin, Mao Tse-tung (rather than Stalin who was no thinker; Mao's thought has not reached us, but it is seminal in Latin America, for instance in the ideology of Castroism). We should also mention Bergson, Dewey, Croce, Ortega de Gasset; then Sartre, Heidegger, Buber and other leading existentialists. Finally we find Teilhard de Chardin, mediating much of modern thought to Catholics, with Mounier, G. Marcel and on the evangelical side men like Bultmann and Tillich.

Catholicism, at least on the seminary level, has tended to ignore these men or to dismiss them airily, except perhaps for Teilhard who is immensely popular. But we must frankly recognize the importance of these thinkers: they have all in one way or another concerned themselves very deeply with the predicament of modern man: with his special needs, his peculiar hopes, his chances of attaining these hopes. This concern in itself is by no means incompatible with a Christian outlook. Christianity too must be profoundly concerned with twentieth-century man, with technological man, "post-historic" man, indeed what is sometimes called "post-Christian" man. In the Church there can be no "post-

Christian" man, no mere technological pagan. There is only man redeemed by Christ.

If modern man has a peculiar outlook appropriate to his rapidly developing world, Christianity cannot and does not ignore him or his ideas. The Church seeks to understand his ideas and to share them. We in the monasteries cannot ignore them. Schema 13 of Vatican II makes it an obligation to understand contemporary man as he is, not as we want him to be.

The American bishops who discussed religious liberty in the third session of the Council all frankly accepted the "modern outlook" on the dignity of the person and the rights of conscience. We too must be concerned with this outlook as expressed in the lives of our postulants.

There is more at stake than "human dignity" and the "rights of conscience." We do not merely confront nineteenth-century liberal man and his simple belief in self-realization by freedom in a free economy governed by inherently reasonable laws. We confront twentieth-century man in his desperation and despair, his hopeless quest of an identity, perhaps his renunciation of identity: Not only may we meet him halfway in his desire that his freedom be recognized and developed, but we may even have to restore to him a basic hope in his very capacity to be a person, to have an identity and to dedicate himself fully to the service of God.

The nineteenth century declared that God was dead, and now the twentieth, in consequence, has come to discover that without God man himself doubts the validity and meaning of his own existence. When "God died" there was something in man that died also. If we do not resuscitate these dead men—our own dead selves—with the word of the Gospel, we will only consecrate dead men to a "dead God." And those who come to us will ask themselves what profit there can be in seeking the living among the dead.

Hence it would be both useless and absurd simply to cry out that the atmosphere is polluted by modern errors and try to disinfect it. It is not only impossible to get rid of all the influences exercised on modern man by the thinkers we have mentioned, but also there is no need to do so. On the contrary, we have to take these influences into account, and try generously to make use of them to the extent that modern thought can serve the purposes of truth and of the monastic life.

We cannot, for instance, neglect or overlook the tremendous effect that the world view of modern science has had. Monastic life and liturgy especially belong to the days of the Ptolemaic, earth-centered universe, with God in the empyrean perhaps not more than one hundred miles above us! The Anglican bishop John A. Robinson, in his book *Honest to God,* struggled rather naively with the problem of a religion that conceives God as being "out there." However, this is not too urgent a problem for us at the moment, since in fact the universe of relativity and quantum physics is not what is upsetting our young monks. On the contrary, they find it awe-inspiring, as we all should and do.

"Scientific atheism" is certainly no real problem any more, except in those who still cling to the complacently oversimplified illusions of nineteenth-century liberalism. What is more important and disquieting is the blank passivity and indifference of modern mass man, who is in a confusion in which serious concern for truth on any level may become impossible: the greatest problem is the despair and languor of a depersonalized man incapable of authenticity. But such men do not ordinarily enter monasteries. We must assume in our postulants at least a beginning of capacity for some thought of their own, some authentic religious concern. And we have supposed that this thinking and concern will inevitably be influenced at least unconsciously by "modern thought."

Who were some of the makers of modern thought and what were they saying?

We think of Marx as simply saying that capitalism must be overthrown, and as being "against private property," therefore against the natural law, but one idea that he investigated in depth was the dehumanization of man in industrial society. His remedy was not just revolution, but that man must own the means of production which he uses; he must not be reduced to the level of an object or a machine to be used by someone else: he must preserve his dignity as man.

He must be the master of the means of production and not their servant. He must live among machines in such a way as to acquire and preserve his full human identity and responsibility to his fellow man.

We usually think of Freud as saying that the restrictions of conventional morality are bad for man since they prevent him from carrying out his sexual desires. In point of fact, that is not what Freud is saying. Freud is deploring a social situation in which man does not learn to love in a full and mature manner in so far as his passions remain in a crude infantile state which keeps him from being fully human, fully able to give himself in love. Sexual indulgence is not for Freud a good in itself. On the contrary, it may be selfish and infantile, and hence a source of pathology. In a word, we can see that for Freud too it is a question of man developing psychologically as well as biologically in such a way that his sexuality is in the service of his full identity as a person capable of giving himself and not a blind force that overwhelms and smothers his identity. (Incidentally, depth psychology has certainly had a revolutionary effect on the modern concept of man and on the consequent idea of morality. Whether group analysis should be a normal practice in monasteries is a question I can only mention in passing. The question exists and has its risks.)

Kierkegaard, along with Nietzsche and then later Sartre and Heidegger (though they all approach it in different ways) are telling us substantially that elaborate conventional structures of thought, language, cult, etc., are all doing the exact opposite from what they originally pretended to do: instead of bringing man in contact with reality, and helping him to be true to himself, they are standing between man and reality, as veils and deceptions. They prevent him from facing "anguish." All urge man to discard the impediments of conventional thought in order to face himself directly, take upon himself the burden of anguish and contingency, face the awful reality of death, and use his freedom not as one who is enmeshed in the artificialities of social convention, but as one who sees himself with all his limitations grounded in nothingness and yet in his true dignity, his freedom, his ability to establish his personal identity and "choose" to be him-self, even though he is nothing.

The literature of the late nineteenth and early twentieth century has been deeply concerned with authenticity and the problem of finding one's "true self" in an artificial and inau-thentic society. T. S. Eliot's *The Waste Land* and *The Hollow Men* state the problem. In *Four Quarters,* his greatest poem, Eliot uses traditional spiritualities and symbols to rise above identity, to achieve a personal deliverance from a common-place and fictitious identity in the stream of historical con-tinuity, or rather in the "now" which stands behind all events and includes them all together. For more recent writers, the very existence of a "personal identity" has been called into question. This has resulted in a systematic and destructive questioning of all that seemed to earlier writers to offer sup-port for an authentic identity. For novelists and dramatists of the absurd it is perhaps true to say that the only authentic identity is the recognition that identity itself is an illusion and hence the best man can do with his "freedom" is to accept, and take responsibility for his own despair. Postulants in our monasteries have perhaps not been reading the pessimistic literature, yet can we say that they are totally unaffected by it, when such ideas make themselves felt everywhere?

Meanwhile the nineteenth-century belief in progressive evo-lution has persisted side by side with existentialist pessimism, and one may say that in the United States as well as in the Communist countries the prevailing climate is one of official optimism. Sometimes the optimism of Christian eschatological hope takes on a coloring of evolutionist expectations, looking forward to a spiritual and religious climax at the end of the evolutionary process. Thus we have a combined Christian and evolutionist optimism opposed to the pessimism that sees the world as falling into entropy, meaninglessness and self-destruction. For some, man is only on the threshold of a glorious fulfillment which will for the first time make him really "man." For others, history is already at an end. Man is running down like an unwound clock. He is already in his post-historic inertia.

Both Darwin and Teilhard de Chardin are concerned with

the development of man toward the fulfillment of his true (historic and biological) destiny and Teilhard, mingling Marx and Darwin with Christianity, looks forward to the recapitulation of all in Christ, the eschatological and supernatural goal to which man has been destined by God. This means, for Teilhard de Chardin, a Christianity that fully accepts "the world" and recognizes its destiny as a redemptive force fully rooted "in the world." Hence Teilhard is concerned with the Christian's identity as a Christian person and a member of Christ with a responsibility not only to his fellow man but to the whole of creation and to all the past history of creation. Man, in Teilhard as in Marx, finds himself at a point where the whole fulfillment of the world depends on his enlightened and free choice—a grandiose and noble vision.

All these thinkers, with all their different approaches, with their optimism on one hand and their pessimism on the other, agree more or less in one basic emphasis: upon the problem of authenticity, the predicament of man in technological and mass society in which in fact he is not reaching maturity but on the contrary becoming fixed in infantilism and irresponsibility, in which he passively submits to systematic stultification. Hence they all concern themselves with the need for man to discover his identity (or at least his lack of "identity") and assume mature responsibility for himself in his world and in history. All tend to look upon man, whether individually or collectively, not as a static essence fixed in a stable condition, but as a dynamism or a "project," a "freedom," a person responsible for "creating" a world and an identity proportionate to his plight. Now, though this "humanism" and "personalism" may occur in a frankly atheistic context, we must learn to distinguish, more carefully than we do, what is "godless" in Marx and Freud, for instance, and what proceeds from implicitly Christian roots. It has been said that the revolt against Christianity is a form of "judgment" pronounced in and by history upon the failure of Christians to meet the demands of God's Word in their time. Hence it is that Marxism, for one, frankly seeks to achieve the aims and promises of Biblical messianism (world unity, peace, harmony, justice, love) by the formal rejection of Christianity and indeed of all religion. The Marxian idea of man postulates that religion, being essentially a mystification, actually prevents man from realizing the ideals which it proposes to him. Hence, in a way, to abandon the "mystification" and work for the proposed ideal is to fulfill the spirit and genuine claims of religion. Naturally Marxism does not look at it in this way, but Christian thinkers influenced by Marxism tend to do so. In any event, the personalist and humanist ideals of modern thought are not always radically incompatible with the Christian ideal. The rejection of God and of the Church is of course frankly anti-Christian. But the goal of human freedom, peace, and unity is not unchristian in itself. On the contrary it stems from the New Testament idea of freedom before God, the freedom of the sons of God, the dignity of man redeemed in Christ and man's vocation to work out historically, in harmony and love, the redemption of the whole world in Christ. Hence these characteristic modern aspirations should present no special difficulty to us. We should be able to "save" and "redeem" those aspirations which are authentically germane to Christianity even though buried in a matrix of atheism.

The real problem then is not that young men come to us and find the life boring, or insipid, and leave in order to go back where they can have a good time. It is not simply that they feel themselves hemmed in and suppressed and reject all forms of discipline in order to go back to the world where they have every chance to seek fulfillment of their desires and of their will, unhampered by authority and restrictions. This is not the point at all.

On the contrary, they usually come (except for those so young and callow that they have no notion what they are doing in the first place) seriously concerned with one thing above all: they want to *give their lives a religious and human meaning*.

They recognize that life in the world as it is today tends to be confused and meaningless even on a human level. Hence they come to the monastery not only to save their souls in the next world, but before that to save their dignity and integrity as human beings in this life, to discover their true identity, so that they will be able to know themselves and give themselves fully and maturely to God.

This is perfectly in accordance with the teachings of the Fathers, especially of the first Cistercians. St. Bernard makes clear that the monastic life first of all restores man's nature in its capacity to know truth, to experience the truth in ourselves, to experience the truth in our normal, human relations with other people. St. Bernard definitely stresses the natural aspect of this restoration which must come before the supernatural elevation of man (of course he does not use Thomist terminology). When we have experienced the truth in ourselves and in others we are ready for the (mystical) experience of Truth in itself, that is in God.

Other Cistercians follow this line of thinking. For instance, Adam of Perseigne: his letters describe the monastic formation as "therapy" for people who in the world have been seriously disordered and have lost the balance and sanity proper to their nature.

Here is where the problem arises.

Young men come to the monastery seeking truth in themselves, seeking to experience themselves as real and authentic human beings. They come seeking identity, and an experience of identity which is largely denied them or frustrated in the world.

However, we must not misapprehend the nature of their quest and assume that they come to the monastery seeking a different "answer" or a different explanation of life. They themselves may be unaware of this, and they may at first seem to expect "answers" and indeed a whole new set of explanations, a systematic outlook on life, in which everything "fits" and "makes sense." Thus for instance if we assume that modern man is simply rootless and disoriented and try to give his life direction and meaning with a logical, scholastic view of the universe and of the economy of salvation, we may at first arouse his curiosity, but we must take care not to lead him into what he considers a further and more radical disappointment. The "answers" that modern man seeks and needs are not those of the neat verbal formula or the logically constructed system. There is in his very being a profound distrust of logic and of system. His need and his hope are in a realm of paradox where strict logic cannot reach, because it is the realm of the personal and the unique. The very meaning of personal identity is lost if we suppose that it conforms to precedent and to the general type. The question of identity and of meaning in our personal life can never be adequately answered by logic but only by life itself. Yet we live in a world where words, formulas, official answers and a seemingly logical system may pretend to decide everything for us in advance. If modern man, seeking his true self, seeking the existential atmosphere of an exploration that has not been determined beforehand, comes to a monastic life and discovers that all his questions are answered in advance, all his decisions are made for him, all his movements are expected to fit in with a rigid logical necessity of black and white, absolute right and wrong, he may try earnestly to accept the answers, and may seem to succeed for a few years. But in the end he will feel as frustrated in the monastery as he did in the world. He will not find himself because he will not be able to seek himself. He will simply have been told who and what he is expected to be.

We must not be too quick to think that because modern man is in a state of uncertainty, that what he wants is absolute certainty at any price. In an age when science has discovered the utility of an "uncertainty principle" to correct the errors and false perspectives engendered by the logical certitude of classical physics, there is also felt to be a need for a more existential spirituality in which uncertainties and hesitations are to some extent accounted for, and in which everything is not immediately and forever settled by good resolutions, and categorical affirmations that see all things in black and white.

It is quite true that most Americans suffer a prolonged and severe identity crisis and many never really pull through it at all. Hence we can expect postulants to come to us in the midst of this crisis. But we will not solve it for them (and indeed no one can solve it for them anyway) if we assume that "identity" means something akin to "character building" as propounded in the do-it-yourself manuals for success in dynamic "strong personality" (whatever that may be). A monastic spirituality that assumes that the individual is a center of volitional force that is supposed to exert itself upon or against a world outside and around it can at best only perpetuate the illusory identity which no man in his right mind would consent to have: that of a mythical and detached "subject" existing entirely outside all "objective" reality, able to understand everything by pure reason and to dominate everything by his own will. Such an identity could not exist except as a caricature of God. And it is unfortunately true that many men have tried to solve their identity problem by this fraudulent imitation of what they imagine their Creator to be. The problem is much more subtle than that. It is resolved only by a much deeper and much more mysterious commitment that begins with the acceptance of a place and a destiny which one can never completely understand because it belongs not simply to an ordered and natural system of laws, but to a supernatural order of grace and love, an order of freedom in which nothing is scientifically predictable and everything has to be taken as a wager, with daring and with unbounded trust.

To decide everything beforehand and to say just what precise form the challenge of grace will necessarily take, is to empty grace of its meaning and reduce the Gospel of love to a system of legalistic security. We must take care not to reduce the monastic life to a purely common-sense machinery of rules and official decisions in which there are only token sacrifices and formal worship, and in which there is no longer anything unpredictable except the day-to-day detail of trivial and absolutely necessary frustration.

The monastic life attracts people who look for meaning and identity precisely because it is a life of solitude. But if it is too completely and minutely organized, it will in actual fact prevent the monk from ever entering into the authentic solitude of heart in which alone he can find himself in finding God.

A Jesuit author, writing of the prevalence of the identity crisis in America, and of the American fear of solitude, says:

Critics have also noted the American fear of loneliness. Individual identity is sacrificed in an effort to stay close to the herd, to be no different from others in thought, feeling, or action. To stand aside, to be alone, is to assert a personal identity which refuses to be submerged. Society will not tolerate this. Innumerable social features are designed to prevent it: stadiums to accommodate thousands at sport events, open doors of private rooms and offices, club cars on trains, shared room in colleges and boarding houses, countless clubs, organizations, associations, societies, canned music (for silence is unbearable) piped into hospitals, railway cars, and supermarkets.

Yet one of the surest signs of the resolution of the identity crisis is an increased capacity for being alone, for being responsible for oneself. The gradual process that will end in perfect identity involves an awareness of the fact that there are decisions in life and aspects of life's struggle that a person must face alone.

For as a young person becomes clearer in his own mind of his role in society and of his personal identity, he is likely also to become more aware of how he differs from others. Gradually he becomes conscious of his isolation from others, not because others are pulling away, but because the fullness of personal identity cannot be achieved without some degree of aloneness. Here there is a paradox: the more richly a person lives, the more lonely, in a sense, he becomes. And as a person, in this formative isolation, becomes more able to appreciate the moods and feelings of others, he also becomes more able to have meaningful relationships with them.

But the unwritten code of our national culture prohibits aloneness, and this is the second causative factor for a prolonged identity crisis: the obstacles our society imposes to prevent personal reflection.[2]

One of the most characteristic American ways of evading the identity problem is conformism, running with the herd, the refusal of solitude and flight from loneliness. This exists even in monasteries and can create a serious problem if for renunciation and inner solitude it tries to substitute a false atmosphere of collective euphoria and corrupt our cenobitic life with a vapid "togetherness." Togetherness is not "community." To love our brother we must first respect him in his

[2] Barry McLaughlin, S.J., *Nature, Grace and Religious Development*, pp. 46–47.

own authentic reality, and we cannot do this if we have not attained to a basic self-respect and mature identity ourselves.

Are our efforts to be more "communal" and to be more of a "family" really genuine or are they only new ways to be intolerant of the solitude and integrity of the individual person? Are we simply trying to submerge and absorb him, and keep him from finding an identity that might express itself in dissent and in a desire for greater solitude? Are we simply trying to guard against his entering a "desert" of questioning and paradox that will disturb our own complacencies?

We are likely to meet postulants in two kinds of identity crisis, those whose adolescent identity problem has not been solved and practically cannot be solved because they are too neurotic and those with an identity crisis on a deeper spiritual level. The former do not really want an identity. They do not want to be mature and we can do nothing with them. Unfortunately, since they generally appear to be docile and obedient, and even seem quite "spiritual" sometimes, they are too often accepted, with bad consequences.

The latter people are capable of maturing spiritually. They have excellent qualities, and they are handicapped only by the deep self-doubt and inner confusion that come from not experiencing themselves as really having a mind and a will of their own, as being fully persons with true personal convictions and the ability to love, to give themselves, to surrender to God.

They may perhaps be slightly neurotic, but they can be helped and they can make a good adjustment. These are the ones we are concerned with. They come to the monastery hoping to find a real meaning for their life as men. They come with some of the critical ideas and some of the hopes sown by Marx, Freud, etc., in the air of our times, and they have some of the demands and expectations which have been created by modern thought. They bring with them the confusions and contradictions of modern thought. They do not usually have the "unchristian" presuppositions of secular thought, and so we ought to accept them as they are, face their needs as reasonable and valid. We ought to try to do something for them.

At the same time we must, while respecting their personal integrity, recognize that they may be strongly impregnated with the romantic sense of need and longing. The "self" they seek to "realize" is perhaps an unreal, an impossibly "pure" consciousness (which they may momentarily confuse with Cassian's *puritas cordis*). They may, on the basis of this quest for romantically pure feeling, justify every rebellion against whatever disturbs them and divests them from that quest of narcissistic peace. In this case they need to know that what they seek is unauthentic, and that its inauthenticity cannot be excused by appeals to modern writers whom the "monks do not understand."

But suppose the young monk wakes up to the fact that he came to the monastery with romantic illusions, that he is being kept there by suggestions and directions which point to an impossible goal of "pure contemplation," a narcissistic or platonic beatitude of pure self-consciousness, masking as consciousness of God? Surely this awakening is serious, and requires to be understood.

In any event, these distinctly modern young men are going to come to us with certain modern questions and difficulties. Their questions and difficulties are going to focus a spotlight of criticism on some features of our monastic life. In point of fact these difficulties will call in question the very meaning of the monastic life of "contemplation," and indeed of religion itself. Basic ideas such as that of obedience to religious authority, of liturgical worship, of interior prayer, of poverty may be called into question. If these concepts are found in fact to be somewhat formalistic and arbitrary, if they have lost their value as signs, if they are reduced to a pious routine substituting for true love of God and genuine worship, their "mystery" will be reduced to "mystification." The modern young man will be wounded with a profound resentment, and will begin to think that all these things have been imposed on him by a religious system which does not really have his true interest at heart, but only requires that he become a submissive cog in a religious machine.

This of course may and often does imply a failure of faith, a movement of withdrawal and doubt, a refusal to encounter the demands of God's Word and to make the fundamental sacrifice of one's own will without which no monasticism is possible. Nevertheless, there may also be an element of genuine scandal in the way monastic observance is understood and carried out by a given community.

What can we do about this?

It is usually at the point when we realize that there is definite criticism and challenge implied by these problems that we run into difficulties with these young monks.

First, in so far as their problems themselves imply criticism of the life (they could not have the problem in that form unless they experienced the life as "wrong" for them), we may tend to deny the existence of the problem, or even the reality of their subjective experience.

Here we must be careful of manipulating the word "neurotic" with too much abandon. Maybe the problem is not pathological at all. On the contrary, it may very often happen that the awakening of the problem, the ability to experience it as a problem after several years in the monastery is the sign of an awakening of identity. It is precisely the reality and importance of the experience that ought to engage our attention. This is a sign of growth, and hence a sign that the monk is reaching out for a truth, a good that ought to become his. He is now at a point of critical confrontation, not only with his own human condition but with the Word of God addressed directly and in mystery to his own human freedom, asking his free adherence to the Law and Love of Christ, inviting him to follow Christ in sacrifice.

But if we refuse to accept his problem as valid, if we try simply to dismiss it, and even to question his sanity or his sincerity, we immediately aggravate the crisis. One thing the young monk knows and experiences is the human reality and urgency of his problem. At the same time he profoundly and earnestly doubts that our observances and our obedience have any further relevance to his problem. This doubt is, in fact, at the heart of the problem. Hence we only intensify his ambivalence and his torment if we implicitly say, "Renounce your doubt, accept obedience and monastic observance on our terms, and you will have peace." This will almost fatally drive him out of the monastery if, in fact, what he needs is precisely to see and understand the monastic life not in our terms but in his, that is to say, in terms of his own capacity to find it meaningful. In a word, if we simply reduce the choice to the acceptance of monastic life because we say it is meaningful, if we insist that he must take our word for this or else stand convicted of faithlessness and cowardice, he will finally decide that our monastic observance is nothing but a mystification. And he will leave. His departure will perhaps be more our fault than his. He will almost have to leave in order to be true to himself. Our refusal to listen to his problem, our demand that he should simply cease to have this problem, is in effect a confession of our own inadequacy, our own incapacity to meet him on a fully personal level.

Secondly, we treat this critical awakening as the beginning of rebellion that has to be firmly put down. And in order to do so we demand not understanding but unconditional submission. We do not see that what the monk is asking of us is not so much a magic and official solution to all problems, but the recognition of his new identity (as a person who experiences this thing about the monastic life, who sees the monastic life in this new and difficult light) and the loyal effort to cooperate with him in trying to clarify something that is as yet clear neither to him nor to ourselves. We refuse him this recognition, and demand that he cease to question "the system" and our official interpretation of it. We demand that he simply accept our answer even though to him it seems to have nothing to do with his question.

Then when the young monk begins to raise questions that we ourselves do not want to face, we not only try to impose an answer but we even try to change the question. Our answer consists in reformulating his question in a way that seems acceptable to us, because then we can give it an answer that we approve of—and that requires no new adjustment!

What then should we do? If we recognize that in questioning his vocation the young monk is also seriously questioning us and our vocation, should we then enter into his doubt, and share his own perplexities? Should we too call everything into question, re-examine everything, and wonder what we are doing in the monastery ourselves?

It seems to me that what is called in question is not our monastic life but rather some of the presuppositions which we, as slightly dated moderns, have read into it. And the most questionable of these is our persistent conviction that life consists of questions and answers, and that "problems" and "decisions" and "choices" are of overwhelming importance, so that at every moment we have to be thinking of right and wrong, commitment or evasion, sincerity or insincerity, maturity or immaturity. We keep all these questions going full blast every waking hour of the day and even during the hours when we ought to be asleep, and we drive the young monk to torment himself with these questions even more than we torment ourselves. Perhaps our problem consists in wanting to have problems and consequently creating them out of nothing in order to seek solutions!

Thus we begin earnestly to reconsider the young monk's questioning of our life. Sincere efforts to understand the "problem" are made. We try to answer the objections of the young monk, but usually on a level where our attempt tends to be meaningless. We strive to meet him halfway in his difficulty with our life and to try to work out some way of changing the pattern of the life so that it will make more sense to him. Our changes in observance, liturgy, horarium, work and so on are generally our well-intentioned response to the "difficulties" of young monks. We intend thereby to help him answer his questions and find happiness in a "meaningful" dedicated life.

Without being a prophet of gloom, I must say that legislated changes in the externals of our life are not going to solve this problem as long as our mentality itself is not deepened and clarified. The restlessness of the new generation has finally awakened a response, but is it the response of Christian and monastic wisdom? or is it simply a protective reflex of our own insecurity? It seems to me that we are now becoming self-consciously and naively "modern," hastily and uncritically adjusting any and every formula that seems to fit the new situation, without "changing our minds" in any deeper sense.

Basically our trouble remains the same: an obsession with questions and answers, with problems and solutions, with momentous decisions, and even with "identity" raised to the level of a kind of absolute. The traditional wisdom of monasticism and of the Gospel ought to help us see through this mystification and bring us back into contact with reality. Our life does not consist in magic answers to impossible questions, but in the acceptance of ordinary realities which are, for the most part, beyond analysis and therefore do not need to be analyzed.

We will help the monk through his "identity crisis" only if we refrain from making him too conscious of his identity or his lack of identity, and of his crisis. And we will prove ourselves wise and discreet monks if instead of making a problem out of everything in the monastic life, we are first content with living it in the spirit of the Gospel, with a sincere and healthy realism, refraining, as far as possible, from judging everything and everyone at all hours of the day and night.

The act of judging is an act by which we set ourselves apart as unique, as "outside" the common run of beings, as something totally special and apart, taking a godlike view (*eritis sicut dii*) of men and events. We ask questions, we "have problems," we seek to make "authentic decisions" because we believe in this mystification, this spurious and romantic "identity" of the self that stands apart and affirms itself by judging others. As long as man thinks that the solution of his "identity crisis" consists in achieving this capacity for self-assertion, we can have no peace in our monasteries. "Judge not, that you be not judged."

Nevertheless, the monk does judge, and before he can learn to stop judging he must realize that this is what he is up to. He must become able to get along without it.

All explanations and "definitive answers" on a religious level will remain meaningless and inadequate to the monk as long as in his heart he experiences an "existential doubt" of the value of the monastic life for him. Many of those who are tempted to leave can easily articulate their problem in these terms: "What is the use of my undergoing all this suffering and hardship (in my mind, struggling with the apparent meaninglessness of this life) if in the end it will not be worth anything anyway?" They are seriously confronted with what they feel to be the problem of useless suffering. The answer of "dark faith" and "believe what you cannot see" fails to convince them because it seems to them to be little more than verbalization. On the contrary, they are deeply affected by what seems to be the failure and inauthenticity of others who have, in all docility, contented themselves with this advice.

What do they see? Too often they see men who have abdicated their human identity and reality (in good faith) and are leading lives without human authenticity, simply passive, evading responsibility, and humanly impoverished, often to a serious degree. For example, they may sometimes see men who have been in the monastery for years and whose simplicity is not that of spiritual childhood but frankly that of neurotic infantilism.

They may see men who seem to be obeying and who, in fact, are simply the products of a life of overcontrol. (The idea that every slightest move of the monk and even his inmost thoughts are not supernatural and monastic except when subject to complete control is disastrous for modern man. This proceeds from a false supernaturalism.) These people cannot be entrusted with the simplest job, without expecting instructions and commands at every step. They lack sound judgment and even common sense. They are often eccentric and their spirituality tends to be both naive and bizarre. Yet because they maintain a servile attitude they are praised and rewarded. In point of fact the emptiness and futility of their lives are a real scandal to the young monk. How often do we not hear novices and young monks saying: "If I remain in the monastery will I become like Father so-and-so?"

If all these things are true, should they not be admitted and faced? Certainly the solution is not simply to tell the young monk to close his eyes and act as if these realities were not real. But if we want to get to the root of the problem we have to ask why these inevitable human failures attain to so great an importance and become so great a problem. After all, if you have failings I may notice them and be sorry for you, but do they have to upset my whole life?

It is the conviction that we have to confront all problems and definitely settle them that leaves young monks disturbed and unhappy about the failures of others. But a true and mature identity does not consist in the ability to give a final solution to everything—as if the "mature person" were one for whom there were no longer any mysteries or any scandals. We discover our identity when we accept our place and our way in the midst of persons and things, in a historical situation, that we do not have to completely understand. We simply see that it is our own place and decide to live in it, for better or for worse. In the light of this simple and primordial acceptance, a natural consent, an obedience to reality that is already analogous to the obedience of faith, we can finally "be ourselves." Our mind is "made up" and so we do not have to keep unmaking it and putting it together again with new judgments, many of which are irresponsible and rash.

Of course when a monk is making up his mind to leave his monastery he easily finds all kinds of bad examples to persuade him that he is right. He may tend to ignore the really mature and well-adjusted monks, the serious and solid ones who are living an authentic monastic life. Yet a further problem arises: for practical reasons, the ones who are solid and mature are usually officers or have some important job. Hence the others argue that in fact one has to have a job to "become mature," and that hence activity is the solution. This may even become a generalized response to the problem and a whole monastery may get the idea that all the monks will benefit if all are more active, more outgoing, more in contact with outsiders, perhaps even engaged in parish work.

But in any event, it is a sign of immaturity and lack of identity to remain so dependent on the good and bad examples of others that we allow their lives to influence our own lives in a decisive manner. The fact that some other monks are unhappy or lead fruitless lives has nothing to do with my staying in a monastery or leaving it, if I am a mature person capable of assuming responsibility for my own life and my own response to the call of God.

Another point of great importance is the question of monastic priesthood in the light of the identity problem. Because of the background of the postulants and the very important part formerly played by the priest in immigrant communities in America, the ideal of "being a priest" is deeply rooted in the psychology of the American Catholic—for religious as well as for social and personal reasons. Often the idea of "becoming a priest" is one and the same as the idea of fully becoming a person, of being someone who really counts, whose life has a full meaning. This ingrained presupposition has a great deal to do with psychological conflicts in the community, including the question of status of the brothers, which is made more ambiguous by it.

It seems that we ought to examine some of the main features of our monastic life, liturgy, study, formation, silence, enclosure, conversion of manners, and especially monastic work in order to see how these can all be rethought in such a way as to meet the problem of identity and authenticity.

As matters stand, I can say that of the observances which most young monks feel to be artificial and inauthentic, the Chapter of Faults easily takes first place. Then we must run the whole gamut of monastic community relations, affected by silence, by artificial and archaic customs, etc. The choir, too, is the scene of much depersonalization and anguish. Much trouble is had with distorted and conventional notions of asceticism. A wrong use of superficial mystical ideas can play havoc with some who are suffering from the "emptiness and *angst*" of depersonalization and neurosis.

After merely touching upon these points as topics for further thought, I would like to suggest one area where we can hope for good results, and that is monastic work. Work that is productive, properly organized, and remains in contact with nature, work that is truly physical and manual, outdoor work, work that is properly learned and well done, work that is managed and taught on a human and monastic level, and not carried out like factory-type drudgery or office routines—such work can do much to help the young monk find his identity and grow in Christ, by teaching him to accept himself, work in harmony with others, and feel himself fully part of a world made by a loving Father in which his own work has a redemptive and sanctifying quality because it is united with the labor and sacrifice of the Incarnate Son of God.

Whether or not the postulant who enters our monastic life is himself using such concepts as "identity crisis," "authentic personal existence" and "meaningful choice," or is even aware of them, they are common currency in the realm where psychoanalysis and existentialist thought work together to explain some of modern man's confusions and to render them more tractable, and he is at any rate one who is prepared to think in such terms. He is perhaps, in actual fact, still in the midst of an identity crisis himself, and his vocation may be due in part to such a crisis. He has come to the monastery in the hope that here he can be true to himself, or at least discover whether or not he is anybody at all. In other words, he has a soul to save, a life to be endowed with meaning not only on the supernatural level but even in terms of nature, "the world" and this present life. In other words, whether or not we want to take this phraseology with complete seriousness, we might as well face the realities which it attempts to describe, even if we ourselves want to see them somewhat differently ourselves.

After all, the traditional and popular language of the Gospels speaks of "losing" one's inmost self, one's soul, one's personal and spiritual reality. To "find" and to "save" this inmost and secret reality, one must hear the word of the Gospel, the word of the cross, the message of salvation and grace. To become aware of oneself as a Christian is to discover one's full identity as one who has been sought and found by the inscrutable mercy of God. The discovery of this "true self" is also a discovery of one's responsibility to other such selves, one's brothers in Christ, one's fellow men, including those who are still lost, who have still not entered the light of this saving and supernatural recognition.

There are some men who cannot sufficiently deepen and

clarify this discovery of themselves in Christ until they enter a monastery and devote their whole life to an existential realization, a living out in deed and in fact, of this mysterious relationship to God and to other men. Such persons desire to express their identity in a paradoxical recognition that they are a "nothing" that has been called to a life of pure love and praise, so that their very identity, like the identity of the angels, is that of beings who praise and thank the Source of all Life for being just that: the Source of all Life.

Thus in the highest sense the monastic and contemplative life seems to be a sacrifice of identity, a "loss of the self" in order that there may be no self but that of God who is the object of our contemplation and of our praise. And this, paradoxically, is not self-alienation but the highest and most perfect "self-realization." Unfortunately when this dimension of the spiritual life is grasped only verbally, as a proposed ideal which is "conceived" and "imagined" but not actually experienced, it may be grossly misunderstood and the misunderstanding may lead to grave distortions of the personality.

The mystique of humility and contemplation is good only for those who have an identity which they are capable of surrendering as though it were a nothing, in exchange for the "all" of God, in which they too are found and recovered, with all the world besides. To the immature man for whom the accession to full identity is too difficult a step, a role of passivity and anonymity, a laudable and highly respectable "nothingness" can become a very convenient evasion. In these pages we have not paid much attention to those who have succeeded in playing this role in a monastic habit. They exist, and they are at times a scandal to others who are more seriously concerned with not keeping the talent of identity and personal being buried in the routines of a trivial and forfeited existence.

This chapter has concerned itself chiefly with monks who have a known capacity to live the monastic life tolerably well but who, coming face to face with what can be called the "crisis of identity" after they have been for some years professed, come to believe that the only honest solution, the only "authentic" way of confronting the problem, is to admit frankly that they were mistaken when they entered the monastery, and return to the world to begin life again outside as mature and sober beings who have sloughed off their illusions.

This is a formula that is quite modern, and is becoming very familiar. In some cases we cannot doubt that in order to be fully honest and true to himself, as well as to God, the young professed may as well frankly admit his mistake and leave. But in many other cases it seems probable that the conclusion, ringing with earnest appeals to authenticity and identity, has been arrived at by pure rationalization. In other words, it is fraudulent. It is "inauthentic." And it constitutes an infidelity to the Word of God and to grace.

There will always be evasions. There will always be reasons why we can never be competent to judge these evasions. But it remains for us to recognize that a climate of questions and answers, problems and solutions, a climate of seemingly infallible logic, order, efficiency and clarity may be quite deceptive. It may tempt men to rationalize. It may corrupt in them a capacity for humility and sincere obedience to God's truth and God's will as it is encountered in the existential mystery of daily life.

It is natural that a younger generation should respond to rationalizations about authority with other rationalizations about authenticity. In such cases, there is not only a problem of the younger generation, but a problem of all generations. It is the problem of substituting verbal questions and answers for the reality of life itself in which questions will often answer themselves if we let them alone.

It is our habit of treating everything as a question—in other words, of always tugging at things for an "answer" instead of letting them be themselves—that quite often provokes vocation crises in the monastery. After one has become sufficiently frustrated by a useless search for answers and solutions where there are really few problems or none at all, it is easy to conceive that the biggest and most authentic answer is to question one's original commitment and to go back on it.

The primitive simplicity and authenticity of the monastic life itself should eventually calm the enraged hunger for "answers" and allay the itch to be having and solving problems. Unfortunately the very hope of "primitive monastic simplicity" seems to present itself only as a problem and as a decisive question to end all questions. The only answer is not a new formula or a new program, but simply life itself in peace, humility, simplicity and silence.

In the end, while admitting the reality of the "identity crisis" and of the "need for authenticity," and while adjusting our own view of the monastic life by a sage consideration of these concepts, we will relax our rather obsessive grip on some of the more obdurate myths of authoritarian logic, and return to the basic respect for life, for faith, for truth, for experience and for man himself which is implied in the teachings of primitive monastic tradition. The monastic life itself has retained its primitive validity, or can easily recover it where the basic principles of the life are respected. Where there is a genuine life of solitude, poverty, prayer, silence, penance, work, charity, obedience: where the Law of the Gospel, which is a law of love and grace, is fully and fervently kept and not obscured by legalism and sermonizing, it will be easy to see that here is a way of authenticity and truth in which man does not merely discover and assert a private identity, a "personality" in the sense of a successful role, but learns that the truest way to find himself is to lose the self he has found in Christ.

THE IDENTITY CRISIS

The crisis of religious vocations is no secret. It is everywhere the same. The departure of professed, including very many who have proved themselves capable of living a good religious life and apparently of successful adaptation, constitutes a vexing problem in all Orders, not excluding our own.

If we try to study this problem in terms of the thinking, the mentality, the outlook, the psychology of the postulant, which all play an important part in his vocation and adaptation, perhaps we can evaluate the problem in some depth, and not be content with superficial analysis. Naturally we will have to be content with only one or two aspects of the question.

It would be a mistake to presuppose that it is important to pinpoint the "fault," for instance, by "blaming" all the trouble on "modern youth," or blaming it on a retarded form of spirituality in the monasteries. It is rather a question of finding out the genuine and new needs of a new generation, and of discovering how God asks the monastic life to meet these needs.

It is not enough to point to the moral disintegration of an affluent society, to broken homes, alcoholism, irresponsibility, delinquency and other widely prevalent evils, and then simply say that the modern postulant, even when he has the best kind of good will, is really deprived of the moral fiber and courage which the life requires.

Nor is it adequate to assume that in "the world" everybody is abandoned to strong and lusty passions and all are carried away with animal spirits, seeking unrestrained pleasure and infallibly getting what they seek. This is a totally misleading picture of the modern world in America, where in point of fact, though pleasure is presented and marketed under the most glowing colors, it eludes even those who can afford everything they desire. What is wrong with the world is not the satisfaction of carnal desires but universal confusion and frustration, leading to a collapse of real interest in life, the danger of despair, and the search for an outlet in various forms of extremism, fanaticism, or nihilism: or else, more commonly, a mindless and routine conformity to the demands of a highly organized social machine. These are symptoms. They are not the problem itself.

One might also be tempted to point to modern thought in all its various manifestations, and to see in it nothing but so many incitements to revolt, to the assertion of self-will and lust, the love of anarchy and rebellion against all authority and all morality. All the most influential thinkers of modern times are thus regarded as disciples of demons and prophets of evil. Though we are not acquainted with them, we feel we "know" enough about them to reject them without further investigation. We feel we can say, without even a second thought, that they are in great part responsible for the mystery of evil, restlessness, dissatisfaction, doubt and rebellion in modern youth. They have "poisoned the mind of man." And there is nothing for us to do but counteract the poison of anarchy and self-will by the medicine of obedience, authority, control, etc.

Is it really that simple?

Who are these thinkers? Let us just name a few, going back a hundred years. Marx, Darwin, Kierkegaard were flourishing then. Nietzsche came soon after. Then Freud, Jung and Adler along with Lenin, then Sartre, the existentialists (Christian and otherwise). There is no question whatever that these thinkers have completely revolutionized the thought of modern man. They have created a whole new climate of thinking, and the chief reason for the impact of Teilhard de Chardin on modern thinking both in and out of the Church is due to the fact that he knows his Marx and Darwin.

But let us ask: Are all these men simply madmen or villains? Is it true that they are simply trying, out of malice, passion or envy, to undermine a beautiful and well-ordered world? Is not their concern for man something very genuine and are not their insights extremely valuable on occasion, even for us? Whatever may have been the remedies they prescribed, we ought to attend to their diagnosis of modern man. All of these thinkers are deeply concerned with the problem of man since the industrial revolution. They are trying to understand and explain the progressive dehumanization of man in the world of the machine, and trying to tell him some way to get control of himself and of his world so that he can be himself again.

Right or wrong, these prophets are all concerned with the main problem that faces us: Man is not himself. He has lost himself in the falsities and illusions of a massive organization. How can he recover his authenticity and his true identity? All these thinkers, even the Christians, tend to regard conventional forms of religion as being in league with the forces which have diminished and depersonalized man.

Whether we like it or not, their thought applies to us, and it is bound to affect us, even if only by the fact that they have created a climate of questioning, criticism and doubt, in which the best of our postulants are going to come to us asking for authentic values and demanding not that we meet the requirements of an ancient written code, but that we be genuinely and spontaneously human first of all. This is a challenge rather than a problem.

Most postulants who come to our monasteries (with the possible exception of teen-agers who have spent several years in a minor seminary) are deeply conscious of their need to give their lives a meaning which they cannot seem to find in the world outside. More and more postulants come to the monastery with the vague sense that they have not yet fully confronted the problem of identity. They are hoping that in the monastery they can finally work through their identity crisis. But it must be said at once that the monastery is not the place for that. Monastic life presupposes that one has found his identity and has profound personal convictions and personal standards to go on. Many postulants who have this problem are only vaguely aware of it. Others are more conscious of it, but cannot explain it. Obviously, few are able to be articulate about it. If they were, it would mean that the problem was already half solved. Yet even then, does their experience in the monastery help them to develop a deeper insight?

The crisis of identity which is everywhere normal in adolescence has become a grave problem in America extending far beyond adolescence and through young adulthood. Possibly there are many who never really resolve this problem in our society. One of the characteristics of "mass society" is precisely that it tends to keep man from fully achieving his identity, from operating fully as an autonomous person, from growing up and becoming spiritually and emotionally adult.

What is meant by identity? Many facets of the concept could be considered. For practical purposes here we are talking about one's own authentic and personal beliefs and convictions, based on experience of oneself as a person, experience of one's ability to choose and reject even good things which are not relevant to one's own life.

One does not receive "identity" in this sense along with life and vegetative existence. To have identity is not merely to have a face and a name, a recognizable physical presence. Identity in this deep sense is something that one must create for himself by choices that are significant and that require a courageous commitment in the face of anguish and risk. This means much more than just having an address and a name in the telephone book. It means having a belief one stands by; it means having certain definite ways of responding to life, of meeting its demands, of loving other people, and in the last analysis, of serving God. In this sense, identity is one's witness to truth in one's life.

This does not mean merely the capacity to cling with conviction to official or external standards, to values which one does not personally experience as good but which one accepts in order to experience security, in order to please authority and so on.

The monk or novice who thinks he strongly feels certain values in our life and apparently embraces them simply because he experiences the security of "belonging" and of pleasing someone else, or pleasing the community, or the superior, etc., is perhaps evading the identity crisis. He is not in a position to make a serious choice of his vocation. Yet many have gone on to vows in this state of mind, urged by superiors to do so.

On the other hand, the problem of opposition raises an identity crisis for many. They confront things in the life that raise serious questions. These questions are perfectly reasonable and legitimate questions. But a person who has not really matured thinks that the mere presence of such questions is a problem, an infidelity. He may choose to question the values of the monastic life, but in doing so he imagines that he is automatically rejecting them, and then the life becomes unbearable because though he cannot apparently accept the monastic life he also feels he cannot commit himself to anything else. Since he has no definite ideas or standards of his own he has nothing to "stand by" and hence in that sense feels himself to be "unreal" and without identity. He is not able to question, to doubt, and to make a choice. The fact of questioning seems to him to dictate a negative choice, especially if he is surrounded by others who communicate the same insecurity and doubt to him. Of course there is no real solution to the identity crisis simply in opposing authority. This is an adolescent trait. In a supposed "adult" who simply wastes time pitting himself against authority in trivialities there is a real lack of identity, or a false identity which maintains itself by provoking resistance (attention) rather than by flattering or cajoling authority. In either case, the "center" of identity is experienced to some extent not in oneself but in the other. This is "alienation" in a psychological sense.

In the Middle Ages, the mentality of the monastic postulant was much less confused than it is today. Society was homogeneous. There was a great deal of violence and disorder, but one moral and religious standard was accepted as relevant. The meaning of the monastic life was hardly questioned, though an individual might conceivably doubt its relevance for him. Today everything is in question: monasticism, Christianity, reason, all values, humanity itself. Hence it is no longer easy for a person to discover his identity by choosing and embracing certain well-established traditional standards which no one doubts, and simply experiencing these as his own.

To choose a value that is questioned and doubted is to place oneself in the position of being doubted. The mature person is able to assume this risk. He can embrace an unpopular idea, commit himself to it and to its consequences, and accept the fact that it means becoming a problem and even in some way a "scandal" to others. It is in this way that most people today have to establish and affirm their identity. But it takes courage to do this. Hence *all* values are questioned, or can be; to embrace any of them is to become an object of questioning and doubt. Those who shrink from personal responsibility shrink from this also. They seek to rest on an infallible authority or else take refuge in an area where questions are not asked.

What we are now about to say is in no sense an attack on "regularity" and exact observance of rules and customs. We are taking for granted that a mature and responsible man accepts the obligations of his state of life objectively and seriously fulfills them. A good monk keeps his rule, and has mature and serious spiritual motives for doing so.

But there are others who in actual fact welcome the passivity and irresponsibility that are possible in a strictly controlled and organized life. For these the monastery offers opportunities for a false solution to the identity problem. Their obedience may be an evasion. These persons fear insecurity, and seek security from a well-established and approved system that nobody questions. Rules clearly say what is right and wrong. The monk can turn his back on the world with its problems and forget it. He can simply follow the rules, do what he is told, and have security because everyone around him holds that this is "right" and that to do anything else is "wrong." He no longer has to think. Choices are made for him. Others are responsible. He need not care.

Furthermore, this conduct on his part is rewarded. He causes no trouble. He is therefore approved. His "rightness" is confirmed by the approval of superiors, and he feels he is "a good religious." His one source of insecurity is the apparent questioning of rules and standards by those who are less regular. He worries if these people are not firmly corrected, and he seeks to have them corrected. He worries if the work is not precisely regulated so that at every moment everyone knows exactly what is right and wrong, etc., etc.

His solution is to enter into a system where doubt is impossible. This looks like "faith," but is it?

Someone will say: Why be so subtle about it? Why split psychological hairs? Even supposing they are artificial and immature interiorly, these monks are objectively fulfilling their obligations and it would be hard to tell the difference between them and the really mature monks whose seriousness and regularity are based on fully responsible identities before God and man. These others are at least able to act like good religious, and since they also desire to be good monks, who is to say that they are not so? These people have good will, good intentions and they are "obedient." They do not rock the boat. They help keep order. They are "edifying." Why complain? Let us be grateful that we have so many such monks. They may not be ideal, they may be a little stiff and unnatural, but who knows if they are not saints, after all?

It is quite true that no one can say what God thinks of these men and of their good will. It is not for us to question the fact that He will reward their efforts to love Him according to their own ability. But the fact remains that we are talking about the human and personal development which is in the line of man's natural maturing and which is therefore willed by God for all. If these people, without any moral fault, are to some extent deficient in maturity, the absence of fault does not make their deficiency a good in itself, something that others can accept knowingly as good. If this passive and evasive response to the identity problem is a false solution, then its falsity must be noted for what it is. They may think they want to give God everything, but by their (inculpable) failure to really mature and attain to full personal stature, they are keeping themselves in a state where they really cannot give Him the fullness of service and love to which He is entitled. This is proved by the fact that these people often crack up and become psychotic, which happens when it is no longer possible for them to maintain the artificial and rigid black-and-white, right-and-wrong view of the monastic life on purely external motives. Because they lack inner identity and inner truth, they cannot face the real problems of life if these bear down on them too hard. But the monastery may, it is true, provide them with a permanent refuge in which they can always more or less successfully avoid facing reality in themselves and in others.

It is often evident that such lives are really to a great extent humanly sterile, no matter how much we may rationalize them as "holy," edifying, meritorious.

For example, unlike those who are mature and solid monks and live their vocation with deep personal motives and faith, these people are often eccentric in their conduct and bizarre in their theology. Their devotions are often marginal and queer. They generally lack sound judgment and even common sense. They are often quite incapable of normal human relationships, and their contacts with others are stilted and artificial—or else perhaps they go to the other extreme and become clinging and sentimental. They are always raising strange and useless questions or making naive propositions. They are usually harmless and well-intentioned, but sometimes they become critical and go about ferreting out the "faults" of others and denouncing them. In one word, these people are in many ways deficient and impoverished, and their external regularity is just about all they have. Instead of developing their true identity they have acquired a pseudo identity. They are not persons but only "characters."

What is much more important: the apparent uselessness and sterility of the lives of the externally compliant religious who are approved, who do not rock the boat, who do not raise doubts and questions, who conform, who are passive, is a constant source of doubt to others in whom the identity problem is more acute.

In other words: those who experience doubt, who question their vocation, who have to face the fact that they might be wrong, or even that they might have made profession without sufficient motives, are brought into a state of crisis by observing those who have adopted the false "compliant" solution. They cannot perhaps formulate their serious misgivings, but they know and experience the fact that there is "something wrong with this edifying behavior." (It is important to note that this is for them a genuine and personal experience. It is therefore something real. It is something to work with. It is also important for the monastery and for the community. It is important for us. It may be telling us something we badly need to know.) They may have a valid and disquieting intuition of the real lack of identity and lack of authenticity in these others. They are really aware, however dimly, that the "false solution" of those who have evaded the issue and simply complied, is indeed false. But because they themselves have no deep convictions of their own, because they do not experience their own values as personal and authentic, because they do not fully dare to commit themselves to some other solution which is more genuine, they remain in a state of doubt, frustration, resentment.

It is at this point, we must face it squarely, that the behavior of the externally "good religious" who, in good faith, unconsciously, certainly without guilt, has in fact compromised with one of the most basic demands of his humanity (the demand for authenticity and personal integrity), is a scandal to those who are still deeply aware of their need to attain to a fully human and personal identity, to become authentic human persons in order to give themselves to God as monks.

What follows is of course that the religious truth of monastic profession is brought into question. From failure on the natural level comes a questioning of the supernatural.

Time after time, young monks, novices, postulants, try to express their anxiety and their distress over the fact that, though they cannot formulate it, they feel that the life of some of the older monks as it is concretely lived and "approved," as it is manifested in the monks who have "made it" and are apparently the ones who are most adapted to the monastic life, is inauthentic, an evasion. They feel it is unreal because it is less than human. They feel instinctively that there is something wrong with a sweeping claim that all this rigidity and formality, this artificiality in otherwise good and normal human beings, is really "supernatural." This claim is something that they find deeply disturbing, and gradually they have to admit that they have genuine motives for being disturbed by it. Are they right?

(Here of course an important qualification is necessary: First of all, this intuition of inauthenticity can be greatly exaggerated, and those who have gradually decided that they can't face the monastic life any more do tend to build up too strong a case against the poor monks they see in the community. Even the more artificial ones are not as bad as all that: with their limitations they always retain a certain simplicity, genuineness and goodness which it is unjust and uncharitable to overlook. And then there are in every community a few excellent priests and brothers who, while not being in every respect ideal, are really authentic and genuine Christian persons, mature, simple, direct, honest, and totally human. These are always recognized and respected for what they are, though their presence may be conveniently overlooked by the monk who is intent on arguing his way out the front door.)

Yet these "critics" still love the monastic life. They still see something very real, very desirable, very healthy, in fact something irreplaceable in the spirit of the Rule of St. Benedict (in its honesty and simplicity) and in authentic monastic tradition, in so far as it all reflects the sanity and wisdom of the Gospels. They still want to "truly seek God." But they feel they can no longer reconcile the "search for God" and for truth with an external and routine existence in which they cannot experience in themselves any opening up of their own inner truth. It seems to them that the mere carrying out of actions which they personally find meaningless, in the trust that this will somehow prove meritorious and will be rewarded in heaven, reflects upon God Himself. Can God really ask man to sacrifice the most basic realities of identity and meaning in order to live a life that seems absurd? Does this not call into question the very idea of God? We may try to assuage this doubt by mystical concepts—the "dark night" and so on—but mystical formulations are not called for here. These people are not in the mystical night of the superhuman illuminations, they are in the subhuman and psychological night of depersonalization, of facelessness, lack of identity. God is not asking them to be subhuman and to remain without identity. He wants them to become persons so that they can love Him and give themselves totally to His Truth.

In any event, to resume what has been said so far: it quite often happens that in practice, a young American who enters the monastery and there comes face to face with his identity crisis, tends to solve it "honestly" by coming to recognize that he does not have sufficient motives for staying, or that, even if he has vows, there is such good reason for his leaving that it now seems to be a greater good for him to leave.

If this is in fact true, it is quite an indictment of our system. And perhaps the realization of this is what makes us unwilling to really go too deeply into the question. The question remains: can we adjust our life and our view of our life in such a way that it will be capable of being lived in a more authentic and honest way by modern youth, that is to say, can we offer them a life in which they will really be able to find themselves, realize their identity, authentically grow and develop spiritually as well as mentally and emotionally?

Are we capable of offering modern youth a life in which if they are generous and honest (which they usually are) they can become completely mature Christians and monks?

One might at this point discuss something that always arises in connection with this problem of "authenticity": the question of our "antiquated observances." To what extent can they retain a deep meaning for modern Americans? This is certainly something that people question quite often. The fact that as novices they may at first be willing to accept certain rudimentary spiritual explanations of our monastic behavior does not necessarily mean that they accept the observances in their heart. They are probably just shelving the question—until it comes up later in connection with a post-profession vocation crisis.

But the question of observances and of their meaning is too complex to go into here. And once again, the usages and the way they are observed are symptoms rather than roots of the trouble.

One thing must be said: mere modernization of usages, of liturgical practice, of rules, of behavior, will not solve the

basic problem, which lies much deeper. The agitation and
very active concern with which so many are plunging into
the work of changing our customs, our liturgy, etc., certainly
have a good aspect. It certainly is related to a general
renewal of monastic life which is manifesting itself everywhere. But at the same time, in so far as this need for change
is flavored with a kind of desperation, it may be seen as pro-
ceeding from people who are still struggling with this deep
identity problem and who hope against hope that changes of
rule and ritual will solve it for them.

It must be stated categorically that the problem cannot be
solved from the outside. No amount of "modernization" will
make an alienated personality experience himself as fully
real, though it may help him to confront his problem more
squarely.

Nor can the problem be solved by legislation.

Very often in the efforts made to devise new solutions and
get them legislated we see immature people acting out their
problem in relation to authority, in relation to control, and it
may still be the adolescent problem of identity, which they
are trying to handle is this way.

They are perhaps trying to persuade themselves that they
are "real," that is to say, that their ideas and opinions, their
tastes and needs have an authentic value.

But if I am the kind of person who cannot believe that my
ideas and convictions have authentic value unless they are
the object of a whole gamut of legislative acts on the part of
the Order and the Church, then I prove by that fact that I do
not believe in myself, that I cannot take my convictions
seriously, that I do not experience my own inner motives as
real until they are certified as real by external and official
approval.

This does not mean that a mature person never consults
anyone else and never seeks advice. He certainly asks advice
and accepts it when it is needed and useful. He can also adjust himself to the will and need of another and renounce his
own way in order to do what another wants of him. But in
all this he knows when he himself is convinced, because he
experiences his own convictions as inner realities, not just

as "feelings" or "impressions" or dubious manifestations of something or other needing confirmation by someone else before he can admit that he has them.

It is sometimes assumed as axiomatic that every action of the monk must be subject to external control, even, in some cases, that every thought of the monk must be subject to external control. To renounce one's autonomy to the point of abandoning all spontaneous and independent reflection, intellection, volition, even feeling, is sometimes presented as an ascetic ideal. But this is an impossibility, and even the idea that such a thing is desirable can do irreparable harm. The attempt to live in this manner and to make others do so, is gravely damaging to souls and is a flagrant violation of Christian truth and of the integrity of the human person made in God's image. Our monastic life can at times suffer seriously from this overcontrol.

To be more exact, it used to suffer seriously from it. In practice there is much more spontaneity and variety allowed today. Complete submission to absolute external control is rarely demanded any more in practice, but it is still accepted in theory as right and good, as the "supernatural" and "monastic" way for a monk to live. This creates problems both for those who are seriously attempting to submit in all things and abandon all responsibility for themselves into the hands of others and for those who are in doubt about the validity of their motives and the honesty of remaining indefinitely "minors" in the religious life.

Overcontrol thus tends to do just the opposite from what it is theoretically expected to do.

In theory it is supposed to be a manifestation of faith and supernatural spirit. It is supposed to strengthen faith and the supernatural spirit. In actual fact it breeds doubt, and it eventually undermines both faith and vocation.

Overcontrol of an immature religious does not make him mature, does not strengthen him. It merely suppresses for the time being the questions he ought to be raising and the initiatives he ought to be taking. And its chief effect is to keep him in a state of doubt. It makes him inert, hesitant, confused, helpless and frustrated.

Actually, there is great harm not only to the religious but also to the community in maintaining him in a state of doubt, ignorance and insecurity.

Here are some of the effects of overcontrol on immature monks:

a. By deliberately withholding information from them, and thus keeping them insecure, superiors unwittingly create in their subjects an altogether inordinate need and desire for information. For instance, the immature monk in his identity crisis now becomes convinced that knowledge is altogether essential for his maturity. Hence the veritable panic with which so many young religious now are hunting for knowledge, for education, for information, for information which they feel they have lacked and which they are trying to catch up with. This is one of the more usual and more urgent symptoms of our present crisis.

b. By keeping the subject in constant doubt about himself, by making him repeatedly experience himself as a being of dubious worth, a questionable object, besides preventing him from having inner peace which is necessary to a solid interior life and for growth, one makes him all the more likely either to doubt everything and everyone, or else encourages a blind dependency which in the end cannot help becoming pathological if the person is seriously vulnerable.

c. By fomenting this constant doubt in the heart of the individual monk, one actually creates in him a very ambivalent attitude toward authority. The young monk may experience himself acutely as not worthy of trust, not worthy of being informed, not "able" to know and understand, etc. This may precipitate all kinds of desperate maneuvers to allay doubt, to change the attitude of authority. It ends by causing a great deal more trouble for the superior.

In résumé: It is likely that in the case of modern American youth the phenomenon of overcontrol in our monasteries will result only in confirmed self-doubt on their part coupled with a deep and eventually hostile suspicion of authority. In a word, overcontrol is dangerous and self-defeating. It is a source of many serious problems and it really solves nothing.

Let us not make the mistake of thinking that overcontrol is really a religious value in disguise, that it really has to do with religious obedience and with surrender to God. Let us not imagine that overcontrol answers a real need on the part of the postulant who comes from an anarchic and libertine society in which there is nothing but license and self-will rampant on all sides.

We must be quite clear about one thing above all: overcontrol is one of the salient features of the secular world today. It is particularly related to godlessness and materialism.

Indeed one might argue that it is the largely unsuccessful but nevertheless thorough systematization of control in secular life that is to a great extent responsible for the apparent lawlessness of certain reactions (delinquency etc.). These rebellions are in their turn frantic and desperate attempts to meet overcontrol with genuine independence and authentic identity. Because overcontrol is precisely so powerful, the attempts usually fail.

The world is dominated by the questionable, but inevitable, power of mass society.

We will not here go into all the manifestations of overcontrol, which is just as evident in our affluent consumer society as it is in the rigid totalitarian societies beyond the iron curtain. The manifestations are different, that's all. With us the control is largely anonymous, and decentralized but none the less effective for being anonymous. It would be easy to cite hundreds of ways in which, by advertising etc., the consumer is treated consistently as a minor and is maintained in a state of psychological passivity and dependence, so that he is "unable to resist." (It is important to keep the consumer from having too much of a mind of his own, yet at the same time to create the illusion that he is in the know by feeding him all kinds of bogus information about the product, plus elaborate and "efficient" instructions about how to open the package and make use of the product.)

To sum it all up in one word, our postulants come to us from a society in which man is alienated, in which he is systematically deprived of a serious identity, in which he cannot believe in his dignity, in which he has good reason to be profoundly skeptical of everything and everyone, and in which he tends to renounce all hope of experiencing himself as real and genuinely worth while. It is a society in which he has not much left but to resign himself with a sigh to passivity with a can of beer in front of the TV.

The term alienation is used of a human being who is systematically kept, or who allows himself to be kept, in a social situation in which *he exists purely and simply for somebody else*.

His reason for existing and for acting is not in himself, but in someone else's profit. That is to say that what he does is vastly more profitable and pleasant for someone else, and he gets little or nothing out of it himself. His life lacks meaning. As far as he personally is concerned, there is no reason for him to exist at all. Life is not worth living. (Of course he can manage, if he is strong, to salvage a little meaning and satisfaction. This was possible, as Victor Frankl has shown, even in the ultimate meaninglessness and alienation of the concentration camp. The prisoner in the concentration camp is the type of the completely alienated man, who is totally under the control of the power of mass society. Is this the monastic ideal?)

(Let us not imagine that this "existing for another" is compatible with perfect love. The alienated man cannot love. He has nothing to give. Nothing is his. The lover is able to give himself completely to another precisely because he is his own to give. He is not alienated. He has an identity. He knows what is his to surrender. The alienated man has no chance to surrender. He has simply been "taken over" by total control.)

How will an "alienated" person act and experience the realities of life in a monastery?

In his spiritual life he will tend not to experience realities directly, but secondhand. In the liturgy, for example, instead of deeply feeling and understanding the meaning of the chants, texts, rites, and sacred action directly and personally as relevant to his own response to Christ the Savior and his relationship of brotherhood with the other monks as fellow disciples of Christ, he will experience the fact that in doing these things he is doing what is right: he is doing what is approved by the Church; he is doing what the superiors and professors of liturgy have described as the highest form of worship.

In his reading, he will not so much read books that deeply interest him and arouse a profound intellectual, affective and spiritual response, which is personal to him and which he experiences as light to follow God's paths. He will rather experience the fact that what he is reading is entirely familiar and safe, that there is nothing about it that is disturbing. It echoes the ideas and experiences that have been publicly praised and approved by others, especially by Reverend Father, Father Master, etc.

In the question of monastic renewal, the "alienated" person may doubtless take a fairly active part in new movements, yet without abandoning his alienation. Let us suppose that he admits to consciousness just enough realization of his condition to suggest that a change is needed. He will then "experience" in himself not the real, profound and personal need for a radical change that goes with genuine renewal and implies a certain anguish, insecurity, and risk. He will rather experience the fact that a certain line of change is now approved by forward-looking theologians and publicists. Hence he will accept these ideas not with any intention of involving himself in the anguish and uncertainty of a real renewal, but simply in order to experience himself as "with" the approved ones. His very desire for change is a desire not for the anguish of renewal and self-commitment, but for the safety of having made the right change, the right adjustment, without too much difficulty. "Everything will have changed and it will be all right." Everything will have changed except his alienation.

After having at considerable length studied aspects of the identity problems (without by any means exhausting them, or indeed even scratching the surface), let us briefly conclude with some of the implications for the monastic life and for renewal.

Monastic renewal must now more than ever aim at authenticity.

But we must take care to note a very special aspect of authenticity which has become crucially important now. It will no longer be enough to guarantee a kind of "juridical authenticity," that is to say, a monastic practice which is faithful to the documents of the past. More than ever a merely literal authenticity (fidelity to the letter) will be not only unsatisfactory but disastrous.

The authenticity which the modern monk sincerely and rightly desires, whether or not he may be fully conscious of it, is first of all a fidelity to his own truth and his own inner being as a person. The very first thing of all (something that was much less precarious in the past) is the authentic affirmation of his own identity. Without this starting point, everything else will be lost.

But a monastic life that tends systematically to deny and frustrate the monk in this quest of his own inner authenticity first of all, will necessarily threaten the authenticity of his vocation. It will leave him confronted with the choice: either to submit, sacrifice his integrity and his fidelity to ths first demand of conscience, and live like a zombie—or else to leave the monastery. For many it will reduce itself to this hard choice. Only the mature will be able to adjust to the monastery in spite of everything and live as true monks even though the spirit of the community may be to some extent inauthentic.

We cannot even begin to understand the task of monastic renewal and of a really meaningful aggioramento, unless we take account of this danger.

Being aware of the need of the postulant for inner and personal authenticity first of all, and taking account of the fact that we cannot afford to admit people who are not capable of seriously confronting the problem themselves, we will conclude that we must in no circumstances tolerate the survival of a spirituality which seems, either explicitly or implicitly, to require the sacrifice of personal authenticity and integrity. That would be the sacrifice of truth. It would be a living lie.

We must be very careful indeed not to tolerate any ambiguity on this score, for example by approving concepts of humility and obedience which seem to say that the complete abdication of one's personal autonomy and dignity is a basic value in monastic asceticism. We must not preach an obedience that is mere passive compliance, a humility that is the glad acceptance of depersonalized abjection, a spirituality that glorifies, as "abnegation," the total abdication of all human worth and all identity. This must be seen for what it is: a debasing of man which gives no glory to God, but is bad theology and false supernaturalism, and which seriously endangers the faith of those who allow themselves to be caught in it for a while, only to leave later disgusted and disillusioned.

This has very important theological implications, because a spirituality which despises nature and contemns the human person is basically divisive and Manichaean. It implies a strongly dualistic concept of God and His creation in which creation seems to be opposed to the goodness of God and completely *alien* to God; indeed creation seems in this light to be cursed by God rather than blessed and redeemed. Thus instead of using the goods of nature which God has given us, we tend to fear and despise them. We reject them and trample on them with contempt. But when it comes to our own freedom, our integrity, our dignity as persons we cannot afford to do this! To contemn the human person and his identity is to contemn the image of God reflected in man, His creature and His Son.

We must on the contrary recognize that nature is not irreconcilable with grace, and on the contrary, by the Incarnation and Redemption nature has become penetrated and hallowed by grace. Nature has become the rich field in which grace brings forth its harvest. To sterilize the fruitful capacities of nature is then to sterilize grace itself by depriving it of the ground in which its seed will grow and fructify.

In the contemplative life above all, lack of identity is a disaster.

The monastic life demands first of all a profound understanding and acceptance of solitude. The spirit of the monastic life, even of the cenobitic form of the monastic life, is the spirit of solitude and of the desert, the spirit of the life lived like that of St. John the Baptist, Elijah, and St. Anthony, alone in the presence of God ("By the Living God in whose presence I stand," said Elijah, in I Kings 17:1).

But this capacity for solitude is nothing else than the full affirmation of one's identity, that is to say, the complete acceptance of oneself as willed by God and of one's lot as given by God. It is also the complete and loving acceptance of the ability to choose and to love, the capacity and the necessity for choice which one must make in the presence of God, under the eye of God, in the light of His truth and of His redemptive love.

This affirmation of identity is not proud, on the contrary; it is not by any means a *non serviam*, for the fullest identity is found only in the readiness to serve. It is the *Ecce ancilla Domini* of the Mother of God. (*Non serviam* means in effect the refusal to accept oneself and one's identity, one's place and one's mission, as gifts of God. It means the affirmation of a false identity, and therefore of nothingness, set up over against being, and requiring to be defended by prevarication.)

It should therefore be quite clear that the failure to accept and understand the basically solitary character of the monastic life means to some extent a failure of the monk to fully achieve his identity and authenticity in that life.

Those monks today who are conscious of the problem of authenticity and who feel that the only solution for the need of individual monks for identity must be resolved in active apostolic work and dealing with other people, are quite probably thinking realistically in terms of the modern thinkers, from Marx down to Teilhard de Chardin, Emmanuel Mounier, etc., whose thought is essentially oriented to activity and even to some extent suspicious of contemplation. This is perhaps due to the deformations and evasions that have been tolerated and preached in the name of "the contemplative life." It is true that our life can be made to seem nothing more than canonized inertia. But this is a total falsification of the meaning of monasticism.

It is for us not to surrender our monastic life and its tradition, but to get down to its real meaning and to revive its genuine values.

The choir, we must admit it, is at least for choir religious and novices quite often the scene of the most serious difficulties with personal integrity and authenticity of prayer.

It is in choir that the monk often feels himself most completely depersonalized, most totally subject to overcontrol, most thoroughly alienated.

This of course may be due to the accumulated failures of many monks over many years, creating an atmosphere of frustration, negativism, and thinly veiled despair in many choirs. There is no question that the choir is and can be very trying. But is this not due in large part to ignorance and even to a kind of refusal to consider the real nature of choral prayer?

Is this not in turn due to a deeper ignorance not only of Christian asceticism but of the basic truths of theology?

The purely individualistic concept of asceticism and of prayer is, paradoxically, very harmful to the development of true personal identity. The identity of the person is fully realized only in a conscious and mature collaboration with others. The "atomized" concept of the choir as a group of individuals, each enclosed in his private solitude and recollection, results in depersonalization, stupor and indifference. The phenomenon of sleep in choir and in meditation is simply an evasion from identity and presence.

It is true that American vocations are ill-prepared for genuine collective prayer, praying with others in any real communal sense.

Is this not due in great part precisely to the problem we have been discussing? It is the person who has fully realized his identity and accepted it, that is able not only to face God in solitude but also to meet his brother in love and collaboration. He is the one best fitted to "pray with" others in unity.

The person who has an identity crisis will have it in choir more than anywhere else, because there it is most difficult to evade.

In choir he is apparently reduced to nonentity (in terms of the individualism with which he is familiar). The prayers are "not his" and yet they are so "universal" that they tend to escape him and he cannot even get the secondhand experience of satisfaction with them because they are "official." He may feel totally disoriented and lost.

For this reason, of course, there is a tremendous push for the vernacular in the monastic liturgy, a push so anguished and so concerted that it surely represents a real need. Those of us who are satisfied with the Latin liturgy and who have been able in the past to taste its deep and genuine realities, will probably have to content ourselves with an English office that will be in itself much less excellent, but which will better serve the needs of a new generation no longer capable of tolerating a Latin office that is not understood. We must frankly admit that we owe them this, and that it is only right to let them have it. It is to be hoped that the Latin office will not altogether disappear: there may still be room for one community or other here and there where it could be kept up, precisely because it has such great intrinsic worth (as artists and musicians in the wicked world frequently remind us).

In the most characteristic practices of the contemplative life of the monastery, silence, enclosure, *lectio* and *oratio*, and even *contemplatio*, the identity crisis poses very serious problems.

First of all, the identity crisis makes monastic silence almost intolerable for someone who is anxiously seeking to experience his own reality by seeing himself understood and accepted by others. This is a very normal adolescent trait, and it accounts for the fact that young novices and professed are often so wildly communicative. If they have to remain silent and alone, they become overwhelmed with doubt of their own reality (not in a metaphysical sense, but in our life they cannot experience themselves as "being there" with any certitude because they just have no way of really telling where they stand and what they want and what they really mean).

The immature person, when forced to be silent, tends to experience his inauthenticity and has no escape from it. Communication with others, even about nothing, at least offers some diversion. No need to insist on this common and rather well understood fact of our life. It simply indicates that those who are not mature enough to accept the discipline of silence cannot be admitted. To admit them and then provide recreation for them will not solve the problem, it will simply diminish the seriousness of the monastic life for the more mature ones, without helping the immature to become serious monks.

In the matter of prayer, contemplation and "mystical theology" one extremely important point must be mentioned.

The "alienated" and somewhat immature person, the one who may still be trying to negotiate his identity crisis, may and often does, in the beginning, seem to have some evidence of contemplative prayer. And if this is not the case, their "dryness" and "darkness" may very easily be taken for the kind of thing mystical writers have characterized as the Night of the Senses. (An incautious director might even take the extreme distress of a depersonalized monk as "Night of the Spirit.")

Of course there is absolutely no point in trying to determine whether these people, usually good and sincere, are receiving real graces of prayer. Whether they are or not, the pattern is usually this: they come to the monastery, they find themselves sheltered, their lives are completely regulated, the burden of responsibility is lifted from their shoulders, they are surrounded by benign authority figures who give evidence of liking them and even of taking them seriously. In this situation, these novices and young monks may experience a new feeling of relief, of self-acceptance, and they assume that their troubles are over. Strongly supported, they relax, they remain passive in an experience of contentment and love (which is rooted in the fact that they feel "safe" and "accepted" for the first time, perhaps, in their lives). This contentment is of course most evident in moments of prayer, and their prayer is easily prolonged. This happiness has a place in their lives no doubt, but it may turn out to be completely meaningless, in so far as it represents nothing but the momentary renunciation of self-concern and anxiety that comes from totally lean-

ing on another—not God in this case but the superior, the
rule, the ambient of safety provided by the community.

One might say that this respite might quite possibly be
used, and a good spiritual father can perhaps take advantage
of it to help in solving the identity crisis, by bringing the
young monk to face himself.

It would however be a very great mistake to take the dryness and trials of an anguished, depersonalized young monk
for a "mystical purification." It is not so at all. The alienated
man can certainly feel in himself an awful sense of meaninglessness, of dryness, helplessness, void. But this is because he
is not fully a person, and because he lacks some of the normal
natural resources of a mature person. He is a diminished and
spiritually handicapped man. He can certainly be helped, but
it will not help him at all to encourage him by the false as-
surance (often given in perfectly good faith) that his emptiness marks him as a higher kind of being, a "contemplative"
and a "mystic."

Nothing is more disillusioning than persons of limited and
mediocre humanity, less than mature, incapable of genuine
love for others, narrow, impoverished, lacking in imagination
and even in common sense, who have been taught that they
are somehow quite extraordinary beings and that their very
limitations are signs that they are in the "mystical way." Established firmly in complacency and illusion by this error,
they remain as a scandal and a portent to those whom God
has perhaps brought to the monastery with real potentialities
for the life of prayer.

One final word about work.

It is in our work above all that the most obvious and most
tangible opportunities for personal development exist. This
does not mean that we should therefore get more and more
involved in work and even go out into the parishes. But it
does mean that we must take frank and honest advantage of
the real value of monastic work.

First of all, let us recognize the profound human importance of hard manual labor in a natural setting! Factory
work and office work are not the same thing and will not fill

the bill. They may be to some extent unavoidable, but we should take care not to reduce our work merely to "making money" and therefore doing what is most profitable.

At least in a monastery, the spiritual, psychological and biological value of physical work ought to be recognized. Work is for the spiritual good of the monk first of all and therefore it follows that even though the profit of the monastic business may be somewhat reduced, there should always be a good proportion of field work and work in the woods, even though these operations may not pay. It would be totally shortsighted, unmonastic and un-Benedictine to "take more care for temporal things" and deprive the monks of outdoor work in the midst of nature on purely materialistic grounds. On the contrary, the greater profit of the monastery, in all respects, will certainly be safeguarded in the long run. The monks will be healthier, they will be more at peace, they will pray better, they will work better in every job.

Also it must be admitted that it is at manual work that the monk can best deal with the identity problem. It is at work that he can begin to experience genuine responsibility (assuming he is allowed to do so). It is at work that he can begin most simply and spontaneously to experience himself as a real person, by seeing before him the results of his efforts, in a concrete contribution to the life of his brothers. This is certainly most important. It accounts for the fact that at least here in this community quite a few novices ask to pass from the choir to the brothers, and assert that they feel that the "brothers life is much more real." This is precisely because of the work and because of the relatively less control to which the brothers are subjected.

Finally it is in manual labor that the young monk can come to appreciate his identity by respecting the identity of others in collaboration with them on useful tasks. It is here too that a certain amount of leeway in talking can be a great help (instead of the nonsensical ideal of an artificial and depersonalized "recreation" which would only make the problem of authenticity more acute). If a young monk or novice is placed as apprentice under an older monk who really knows his job and from whom he himself can learn to become a good workman, it will do more than anything else to help him mature and grow in his vocation.

In conclusion, let us recognize that if in the monastery the work, the liturgy, the study and so on are all overorganized and made artificial, if they are more and more removed from the sphere of *nature* and brought indoors to the office or assembly line, if the monastery comes to resemble a big business and a plant surrounded by noise and clatter, the monks will certainly lose very much. They will tend to be more and more alienated, taking refuge from routines in which they cannot take a serious human interest because they are the same impersonal and organized routines they left in the world.

If this happens to a monastery, then there is no hope of renewal no matter how much you tinker with the liturgy, no matter how much you psychoanalyze the monks, no matter what trivial rewards you grant them in the form of amusements and diversions, or trips and vacations.

The monastic life today stands over against the world with a mission to affirm not only the message of salvation but also those most basic human values which the world most desperately needs to regain: personal integrity, inner peace, authenticity, identity, inner depth, spiritual joy, the capacity to love, the capacity to enjoy God's creation and give thanks. If the world fails to find these things in the monastery, then there is little value in following the latest in liturgy, having the most efficient machines and operating a profitable business.

Our first task is to be fully human, and to enable the youth of our time to find themselves and develop as men and as sons of God. There is no need for a community of religious robots without minds, without hearts, without ideas and without faces. It is this mindless alienation that characterizes "the world" and life in the world. Monastic spirituality today must be a personalistic and Christian humanism that seeks and saves man's intimate truth, his personal identity, in order to consecrate it entirely to God.

IV

DIALOGUE AND RENEWAL

The task of renewal in the monastic and cloistered Orders is just as urgent and just as challenging as it is everywhere else in the Church, though the problems and risks involved may in fact appear to be less dramatic. In order to understand this task of renewal we have to remember that the Vatican Council did not simply command religious to reform from the top down. The renewal of religious life, including the cloisters and monasteries of contemplatives, is a work in which the religious themselves must actively share. Indeed, it would seem that the share of the "ordinary religious" may prove in some sense decisive. In other words, there is a big difference between a "renewal" which requires active participation at every level, and a reform which starts at the top with the action of superiors and reaches the subject passively through new laws and new decrees to be accepted and obeyed. Ultimately, of course, there must be new legislation. But it is understood that the legislation should be much more flexible and that it should leave room for a larger measure of self-determination in communities where the subjects themselves will (we hope) play a more active role in guiding their own communal destinies.

Not only are subjects participating in the work of giving their lives a new shape and a new scope, they are also to some extent going to the root of their contemplative vocation trying to rediscover its true meaning. This means a re-examination of the very essence of their life and vocation. Not that the essence of the life will be necessarily changed: but a new understanding of that essence has to be arrived at. In other words, it is no longer sufficient to take for granted the accepted and conventional ideas of what the contemplative life is all about. The contemplative ideal must be rediscovered in new terms. There is a difference between what stems from living tradition (from tradition as fully alive now) and what is accepted passively and without question from a dead past. What is valid is Spirit and Life. It is from God. What is invalid is dead—it is mere human custom.

It is no longer possible merely to impose sixteenth-century ideas on the postulant who enters the cloister from "the world" of the twentieth century, and expect him to accept everything without question. The modern world, speaking through the modern postulant, will make itself heard in the cloistered dialogue—perhaps with devastating effect. But the cloistered Orders, like all others, must take this voice into account if dialogue and renewal are to be effective. On the other hand, this voice is not the only one that deserves to be heard, nor is it automatically and in every case entitled to say the last word on the grave problems of contemplatives.

There are two ways in which the monastic community can look at the postulant whom it expects to recruit from "the world"—ways which may reflect differences, and perhaps rather profound differences, in one's concept of the Church, the monastic life and the "world." The first way considers the monastic Order (the Church too, by implication) as the embodiment as well as the guardian of a fixed traditional ideal which can never be questioned. It also considers that this ideal can be easily discovered—by asking those who know: the superiors.

Without examining too closely what the authentic monastic tradition really is, this outlook simply assumes that what "is there," what is "given," what is more or less "established" is also in fact perfectly traditional. Thus we find that an "accepted spirituality" is considered without investigation or question to embody a living tradition and to say the last word on what is and is not "contemplative" or "monastic." Though not really official, this "spirituality" has common currency in the Order, is taken for granted by superiors and is received by subjects without question and even without serious interest, as if it could not really be questioned. As a result, the real monastic tradition becomes drained of life and sap and becomes more or less inert. By virtue of a passively accepted, vague, indefinite "spirituality," tradition tends to be transformed into routine. Yet this accepted attitude toward monastic observance, embodied in formal regularity, and in a somewhat schematic teaching, stands radically opposed to all other ideologies, especially to that of "the world."

Hence the postulant is regarded as one who comes to the Order with the intention of being stripped of an old ideology and clothed with a new one—the "accepted spirituality." And of course, more than ideas are at stake: a whole new way of life will reflect the new ideas or indeed the new ideas will perhaps come as a result of the new behavior. If the novice learns to walk humbly, sit humbly, cough humbly, etc. he will also think humble thoughts. At least we hope so. But in any case, he now has wrong ideas and he will soon be given right ideas.

There is of course a genuine charitable concern for the spiritual needs of the postulant, but it is taken for granted first that the community perfectly well understands his needs and his possible problems (they are all characteristic problems of "the world" and can all be schematically reduced to a few simple headings: pride, self-satisfaction, self-seeking, self-will), second that the solution to his problems and the fulfillment of his needs is ultimately a simple matter. It is in fact assumed that the postulant, by the mere fact of desiring to enter the monastic Order, thereby signifies his recognition that he is "wrong," that he wishes to escape from the errors and the ambiguities of his worldly state, that he is resolved to have done with these errors in their totality, and indeed he recognizes that all that is of the world is simply error and sin. Thus there is no necessity to examine his needs with subtle and discreet analysis. He has one need: the need for the doctrine and discipline he is to receive in the monastery. And in order to do this he needs to escape from the world. Having once escaped it, there remains one need above all: the need to be kept from returning to it, at any cost.

Therefore the novice has only to embrace the rule and the observances, to renounce and foreswear his own ideas and opinions, and accept with perfect docility any teaching, however superficial, that is given him. Whatever he is taught is "right." This teaching need not be especially stimulating or "intellectual." Indeed the value of intellectuality is questioned, though learning is respectable, provided that it means the learning of acceptable and well-understood time-tried attitudes: the "accepted spirituality." (Note that the teaching given tends to be not so much the personal doctrine of a "spiritual father" based on his experience, but rather what is taken for granted by a whole generation. Not that this "spirituality" has a definite authoritative status—a precise teaching: it may be comfortingly vague. Its chief advantage is that it is not likely to get anyone excited. It is safe. And you can live by it without having to think!)

Why is this doctrine rather than another to be taught? First, because it is already accepted. In actual fact, this accepted spirituality recommends itself because it is the most complete justification of the community in its actual condition. If it permits changes, they will all be very slight, because in fact only the slightest changes are felt to be needed. Anything else would strike at the "essence of the monastic life." It is true that "times have changed," but are they not rather the "times" of the "world?" The truth is one and eternal. It does not change. Of course there must be accidental changes. But they are worth while precisely in so far as they can be made with the minimum of disturbance. In fact their chief recommendation is perhaps that they are more apparent than real. They can be made without anything really happening.

A "good monk" is then one who has thoroughly learned this accepted spirituality and put it into practice, thus becoming at once an exemplar of the current teaching and its confirmation. The presence of the "good monk" is a kind of concrete guarantee that the teaching itself is practical, and that it can and does succeed (if it can succeed in some cases therefore it must be capable of succeeding in all cases). The successful carrying out of this program is rewarded by a life of happiness and peace, since the monk feels that he is approved, accepted, and that his efforts are rightly directed, in fact blessed by God. The orientation of faith, in this situation, is toward what has always been there. It is consequently accepted and unquestioned. This being the case, the average postulant can be judged by his willingness to understand, accept and follow the accepted spirituality and the ordinary rules. The ability to do this is a sign that he is capable of being formed "according to the spirit of the Order."

To put it quite simply, such a one shows unmistakable signs of having a divine vocation. He agrees with us from the very start and we have reason to be assured that he will cause us no trouble, nor will he raise any doubts in our own minds as to the absolute rightness of what we have always accepted ourselves.

There is no question that this approach is in many ways quite simple and practical. It may, in its application, be somewhat oversimplified, even to the point where it becomes slightly inhuman in its apparent indifference to the peculiar and personal needs of some modern vocations. But it assumes that these special needs can legitimately be sacrificed to the common good, which is reduced to the peaceful efficient application of the accepted norms to all without exception or difference. And, in times of general stability, it may happen that in fact exceptional vocations consent to this without too much anguish, though of course not without effort and self-immolation. They can accept the sacrifice demanded of them without too much questioning and are able to adjust their motives. And because this happens in some cases, or many cases, it is taken to be reasonable evidence that it ought to happen in *all* cases. It is even elevated to the rank of a universally valid principle, for all situations and at all times.

But when for various reasons the Church herself, in a time of crisis and of reform, calls into question certain human customs and practical principles that have been accepted for a long time, and when some of these are seen to have possessed a validity that was temporary rather than permanent and universal, then immediately the force of an "accepted spirituality" tends to be questioned, all the more so because in becoming quasi official it may in fact have lost some of the necessary elements of suppleness, of life and of *charis* (in the sense of spiritual beauty, attractiveness, appeal) which inspire genuine love of the monastic vocation. Then at the same time it may become apparent to younger religious that those who have devoted themselves with all sincerity and trust to carrying out the teachings of the accepted spirituality, have suffered certain human impoverishments and limitations in consequence, though they have perhaps developed and have attained to an admirable poise and even wisdom, supported by the observances which they faithfully practice, this wisdom suddenly seems to have no reference to the realities of life whether in the monastery or anywhere else. Thus the relevance of the monastic ideal itself comes to be questioned, and young religious begin to wonder whether the most basic doctrines of the spiritual life, as taught and practiced in the monastery, have any real significance. When this questioning begins, as we have seen, the whole structure of faith suddenly seems to be threatened, in so far as the mere questioning of the validity of an accepted spirituality seems to involve a doubt of the principle of authority, doubt of the Church, doubt of God revealing Himself in and through the Church, and ultimately doubt of God Himself. Thus the monk who is convinced that he must identify everything that is "accepted" as traditional and therefore as the teaching and the will of God Himself, suddenly finds that in doubting the meaningfulness of this or that monastic observance, he appears to be doubting God. But this lamentable misapprehension can hardly be articulated. Nor is any encouragement offered for it to be so. It sometimes remains unspoken and often unconscious. Perhaps more often the monastic conscience is formed to such a way that the mere "temptation" to question the absolute and eternal validity of this or that practice may cause terror in the heart of the monk who sees himself as it were putting his foot on the slippery path to total apostasy. In any case, conscious or unconscious, where this misapprehension exists, it becomes the cause of grave difficulties. These can seldom be resolved once they have deeply taken hold on a young monk, and as a result the monastery becomes, for him, the only solution.

Unfortunately, he has learned to accept as axiomatic the idea that he belongs in the monastery, that his needs can be satisfied only in and by the monastery, and that any needs he may have which cannot be fulfilled in the monastery are highly questionable, indeed "natural" and therefore suspect of degeneracy or at least of uselessness. When it becomes necessary for such a monk to leave the monastery, in which he is no longer able to extricate himself from intellectual confusion and spiritual anguish, he returns to the world without really getting rid of his doubts and his hesitancies. He goes back to secular life with a heart full of ambiguity, self-questioning, perhaps self-hatred, and in any case profound distress.

The consequence of this first way of looking at the postulant and at the Order's obligation to him is that at the present time there will be very few postulants who will be able to assimilate this rigid and absolute idea of monasticism and resign themselves to live by it. One can simply tighten up the requirements, writing off the new generation as more or less monastically hopeless, and then at the same time attempt to quietly and unobtrusively adapt the accepted spirituality, relaxing its rigidities and making room for a more tolerant consideration of the needs of the modern postulant, while assuming it to be obvious that this is what we meant to do all along.

The principle, however, remains this: that the postulant comes to the Order with "wrong ideas," and consequently even his expression of what he feels to be urgent personal and spiritual needs will usually be wrongheaded and inspired by unregenerate self-love (or perhaps by a neurosis), which cannot be reconciled with the monastic life. The right idea of the monastic life is the idea which is commonly held by and taught in the Order and the first requirement of faith and humility in a prospective monk is to accept this in all docility as an unquestionable premise.

There is, however, another concept of the monastic life, which implies a somewhat different view of the Church, and which is perhaps more complex and less absolute. It is doubtless more difficult to understand in theory and certainly more difficult to put into practice. It involves definite risks of misinterpretation and of misapplication, and from the institutional point of view it may seem, and indeed may actually be, less practicable and more hazardous than the other.

Basing itself on more general principles from the Bible and from the Rule of St. Benedict and primitive monastic documents (rather than on detailed and more recent legislation, observance and spiritual doctrine), this view understands the monastic community as an assembly of Christians called together by the grace of God in order that they may live the life of discipleship together under a Rule and an abbot, helping one another to attain to eternal life by means which will (in their minor details) depend largely on the situation in which they are actually living.

According to this view, the monastic community is in possession not so much of a body of detailed and more or less infallible and rigid principles, governing all the minutiae of one's daily life and worship, and systematizing all one's communal relationships: but rather the Holy Spirit, working through the humility and charity of the brethren in their loving acceptance of their Rule and their spiritual father, enables them all to keep the commandments and counsels of Christ within a framework of rather flexible observances and practices which are not regarded as so perfect that they cannot be changed without extraordinary legislation.

Depending less on the support of legislation in black and white, the community puts its trust in the love and grace of Christ. Believing that the Holy Spirit has been granted to the community to be a source of light and life and acting in a spirit of openness and sincerity, the brothers under their spiritual father seek to work out together actual solutions to their own problems. They may certainly come up with answers that are far from ideal in theory, but it may happen by God's grace that these are the particular answers which bring to all of them a possibility of authentic peace, fruitfulness and growth in Christ. Naturally these solutions will not lack the support of whatever official approval may be necessary.

Into this conception of the monastic life enters a correlative conception of the world. There is no question, of course, that the monk lives as one who is basically alien to the ways of the world (*a saeculi actibus se facere alienum*). So says St. Benedict. But nevertheless the peculiar difficulties and vicissitudes of life in the world are relevant to the monastic life which is considered precisely as a remedy and as a fulfillment: a remedy for the ills contracted in the world, and a fulfillment of legitimate needs which the world of this particular time arouses without being able to satisfy them.

The first concept of the monastic life also promises a fulfillment which the world cannot give, a fulfillment which is attained by the simple and uncompromising way of renunciation (of the world) and obedience (to the accepted observances and practices of the monastery, as applied in detail by the superior). But in this first case there is no concern for needs, legitimate or otherwise, that may have been brought to consciousness by the mentality of "the world." Whatever came to mind in the world remains more or less irrelevant to the monastic calling which is so far "out of this world" that it has nothing more to do with it. So the "needs of modern man" precisely as modern and contemporary are regarded as irrelevant.

Contemporary man is regarded, by the first view, as "contemporary" precisely in his worldliness. In having a "need" to renounce his worldliness, he has *ipso facto* a need to renounce his contemporaneousness. He ceases to be contemporary with his fellow man in entering the monastery, just because in that same act he ceases to be worldly, and becomes an unworldly being, concerned only with the needs of his soul and with eternity. Of course, it can be argued that eternity is contemporaneous with all time and in this sense the monk becomes contemporary, in an abstract and universal way, with absolutely all ages and all times. A malicious intelligence might also conclude that in so doing the monk became contemporary with no one and, in fact, altogether abandoned the realm of the human.

The second view, on the contrary, recognizes, not without a certain anguish, that there is no other time than the present, and that to be contemporary is the price of existence itself. Man has a responsibility to his own time, not as if he could seem to stand outside it and donate various spiritual and material benefits to it from a position of compassionate distance: but man has a responsibility to find himself where he is, namely in his own proper time and in his place, in the history to which he belongs and to which he must inevitably contribute either his responses or his evasions, either truth and act or slogan and gesture. Even his gestures of evasion and withdrawal may unfortunately be decisive contributions to a void in which history can take on a demonic orientation. And so the second form of monasticism exists in confrontation with a world and with a time to which it feels it must respond. Not that it must become implicated by a loss of its own special perspective. For the first thing that the monk can contribute to the world of his time is precisely a perspective that is not of the world. The monk owes the world of his time an unworldliness proper to this time, and the contemporary monk is real in so far as he manages by the grace of God and the charism of his vocation, to achieve a contemporaneous unworldliness. He is in the world and not of it. He is both in his time and of it.

Hence we see the error of imagining that being out of the world also involves being out of one's own time—i.e. in the past, since the past is imagined as having acquired an eternal validity by the fact that it is past.

It would perhaps be more truly monastic to say that the monk who is effectively liberated from the servitudes and confusions of "the world" in its negative and sterile sense, ought to be enabled by that very fact to be more truly present to his world and to his time by love, by compassion, by understanding, by tolerance, by a deep and Christlike hope.

The second view of monasticism can therefore be called in a certain sense "worldly," not that it concerns itself with the ends and means of secular life as such, but it takes into account with sympathy and understanding the legitimate aims which "the contemporary world" feels itself called to obtain for man, such as peace, personal fulfillment, communion with other men in a warm and creative social environment, etc. It regards these aspirations as real and relevant to everyone and therefore to monks, and it sees with compassion that man today is frustrated in his most sincere efforts to attain these things. It does not despise or condemn him because his efforts are undertaken seemingly "without God" or in an "irreligious" spirit since it sees that he is basically sincere and in good faith and that these aspirations, good in themselves, doubtless come from God. The monk should be in the world of his time as a sign of hope for the most authentic values to which his time aspires.

Thus the monastic community will take seriously the earnest and valid effort of secular thought to reach out toward these values, but will understand that thought in the light of the Bible and of the Fathers, finding there a very propitious climate for ideas which seem to a great extent doomed to sterility in the aridity and violence of modern urban and technological life.

This is not the place to develop this idea in all its implication. One consequence of this attitude concerns us here: in looking at the postulant, the monastic community will no longer assume that he comes to the monastery with ideas and aspirations that are all wrong, but that some of the deepest needs of his heart, even though they may not be explicitly religious needs, are genuinely human and specifically contemporary needs which the monastic life is also called upon to fulfill. And so to ignore these human needs, to reject them as irrelevant, and to turn the whole attention of the postulant to other seemingly more lofty, more eternal, more unworldly, more spiritual and more religious aims, may in fact turn out to be arbitrary, unjust, and even unrealistic. For that reason, this procedure will ultimately tend to vitiate the postulant's vocation precisely in its religious and spiritual authenticity. For one cannot establish the religious authenticity of a vocation by trying to distill away all the human and contemporary components that may be there in it. On the contrary, the truth of a vocation, its religious truth, depends on the fundamental respect for the human components which have been placed there by heredity, by the postulant's history, by his own freedom acting in union with grace, and therefore by God Himself.

There is no question that in implementing the post-conciliar legislation on the religious life, the monastic Order will naturally adopt the second of the two attitudes we have outlined above.

The Council decree *Perfectae Caritatis* on the renewal of

the religious life praises the contemplative Orders and urges them to maintain "at their holiest" their "withdrawal from the world and the practices of their contemplative life." But it also states that the language of praise and approval for the contemplative Orders as "the glory of the Church and an overflowing fountain of heavenly graces" does not exempt them from the obligation of complete renewal. The decree says significantly: *"Nevertheless* their manner of living should be revised according to the aforementioned principles and standards of appropriate renewal" (n. 7).

Among the principles referred to are the following:

"Communities should promote among their members a suitable awareness of contemporary human conditions and of the needs of the Church" so as to enable the members to make "wise judgments in the light of faith concerning the circumstances of the modern world [and] come to the aid of men more effectively" (2 d).

"The manner of living, praying and working should be suitably adapted to the physical and psychological conditions of today's religious. . . . The way in which communities are governed should be re-examined in the light of these same standards. . . . Constitutions, directories, custom books . . . are to be suitably revised. . . . This task will require the suppression of outmoded regulations" (3).

But also: "The fact must be honestly faced that even the most desirable changes made on behalf of contemporary needs will fail of their purpose unless a renewal of spirit gives life to them. Indeed such an interior renewal must always be accorded the leading role even in the promotion of exterior works" (2 e).

In the section that deals specifically with monks, the decree says:

"While safeguarding the proper identity of each institution, let monasteries be renewed in their ancient and beneficial traditions and so adapt them to the modern needs of souls that monasteries will be seedbeds of growth (*seminaria aedificatiois*) for the Christian people" (n. 9). (The injunction to "safeguard the proper identity" of each "institution" refers to the previous sentence in which the decree says some monks serve God "by devoting themselves entirely to divine worship in a life that is hidden" and others "by lawfully taking up some apostolate or works of Christian charity.")

Note that in speaking of papal cloister for nuns the decree says that while the cloister is to be maintained, "outdated customs are to be done away with" and "in such matters consideration should be given to the wishes of the monasteries themselves" (n. 16).

Without doubt a notable change of attitude has already taken place. Communities certainly show an increased willingness to consider realistically the needs of the new generation, and one no longer categorically assumes that the new wave is made up entirely of morons, rebels, neurotics and dope fiends. It is almost conceded that in their quixotic way the young manifest a certain amount of good sense. Unfortunately there is still very much of a spirit of patronage in this benign endeavor to recognize the engaging and positive qualities of youth. Do we really believe that monasticism can actually survive in an actual *dialogue* with the modern postulant? Or with the novice? Or with the young monk?

Here we must admit there are problems, some of them rather complex. It would be a little silly to take for granted that one who has no experience whatever of the monastic life is, upon entering, in a secure position to reform everything in the first week. When all monastic tradition unanimously assumes that the worthy postulant manifests a sincere desire to listen and to learn rather than immediately to teach, this is surely not to be taken as an eccentric and antique formula fit for the museum. It is after all not unfamiliar to modern man, for example, in the world of athletics. Coaches are not normally patient with temperamental freshmen who know more about football than anybody else.

On the other hand, let us admit we can no longer safely insist that the postulant passively accept our cursory diagnosis of his ills just because we have a familiar remedy at hand to fit that particular diagnosis. ("You are proud, therefore you need to submit to humiliation, and to begin with you must accept the fact that I know you better than you know yourself, and if you don't agree on that point, it shows from the very start how proud you really are!" A most convenient vicious circle which dispenses with all effort to understand the subject's real needs!)

The postulant who has come to the monastery looking for something, may not necessarily be looking for what we think. Yes, of course, *si revera Deum quaerit.* "Does he truly seek God?" But what entitles me, as novice master, to imagine that *my* particular way of seeking God is the only way possible and that *my* spirituality, *my* prayer, *my* idiosyncrasies, *my* monastic likes and dislikes, *my* interpretations, are normative for all monks of all time? Such an assumption teaches, louder than any words, that I have no humility myself and am therefore disqualified from trying to teach it to another. I do not have the elementary humility to respect his own personal integrity, his uniqueness, his differences, his own singular and personal need.

All this is quite simply to say that the Holy Spirit speaks in very many ways, and one of the ways in which He speaks is precisely through the need, the poverty, the limitation of our fellow man.

A merely external practice of silence and enclosure will never do anything by itself to guarantee the inner transformation of consciousness which the contemplative life requires. We have to re-examine all our practices with a serious willingness to admit that our present conceptions may simply be inadequate. They need to be made much deeper and much more alive—and perhaps given an entirely new perspective. In this way we will show ourselves truly alert to the new needs of a new generation, aware that in this alertness we are being open to grace, obedient to the love of the Holy Spirit, and in the end more authentically monks than if we simply insisted on making two fatal assumptions: (1) that the idea of monasticism which we happen to hold, and which happens at the moment to have a quasi official look, is the only right view and is therefore of the essence of the monastic life and therefore unchangeable; (2) because we are right in this respect, we are right in every other respect too: we can safely assume that the man who comes in from the world is infected with every error, and that if he does not manage to assimilate our own favorite view of monasticism this is merely a proof that he is bad material, dead wood, a fruitless tree, fit only to be rooted up and cast into the fire. Attachment to these two rather arrogant assumptions will guarantee the early end of the monastic life in any community that clings to them with perseverance.

V

RENEWAL AND DISCIPLINE[1]

The monastic life can be seen as a dialectic of freedom and discipline if we remember that it implies, by its very nature, some kind of distance and transcendence with regard to ordinary social and cultural life. The monk is "out of this world" in so far as he is liberated from the routine demands of "worldly" life. His liberation enables him, however, to give to the world something it needs: a capacity for creative and spontaneous celebration, a deeper understanding, a freer response to the basic existential challenge that summons us to make sense out of our life—to make our own sense out of life. Not just to accept someone else's answers, but to discover by personal experience and to verify existentially the inner meaning and value of human life on earth. Note that I am speaking of the monastic ideal, not of the actuality, which can easily turn out to be the exact opposite.

The element of "distance" from the ordinary unthinking way of life—the element of solitude, withdrawal "into the desert," of silence, of ascesis, of poverty, humility, obedience —all this is necessary for the monk. But why? Simply because "monastic tradition says so?" or simply to give the monk "something to do?" or to "make him more virtuous?" The traditional ideas of worldliness and asceticism, of discipline, renunciation, self-denial, prayer, have come under criticism because of the way they have been presented: now in terms of arbitrary and compulsive perfectionism, now in terms of formalist institutionalism. Obviously there is no point in the vicious-circle argument which postulates an austere Trappist image and then practices austerity in order to keep the image

[1] The author noted that the following pages' informal, offhand observations intended in part to answer some question raised by the lively exchange on the "decline" of the Trappists in the *National Catholic Reporter*, January 11, 1968. "In a letter of mine, published in that issue, I stressed the element of freedom essential to the monastic life, but also remarked on the importance of discipline."—Ed.

authentic. It is not a matter of image. It is not a matter of putting up a front, or even of making a contract (to live austerely) and then living up to it. The reasons for discipline lie deeper.

St. Paul long ago remarked on the obvious analogy between the training of athletes and the discipline of Christian self-denial. Over the course of long ages of routine understanding, Paul's analogy was somewhat materialized and his self-denial came to be regarded, by those who thought only superficially, as a matter of "payment" for an ultimate commodity: beatitude. This materialistic view of sacrifices as *quid pro quo*, for which one would "collect" in the afterlife, influenced the nineteenth-century view of Christian asceticism in monasteries. But really, there is more to it. If one "trains" and disciplines his faculties and his whole being, it is in order to deepen and expand their capacity for experience, for awareness, for understanding, for a higher kind of life, a deeper and more authentic life "in Christ" and "in the Spirit." The purpose of discipline is not only moral perfection (development of virtue for its own sake) but self-transcendence, transformation in Christ "from glory to glory, as by the Spirit of the Lord." The death and crucifixion of the old self, the routine man of self-seeking and conventionally social life, leads to the resurrection in Christ of a totally "new man" who is "one Spirit" with Christ. This new man is not just the old man in possession of a legal certificate entitling him to a reward. He is no longer the same, and his reward is precisely this transformation that makes him no longer the isolated subject of a limited reward but "one with Christ" and, in Christ, with all men. The purpose of discipline is then not only to help us "turn on" and understand the inner dimensions of existence, but to transform us in Christ in such a way that we completely transcend our routine existence. (Yet in transcending it, we rediscover its existential value and solidity. Transformation is not a repudiation of ordinary life but its definitive recovery in Christ.)

Monastic discipline and freedom are correlatives. In traditional ascetic terms, our passions, appetites, needs, emotions, create certain limitations which hamper and frustrate a certain kind of development if we allow ourselves to remain too dependent on them. They blind us, weaken us, unnerve us, make us cowards, conformists, hypocrites. They are roots of bad faith. The craving for a certain kind of comfort, reassurance and diversion can be satisfied only if one is willing to accept certain social conditions: to fulfill a prescribed role, to occupy a definite place in society, to live according to acceptable social norms. If we fulfill the role imposed on us by others, we will be rewarded by approval. These roles impose definite limitations, but in return for accepting the limitations, we enjoy the consolation of companionship, of understanding, support and so on. We are made to feel that we "belong" and are therefore "all right." The monastic idea, originally, was to explore the possibilities that were opened up once these limitations were removed, that is to say, once one "left the world." The comforts and joys of ordinary social life, married love, friendly converse and recreation among other people, business, a place in the city and the nation, were to some extent renounced. Sometimes the renunciation was made in crude terms, as if ordinary social life were "evil." This must not mislead us. It was simply a question of obscurely realizing that, in some way, the limitations imposed by social life stood in the way of something else, and the monk was one who wanted to look into this "something else."

The monastic life has always had something of this element of "exploration" about it (at least in periods when it has been *alive*). The monk is a man who, in one way or other, pushes to the very frontiers of human experience and strives to go beyond, to find out what transcends the ordinary level of existence. Aware that man is somehow sustained by a deep mystery of silence, of incomprehensibility—of God's will and God's love—the monk feels that he is personally called to live in more intimate communication with that mystery. And he also feels that if he does not respond to this summons, he cannot be happy because he cannot be fully honest with himself. To evade this would be to reject a certain kind of truth, a certain inner reality, and ultimately to forfeit his self-respect as a human being.

I am simply trying to translate into more modern terms

the familiar idea that has hitherto been expressed in the words "a monastic vocation" or "a contemplative vocation." The idea of this vocation is not necessarily confined to one special kind of discipline. There may be various different ways. Different aspects of training may be emphasized: now community life, now solitude; now ascesis, now work; now *lectio*, now silent prayer; now liturgy, now meditation; now a thoroughly sacramental piety, and now a life of spiritual risk outside the cadres of ritual and institution. But all these, some more and some less, are oriented to a kind of exploration "beyond frontiers." The claim of a cenobitic and liturgical monasticism is that it is safer and more universal because it does not push the frontiers too far and maintains a more normal human (social) measure. Yet the cenobium itself is a little Church, a sacred community, in which the Lord is present to His own in the breaking of the bread. The frontiers are dissolved, not from our side but from His. And of course this is a universal truth underlying all the paradoxes about "monastic exploration." In the end, there really are no frontiers. We would not seek God unless He were not already "in us," and to go "beyond ourselves" is just to find the inner ground of our being where He is present to us as our creative source, as the fount of redemptive light and grace. Whether as hermit or as cenobite, as pilgrim or as laborer, as hesychast or liturgist, the monk seeks in some way to respond to the summons: "Behold the Bridegroom comes: go out to meet Him!" The need for discipline is the same need for watchfulness, for readiness, as in the parable. The ones who wait for the Lord must have oil in their lamps and the lamps must be trimmed. That is what monastic discipline is all about. It implies the cultivation of certain inner conditions of awareness, of openness, of readiness for the new and the unexpected. Specifically, it implies an openness to, a readiness for what is not normally to be found in an existence where our attention is dissipated and exhausted in other things. True, one important new insight in the current monastic renewal is an awareness that "the world" cannot be summarily dismissed as irrelevant to the Christian life. But this is above all a salutary reaction against a kind of sclerotic, arti-

ficial, automatic routine of pious thinking: the mechanical
assumption that to put on a religious habit, retire to a cloister
and embrace a complex set of observances somehow guarantees a deepening of life and gives our existence its true meaning. As if one automatically became enlightened and liberated
merely by the rote learning of a cloistered ideology.

Here we might pause a moment to consider something
that, to my knowledge, has never been studied: the influence
of science and scientific method on the monastic mentality
and on the monastic concept of discipline. Anyone who is
acquainted with early monastic and patristic literature is
aware that, for the Fathers, discipline and ascesis were not
simply sure-fire methods which paid off in results, provided
you followed all the instructions and carried out all the proper
steps in the right order. This concept of discipline in the life of
prayer did however arise in the fifteenth and sixteenth centuries, about the same time as the concept of scientific method
developed (Bacon, Descartes). It quite evidently influenced
the Jesuits—perhaps not so much Ignatius himself who was
more subtle and more experienced—but doubtless the Igna-
tian school. The idea was that if you set up the right conditions, a kind of laboratory for prayer, and if you carried out
the experiment according to instructions, you would get the
desired result. You could work things out efficiently so that
you obtained the precise kind of grace you were looking for.
This concept has by now evolved into the simple pharma-
cology of contemplation: you take the right pill and you turn
on. Hence the idea of discipline was corrupted into a kind of
methodology, and, as in the case of social sciences, for instance (where the same kind of transposition took place),
instead of really praying and meditating, people became obsessed with their "method" and observed themselves at prayer,
checking on the method and wondering why they were not
getting the desired results. Without going further into this
important question, it has to be said here and now that this
transformation of a discipline in a broad, human measure and
in a theological climate of love and grace into a methodology
of will and concentration has been fatal to Catholic contemplation. Fortunately a few rare people like Caussade per-

sistently and quietly counteracted this error, led by a kind of sanity and tact which emphasized openness to grace, passivity, and a deeper, less rationalistic kind of attention. For the discipline of prayer (especially in the old monastic tradition) is not a matter of forcing the issue and getting what you want, but of learning the ways of the spirit and of grace, and of being ready and open to respond to the unpredictable working of a God whose ways are "not our ways."

It can be seen that the long centuries in which the monastic order was deeply embedded in the structure of Christian civilization, while very fruitful and rich both for monasticism and for European culture, did in the end produce a kind of routinism which can only be overcome by a thorough return to sources. The whole issue of monastic discipline has been confused, especially for Americans, by the fact that it has in practice been reduced to blind submission to a set of nineteenth-century customs. Fidelity to the monastic vocation has been too often confused with the ability to swallow, without criticism or question, a bitter-sweet and rather unpalatable mixture of quasi-Jansenist rigorism, pietistic formalism, a literal-minded, myopic theology and anthropology plus a certain self-complacency about admitting that one was indeed the salt of the earth and that one's prayers were really keeping the cosmos from falling apart. At the price of a dogged insistence on devout observance and a head hard enough to resist severe nervous breakdown from one year to the next, one could thus rationalize his existence as thoroughly monastic, pleasing to God, and even, in some sense "contemplative." After all, one never went anywhere or knew anything. One had all but forgotten the wicked world. Presented in this light, monastic discipline was self-discrediting. Those who have broken away from the ordinary monastic patterns and have tried to open up new perspectives, have naturally discarded this idea of discipline before everything else. Rightly so.

At this point we must face one of the main dilemmas of the "monastic order" or of monasticism as institution. The monastic vocation is a summons to *metanoia, conversatio morum*, a whole new life. If this new life is nothing more than a change on the cultural and religious levels it will fail to satisfy the deepest and most authentic demands of the monastic vocation. In other words, the postulant who feels himself called to become a new man, a more authentic person, more profoundly true to his Christian calling and to the Gospel, feels an obscure dissatisfaction with his former life "in the world" and entrusts himself to the monastic community believing that it will show him the way to deepen and expand his awareness as a Christian by developing his whole being "in Christ." What happens is that he is instructed in the observances and ideology of a very specialized, cloistered style of life. He receives a special formation which adapts him to life according to a particular cultural and religious pattern. This monastic and religious culture, handed down from the deeply Christian Middle Ages, has certainly a real validity of its own. Nor is it totally irrelevant to *all* modern men. Many, especially in Europe, have been able to take full advantage of these cultural and religious means, and have profited by them in the same way that the monastic fathers did in the past. They have found that Gregorian chant, the reading of the Fathers, monastic ascesis as understood in terms of early Benedictinism and twelfth-century Cîteaux, the Bible, have helped them find the way to a real self-transcendence, an interior transformation, which has met the requirements of their interior call from God. Within the structure of monastic life, but not enslaved by externals, they have developed interiorly and acquired a kind of wholeness, certitude and peace. They are fully mature Christians and monks because they have made use of these cultural means and at the same time gone beyond them in their own personal way. But many of the younger generation, while embracing the monastic observance and "culture" with complete generosity, have not managed to find the same kind of meaning in them. In the past, the tendency was to blame the young for this. Now we are more ready to understand that it is nobody's "fault." These young monks have felt, perhaps more rightly than we realize, that entering a monastery has meant little more than leaving one kind of culture and society in order to learn the complex rubrics and roles of another. They have felt that this amounts to little more than an external change, and that religious rationalizing and purification of intention really do nothing to make it interior and profound. They learn a whole new role, a whole new system of attitudes and ideas, but interiorly they remain dissatisfied, disoriented, empty, and in the end they feel not only that they have somehow been cheated, but that if they continue to play the same external roles, they themselves are cheating. For one reason or other, the external role does not betoken—still less bring about—any interior renewal of a very deep kind. Merely to lead sheltered and more or less sinless lives—this is not what they can accept as a valid transformation in Christ. (Perhaps in this respect the older generation was more patient and less demanding. The young are less easily satisfied.)

In any case, what happens is that the learning and practice of monastic observances, rituals, do not constitute a real discipline though they may indeed provide an appropriate setting for the learning and practice of such a discipline. True discipline is interior and personal. It is something more than just learning a certain kind of conduct and possessing coherent religious justifications for that conduct. It is one thing to say that when I make a profound bow I intend to express love and adoration for God, but another to really grow and develop in that love and adoration. For some people, the bow and its explanation may tend to become more of a hindrance than a help. In other words, there may come a time when the young monk realizes that in order to meet the real, deep demand of the call that once brought him to the cloister, he has to leave the cloister. The machinery of cloistered life is now imposing limits that prevent his authentic development. The tragedy may be that when he leaves he gets into a still less profitable situation and loses even the little that he had in the monastery.

Monasticism after Vatican II[2] will obviously pass through a transition in which there will be a great deal more permissiveness since, in fact, people will be trying out all kinds of new formulas. This permissiveness will (and in fact does) vary from community to community. On one hand, there will be communities which, for one reason or other, will effectively try to work out the problems of renewal within the familiar institutional framework of the large monastery with its multiple projects, big plant, varied commitments and its fidelity to established cultural patterns. In Europe, this will mean a certain evident continuity with a millennial past. In America it will mean more or less continuity with the nineteenth century of which we are, nevertheless, somewhat dubious and ashamed. It is after all a notable monument of religious camp. And it is at the same time all we have as "tradition." The tendency will be to modernize in the sense of to "Americanize" and to tend more and more to "protestant-ize" our life, to liberalize it with borrowings from sociology, psychotherapy, etc.: in a word, to suburbanize the monastic life. This will be the case because people, after all, need to have some bearings to identify themselves by, and having renounced the crude otherworldliness of the nineteenth-century immigrant and ethnic Catholicism, American monks are situating themselves, naturally enough, where they are: twentieth century in America. But if a Trappist monastery becomes after all indistinguishable from any other marginal, seminary-type outfit in the Great Society, it will have lost its reason for existing. Thus, while we will certainly be flexible, permissive, tolerant, open-minded, and will explore in the sense of experiment with new patterns, we must nevertheless remember our identity as monks. That identity cannot be preserved without a discipline oriented to real inner transformation, to the development of the "new man."

In this connection, I think we ought to be more conscious of and attentive to the kind of para-monasticism which is very alive in this country. I mean, frankly, movements like the hippies, like the beats before them, like all those who are interested in Yoga and Zen, like (in other respects) the peace movement, the civil rights movement. All these movements have elements that can be called monastic in the sense that they imply a very radical and critical break with ordinary social patterns. They have their asceticism, their "discipline," in the various kinds of sacrifices they make in order to "break" with their own past, with their normal milieu, with the society of their parents, or with a social order with which they violently disagree. It is common knowledge that while monks have largely given up fasting, kids in the peace movement are liable to fast several days (with *no* food) on a peace vigil which may also be a prayer vigil. Whether or not one may agree with those who burn their draft cards, they are certainly making a more radical "break with the world" in this particular area than the postulant who walks into the monastery, is automatically exempt from all further concern about the draft and is fully approved by society. I do not mean to say that all these things are necessarily "right" and that monks are "wrong." I am just saying that the monks cannot afford to ignore these poor relations. They represent an attitude toward the world which is analogous to that of the monk. They also, in many cases, seek to explore the frontiers of experience and perception in ways at once more serious and more dangerous than monks do. Whatever one may think of psychedelic drugs, as a sociological fact they clearly indicate that the desire for inner experience is not something buried in the medieval past. The fact that the Beatles took LSD and then went to an Indian monk and guru for guidance, then dropped LSD when he told them to, and practiced meditation under his instruction, is certainly salutary for so-called contemplative monks. And it is a simple illustration of what I mean in talking of discipline. This edifying scenario has a special interest because it reminds us of something too often ignored in practice. Monastic ascesis has tended to be in general what one might call an ascesis of virginity, presupposing that there is a special excellence in a life in which passion has never reached full expression and satisfaction but has been sublimated from the beginning in divine love. Such excellence is certainly real, but it is a special charism. It is not the only formula for monastic ascesis and perfection. We remember that in the religious tradition of Hinduism, for example, it is considered normal for a man (or woman) to undertake the solitary and ascetic life of prayer after having been married, and having brought up children. The charismatic life of virginity retains its own value, but we must also emphasize that for modern people a monastic life that is embraced when there has been no fully normal and mature sexual development, may remain ambiguous and problematic. Paradoxically we often find that young men come to the monastery is order to discover finally, with more reliable certitude, that their vocation is marriage. There are many married people who, after ten or fifteen years of married life (or longer if they are to bring up their children) would definitely like to separate and take on a different kind of life, more solitary and disciplined and perhaps in some sense monastic. Our customs and even the laws of the Church provide them with little or no encouragement. They would probably make very good "monks"—perhaps much better ones than their children.

The idea of discipline implies a clear recognition of an elementary human fact: permissiveness is all right if you are content to drift along with a stream that carries you more or less safely by itself. We can to a great extent trust our nature and culture to guide us once we have learned the relatively easy and habitual norms they impose. But this easy permissive drifting existence is bought at a price: it excludes certain other dimensions of life which cannot be found unless to some extent we work hard to discover them. Of course one must always admit of exceptions. There may be people who drift along permissively and who attain an unusual degree of wisdom. But usually you will find that even their apparent permissiveness is the result of a break, a sacrifice of certain easy adjustments and of a conventional role. The man who wants to deepen his existential awareness has to make a break with ordinary existence, and this break is costly. It cannot be made without anguish and suffering. It implies loneliness, and the disorientation of one who has to recognize that the old signposts don't show him his way, and that in fact he has to find the way by himself without a map. True, the monastic life provides other signposts and other maps: but the trouble is that too often the signposts point merely to a dead end and the maps are like those curious productions of fourteenth-century cartographers which inform us that "here are many dragons." The real function of discipline is not to provide us with maps, but to sharpen our own sense of direction so that when we really get going we can travel without maps.

Monastic discipline is therefore by no means a matter of training in pious deportment and moderation, a system of modesty, prudence and self-control, which guarantees a certain capacity for recollection and pays off in inner peace. Such discipline is nothing more than conformity to rule in a specified style of life. It is simply a matter of learning to play one's part, to fulfill one's monastic role, and, I suppose, to "edify." True monastic discipline does not begin until this leaves off: and presumably one can begin without passing through any formal schooling in "monastic etiquette." Such schooling may or may not be useful, but clearly it is not what I am talking about and I cannot believe it is essential to any serious monastic renewal. It may help, for those who are interested. On the other hand, there does seem to be a definite danger that those who have lost patience with discipline as etiquette and recollection may, in discarding it, get rid of all discipline whatever. The result will then be an entirely casual monasticism without any structure, any forms, and recognizable shape and perhaps even without any serious motivation or real purpose. Even this may have its advantages temporarily, but it will have to be only temporary, a breathing spell in which the experiment discovers its own motives and its own identity. During such a lull, one may hope that a permissive and entirely unstructured situation may be helpful, provided there is real stuff in the men who live in it. On the other hand, if a group of "reformers" are banded together in a nebulous idea with no cohesion except that provided by half-conscious aspirations, fears and resentments held more or less in common, mere permissiveness and casualness will never serve. The danger of acting out neurotic drives will be too great. The result will then be regression and disintegration, both for the group and for the individuals in it.

The question of discipline naturally raises another, and even more critical, question of authority. Indeed, the discrediting of discipline, the suspicions attached to it, are largely the result of crude authoritarianism. Those who are distrustful of authority are distrustful of discipline, and vice versa.

Usually there are at least a few plausible reasons for their distrust. But in the end, we must admit that monastic training demands some kind of authority as it demands some kind of discipline. Obviously, the concept of the Lord Abbot vested in pontificalia and graciously offering his ring to be kissed for a thirty days' indulgence—or perhaps forbidding his subjects "by virtue of the vow" to read *The New Yorker*—this has had its day. But such authority never had any real inner strength. It was bolstered up externally by legal sanctions. What is needed in monasteries is a recognition of authority that is strong with the strength of love and of Gospel truth. This authority may be seen perhaps in the rare charismatic teacher, but we will be more practical if we look for it in the believing community, united in Christ, in the humility of Christian love and of the spirit, serving one another in the obedience of faith and gathered around one they have chosen to make the final practical decisions in running their community. Discipline in such a setting is less a matter of personal austerity and will ("character training") than of openness to the demands of the Spirit of Love, to the needs of one's brothers and of the community.

Nevertheless we cannot neglect the importance of personal ascetic training, as also of spiritual fatherhood (where this can be found). The life of inner contemplative prayer is something that has to be learned by trial and error, under some sort of experienced guidance. One of the great problems of "the contemplative life" is that such guidance has usually been too rudimentary, too superficial, too improvised, too slack—or else too arbitrary, too compulsive, too legalistic and too insensitive to the real needs of the individual vocation. Hence monks never really learn to pray, to meditate, to "discern the spirits" and to find their way in the uncharted territory they have come particularly to explore. The spatial metaphor must not mislead us. Obviously, there is no "territory" at all "within us" and we do not "travel." Nevertheless the idea of development is something we naturally tend to visualize in spatial terms (for instance in a graph). The purpose of discipline is, however, to make us critically aware of the limitations of the very language of the spiritual life and of ideas about that life. If on an elementary level, discipline makes us critical of sham values in social life (for example, it makes us realize experientially that happiness is not to be found in the usual rituals of consumption in an affluent society), on a higher level it reveals to us the limitations of formalistic and crude spiritual ideas. Discipline develops our critical insight and shows us the inadequacy of what we had previously accepted as valid in our religious and spiritual lives. It enables us to abandon and to discard as irrelevant certain kinds of experience which, in the past, meant a great deal to us. It makes us see that what previously served as a real "inspiration" has now become a worn-out routine and that we must go on to something else. It gives us the courage to face the risk and anguish of the break with our previous level of experience. It enables us, in the language of St. John of the Cross, to face the Dark Night in full awareness of our need to be stripped of what formerly gratified and helped us. To adjust to a new level of experience is at first painful and even frightening, and we must face the fact that the crisis of real growth in the contemplative life can bring one perilously close to mental breakdown. That is why it is so helpful to have the support of someone who knows what it is all about.

Growth in experience implies a serious self-doubt and self-questioning in which values previously held seem to be completely exploded and no other tangible values come to take their place. This may even take the form of a crisis of religious faith in which our whole conception of God and of our relationship to Him may be turned upside down. There may seem to be "no God" at all, or else our relationship to Him may seem so desperate that we feel as though we are damned, in our moments of darkness. This, as St. John of the Cross shows, marks the beginning of a whole new experience of faith on a completely different level. The passage from a stage in which one loves and worships God as a beautiful object of desire to a stage in which God ceases to be object and loses all definite limitations in our mind is something which cannot easily be described: but it is a perilous, though necessary, experience. Discipline prepares us for this.

But the passage itself is not a matter of discipline. It is brought about "mystically" by the secret action of God in a way of which we cannot be fully conscious. Obviously, serious problems will be raised by any kind of "discipline" which simply seeks to maintain one at a single satisfactory level of experience (that of a fervent novice) and represents any "going beyond" as illusion or infidelity. A discipline that in fact *blocks and prohibits* development can produce nothing but tragic inertia. In such a case, crisis and upheaval are desirable reactions! They keep us in touch with reality. If in fact many monks have (in quiet despair) sought psychiatric help rather than spiritual direction, this is not to be wondered at. Psychiatry has advanced more valid claims to seriousness than most contemporary "spiritual direction." The two are entirely distinct. We need only remark on the obvious fact that some psychiatric help may be an absolutely necessary preliminary to a serious spiritual life, and psychiatry may (with important qualifications however) usefully intervene in the grave crises of mature contemplative development. (Obviously the psychiatrist must be one who knows what the monastic life is all about!) But spiritual discipline is something else again. And we must not lightly set aside the possibility of mystical prayer and charismatic developments in the course of a monastic life. The purpose of discipline is to favor such developments. One of the faults of the old narrow and rigid nineteenth-century spirituality was that it excluded all this a priori (while venerating the most naive accounts of it in the lives of the saints). The modern activistic approach also takes up a categorically anti-mystical position—and does so, if possible, even more savagely than did our fathers. Contemplative nuns are repeatedly assured that if they like to spend a long time in silent, thoughtless prayer, they are just neurotic, and no distinction is made between narcissistic absorption and genuine, intuitive, simple prayer.

The overemphasis on rationalizing and logic to the exclusion of everything intuitive, the repudiation of the aesthetic from the contemplative life has perverted the idea of monastic discipline with a kind of arid rationalism. Descartes has laid a curse on the Catholic life of prayer. What has to be rediscovered is the inner discipline of "the heart," that is to say, of the "whole man"—a discipline that reaches down into his inmost ground and opens out to the invisible, intangible, but nevertheless mysteriously sensible reality of God's presence, of His love, and of His activity in our hearts. The old familiar literature in this field (the debates of people like Saudreau, Poulain, and Garrigou-Lagrange) may have lost all sense and savor for us, and there is not much new literature of any real value about the mystical life. Nevertheless the classics of monasticism and contemplation are there to be reinterpreted for modern readers, and above all the Greek and Russian (hesychast) tradition can infuse a new life into our rationalist Western minds. Oriental ways of contemplation (Zen, Yoga, Taoism) can no longer be completely neglected by us. Sufism and Hassidism have a great deal to say to monks because of their explicit or implicit Biblical content, and because they are so closely related to a monastic type of spirituality. (Hassidic and Sufi communities are not strictly monastic in our sense, but very interestingly provide a monasticism for people "in the world but not of it.") Modern psychoanalysis, social anthropology, comparative religion, some schools of philosophy, also have much to contribute to a rethinking monastic discipline. Contact and communication of monastic communities among themselves, dialogue with one another and with other groups, scholars, psychoanalysts, Zen People, hippies, etc., can be of great importance for monks today. A concept of monastic discipline that merely excludes and rejects all that does not take place within the walls of the monastery is definitely not for our age (except in individual cases when a mature—or maybe just an old—religious may have found his or her "way" in this kind of isolation).

Much more could be said about all these points. My purpose is simply to reaffirm that without discipline the monastic quest, which seeks typically to explore regions of faith, of love, of experience and of existence beyond the limits of ordinary Catholic routine, can never lead to anything serious. Let us be quite clear that although there may be a real need for new attitudes and new approaches and though the whole question of the *how* of monastic discipline needs to be rethought, there is no change in the need for discipline itself. This means first of all a need for control and liberation on the level of appetite and physical need. One cannot seriously pretend to "explore" unusual realms of experience if one is enslaved by a need for kicks on the sensual level. There is also no change in the need for those values which have traditionally been described in terms of humility, obedience, detachment, poverty, etc. It is quite true that the whole idea of humility needs to be rethought in terms that will make it real to modern people. It is true that obedience must be rediscovered, not as submission to legalistic authority but as openness to the hidden will of God. But basically, the discipline involved here is that of a crucifixion which eliminates a superficial and selfish kind of experience and opens to us the freedom of a life that is not dominated by egoism, vanity, wilfullness, passion, aggressiveness, jealousy, greed. Finally, discipline means solitude of some sort, not in the sense of selfish withdrawal but in the sense of an emptiness that no longer cherishes the comfort of various social "idols" and is not slavishly dependent on the approval of others. In such solitude one learns not to seek love but to *give* it. One's great need is now no longer to *be* loved, understood, accepted, pardoned, but to understand, to love, to pardon and to accept others just as they are, in order to help them transcend themselves in love. Anyone who undertakes to be a monk knows, by the very fact of his vocation, that he is summoned by God to a difficult, lifelong work, in which there will always be anguish and great risk. If he evades this work, under any pretext whatever (even under the pretext of conforming to an exterior ritual or ascetic observance which does not really suit his inner needs), he must know that he cannot have any peace with himself or with God because he is trying to silence the deepest imperative of his own heart.

We must not (in thinking romantically and emotionally) make discipline an absolute good in itself. Discipline has its uses. What we want is to rediscover the right use of discipline, and this implies a recognition that it may in fact be used wrongly. For instance: suppose that one has certain objectives in the life of prayer, and is set on obtaining these. He tries first one kind of discipline, then another. The discipline that appears to him to be "good" is the one which seems to bring him closest to his objective. But one may in this way use discipline to one's own (and the community's) great disadvantage if it turns out in fact that the objectives sought are irrational, or unreal, or self-contradictory, or unproductive, or simply not viable at all. This would be the case with disciplines whose effect would simply be to create, rapidly and convincingly, an illusion of holiness, of prayer, of union with God—in other words, of disciplines whose chief effect would be to enable one to "turn on" with a minimum of delay and inconvenience. This is the problem of psychedelics, and it is also a problem of ascetic methods. I would therefore, without going into details, suggest that we need to apply the cutting edge of discipline a little closer to the root and make use of it first of all to question our objectives themselves. Monastic discipline today will have to concern itself not with obtaining unquestioned contemplative "goals" that are accepted as valid merely because they are thought to be ideally "monastic." Rather, discipline must question these goals themselves, and find out not whether they are "monastic" but first of all whether they have, or can have, any reality whatever. In this sense it is to our advantage to accept, at least provisionally, the rather severe critique which is directed against the contemplative life. Instead of simply trying to repel all hostile arguments by forcing the issue and tightening up discipline to prove that we mean business and that therefore our goals must be sound (this is no logic at all—nor can it be justified as a mystique), we might profitably admit that much that passes for "contemplation" is mere narcissism and self-love, placed at a convenient remove of subjectivity and mystery where it cannot be reached by criticism. ("Oh, you just don't understand. One has to experience these things to understand them.") Discipline and experience must, on the contrary, reach into this area and criticize what goes on there. The problem is then not to barricade oneself in cloistered subjectivity and in a silence from which the critic is excluded: one must learn to make "silence," "solitude," the "desert" and so on areas of more relentless criticism. Effective discipline will then not confirm us in error (which would be the case if we merely used it to "get what we want") but will enable us to unmask and correct our errors. This may sound very obvious, but as a matter of fact it is not obvious at all in practice. Discipline can so easily be used in the service of bad faith and religious hocus-pocus, with the emotional assumption that the intensity of one's conviction is a proof of its rightness (and discipline is used merely to intensify one's conviction). Thus for example the ascetic who punishes himself and then gets a nice warm feeling in the solar plexus as a reward, becomes mechanically self-justifying —and confirms himself in illusion. Our discipline needs first of all to question and if necessary to discredit some of these "good" self-justifying feelings and convictions of ours. Our discipline should lead us to discover not how right we are but how wrong we are. If in the course of this discovery we give up our monastic enterprise altogether, well, perhaps it was never real in the first place. If on the other hand, we radically revise our whole idea of what we came here for and continue to seek what we came to seek, but in a different way and with an entirely different (and more humble) understanding, our discipline will be serving a useful purpose.

VI

THE PLACE OF OBEDIENCE

The draft schema on Religious presented in the Third Session of the Second Vatican Council was severely criticized because it did nothing to meet a desperately felt need for a renewed theology of the religious life. Such a theology is obviously demanded if the religious life is going to be brought up to date in accordance with the *Constitution on the Church*.

The remarkable thing about this *Constitution* is the shift of emphasis which, instead of considering the Church primarily and principally as a hierarchical society and a strictly organized institution, affirms that the Church is the community of the faithful, the Mystical Body of Christ, the people of God. It thus affirms the primacy of spiritual life and its fruitfulness over organizational rigidity, juridical exactitude, and temporal power. Certainly the Church is a society with laws, an organized institution; but the laws and organization are for the sake of love, of life. They exist to safeguard the freedom of the Spirit within the framework of earthly society. Thus the institution, its power and its influence, do not become ends which every Christian must serve, even at the cost of his own inner spiritual fruitfulness and growth. The end is the transformation and consecration of all life to God by the leaven of holiness, and hence by the spiritual vitality and fruitfulness of the members of Christ. Thus a static concept of the Church as organization is replaced by a dynamic concept of the Church as a living Body moved by the invisible and divine Spirit of Truth and Love imparted to her by the Risen Christ.

This is why we do not speak today of the *reform* of religious life but rather of its *renewal*. Renewal is something deeper, more living and more total than reform. Reform was proper to the needs of the Church at the time of the Council of Trent, when the whole structure of religious life had collapsed, even though there was still a great deal of vitality among religious. Today the structure and the organization are firm and intact: what is lacking is a deep and fruitful understanding of the real meaning of religious life. Simply to imitate the Tridentine reform and legislate a tightening of discipline within the now familiar framework would ignore the very real problem of religious, and not least the problem of obedience and authority in the modern context.

The obedience which is vowed by a religious is not the obedience of a child to a parent, nor the obedience of a citizen to civil authority, nor is it properly understood merely as the obedience of a subject to juridically constituted authority, even though this may be within a religious framework. Hence, the renewal of religious obedience will not be accomplished simply by an increase of promptitude and exactness, though these are certainly not to be overlooked. The religious, and particularly the monk, desires the *bonum obedientiae* (one might almost translate St. Benedict's phrase as the "benefit of obedience") because it is a means to closer union with God. It is, in fact, the chief way by which the monk returns to God, as St. Benedict says in the opening sentences of his Prologue. Now a merely external and juridical obedience, no matter how exact, is hardly to be prized as an especially efficacious way to union with God. The obedience of the monk must therefore be the obedience of faith, deeply rooted in his belief in Christ as his Lord and Savior, in his earnest desire to live as a perfect disciple of Christ, in his love for Christ who for our sakes became "obedient unto death" (Phil. 2:8).

Monastic obedience is seen by the monk as a way to imitate the obedience and love of Christ his Master. Since Jesus "emptied himself taking the form of a servant" (Phil. 2:7), the monk will seek also to empty himself of his own will and to become a servant, above all because this is Christ's "new commandment." "The Son of Man came, not to be ministered unto, but to minister" (Matt. 20:28). At the Last Supper, Jesus plainly demonstrated his meaning to his disciples when he washed their feet and told them: "If I, being your Lord and Master, have washed your feet, so you should also wash one another's feet: for I have given you an example, and as I have done, so must you do also" (John 14:14–15).

The monk who desires to live as a true disciple of Christ will therefore seek to humble himself before all his brothers, and to serve all his brothers, and not only his superiors, because if he does not do this he is "putting himself above the Master" (John 14:16–17).

Religious obedience must be seen first of all in this context of love and discipleship. Only then do its formal and juridical aspects fall into the right perspective. The monk must obey, not because he has become the subject of the Abbot who has all the authority of a Roman *pater familias*, but because he is a disciple of Christ, and because, in faith and humility, he wishes to see his own function as a service to be exercised in all humility and love. The Abbot desires not only to get his own will carried out, or to see that the Rule is strictly enforced, or to guarantee that the community is well-disciplined and prosperous, but to help his monks to seek and find God more truly, more sincerely, more intelligently, and more efficaciously.

It is to be expected that this crisis of obedience will loom very large in the views of superiors. But this very fact may tend to perpetuate certain unfortunate confusions if superiors continue to regard obedience, consciously or unconsciously, as ordered primarily to the good order and efficient functioning of the religious institute. Any "renewal" of obedience that begins from such a viewpoint will hardly be more than a consolidation of what amounts in fact to a spiritual disorder. This disorder consists in considering that the monk exists for the sake of his institution and in order to keep it going, and that his good and his sanctification are to be found above all in the obedience which places him totally at the service of his superiors in working for the interests—and, we may add, the prosperity and prestige—of the community. While this concept of obedience may perhaps be more justified in modern active congregations (though even there it would lead easily to abuse), *it has no justification whatever in the monastic context.*

The whole purpose of monastic obedience, the *disciplina* of the regular life, the docile acceptance and following of spiritual and traditional norms, is the sanctification of the monk and in fact his liberation from temporal agitations and concerns in order that he may learn to listen to God in his heart and to obey God.

The unfortunate tendency to regard the problem of obedience and authority as primarily one of *order* obscures much deeper theological implications. Religious, especially in America, tend to seek immediate practical solutions and adjustments that will make their life run more smoothly and effectively here and now. Hence there is considerable interest in psychology and psychiatry, and great trust is placed in techniques that have been used in social sciences. It is certainly good to know what may be the less obvious motivations and forces at work to generate our common problems. But basically the problem of obedience is inseparable from the theology of the religious life, and solutions on the level of psychology, sociology or even canon law and disciplinary reform, will all be useless without new theological perspectives. However, let us consider first of all the concrete and psychological dimensions of the case.

It is quite possible that the whole Church is now facing a crisis of authority—a crisis of order. If so, the crisis will doubtless be especially acute among clerics and religious. But it will probably be a crisis of *understanding* even more than one of *will*. The hesitations, doubts, and outspoken questions of so many religious (in this matter of authority and obedience) arise not from a simple refusal to comply, or from a rebellious assertion of self-will—though they are often seen in this light only. They more often arise from a fundamental lack of understanding and agreement concerning the real meaning of the religious vocation.

Let us not forget that modern man, or modern woman, at least in the "advanced countries," is desperately concerned with the problem of giving meaning to a life that is so easily reduced to mere empty routine by the alienating pressures of commercial and technological organization. We are often very keenly aware of the danger of becoming mere "mass men," frustrated, unidentified cogs in a huge impersonal machine.

Hence the religious often develops the same unformulated objections and resentments that characterize the "mass man."

He finds himself deeply involved in the very futility and alienation he came to the monastery to escape. (In this case the
desire to "escape" a meaningless existence is surely legitimate.)
His feeling that his vow of obedience means more than a
commitment to work for the organization and the prestige of
the order is basically sound—but he does not know how to formulate it. And in fact he confronts a theology that has developed as an unconscious justification for the state of affairs
in which he finds himself.

The summons to offer himself as a victim of holocaust on
the altar of religious perfection, without even a reasonable
hope that the sacrifice will make sense or be of real use to
human persons, but only to the impersonal "Institute," leaves
him in a state of serious doubt about the worth of the religious life itself. To diagnose this as cowardice or lack of
generosity is more often than not equivocation. These same
religious, in a situation that they are better able to compre-
hend, can give themselves most generously. Clichés about
"blind obedience" make the modern religious feel, and not
without reason, that his objections are simply being waved
aside without even being considered.

Theology has, up until recently, viewed the religious life
almost exclusively in terms of sacrifice and immolation (an
outlook that corresponded to the medieval liturgical forms in
which the Host was primarily a Victim immolated in the distant and invisible sanctuary, in the midst of mysterious words
and rites which the faithful observed in devout, uninitiated
silence). Certainly the religious life is a sacrifice, and so is the
Mass. But just as theology now stresses the Eucharist as a
sign of fraternal unity and demands active and intelligent
participation in a common act of worship, so the old theology of the religious life needs to be completed and filled
out with a new perspective in which the obedience of love
rooted in faith becomes at once a sign and a principle of
living unity in Christ, and a way of "returning to the Father"
in and with the loving obedience of Christ. This "Eucharistic" concept of obedience is aimed not at an abstract, impersonal "common good" but at a concrete personal, indeed mystical unity of love in Christ. Instead of a "common

good" that remains external to the religious and affects his life only superficially, the fruit of obedience is the living and life-giving Spirit who is at once God's gift to each and the unifying bond of all.

Here, instead of the religious being forced back into the isolation of his individual will, which he exerts in order to obtain for himself an abstract and juridical reward, he is drawn into the living dynamism of fervor and love which gives meaning to his own life by enabling him to contribute personally to the meaningful life of his brothers in Christ.

Obedience then becomes an expression of the new life and the new creation which restores the simplicity and peace of paradise (*paradisus claustralis*) to a communal life in which each is the servant of all, and each finds fulfillment in a meaningful service of love that is inspired and vivified by the presence of Christ in his Spirit.

The end of Christian obedience is then not merely order and organization, not the abstract common good, but God Himself, the epiphany of God in his Church, and in the microcosm of the new creation which is the monastic community.

Once this is understood, the totality of the demand of obedience becomes obvious by itself. Evidently the individual must renounce his own will in everything and obey God in everything. His obedience *to God* is without limit because it is simply a fulfillment of his basic orientation to God by baptism, made more specific and concrete by his religious vow.

This *in no sense* means all abdication of his basic human rights and dignity in order to become an inert and uncomprehending utensil in the hands of a religious superior. It means a dedication and consecration of liberty in which the superior first of all must see that he is obliged to serve and preserve the spiritual liberty and dignity of his subjects. The superior cannot demand blind and total subjection to his own authority, in order that he may make an arbitrary use of his subjects for his own ends or for those of the organization considered as such (for example, in order to make more money). He has to enlist the freedom of his subjects for the service of God and of love. He must realize that all other ends are subordinated to the spiritual good of the subjects as persons and as a community, and to the good of the souls they serve.

This does not by any means eliminate either the element of sacrifice, of heroically difficult obedience, or of complete immolation; but it presents them in a totally different light. The religious spends himself and devotes himself to the work of God in Christ with all the more good will and energy since he is able to see how he is in fact fulfilling his vocation and responding to its deepest exigencies of love and surrender to the truth of Christ. His work is not a blind, uncomprehending act of submission to the mandates of an inscrutable authority —mandates in which he has fundamentally no interest whatever because they really have no vital relation to his own vocation or to the true good of souls.

The work of obedience implies a loyal collaboration between superior and subject, in which *both* strive, each according to his function, to understand and carry out the will of God. It is not that the superior arbitrarily makes his own will the will of God by issuing a command, but that he objectively and in the fear of God seeks the divine will, and in doing so does not neglect to consider first of all the spiritual good of his subjects. The subject, on the other hand, must remember that he is not on a plane of democratic equality with his superior, and that collaboration with his superior must mean more than an informal dialogue in which the subject may decide, if he likes, that he is not bound to do the will of the superior even when the command is objectively legitimate.

However, obedience is in truth a dialogue between two responsibilities—that of the subject and that of the superior— and in carrying out his superior's command the subject cannot allow himself to abdicate moral responsibility and act as a mere utensil. It is also a dialogue between two forms of *service*. Superiorship is a service, just as much as the obedience of the subject. The superior serves God and his subjects by assuming the responsibility of decision and command. The subject serves God within the framework of law and command, but not without making mature decisions of his own. His decision to obey is not an abdication of freedom but a mature use of freedom. The superior owes his subject the information and confidence which will make mature obedience possible, and the subject owes his superior intelligent and loyal cooperation.

If this is true in ordinary everyday religious life it is also true in the special work of *aggiornamento* and religious renewal which has been undertaken by the Church today. While the major superiors and the competent councils and chapters must of course finally decide what adaptations are to be put into effect, in accordance with the Rule and Constitutions, it is nevertheless essential that all the members should actively participate in the renewal of religious life by assessment of the meaning and value of their vocation, clarifying the relevance of their particular religious ideal for themselves and for their time, evaluating the contribution they might make to the understanding and aid of the contemporary world, defining the relevance in a present-day context of certain observances belonging to the past, and bringing to the attention of superiors the real everyday needs and problems of subjects.

The true monk is one who, fully aware of his own limitations, has surrendered to the love of Christ, in order to praise the mercy of God and serve Him joyously in common with others who have made the same surrender. This is simply a special modality of the ordinary Christian life, in which the vows are to be seen not just as peculiar and difficult obligations, but as means to guarantee the authentic purity of the Gospel life in religious communities. It is here above all that renewal is demanded because in point of fact, as theologians observe with increasing frequency, the vows have often come to be used as evasions and pretenses—for example, where poverty becomes a purely abstract formality, by virtue of which the religious enjoys all the comforts of life "with permission" and without the exercise of juridical proprietorship—or the burden of responsibility.

The authenticity of the religious commitment is what makes all religious life (even that which is contemplative and cloistered) apostolic. So, the measure of apostolicity in religious communities is not to be sought purely and simply in the amount of active work they accomplish but in the purity of their faith as expressed in the genuine simplicity of a truly humble and open Christian life.

Hence it would be an illusion for the monastic orders to increase their commitment to active life at the expense of their essential monastic *conversatio*. This is not addressed to those monastic congregations which have schools and parishes. Their problems are of a different and special order, since they do in fact commit themselves to provide an active and apostolic service, whereas the contemplative monasteries have quite another function—that of preserving the purity of the monastic and contemplative tradition in a world in which that tradition is increasingly misunderstood and menaced, not only by people outside the monastery but even by the monks themselves.

A spirit of *openness* is most important in any renewal of monastic life. Observances which are "closed" and incomprehensible even to the religious themselves will almost inevitably generate a spirit of pretentiousness and artificiality which is incompatible with true Gospel and monastic simplicity. Such observances must either be re-thought so that they recover a living meaning, or they must be discarded, and if necessary replaced by others that fulfill the function which they have ceased to fulfill.

In any case it is clear that one of the central concerns of the Church in the monastic life, as in the liturgy and everywhere else, is to ensure that renewal is more than tightening up the exactitude of rubrical or juridical observance. In monastic life as in liturgy, renewal means a restoration of authentic meaning to forms and acts that must recover their full value as sacred signs. And these signs, whether in religious observance, monastic witness, contemplative solitude or liturgical worship, should always be clear and evident not only to those who give them form and shape by their living practice, but to all who may happen to see them. The renewal of the monastic life must be first of all a renewal of authentic meaning and of understanding, and only after that a renewal of zeal in carrying out what is understood.

In considering this renewal of the "significance of signs" in the monastic life we must remember that the sign and the thing signified are always inseparable. No matter how much we may attempt to renew the meaning of the sign, the meaning will not change in any real way if the thing signified does not change. Thus if the actions and ceremonies of monastic liturgy are informed by a spirit of institutional ambition, if they spring from charity and from an earnest desire to obey the Gospel of Christ, then no matter how one may alter the "sign," it will still proclaim the thing that is really signified. Hence one cannot renew the religious life in depth merely by superficially altering some of the ceremonies and rites which are meant to bear witness to the inner spirit. However, once the change of the inner spirit has seriously begun, a renewal in the clarity and significance of the sacred signs will be of great help in bringing all to a clearer understanding and deeper appreciation of the work of renewal.

The meaning of communal life, of the vows, of monastic work, of worship, meditation and prayer can therefore not be permitted to remain arbitrary or abstract. Everything must converge on the central living mystery of unity in Christ and illuminate it—or rather spread the illumination which it receives from it. The function of the monastic community is to manifest this mystery, and the "spirit" of each Order is in fact simply the way in which the Order interprets its vocation to understand and to live some particular aspect of the mystery of Christ. Usually this "spirit" was manifested to the Founder and made itself fairly clear in the first generations of the Order's history. And so, for example, the sons of St. Benedict pray in the liturgy of his feast, "that the Lord may renew in his Church the Spirit that St. Benedict served, so that we, being filled with the same Spirit, may strive to love what he loved and to carry out in our works the things that he accomplished." So in the monastic life, renewal consists in rediscovering the meaning and spirit of monasticism as it was understood and lived by the early monks. Obviously the "return to sources" has been an important element in the monastic movement of the past hundred years.

The Church in recent years has insisted upon two essential aspects of the contemplative life: first that it must be and must remain what it has always traditionally been: a life oriented directly to God alone (*si revera Deum quaerit!*) in physical separation from the world, i.e. in solitude. But at the same time the Church insists that the contemplative life is and must be fully and completely apostolic. My purpose is not to define the "apostolate of contemplatives" or to introduce nuances into the rather crude idea of the monastery as a "dynamo of prayer" in which the monks are generating spiritual power for the workers in the active ministry. If the active apostolate does not proceed from the apostle's own union with God, the lack cannot be supplied by somebody else's holiness. The monk's prayer of petition and his inner consecration doubtless bring down grace upon the world. But the ancient monastic idea of the *vita apostolica*—source of the traditional understanding of our "apostolic vocation" —is centered in the witness of complete renunciation in obedience to the Gospel, what the early Cistercians called the *formula perfectae paenitentiae,* the life of obedience to the Gospel in humility, poverty and love.

It is by this spirit of apostolic renunciation that the monk, in spite of his essential solitude, can be open to the needs and to the anguish of the world and hence exercise his apostolate which is above all the apostolate of understanding and of compassion.

Here again, what is demanded of the monk is not the cold and perhaps stupefied "unworldliness" which may at bottom be no better than egoism, but a Christ-like selflessness and purity of heart which can take upon itself the sins and conflicts of the world and "baptize" them with the tears of repentance.

VII

OPENNESS AND CLOISTER

The work of religious renewal is naturally geared for the tempo of the majority who are in the active, apostolic life. The terms in which programs of renewal are articulated will therefore be dynamic, outgoing, aggressive, even in a certain sense "worldly." Since the contemplative Orders (especially communities of cloistered women) have unfortunately come to depend on others to formulate and also to solve their problems for them, this may put them in a rather awkward position.

Speaking as a member of a contemplative Order, I think this can teach us something. It is high time we contemplatives (and I include the nuns) learned to stand on our own feet and solve our own problems in our own terms. We have to think for ourselves and help one another. We would be very mistaken if we tried to apply the norms and solutions of active religious to the very different problems of the contemplative life.

Many cloistered communities have been seized with panic and confusion when confronted with the demands of renewal, simply because these demands have been formulated in terms that do not really apply to contemplatives. Instead of studying these demands in the light of our own special vocation, and learning to translate them into terms viable for the renewal we ourselves need as badly as anyone else, some of us have tended to reject them en bloc and to hold on desperately to the only solutions whose validity we can vouch for by experience. In many cases this means simply clinging to the past. But our younger religious have very grave problems with the legacy of the past, however valid it may once have been. Experience has shown us that if we simply *refuse* the challenge of renewal, and do no more than maintain archaic values, the cloistered life has no future. The day of grilles, double locks, conversations through veils and curtains, mysterious whisperings through the turn, even more mysterious Masses celebrated out of sight behind a wall—this day is done.

What does aggiornamento mean for contemplatives? Naturally, this is a very big question, and it is one which radically divides whole communities—usually along the lines of seniority. The young are a little more inclined to impatience and desperation. They may desire change at any cost, and demand the introduction of new ideas that work in the active life, on the assumption that these must be valid for everybody. The old, on the other hand, have an existential appreciation of certain values that are fully known only to those who have lived under conditions of discipline and sacrifice which no longer prevail. The more intelligent of these older religious are aware that these values can perhaps be preserved in a completely new form: but others identify the values with the framework of rule and discipline of the "old days." They cling to externals of observance that the new generation cannot understand and cannot accept. This is particularly true in the matter of "openness" and "dialogue."

Should contemplatives be "open to the world"? This is a question that has plunged some communities into what amounts to an identity crisis, because it has been formulated in the wrong terms. It is interpreted to mean: Should Carmelites leave the cloister and teach school? Should Trappists run parishes? In other words, are cloistered religious now going to be drafted for service in routine organized work for which they do not feel themselves qualified and for which, in fact, they have no vocation? Stated in such terms, the question is merely silly. The Church has no intention of abolishing the contemplative Orders, and she hopes that they will have the good sense not to abolish themselves. What the Church wants is not the destruction of the contemplative life, but its renewal. Now, the renewal of the contemplative Orders does fit into the overall program of renewal in the entire Church. One important element in the program, as formulated by Vatican II, is "openness to the world." Contemplatives are not exempt from this, but they have to understand it in their own terms. In other words, they must consider how, and to what extent, they can be "open to the world" without losing their identity as contemplatives.

To some contemplatives, the idea of "openness to the world" is incomprehensible. It contradicts what they believe is fundamental to their vocation. The essence of the cloistered life consists in their being "enclosed." They argue that the cloistered life cannot be open in any real sense without ceasing to be cloistered. This seems to them a matter of simple logic. When you embrace the contemplative cloistered life, you turn your back on the world, you renounce the world, you forget the problems and concerns, you pray for it without needing to know what you are praying for.

You turn away from the world to God, because the world is opposed to God. The cloistered ideal then becomes an ideal of "pure contemplation" in which everything is organized in view of a state of perfect recollection: everything is arranged so that one will be entirely purified not only of attachment to the world but even of all interest in it, all concern for it, all memory of it.

But "openness" to the world means involvement in the affairs of people outside the cloister, identification with them in their desires, problems, struggles, dangers; it means vital concern about a world of total war, genocide, race riots, social injustice, misery, poverty, violence, lust, every kind of disorder. All this is wicked and ungodly. Far from divine, it is diabolical. How can one think of such things and maintain the inner peace, the purity of recollection, the serenity of spirit in which one will hear the sweet ineffable call to divine union?

Rejection of the world, "contempt for the world," then results in a crudely automatic polarization: everything that happens outside the cloister is considered hateful, ridiculous, erroneous, ungodly, or at least trifling. Everything that happens in the cloister and according to the sacrosanct rules of the cloistered life is wise, pleasing to God, full of redemptive power, and supremely significant. The God who is nauseated by the actions of worldlings outside the cloister is consoled and delighted by the actions of observant religious within the cloister. This distorted interpretation of the Gospel texts about renouncing the world in our own hearts becomes an excuse for pharisaical complacency. Contemplatives despise the world because they imagine themselves to be superior to it in every way. The cloister is the guarantee of that superiority. If they resume contact with the world, they lose their superiority and become like everybody else. The beautiful image is tarnished. They no longer feel secure in the thought that God loves them better than anybody else.

Obviously, this is caricature. But this distortion has been made positive by a valid traditional concept of the contemplative life—one which has been taken for granted for sixteen hundred years! Yet there are many things which have been taken for granted longer than that which the Church is now questioning.

Is the contemplative life to be considered a state of interior recollection and an affective absorption in God considered as Infinite Love, or is it a response to the concrete *Word of God* manifesting to us His will and His love not only for ourselves as individuals but for the whole family of man redeemed by the cross of Christ? Is our love of God to take the form of blissful repose in consolation and inner peace or is it a total response which draws us out of ourselves beyond all concern over how we happen to *feel*? Is the cloistered life a mere cult of ordered serenity, or is it complete self-forgetfulness in obedience to God? Is the cloistered life merely to escape from the troubles and conflicts of the world to a condition of security and peace in which we "rest" and "taste" the consolations of intimacy with God? Or does it mean sharing the anguish and hope of a world in crisis in which millions struggle for the barest essentials of human existence?

Should not the contemplative life be seen in terms of *event* and *encounter* rather than simply as a "viewing" and "tasting" of essential love? Is love an *object* or is it a *happening*? Is God present to us in *idea* or in *act*? Is the contemplative life built on a dynamic of word and obedience, call and response, or is it a static project in which minds and hearts seek to become impregnated with a spiritual essence of love? If contemplative love is some*thing* which one acquires or receives in secret and jealously preserves from contamination, then one can build walls around it for safekeeping. But if contemplative love is a response to some*one* who is supremely free and whose "thoughts are not our thoughts, whose ways are not our ways," then we cannot really pin Him down to purely predictable relationships. We have to be "open" in the sense that we are ready and available in all possible situations, including those of human encounter and exchange. Christian love, including contemplative love, starts from the basic realization that those who are unable to relate to others in a valid human encounter are also handicapped in their relations to the encounter with God.

The current problems of the contemplative life stem in large measure from the way these questions have been answered in the past. Everything now depends on our capacity to reconsider them in the light of the Gospel and of contemporary human problems.

Most of the statements proposed about the contemplative life as a life of withdrawal, of "perfect recollection," with stress on negation, with being "undistracted" and so on, tend to have a Platonic rather than a Christian emphasis. These conceptions were valid as long as they fitted into the framework of a consciously religious civilization.

The whole world view of medieval civilization was structured on the ideas of eternity and divine transcendence. Secular life itself was understood in this framework of unworldliness. At the same time we have forgotten how completely the monks of the Middle Ages were integrated into the secular life of their time. The Cistercians of northern England in the twelfth century played somewhat the same role in their society as General Motors plays in American society today. The wool from the Cistercian granges was one of the most important factors in the economy of medieval England. The renunciation of the world practiced by the Cistercians of the Middle Ages paradoxically gave them a key place in the world of their time, and their asceticism, their mystical life, were understood to be an essential contribution to a religious culture in which everyone participated. The same is true in a different way of the Carmelite reform in sixteenth-century Spain. But today the symbolic dramatization of the contem-

plative witness, appropriate to a different kind of culture, has
acquired a different meaning in a specifically irreligious culture.

We must now learn to distinguish between "religiosity"
and "discipleship of Christ." "Religion" was an essential part
of medieval culture. "Irreligion" is an essential part of modern culture. What is of importance today is not to get modern
man to accept *religion* as a human or cultural value (he may
do so or he may not) but to let him see that we are witnesses of Christ, of the new creation, of the Resurrection, of
the Living God: and that is something that goes far beyond
the cultural phenomenon of religion. The contemplative life
will therefore need to be understood not in terms of religious
observances which dramatize the more devout attitudes of a
bygone society, but in terms of living experience and witness, that is to say in terms of complete Christian authenticity.
What is important now is not so much to preserve order and
regularity in observance, but to produce *real contemplatives*,
disciples who have found and have known Him whom the
Father has sent into the world and who are able to bear witness to His reality by their characters, by their lives and by
the transformation of their consciousness.

Today a new and more Biblical understanding of the contemplative life is called for: we must see it as a response to
the dynamic Word of God in history, we must see it in the
light of Biblical eschatology. The contemplative finds God
not in the embrace of "pure love" alone but in the prophetic
ardor of response to the "Word of the Lord": not in love
considered as essential good but in love that breaks through
into the world of sinful men in the fire of judgment and of
mercy. The contemplative must see love not only as the highest and purest experience of the human heart transformed
by grace, but as God's unfailing fidelity to unfaithful man.
The contemplative life is not only Eros (the yearning of the
human heart for the vision of beauty), but also Agape (surrender to the inexplicable mercy which comes to us from
God entirely on His own terms, in the context of our personal

and social history). Once this has been said, Eros cannot be excluded. However, it remains always secondary.

God speaks to us not only in the Bible, not only in the secret inspirations of our hearts, but also through the public and manifest events of our own time, and above all through the Church. The radical change in the Church's attitude toward the modern world was one of the significant events that marked Vatican II. In the light of the Council it is no longer possible to take a completely negative view of the modern world. It is no longer possible, even for contemplatives, to simply shut out the world, to ignore it, to forget it, in order to relish the private joys of contemplative Eros. To insist on the cultivation of total recollection for the sake of this Eros and its consolations would be pure and simple selfishness. It would also mean a failure to really deepen the true Christian dimensions of Agape which are the real dimensions of the contemplative life. This is where so much confusion arises.

Lack of theological knowledge, ignorance of the true riches of Christian tradition and of the Church's wisdom, have made contemplatives take a short view of their vocation, one that is almost "materialistic" (emphasis on walls, grilles, veils, withdrawal, mutism). But the same ignorance may well carry them to the opposite extreme. Some apparently imagine that by throwing off the veil, running around talking to everyone, and getting themselves involved in every kind of official active task, they can justify their existence in the eyes of the world. To please "the world" they repudiate their call to contemplation. We have to be careful not to discredit a false idea of contemplation in such a way that we discredit true contemplative life and get rid of the cloister so that everyone can plunge into action, but to renew the true contemplative life as an authentic, rare but vitally necessary charism in the Church. Now, the call of the Church to "openness" is essential to renewal itself, even for contemplatives. Hence "openness" is *necessary* for contemplatives. It is by no means a mere concession, something permitted to modern people who would otherwise become tense through too much concentration and withdrawal. In one word: openness is now seen to be not only opposed to cloistered contemplation but even as necessary for its deepening and its renewal.

But why is this the case? Once again, the only way to validate such a claim is by appealing not to psychology, not to the pragmatic necessities of the moment, but to theology itself. Openness to the world is demanded by the realization that the world of today, in which man's whole future for good or for evil now rests in his own hands, is for all men the place of God's epiphany as Judge and as Savior, as the Lord of History. On the other hand, as we all know too well, those who are completely immersed in the world with its violence and confusion, may certainly have a very real experience of its problem, but they may also see these problems so close at hand that they lose their perspective. Their view of things needs to be completed by the perspective of those who see life from another angle. In order to see the world from this "other angle" there must necessarily be places where people live, under special conditions, devoting themselves to meditation, study, prayer and worship, not for themselves but as a service to the entire Church. This service is what now needs to be properly understood and defined. Here is where "openness" is important. If the contemplative is totally out of touch with the realities and crises of his time, he loses all claim to that special fullness and maturity of wisdom which should be his. The Church has always expected that her contemplatives should be men and women who have attained a greater depth of prophetic wisdom, a more profound understanding of the Word and love of God, so that they may be more perfect witnesses of the Kingdom and of the new creation. That is why John the Baptist—"the voice of one crying in the wilderness"—has traditionally been the model of monks: not just because he fasted and lived in the desert, but because it was he who was first able to recognize the Messiah. Needless to say, our contemplatives are not always distinguished by this superior wisdom at all, and the charism of prophetic wisdom has unfortunately too often become distorted by eccentricity and illuminism. (No need to retail here the taste for bizarre devotions, for curious inner feelings, for apocalyptic surmises, or for preternatural happenings which have flourished in the cloister due to excessive rigidity and too much enclosure.)

There is therefore a twofold need for "openness" in contemplative communities. Contemplatives need to be more "open" for their own good and for the renewal of their contemplative life by a saner contact with contemporary reality. But also, assuming that the contemplative life itself is authentic, others need to share in its advantages. Openness works two ways. On both sides there is giving and receiving. The result is, or should be, a real increase of charity, a greater love of the contemplative for the world created and redeemed by God, a greater love of the non-cloistered person for God found and experienced more deeply in temporary contact with the cloister. Needless to say, those who have been deputed by the Church not only to pray for the world but also to attain a deeper level of experience and understanding, should also, at least in some cases, be able to teach the ways of prayer to others living outside the cloister, besides providing them with a place of quiet and rest and interior renewal.

There can be no question whatever of the Church asking contemplatives to engage in work for which they are not qualified, work which others can do far better than they. There is no need for contemplative Carmelites to teach third-grade arithmetic. There is no need either for Cistercians to get out into the parishes and preach. What the Church needs is for contemplatives to share with others their privilege of silence, worship and meditation, their ability to listen more deeply and more penetratingly to the Word of God, their understanding of sacrifice, their inner vision.

Anyone who has been called to share with others the fruits of contemplation knows well enough that this sharing is not a distraction and not a threat to the contemplative life. On the contrary, much discipline and humility are necessary for one who tries in all honesty to share with others an undistorted view of the truth. The task of conveying to others clearly and sincerely what one knows of the problems of the Christian life, without saying more than one knows and without resorting merely to catch phrases borrowed from books, is a great help for one's own life in Christ. Of course, not all are called to do this kind of thing habitually, and many members of contemplative communities will have no reason to worry about it.

Now an important question: What is meant by "openness"? As a matter of fact, it is not quite certain just what openness is going to mean in practice for contemplatives: that is something we have to discover by experiment. I would suggest the following as a useful description of what openness might imply for cloistered orders. Here I am not making nice distinctions for men and women, but just taking the contemplative life in general.

a. First of all, being "open to the world" means being aware of and responsive to the real situation of people in the world, the critical problems of the world. These problems are basically spiritual problems. The world is in a state of spiritual crisis. In fact we are now in one of the most crucial periods of development in the whole evolution of man. We are literally at the crossroads of our destiny. Most people either ignore the spiritual dimensions of the crisis or else they are incapable of apprehending the real issues in any way whatever. The contemplative, by *selective* information and *well-chosen* exposure to sound commentary, should be able to identify intelligently and compassionately with modern man in crisis. Simple aloofness, withdrawal, and refusal of concern would make the contemplative a scandal to his brother in the world.

Parenthetically: this is another case where the lack of originality and initiative are grave handicaps in the contemplative life. There is obvious risk in an uncritical use of modern media: we have to face the fact that what passes for news is often merely the retailing of pseudo-events. What passes for entertainment is the subject of articulate and constant protest on the part of intelligent people. It would be absurd for naive contemplatives to be agog over material which those outside the cloister regard as cultural garbage, and there is very real danger of their doing so, since they lack the critical sense to discern what is valuable and what is not. There is need for qualified persons to select and distribute information that would be really pertinent in the contemplative life, and to provide a minimum of intelligent comment showing its relevance to our life in Christ. Someone ought to undertake a weekly mimeographed newsletter for contemplatives: this would be a real service. It would save religious the tedium of plowing through the newspapers and magazines to find something useful amid the bewilderment of pseudo-events and religious fads. This mimeographed service could also include a list of references to articles in useful sources like *Herder Correspondence, Informations Catholiques Internationales,* etc.

b. Being "open to the world" means being more accessible to people of flesh and blood who are brought by God, in one way or other, to our doorstep. The poor, materially and spiritually. Our relatives and friends. Men and women who are looking for something they need, without being able to identify it precisely, and who came to the cloister for rest, reflection and retreat. Here, too, there have to be certain limits, and contacts with the outside must be *selective.* There is no point in simply turning the monastery into a busy retreat house. In any case, it would seem that "retreat movements" and "closed retreats" are losing their significance. What people seek today is not so much the organized, predigested routine of conferences and exercises, but an opportunity to be quiet, to reflect, and to discuss in informational, spontaneous and friendly encounters the things they have on their minds. At this point we might add that there is today a far greater interest in contemplation among non-Christians and even nonbelievers than there is among the ordinary run of Christians. Contemplative communities may find that they have a great deal to say to these people who seek spiritual insight but who, generally speaking, are bored to death with preachers and utterly deaf to Christian apologetics. The only Christian communities that still retain some meaning for these people are contemplative communities.

c. Does openness to the world imply going out of the cloister more freely? The contemplative life would lose its meaning if it did not preserve a certain amount of solitude and silence. But we must admit that merely keeping everyone locked up is no guarantee of an authentic contemplative life. There are times when a contemplative needs to leave the cloister. Obviously there is no point in a contemplative merely going out "socially" and spending time in idle conversation or "having fun." But there may be reasons why a contemplative should leave his cloister in order to obtain information or experience that would be valuable for him and for his community. Obviously this too will be a highly selective matter. But it should be quite normal to go to other monasteries in order to take courses in theology, Scripture, liturgy and so on. This should be possible for nuns also. Cloistered nuns can and should be open to the extent of attending certain important meetings and conferences (for superiors, novice-mistresses, etc.). Monks might in exceptional cases travel to engage in ecumenical dialogue or discussions where their presence would be really useful. Contemplatives have a special slant on the theological and spiritual problems of the Church and of the world. They should be able to make their own contribution to discussions of these problems, and should be allowed, with other qualified experts, to participate in affecting the good of the whole Church. Above all, they should take a most active part in solving the problems of contemplative communities themselves, and should be able to give help where it is really needed. On the other hand, if a contemplative religious becomes so caught up in these activities that he is no longer able to live a contemplative life, then the reason for his "services" no longer exists. He is not qualified to help others in so far as he is what he is supposed to be: a contemplative. No matter what may be the need for action and service on the part of the contemplative, that need must yield to the minimal demands of the contemplative life itself. In the contemplative life, action exists for the sake of contemplation and vice versa. The openness of the contemplative is justified in so far as it enables him to be a better contemplative, and to share with others the fruit of his contemplation.

Finally, one very important point. In the past, the structures of the contemplative life have acquired too much rigidity and uniformity. Emphasis on exterior regularity and on uniform observance tended to stifle personal development and took little or no account of special needs or personal vocations, for instance to greater solitude. Contemplative "openness" must develop not only in relation to the outside world but also, and above all, within the community itself. Free and spontaneous contacts between the religious themselves are absolutely necessary. Religious must communicate frankly and sincerely in a personal way and not only in the set of formalized relationships which have been favored in the past. The structure of community relations in the contemplative life has been too inflexible, too impersonal, and in many cases artificial to the point of stultification.

Relationships must once more become "natural" and human in the best sense of those words. This means inevitably a greater freedom and tolerance in the matter of communication. In other words, it means materially less silence. On the other hand, to balance this freedom of communication, the legitimate needs of individual religious for greater solitude and silence must also be respected. The community that grows in charity and self-understanding will also spontaneously recognize these special needs—and favor them in a spirit of real love, knowing that they imply no derogation of the common life. The mature contemplative (who may not always be necessarily a very brilliant or gifted person) can contribute a great deal to the common life by his or her silent and solitary prayer. Even those who are not yet fully formed need the experience of periods of solitude and silence in order to grow in the life of prayer. Contemplative communities should recognize the value of encouraging these personal aspirations.

The "openness" that is asked of contemplatives by the Church is then not a mere matter of relaxation, not an expedient for making life more livable. The real purpose of openness is to renew life in the Spirit, life in love. A greater love and understanding of people is no obstacle to a true growth in contemplation, for contemplation is rooted and grounded in charity. A more generous sharing of the values of the contemplative life will increase our love instead of diminishing it. It will also increase our understanding of and appreciation for our own vocation. Obviously, a great deal of prudence will be required, but we should not be so afraid of mistakes that we fail to make necessary changes. If we face change in a courageous spirit of faith, the Holy Spirit will take care of the rest.

VIII

IS THE WORLD A PROBLEM?[1]

Is the world a problem? I type the question. I am tempted to type it over again, with asterisks between the letters, the way H*y*m*a*n K*a*p*l*a*n used to type his name in *The New Yorker* thirty years ago. And as far as I am concerned that would dispose of the question. But the subject is doubtless too "serious" for a chapter title heading a page with "Is the world a problem" running down the middle, full of asterisks. So I have to be serious too, and develop it.

Maybe I can spell this question out politely, admitting that there are still cogent reasons why it should be asked and answered. Perhaps, too, I am personally involved in the absurdity of the question; due to a book I wrote thirty years ago, I have myself become a sort of stereotype of the world-denying contemplative—the man who spurned New York, spat on Chicago, and tromped on Louisville, heading for the woods with Thoreau in one pocket, John of the Cross in another, and holding the Bible open at the Apocalypse. This personal stereotype is probably my own fault, and it is something I have to try to demolish on occasion.

Now that we are all concerned about the Church and the World, the Secular City, and the values of secular society, it was to be expected that someone would turn quizzically to me and ask: "What about you, Father Merton? What do *you* think?"—and then duck as if I were St. Jerome with a rock in my fist.

First of all, the whole question of the world, the secular world, has become extremely ambiguous. It becomes even more ambiguous when it is set up over against another entity, the world of the sacred. The old duality of time-eternity,

[1] On the original title page the author had written:
Et quand donc suis-je plus vrai
que lorsque je suis le monde?
—Camus

matter-spirit, natural-supernatural and so on (which makes sense in a very limited and definite context) is suddenly transposed into a totally different context in which it creates nothing but confusion. This confusion is certainly a problem. Whether or not "the world" is a problem, a confused idea of what the world might possibly be is quite definitely a problem and it is that confusion I want to talk about. I want to make clear that I speak not as the author of *The Seven Storey Mountain,* which seemingly a lot of people have read, but as the author of more recent essays and poems which apparently very few people have read. This is not the official voice of Trappist silence, the monk with his hood up and his back to the camera, brooding over the waters of an artificial lake. This is not the petulant and uncanonizable modern Jerome who never got over the fact that he could give up beer. (I drink beer whenever I can lay my hands on any. I love beer, and, by that very fact, the world.) This is simply the voice of a self-questioning human person who, like all his brothers, struggles to cope with turbulent, mysterious, demanding, exciting, frustrating, confused existence in which almost nothing is really predictable, in which most definitions, explanations and justifications become incredible even before they are uttered, in which people suffer together and are sometimes utterly beautiful, at other times impossibly pathetic. In which there is much that is frightening, in which almost everything public is patently phony, and in which there is at the same time an immense ground of personal authenticity that is right there and so obvious that no one can talk about it and most cannot even believe that it is there.

I am, in other words, a man in the modern world. In fact, I am the world just as you are! Where am I going to look for the world first of all if not in myself?

As long as I assume that the world is something I discover by turning on the radio or looking out the window I am deceived from the start. As long as I imagine that the world is something to be "escaped" in a monastery—that wearing a special costume and following a quaint observance takes me "out of this world," I am dedicating my life to an illusion. Of course, I hasten to qualify this. I said a moment ago that in a certain historic context of thought and of life, this kind of thought and action once made perfect sense. But the moment you change the context, then the whole thing has to be completely transposed. Otherwise you are left like the orchestra in the Marx Brothers' *Night at the Opera* where Harpo had inserted "Take Me Out to the Ball Game" in the middle of the operatic score.

The confusion lies in this: on one hand there is a primitive Christian conception of the world as an object of choice. On the other there is the obvious fact that the world is also something about which there is and can be no choice. And, historically, these notions have sometimes got mixed up, so that what is simply "given" appears to have been chosen, and what is there to be chosen, decided for or against, is simply evaded as if no decision were licit or even possible.

That I should have been born in 1915, that I should be the contemporary of Auschwitz, Hiroshima, Viet Nam and the Watts riots, are things about which I was not first consulted. Yet they are also events in which, whether I like it or not, I am deeply and personally involved. The "world" is not just a physical space traversed by jet planes and full of people running in all directions. It is a complex of responsibilities and options made out of the loves, the hates, the fears, the joys, the hopes, the greed, the cruelty, the kindness, the faith, the trust, the suspicion of all. In the last analysis, if there is war because nobody trusts anybody, this is in part because I myself am defensive, suspicious, untrusting, and intent on making other people conform themselves to my particular brand of death wish.

Put in these terms, the world both is and is not a problem. The world is a "problem" in so far as everybody in it is a problem to himself. The world is a problem in so far as we all add up to a big collective question. Starting then from this concept of a world which is essentially problematic because it is full of problematic and self-doubting freedoms, there have been various suggestions made as to what to do about it.

At present the Church is outgrowing what one might call the Carolingian suggestion. This is a world view which was rooted in the official acceptance of the Church into the world of imperial Rome, the world of Constantine and of Augustine, of Charlemagne in the west and of Byzantium in the east. In crude, simple strokes, this world view can be sketched as follows: We are living in the last age of salvation history. A world radically evil and doomed to hell has been ransomed from the devil by the Cross of Christ and is now simply marking time until the message of salvation can be preached to everyone. Then will come the judgment. Meanwhile, men, being evil and prone to sin at every moment, must be prevented by authority from following their base instincts and getting lost.

They cannot be left to their own freedom or even to God's loving grace. They have to have their freedom taken away from them because it is their greatest peril. They have to be told at every step what to do, and it is better if what they are told to do is displeasing to their corrupt natures, for this will keep them out of further subtle forms of mischief. Meanwhile the Empire has become, provisionally at least, holy. As figure of the eschatological kingdom, worldly power consecrated to Christ becomes Christ's reign on earth. In spite of its human limitations the authority of the Christian prince is a guarantee against complete chaos and disorder and must be submitted to—to resist established authority is equivalent to resisting Christ. Thus we have a rigid and stable order in which all values are fixed and have to be preserved, protected, defended against dark forces of impulse and violent passion. War on behalf of the Christian prince and his power becomes a holy war for Christ against the devil. War too becomes a sacred duty.

The dark strokes in the picture have their historical explanation in the crisis of the barbarian invasions. But there are also brighter strokes, and we find in the thought of Aquinas, Scotus, Bonaventure, Dante, a basically world-affirming and optimistic view of man, of his world and his work, in the perspective of the Christian redemption. Here in the more peaceful and flourishing years of the twelfth and thirteenth centuries we see a harmonious synthesis of nature and grace, in which the created world itself is an epiphany of divine wisdom and love, and, redeemed in and by Christ, will return to God with all its beauty restored by the transforming power of grace, which reaches down to material creation through man and his work. Already in St. Thomas we find the ground work for an optimistic Christian affirmation of natural and worldly values in the perspective of an eschatological love. However, this view too is static rather than dynamic, hierarchic, layer upon layer, rather than ongoing and self-creating, the fulfillment of a predetermined intellectual plan rather than the creative project of a free and self-building love.

In the Carolingian world view it somehow happened that the idea of the world as an object of choice tended to be frozen. The "world" was identified simply with the sinful, the perilous, the unpredictable (therefore in many cases the new, and even worse the free), and this was what one automatically rejected. Or, if one had the misfortune to choose it, one went at once to confession. The world was therefore what one did not choose. Since society itself was constructed on this concept of the world, Christian society ("Christendom") conceived itself as a world-denying society in the midst of the world. A pilgrim society on the way to another world. It was fitting that there should be in the midst of that society, and in a place of special prominence and choice, certain people who were professional world-deniers, whose very existence was a sign of *contemptus mundi* and of otherworldly aspirations. Thus from a certain point of view this renunciation and unworldliness of monks became a justification of worldly power and of the established social and economic structures. The society that, by its respect for consecrated unworldliness, confessed its own heavenly aspirations, was certainly the realm of Christ on earth, its kings and its mighty were all alike pilgrims with the poor and humble. If all kept their proper place in the procession the pilgrimage would continue to go well. This is all obvious to everyone who has ever read a line about the Middle Ages, and its obviousness is presently being run into the ground by critics of monasticism. What these critics overlook is that though the theory was austere and negative, in practice the "sacred" and basically "clerical" and "monastic" Christendom produced a world-affirming, nature-respecting, life-loving, love-oriented, fruitful and rich culture. It had its limitations and its grave flaws. But the monastic and contemplative ideal of the Middle Ages, based on an ideological rejection of the world, actually recovered and rediscovered the values of the world on a deeper and more imperishable level, not merely somewhere aloft in a card file of Platonic ideas, but in the world itself, its life, its work, its people, its strivings, its hopes and its existential day-to-day reality. The world-denying monastic ethos found itself willy-nilly incorporated in a life-affirming and humanistic climate. No one who has really read Anselm, Thomas, John of Salisbury, Scotus, Bonaventure, Eckhart, and the rest can seriously doubt this.

Nevertheless, this stereotyped hierarchic idea of the world's structure eventually ceased to be really fruitful and productive. It was already sterile and unreal as early as the fifteenth century. And the fact that the Church of the Second Vatican Council has finally admitted that the old immobilism will no longer serve is a bit too overdue to be regarded as a monumental triumph. The Constitution on the Church in the Modern World is salted with phrases which suggest that the fathers were, at least some of them, fully aware of this.

In any case, one of the essential tasks of aggiornamento is that of renewing the whole perspective of theology in such a way that our ideas of God, man and the world are no longer dominated by the Carolingian-medieval imagery of the sacred and hierarchical cosmos, in which everything is decided beforehand and in which the only choice is to accept gladly what is imposed as part of an immobile and established social structure.

In "turning to the world" the contemporary Church is first of all admitting that the world can once again become an object of choice. Not only can it be chosen, but in fact it must be chosen. How? If I had no choice about the age in which I was to live, I nevertheless have a choice about the attitude I take and about the way and the extent of my participation in its living ongoing events. To choose the world is not then merely a pious admission that the world is acceptable because it comes from the hand of God. It is first of all an acceptance of a task and a vocation in the world, in history and in time. In my time, which is the present. To choose the world is to choose to do the work I am capable of doing, in collaboration with my brother, to make the world better, more free, more just, more livable, more human. And it has now become transparently obvious that mere automatic "rejection of the world" and "contempt for the world" is in fact not a choice but the evasion of choice. The man who pretends that he can turn his back on Auschwitz or Viet Nam and act as if they were not there is simply bluffing. I think this is getting to be generally admitted, even by monks.

On the other hand the stereotype of world rejection is now being firmly replaced by a collection of equally empty stereotypes of world affirmation in which I, for one, have very little confidence. They often seem to be gestures, charades, mummery designed to make the ones participating in them feel secure, to make them feel precisely that they are "like participating" and really doing something. So precisely at the moment when it becomes vitally important for the destiny of man that man should learn to choose for himself a peaceful, equitable, sane and humane world the whole question of choice itself becomes a stark and dreadful one. We talk about choosing, yet everything seems more grimly determined than ever before. We are caught in an enormous web of consequences, a net of erroneous and even pathological effects of other men's decisions. After Hitler, how can Germany be anything but a danger to world peace? To choose the world therefore is to choose the anguish of being hampered and frustrated in a situation fraught with frightful difficulties. We can affirm the world and its values all we like, but the complexity of events responds too often with a cold negation of our hopes.

In the old days when everyone compulsively rejected the world it was really not hard at all to secretly make quite a few healthy and positive affirmations of a worldly existence in the best sense of the word, in praise of God and for the good of all men. Nowadays when we talk so much of freedom, commitment, "engagement" and so on, it becomes imperative to ask whether the choices we are making have any meaning whatever. Do they change anything? Do they get us anywhere? Do we really choose to alter the direction of our lives or do we simply comfort ourselves with the choice of making another choice? Can we really decide effectively for a better world?

The "suggestion" that has now most obviously replaced that of the Carolingians is that of Karl Marx. In this view, history is not finished, it has just reached the point where it may, if we are smart, begin. There is no predetermined divine plan (although frankly the messianism in Marx is basically Biblical and eschatological). After a long precarious evolution matter has reached the point, in man, where it can become fully aware of itself, take itself in hand, control its own destiny. And now at last that great seething mass of material forces, the world, will enter upon its true destiny by being raised to a human level. The instruments by which this can be accomplished—technology, cybernetics—are now in our power. But are we in our own power? No, we are still determined by the illusions of thought patterns, superstructures, devised to justify antiquated and destructive economic patterns. Hence if man is to choose to make himself, if he is to become free at last, his duty can be narrowed down to one simple option, one basic commitment: the struggle against the (imperialist) world.

With a shock we find ourselves in a familiar pattern: a predetermined struggle against evil in which personal freedom is viewed with intolerance and suspicion. The world must be changed because it is unacceptable as it is. But the change must be guided by authority and political power. The forces of good are all incarnate in this authority. The forces of evil are on the contrary incarnate in the power of the enemy system. Man cannot be left to himself. He must submit entirely to the control of the collectivity for which he exists. "Man" is not the person but the collective animal. Though he may eventually become free, now is not the time of freedom but of obedience, authority, power, control. Man does not choose to make himself except in the sense that he submits to a choice dictated by the authority of science and the messianic collective—the party which represents the chosen eschatological class. Hence though in theory there are all kinds of possible choices, in reality the only basic choice is that of rejecting and destroying the evil "world"—namely capitalist imperialism and, in the present juncture, the United States. Hence the ambiguities of Communist dogma at the moment: the choice of peace is of course nothing else than the choice of war against the United States. In other words, we have turned the page of *Aïda* and we are now playing "Take Me Out to the Ball Game," but it is the same crazy Marx Brothers' opera. Freedom, humanism, peace, plenty and joy are all enthusiastically invoked, but prove on closer examination to be their opposites. There is only one choice, to submit to the decision handed down from on high by an authoritarian power which defines good and evil in political terms.

This, as I see it, is the present state of the question. The Church has finally realized officially that the classic world view, which began to develop serious flaws five hundred years ago, is no longer viable at all. There is something of a stampede for security in a new world view.

In this endeavor the dialogue with Marxism is going to be of crucial importance not only for Christians but for Marxists. For if it is a true dialogue it will possibly involve some softening and adjustment of doctrinaire positions and an opening to new perspectives and possibilities of collaboration. Obviously, however, the dialogue with official and established Marxism—the Soviets or Red China—is not to be considered yet as a meaningful possibility. But the conversations that have begun with the type of revisionist Marxism represented by the French thinker Roger Garaudy may certainly have some effects. But what effects? Good or bad? It is all too easy for enthusiastic Catholics, having tasted a little of the new wine, to convince themselves that "turning to the world" and "choosing the world" means simply turning to Marx and choosing some variation—Maoist, Soviet, Castroist —of the Communist political line. There is no question that since the Council a few Catholic thinkers and publicists in Europe and South America are tending in this direction. Their tendency is understandable, but I do not find it altogether hopeful.

The majority of Catholic thinkers today are, however, working in the direction of a modern world view in which the demands of the new humanism of Marx, Freud, Teilhard, Bonhoeffer and others are fully respected and often heartily endorsed. For them, the tendency is no longer to regard God as enthroned "out there" at the summit of the cosmos, but as the "absolute future" who will manifest Himself in and through man, by the transformation of man and the world by science oriented to Christ. Though this certainly is not a view which conservative theologians find comforting, it represents a serious attempt to re-express Christian truths in terms more familiar to modern man. It demands that we take a more dynamic view of man and of society. It requires openness, freedom, the willingness to face risks. It also postulates respect for the human person in the human community. But at the same time it seems to me that it may have serious deficiencies in so far as it may ignore the really deep problems of collective technological and cybernetic society. To assume, for instance, that just because scientific and technological humanism can theoretically be seen as "perfectly biblical" ("nothing is more biblical than technology," says Père Daniélou) does not alter the profound dehumanization that can in fact take place in technological society (as Daniélou also clearly sees). The fact that man can now theoretically control and direct his own destiny does nothing to mitigate the awful determinism which in practice makes a mockery of the most realistic plans and turns all men's projects diametrically against their professed humanistic aims. The demonic gap between expressed aims and concrete achievements in the conduct of the Viet Nam war, for instance, should be an object lesson in the impotence of technology to come to grips with the human needs and realities of our time.

I have a profound mistrust of all obligatory answers. The great problem of our time is not to formulate clear answers to neat theoretical questions but to tackle the self-destructive alienation of man in a society dedicated in theory to human values and in practice to the pursuit of power for its own sake. All the new and fresh answers in the world, all the bright official confidence in the collectivity of the secular city, will do nothing to change the reality of this alienation. The Marxist world view is the one really coherent and systematic one that has so far come forward to replace the old medieval Christian and classic synthesis. It has in fact got itself accepted, for better or for worse, by more than half the human race. And yet, while claiming to offer man hope of deliverance from alienation, it has demanded a more unquestioning, a more irrational and a more submissive obedience than ever to its obligatory answers, even when these are manifestly self-contradictory and destructive of the very values they claim to defend.

The dialogue with Marxism is an obvious necessity. But if in the course of it we simply create a vapid brew of neo-modernist and pseudoscientific optimism I do not see what has been gained, especially if it leaves people passive and helpless in the presence of dehumanizing forces that no one seems quite able to identify exactly and cope with effectively. In this sense, the world is certainly a problem. Its idea of itself is extremely ambiguous. Its claims to pinpoint and to solve its own greatest problems are, in my opinion, not very convincing. Its obligatory answers are hardly acceptable. I am not in love with them!

When "the world" is hypostatized (and it inevitably is) it becomes another of those dangerous and destructive fictions with which we are trying vainly to grapple. And for anyone who has seriously entered into the medieval Christian, or the Hindu, or the Buddhist conceptions of *contemptus mundi, Mara* and the *"emptiness of the world,"* it will be evident that this means not the rejection of a reality, but the unmasking of an illusion. The world as pure object is something that is not there. It is not a reality outside us for which we exist. It is not a firm and absolute objective structure which has to be accepted on its own inexorable terms. The world has in fact no terms of its own. It dictates no terms to man. We and our world interpenetrate. If anything, the world exists for us, and we exist for ourselves. It is only in assuming full responsibility for our world, for our lives and for ourselves that we can be said to live really for God. The whole human reality, which of course transcends us as individuals and as a collectivity, nevertheless interpenetrates the world of nature (which is obviously "real") and the world of history (also "real" in so far as it is made up of the total effect of all our decisions and actions). But this reality, though "external" and "objective," is not something entirely independent of us, which dominates us inexorably from without through the medium of certain fixed laws which science alone can discover and use. It is an extension and a projection of ourselves and of our lives, and if we attend to it respectfully, while attending also to our own freedom and our own integrity, we can learn to obey its ways and coordinate our lives with its mysterious movements. The way to find the real "world" is not merely to measure and observe what is outside us, but to discover our own inner ground. For that is where the world is, first of all: in my deepest self. But there I find the world to be quite different from the "obligatory answers." This "ground," this "world" where I am mysteriously present at once to my own self and to the freedoms of all other men, is not a visible objective and determined structure with fixed laws and demands. It is a living and self-creating mystery of which I am myself a part, to which I am myself my own unique door. When I find the world in my own ground, it is impossible for me to be alienated by it. It is precisely the obligatory answers which insist on showing me the world as totally other than myself and my brother, which alienate me from myself and from my brother. Hence I see no reason for our compulsion to manufacture ever newer and more shiny sets of obligatory answers.

The questions and the answers surely have their purpose. We are rational and dialectical beings. But even the best answers are themselves not final. They point to something further which cannot be embodied in a verbal ground. They point to life itself in its inalienable and personal ground. They point to that realm of values which, in the eyes of scientific and positivistic thought, has no meaning. But how can we come to grips with the world except in so far as it is a value, that is to say, in so far as it exists for us?

There remains a profound wisdom in the traditional Christian approach to the world as to an object of choice. But we have to admit that the habitual and mechanical compulsions of a certain limited type of Christian thought have falsified the true value-perspective in which the world can be discovered and chosen as it is. To treat the world merely as an agglomeration of material goods and objects outside ourselves, and to reject these goods and objects in order to seek others which are "interior" and "spiritual" is in fact to miss the whole point of the challenging confrontation of the world and Christ. Do we really choose between the world and Christ as between two conflicting realities absolutely opposed? Or do we choose Christ by choosing the world as it really is in him, that is to say created and redeemed by him, and encountered in the ground of our own personal freedom and of our love? Do we really renounce ourselves and the world in order to find Christ, or do we renounce our alienated and false selves in order to choose our own deepest truth in choosing both the world and Christ at the same time? If the deepest ground of my being is love, then in that very love itself and nowhere else will I find myself, and the world, and my brother and Christ. It is not a question of either-or but of all-in-one. It is not a matter of exclusivism and "purity" but of wholeness, wholeheartedness, unity and Meister Eckhart's *Gleichheit* (equality) which finds the same ground of love in everything.

The world cannot be a problem to anyone who sees that ultimately Christ, the world, his brother and his own inmost ground are made one and the same in grace and redemptive love. If all the current talk about the world helps people to discover this, then it is fine. But if it produces nothing but a whole new divisive gamut of obligatory positions and "contemporary answers" we might as well forget it. The world itself is no problem, but we are a problem to ourselves because we are alienated from ourselves, and this alienation is due precisely to an inveterate habit of division by which we break reality into pieces and then wonder why, after we have manipulated the pieces until they fall apart, we find ourselves out of touch with life, with reality, with the world and most of all with ourselves.

IX

CONTEMPLATION
IN A WORLD
OF ACTION

This is not intended merely as another apologia for an official, institutional life of prayer. Nor is it supposed to score points in an outdated polemic. My purpose is rather to examine some basic questions of *meaning*. What does the contemplative life or the life of prayer, solitude, silence, meditation, mean to man in the atomic age? What can it mean? Has it lost all meaning whatever?

When I speak of the contemplative life I do not mean the institutional cloistered life, the organized life of prayer. This has special problems of its own. Many Catholics are now saying openly that the cloistered contemplative *institution* is indefensible, that it is an anachronism that has no point in the modern world. I am not arguing about this—I only remark in passing that I do not agree. Prescinding from any idea of an institution or even of a religious organization, I am talking about a special dimension of inner discipline and experience, a certain integrity and fullness of personal development, which are not compatible with a purely external, alienated, busy-busy existence. This does not mean that they are incompatible with action, with creative work, with dedicated love. On the contrary, these all go together. A certain depth of disciplined experience is a necessary ground for fruitful action. Without a more profound human understanding derived from exploration of the inner ground of human existence, love will tend to be superficial and deceptive. Traditionally, the ideas of prayer, meditation and contemplation have been associated with this deepening of one's personal life and this expansion of the capacity to understand and serve others.

Let us start from one admitted fact: if prayer, meditation and contemplation were once taken for granted as central realities in human life everywhere, they are so no longer. They are regarded, even by believers, as somehow marginal and secondary: what counts is getting things done. Prayer seems to be nothing but "saying words," and meditation is a mysterious process which is not understood: if it has some usefulness, that usefulness is felt to be completely remote from the life of ordinary men. As for contemplation: even in the so-called "contemplative life" it is viewed with suspicion! If "contemplatives" themselves are afraid of it, what will the ordinary lay person think? And, as a matter of fact, the word "contemplation" has unfortunate resonances—the philosophic elitism of Plato and Plotinus.

It is a curious fact that in the traditional polemic between action and contemplation, modern apologists for the "contemplative" life have tended to defend it on pragmatic grounds—in terms of action and efficacy. In other words, monks and nuns in cloisters are not "useless," because they are engaged in a very efficacious kind of spiritual activity. They are not idle, lazy, evasive: they are "getting things done," but in a mysterious and esoteric sort of way, an invisible, spiritual way, by means of their prayers. Instead of acting upon things and persons in the world, they act directly upon God by prayer. This is in fact a "superior kind of activity," a "supreme efficacy," but people do not see it. It has to be believed.

I am not interested, for the moment, in trying to prove anything by this argument. I am concerned only with its meaning to modern people. Obviously there are many who *believe* this in the sense that they accept it "on faith" without quite seeing how it is possible. They accept it on authority without understanding it themselves, and without trying to understand it. The argument is not one which appeals to them. It arouses a curious malaise, but they do not know what to do about it. They put it away on a mental shelf with other things they have no time to examine.

This view of the contemplative life, which is quite legitimate as far as it goes, places a great deal of stress on the prayer of petition, on intercession, on vicarious sacrifice and suffering as work, as action, as "something accomplished" in cloisters. And stress is laid on the idea that the prayers and sacrifices of contemplatives produce certain definite effects, albeit in a hidden manner. They "produce grace" and they also in some way "cause" divine interventions. Thus it happens that a considerable volume of letters arrives in the monastery or convent mailbag requesting prayers on the eve of a serious operation, on the occasion of a lawsuit, in personal and family problems, in sickness, in all kinds of trouble. Certainly, Catholics believe that God hears and answers prayers of petition. But it is a distortion of the contemplative life to treat it as if the contemplative concentrated all his efforts on getting graces and favors from God for others and for himself.

This conception of God and of prayer is one which fits quite naturally into a particular image of the universe, a cause-and-effect mechanism with a transcendent God "outside" and "above" it, acting upon it as Absolute First Cause, Supreme Prime Mover. He is the Uncaused Cause, guiding, planning, willing every effect down to the tiniest detail. He is regarded as a Supreme Engineer. But men can enter into communication with Him, share in His plans, participate in His causation by faith and prayer. He delegates to men a secret and limited share in His activity in so far as they are united with Him.

I am not saying that there is anything "wrong" with this. I have expressed it crudely, but it is perfectly logical and fits in naturally with certain premises. However, the trouble is that it supposes an image of the universe which does not correspond with that of post-Newtonian physics. Now, in the nineteenth century and in the modernist crisis of the early twentieth century there was one response to that: "If our view of the universe does not correspond with that of modern science, then to hell with science. We are right and that's that." But since that time it has been realized that while God is transcendent He is also immanent, and that faith does not require a special ability to imagine God "out there" or to picture Him spatially removed from His Creation as a machine which He directs by remote control. This spatial imagery has been recognized as confusing and irrelevant to people with a radically different notion of the space-time continuum. Teilhard de Chardin is one witness among many—doubtless the best known—to a whole new conception, a dynamic, immanentist conception of God and the world. God is at work in and through man, perfecting an ongoing Creation. This too is to some extent a matter of creating an acceptable image, a picture which we can grasp, which is not totally alien to our present understanding, and it will doubtless be replaced by other images in later ages. The underlying truth is not altered by the fact that it is expressed in different ways, from different viewpoints, as long as these viewpoints do not distort and falsify it.

Now it happens that the immanentist approach, which sees God as directly and intimately present in the very ground of our being (while being at the same time infinitely transcendent), is actually much closer to the contemplative tradition. The real point of the contemplative life has always been a deepening of faith and of the personal dimensions of liberty and apprehension to the point where our direct union with God is realized and "experienced." We awaken not only to a realization of the immensity and majesty of God "out there" as King and Ruler of the universe (which He is) but also a more intimate and more wonderful perception of Him as directly and personally present in our own being. Yet this is not a pantheistic merger or confusion of our being with His. On the contrary, there is a distinct conflict in the realization that though in some sense He is more truly ourselves than we are, yet we are not identical with Him, and though He loves us better than we can love ourselves we are opposed to Him, and in opposing Him we oppose our own deepest selves. If we are involved only in our surface existence, in externals, and in the trivial concerns of our ego, we are untrue to Him and to ourselves. To reach a true awareness of Him as well as ourselves, we have to renounce our selfish and limited self and enter into a whole new kind of existence, discovering an inner center of motivation and love which makes us see ourselves and everything else in an entirely new light. Call it faith, call it (at a more advanced stage) contemplative illumination, call it the sense of God or even mystical union:

all these are different aspects and levels of the same kind of realization: the awakening to a new awareness of ourselves in Christ, created in Him, redeemed by Him, to be transformed and glorified in and with Him. In Blake's words, the "doors of perception" are opened and all life takes on a completely new meaning: the real sense of our own existence, which is normally veiled and distorted by the routine distractions of an alienated life, is now revealed in a central intuition. What was lost and dispersed in the relative meaninglessness and triviality of purposeless behavior (living like a machine, pushed around by impulsions and suggestions from others) is brought together in fully integrated conscious significance. This peculiar, brilliant focus is, according to Christian tradition, the work of Love and of the Holy Spirit. This "loving knowledge" which sees everything transfigured "in God," coming from God and working for God's creative and redemptive love and tending to fulfillment in the glory of God, is a contemplative knowledge, a fruit of living and realizing faith, a gift of the Spirit.

The popularity of psychedelic drugs today certainly shows, if nothing else, that there is an appetite for this kind of knowledge and inner integration. The only trouble with drugs is that they superficially and transiently mimic the integration of love without producing it. (I will not discuss here the question whether they may accidentally help such integration, because I am not competent to do so.)

Though this inner "vision" is a gift and is not directly produced by technique, still a certain discipline is necessary to prepare us for it. Meditation is one of the more important characteristic forms of this discipline. Prayer is another. Prayer in the context of this inner awareness of God's direct presence becomes not so much a matter of cause and effect, as a celebration of love. In the light of this celebration, what matters most is love itself, thankfulness, assent to the unbounded and overflowing goodness of love which comes from God and reveals Him in His world.

This inner awareness, this experience of love as an immediate and dynamic presence, tends to alter our perspective. We see the prayer of petition a little differently. Celebration and praise, loving attention to the presence of God, become more important than "asking for" things and "getting" things. This is because we realize that in Him and with Him all good is present to us and to mankind: if we seek first the Kingdom of Heaven, all the rest comes along with it. Hence we worry a great deal less about the details of our daily needs, and we trust God to take care of our problems even if we do not ask Him insistently at every minute to do so. The same applies to the problems of the world. But on the other hand, this inner awareness and openness makes us especially sensitive to urgent needs of the time, and grace can sometimes move us to pray for certain special needs. The contemplative life does not ignore the prayer of petition, but does not over-emphasize it either. The contemplative prays for particular intentions when he is strongly and spontaneously inspired to do so, but does not make it his formal purpose to keep asking for this and that all day long.

Now, prayer also has to be seen in the light of another fundamental experience, that of God's "absence." For if God is immanently present He is also transcendent, which means that He is completely beyond the grasp of our understanding. The two ("absence" and "presence") merge in the loving knowledge that "knows by unknowing" (a traditional term of mysticism). It is more and more usual for modern people to be afflicted with a sense of absence, desolation, and in-capacity to even "want" to pray or to think of God. To dis-miss this superficially as an experience of "the death of God" —as if henceforth God were completely irrelevant—is to over-look one significant fact: that this sense of absence is not a one-sided thing: it is dialectical, and it includes its opposite, namely presence. And while it may be afflicted with doubt it contains a deep need to believe.

The point I want to make is this: experience of the con-templative life in the modern world shows that the most cru-cial focus for contemplative and meditative discipline, and for the life of prayer, for many modern men, is precisely this so-called sense of absence, desolation, and even apparent "inability to believe." I stress the word "apparent," because though this experience may to some be extremely painful and confusing, and to raise all kinds of crucial "religious problems," it can very well be a sign of authentic Christian growth and a point of decisive development in faith, if they are able to cope with it. The way to cope with it is not to regress to an earlier and less mature stage of belief, to stubbornly reaffirm and to "enforce" feelings, aspirations and images that were appropriate to one's childhood and first communion. One must, on a new level of meditation and prayer, live through this crisis of belief and grow to a more complete personal and Christian integration by experience.

This experience of struggle, of self-emptying, "self-naughting," of letting go and of subsequent recovery in peace and grace on a new level is one of the ways in which the *Pascha Christi* (the death and resurrection of Christ) takes hold on our lives and transforms them. This is the psychological aspect of the work of grace which also takes place beyond experience and beyond psychology in the work of the Sacraments and in our objective sharing of the Church's life.

I am of course not talking about "mystical experience" or anything new and strange, but simply the fullness of personal awareness that comes with a total self-renunciation, followed by self-commitment on the highest level, beyond mere intellectual assent and external obedience.

Real Christian living is stunted and frustrated if it remains content with the bare externals of worship, with "saying prayers" and "going to church," with fulfilling one's external duties and merely being respectable. The real purpose of prayer (in the fully personal sense as well as in the Christian assembly) is the deepening of personal realization in love, the awareness of God (even if sometimes this awareness may amount to a negative factor, a seeming "absence"). The real purpose of meditation—or at least that which recommends itself as most relevant for modern man—is the exploration and discovery of new dimensions in freedom, illumination and love, in deepening our awareness of our life in Christ.

What is the relation of this to action? Simply this. He who attempts to act and do things for others or for the world without deepening his own self-understanding, freedom, integrity and capacity to love, will not have anything to give others.

He will communicate to them nothing but the contagion of his own obsessions, his aggressiveness, his ego-centered ambitions, his delusions about ends and means, his doctrinaire prejudices and ideas. There is nothing more tragic in the modern world than the misuse of power and action to which men are driven by their own Faustian misunderstandings and misapprehensions. We have more power at our disposal today than we have ever had, and yet we are more alienated and estranged from the inner ground of meaning and of love than we have ever been. The result of this is evident. We are living through the greatest crisis in the history of man; and this crisis is centered precisely in the country that has made a fetish out of action and has lost (or perhaps never had) the sense of contemplation. Far from being irrelevant, prayer, meditation and contemplation are of the utmost importance in America today. Unfortunately, it must be admitted that the official contemplative life as it is lived in our monasteries needs a great deal of rethinking, because it is still too closely identified with patterns of thought that were accepted five hundred years ago, but which are completely strange to modern man.

But prayer and meditation have an important part to play in opening up new ways and new horizons. If our prayer is the expression of a deep and grace-inspired desire for newness of life—and not the mere blind attachment to what has always been familiar and "safe"—God will act in us and through us to renew the Church by preparing, in prayer, what we cannot yet imagine or understand. In this way our prayer and faith today will be oriented toward the future which we ourselves may never see fully realized on earth.

X

THE CONTEMPLATIVE
AND THE ATHEIST

In all the great religious traditions men and women have dedicated themselves to contemplative lives in which, under special conditions of silence, austerity, solitude, meditation and worship, it had been possible for them to deepen and broaden their spiritual consciousness. In so doing, they have become able to explore realms of experience which, though unusual, have profound implications for the ordinary lives of their fellow men. Whether from the point of view of psychology, ethics, art, religion, or simply in the development of man's deepest capacities, the contemplative experience is in touch with what is most basic in human existence.

In religious cultures these contemplatives have tended to form recognized elites in special monastic institutions. But it is not necessary that this drive for spiritual discovery be socially organized: it can spring into existence spontaneously outside the cloister or hermitage, even under the most unfavorable conditions. For the contemplative life is not merely a matter of escaping the world, singing psalms, or mastering traditional techniques of meditation: it is also and above all a personal charism.

Thus there are contemplatives not only in monasteries but also in the midst of secular life. But in all contemplative traditions, it has been found necessary that those who have attained to some depth of religious insight should to some extent guide others who seek to attain the same experience of truth in their own lives. Thus though the contemplative lives in silence and seeks to maintain a certain freedom from involvement in feverish and pointless activity, he does not simply turn his back on the world of other men. Like them he remains rooted in this world. He remains open to the world and is ready, when necessary, to share with others something of his own experience, to the extent that this may be desirable or possible. He also realizes his need to listen to other men and learn from them. But above all he seeks to go deeper into that divine source from which all life springs, and to understand the destinies of man in the light of God.

At a time when the Catholic Church herself has entered into a spontaneous and living dialogue with modern man on all levels of his existence, should Catholic contemplatives also speak to modern man and listen to him, question him and be questioned by him?

The "Message of Contemplatives" presented to the Synod of Bishops in fall 1967 reflected a deep concern on the part of men who, though dedicated to lives of silence and solitude, felt they also had a duty to share the fruit of their experience with their fellow men struggling in the modern "crisis of faith." The life of solitude and contemplation, a life in which men listen more intently to the Word of God, immerse themselves in meditation of the Bible, sing the praise of God in liturgy, and devote themselves to work, study and silent prayer, is not a life remote from contemporary reality. Nor is the contemplative exempt from the problems and difficulties of contemporary man. The life of Christian contemplation is not a life of willful concentration upon a few clear and comforting ideas, but a life of inner struggle in which the monk, like Christ himself in the desert, is tested. In a certain sense the monk, alone with God, fully aware of his own poverty, fallibility and blindness, suffers the same trial of faith as other Christians, and suffers it in a more acute and penetrating way. It can be said that the contemplative is often less a "professional of vision" than a professional of crisis and of intellectual suffering. What he learns is not a clearer idea of God but a deeper trust, a purer love and a more complete abandonment to One he knows to be beyond all understanding. Yet in his silence, his simple life, his cloistered peace, the contemplative certainly has access to values which modern life tends more and more to forget, to underestimate or to ignore. He wishes to share his experience of these values with other men who are weary of the pressure, the confusion, the agitation of modern life. He recognizes his duty to his fellow man: a duty to preserve for him an

area which is most threatened in the stormy existence of a
world in a crisis of growth and transformation. The following thoughts can be considered in some sense an extension
of the "Message of Contemplatives" delivered to the Synod
of Bishops.

We contemplatives are fully aware not only of the general
problems confronted by the Christian believer, but also more
especially of the particular problem of the contemplative life
itself. Many Christians, including priests and even perhaps
some bishops, perturbed by the great needs of the Church in
the world today, wonder how the contemplatives can continue to remain apparently aloof from the active conflicts in
which the Church is engaged. Should not contemplatives
abandon their silence and solitude in order to be enlisted in
the busy army of apostolic workers?

We contemplatives feel that this question is, for us as well
as for the rest of the Church, only another aspect of the general crisis of faith. We know this because we have often
searched our own hearts and sought to resolve this question
for ourselves, fearing that perhaps our call to desert solitude
might be an illusion, and dreading that we might be making
our silence a pretext for refusing to others a necessary
service. Indeed we do realize that we cannot be content with
a purely negative rejection of the world. We cannot simply
turn our backs on contemporary man. That is not our intention. We must on the contrary share with others something
of the benefits of our own life of prayer.

Nevertheless, it is clear to us that our greatest and most
unique service to the Church is precisely our life of contemplation itself. Our silence and solitude are not mere luxuries
and privileges which we have acquired at the Church's expense: they are necessary gifts of God to the Church in and
through us. They are that part of the precious inheritance
of Christian truth and experience which God has confided to
us to hold in trust, in order that the spirit of prayer and contemplation may continue to exist in the whole Church and in
the world of our time.

The laity and clergy who are absorbed in many active concerns are unable to give themselves to meditation and to a deeper study of divine and human things. We feel it is our first duty to preserve for them the reality of a life of deep prayer, silence, and experience of the things of God so that they may not themselves despair, but may be encouraged to continue in their own way to seek intimacy with God in loving faith. We also feel it our obligation, at least where circumstances permit, to allow them to share in the peace and silence of our retreats. Some of us may be called to direct or instruct others in the way of prayer, whether by the written word or by oral direction. Some of us, finally, may be called to enter into fruitful dialogue with intellectuals, Christian or otherwise, and perhaps particularly with contemplatives and philosophers of the non-Christian religious traditions. Ideally speaking, the contemplative monastery should present a perfect setting for dialogue and study concerning prayer and spiritual experience.

However, we may be permitted to suggest that it would be to the greatest possible disadvantage for the Church if contemplatives were to be uprooted from their silent and prayerful way of life and precipitated into active works for which they are neither qualified nor prepared and which they can only do badly. At the same time we realize more and more that the contemplative life itself urgently needs inner renewal in order that this experience of mystical love, which has unfortunately grown cold, this contemplative apprehension of divine things which has become weak and vague, may recover their vital power.

In order to do this, it is necessary for us to maintain the purity of monastic common life in which the freedom of fraternal love in Christ, the discipline of monastic formation, and total obedience of one and all to the Holy Spirit keep alive an atmosphere of prayer in which the authentic purity of Christian contemplation can be handed on from spiritual father to spiritual sons. We recognize especially the importance of silence, solitude, poverty, labor, humility, chastity, fasting and all the traditional forms of monastic ascesis, to keep ourselves open and attentive to the Spirit of the Living God. We also recognize that, as contemplatives grow in their

experience of intimacy with God they will need special opportunities to develop their own personal gifts in their own
ways, some of them perhaps living for this purpose in
eremitical solitude. In a word, we not only bear witness to the
living actuality of the monastic experience that has been
handed down to us from the earliest days of Egyptian and
Syrian monasticism, but we solemnly pledge ourselves to preserve that heritage and to develop it in ways that are relevant
to our own time.

The contemplative life is questioned not only in the active
and dynamic West but in the meditative East. In a certain
sense the duty to bear witness to contemplative values and to
a higher experience, is a matter of universal concern, common not only to the Cistercian monk but to the Zen Buddhist
and the student of Yoga. We find that many who do not share
our religious belief, men of the great Asian religions, or even
modern Westerners without faith, tend to have a better appreciation of our life than some Catholics. These men often
deeply value the advantages of solitude, silence and meditation. The appeals of such men urge us to persevere in our
aim of seeking new depths of awareness and meaning in human existence. They also encourage us to study the ways in
which the religious experience of the great mystical traditions,
both Christian and non-Christian, can continue in dialogue
with a world that has ceased to understand the classic language of religious experience. They encourage us to approach
closer to the mystery of God in that desert solitude which is
the place par excellence of revelation, inspiration and renewal.

In this connection we observe that a Marxist thinker
prominent in the Marxist-Christian dialogue has, while clearly
stating that to him the language of Christian theology
seemed irrelevant, admitted that he found the mystical experience and witness of a St. Teresa of Ávila both meaningful
and challenging. On the basis of such statements as these, we
do not feel that we contemplatives are losing our time if we
devote our lives to exploring areas which other more active
Catholics consider a mere no man's land.

Like the rest of the Catholic Church, the contemplative

Orders seek a renewal of their life in accordance with the needs of modern man. The maturity and personal fulfillment sought by one called to the contemplative life are to be found in contemplation itself and not elsewhere. But the discipline of contemplative attention and awareness has to be adapted to the needs of modern consciousness. Contemplative formation today will include a study of the structures of modern consciousness, and its new ways of experiencing itself in relation to other men, to the world, and to God.

It should be remarked that in the contemplative life, while study and intellectual development are of great importance, there is something else more important still: the realm of personal experience which penetrates beyond the limits of speculative thought to "taste" the ultimate realities and to penetrate the inner meaning of what is believed and yet remains obscure. For the contemplative, then, what matters is not speculative discussion of the "problem of God," still less the effort to demonstrate the existence of God in ways that often raise more problems than they solve for modern man. The contemplative is not one who has to do battle with militant atheism and he is thus perhaps in a position to gain a clearer understanding of the confusions now surrounding the whole question of "atheism" and the "problem of God" in the world of our time.

The Christian contemplative is aware that in the mystical tradition both of the Eastern and Western Churches there is a strong element of what has been called "apophatic theology." This "apophatic" tradition concerns itself with the most fundamental datum of all faith—and one which is too often forgotten: the God who has revealed Himself to us in His Word has revealed Himself as unknown in His intimate essence, for He is beyond all merely human vision. "You cannot see my face: no man shall see me and live" (Exodus 33:20). "No man has ever seen God: the only-begotten, who is in the heart of the Father, he has related it" (John 1:18).

The heart of the Christian mystical experience is that it experiences the ineffable reality of what is beyond experience. It "knows" the presence of God, not in clear vision but "as unknown" (*tamquam ignotium*). Christian faith too, while of course concerning itself with certain truths that have been revealed by God, does not terminate in the conceptual formulation of those truths. It goes beyond words and ideas and attains to God Himself. But the God who in a certain sense is "known" in the articles of faith is "known as unknown" beyond those articles. One might even say, with some of the Fathers of the Church, that while our concepts may tell us that "God is," our knowledge of God beyond those concepts is a knowledge of Him "as though He were not" since His Being is not accessible to us in direct experience. We are persuaded that many who consider themselves atheists are in fact persons who are discontented with a naive idea of God which makes Him appear to be an "object" or a "thing," or a person in a merely finite and human sense. Such people are perhaps weary of the complications of language which now surrounds the "problem of God" and find all discussions of that problem fruitless: yet they are likely to be very intrigued by the direct and existential testimony of contemplative experience.

Now, while the Christian contemplative must certainly develop, by study, the theological understanding of concepts about God, he is called mainly to penetrate the wordless darkness and apophatic light of an experience beyond concepts, and here he gradually becomes familiar with a God who is "absent," and as it were "nonexistent," to all human experience. The apophatic experience of God does, to some extent, verify the atheist's intuition that God is not an object of limited and precise knowledge and consequently cannot be apprehended as "a thing" to be studied by delimitation. As St. John of the Cross dared to say in mystical language, the term of the ascent of the mount of contemplation is "Nothing"—*Y en el monte Nada.* But the difference between the apophatic contemplative and the atheist is that where the experience of the atheist may be purely negative, that of the contemplative is so to speak negatively positive. Relinquishing every attempt to grasp God in limited human concepts, the contemplatives' act of submission and faith attains to His presence as the ground of every human experience and to His reality as the ground of being itself. The "absence" of the transcendent God is also paradoxically His presence as immanent. Here obviously we enter a realm of apparent contradictions which eludes clear explanation, so that the contemplative prefers not to talk about it at all. Indeed, in the past, serious mistakes have been made and deadly confusions have arisen from inadequate attempts to explain this mystery. The job of the contemplative today is not to avoid this area out of fear—this is the authentic field of his exploration and the place of his own promised and desired fulfillment—he must enter into it humbly and resolutely, following the call of God and obedient to the divine Spirit, like Moses approaching the burning bush, removing the "shoes" of opinion and rationalization.

There is however a new atheism which has arisen even among Christians in their anxiety to share every dimension of modern men's experience. These "Christian atheists" have asked themselves, in all sincerity, if one could be a truly modern man and not be in some sense an atheist. In other words, is religious belief so essentially alien to the experience and consciousness of modern man that modern man cannot believe in God without a psychological and cultural regression to modes of thought appropriate to former ages but estranged from our own? Since this "Christian atheism" or "religion without God" has had the benefit of a typically sensationalist treatment in the mass media, and since those who have proposed it differ greatly among themselves and do not always mean the same thing, there has been great confusion in the minds of many people. Sometimes the doctrine of the so-called "death of God," popular in American Christian circles, is reduced to a mere sensational absurdity. But at other times an attempt is made to raise a serious question in this paradoxical form. The "problem of God," it is said, has new dimensions today because one can no longer take for one's point of departure the same assumptions as in the past. For instance, in the past it was more generally taken for granted that every man had a basic natural way of looking at reality, and this spontaneous, preconscious outlook included in it the need for a Supreme Being and at least some kind of tacit assumption of a first cause. Men who denied the Supreme Being and the first cause did so at the price of resisting this natural outlook. But now it is asserted that man's outlook has radically changed. It is no longer "natural" for him to assume, as St. Anselm once assumed, that if there are any beings at all there must be a Supreme Being. On the contrary, it is now said that modern man's consciousness is one which no longer needs God and no longer assumes His existence, influence and presence as the basis for a meaningful view of life. What could be said with truth in the past, that the human soul was "naturally Christian," is no longer to be taken for granted: on the contrary, the consciousness of modern man is, according to this theory, naturally atheistic. Therefore it is contended that as far as the experience of modern man is concerned, "God is dead"—he is not present spontaneously as the basis for meaning in human existence. On the contrary, if "God" once becomes present in the consciousness of modern man, so the argument continues, his presence does violence to that modern consciousness in its modernity—hence in its truth. The act of faith by which modern man adheres, in spite of himself, to the idea of God is an act in which he is untrue to himself, is dictated by fear or some other base motive, and is therefore unauthentic. Faith, for the modern man, must then be by definition "bad faith" in the sense given to this term by J. P. Sartre.

We have exposed this argument in some detail because it has rather ironical consequences in the lives of those who are most concerned with being "adult" Christians in the world of today. Obviously one of the first indications of the adult is that he is securely assured of his own identity, and his judgments concerning his own experiences are based on his own awareness of what takes place within himself. The truly modern adult person will surely not allow himself to be treated as an alienated and helpless individual whose inner experience is dictated to him by another and imposed upon him from the outside. It is the surest sign of immaturity, to be imposed on entirely by the ideas and ideals of others and to substitute these for one's own true personal experience and judgment of life. The faith of the Christian is an inner adherence to a truth which is not imposed from the outside. It is a free personal adherence of love "in the Spirit" and it gives power to resist all external compulsion in the realm of thought as well as of life. In this sense, too, faith overcomes the world. This truth makes one truly and authentically free (John 8:32). The adult Christian is perfectly capable of discovering for himself whether or not a modern man can believe in God and experience Him without being untrue to himself. There is a difference between being true to oneself and being à la mode. After all, St. Paul has cautioned us against confusing the wisdom and the experience of God with the slogans of current intellectual fashion (I Cor. 2:6–9).

In actual fact, the gift of supernatural faith does not in any way depend on whether or not man is naturally disposed to accept easily a congenial concept of God. It is after all quite common for us in dechristianized cultures to encounter persons who have never had a serious thought of God, one way or the other, and who have suddenly been struck, in the most unaccountable manner, by the light of faith. It is customary among pious people to imagine that this is always a beautiful and consoling experience. It is sometimes frightening. You fortunate believer! You do not know the confusion, the bewilderment and the suffering of an atheist who has suddenly, without any apparent human intervention, been literally overwhelmed by the reality of God, and who does not know what to do. Surrounded by friends who can only mock him, if he reveals his trouble, unable to pray, unable to trust himself to the Church of which he is highly suspicious, he is in a state of heartbreaking anguish. Perhaps it may be true that he is not a "naturally Christian soul." God does not present Himself to him in a clear and comforting concept, but as a completely disconcerting and inexplicable reality, making a demand for total commitment and trust. His anguish is all the greater, but his faith is no less real. And he turns, instinctively, to the contemplatives who, he believes, are men of prayer and know the ways of God. But when he comes to us, in profound distress, we become aware of our own insufficiency: and we carefully weigh any words we may say, knowing that they must not be sentimental or complacent or merely formal.

The writer of these lines has recently had one of many such experiences: and he knows that it is utterly false to claim that "modern man is incapable of feeling the need for God; or responding to His presence."

We are inclined to ask here, whether these facile assumptions about modern man and his psychology are not totally gratuitous. That would be a matter for psychology, sociology and historical scholarship to decide, in terms of the evidence. But once again, those who are familiar with the apophatic tradition in theology and mysticism are fully aware that the temporary or permanent inability to imagine God or to "experience" Him as present, or even to find Him credible, is not something discovered by modern man or confined to our own age. This view of religion and of the religious consciousness is too narrow and foreshortened, for it once more assumes that the naive conception of God as "object" is somehow claimed as natural to man and essential to Christianity.

Without entering into a polemic with this new school of thought, we can at least recognize that it is doubtless time for the Christian consciousness of God to be expressed in contemporary language. The conceptual knowledge of God is inevitably associated with a certain cultural matrix. The medieval ideas of God were naturally in accord with medieval thought about the cosmos, about the earth, about physics, and about the biological and psychological structure of man. These ideas have been revolutionized. But the reality of experience beyond concepts (though it may call for a different approach in accord with the new psychological and cultural development of modern man) is not itself modified by changes of culture. The contemplative once again has a certain advantage due to the fact that he is less involved than others in changing conceptual structures and less dependent on the complexities of language.

Far from being a merely mental and conceptual approach to God, far from being the fruit of intellectual speculation which seeks to apprehend God as a most rarefied abstraction, the contemplative approach is highly concrete and existential. Where abstract thought and concrete existence enter into conflict, the mark of the true contemplative is that he is on the side of concrete existence. Our God is the living God who has manifested Himself with supreme concreteness to man, not only in words and deeds by which He intervened in human history for our salvation, but above all in His Son whom the Apostles "heard and saw and touched with their hands and recognized to be the Word of Life" (see I John 1:1). The Christian contemplative is not content to explore the depths of the human psyche and to expand the capacities of natural consciousness. The heart of Christian contemplation is the revelation of the invisible God. The Christian contemplative seeks the fullest and most living participation in the experience which has come down from those who walked with Christ on earth, who knew him and saw him as risen and received from him the Gift of the Spirit.

The Christian contemplative life bears witness above all to the deepest and most central truth of all Christian revelation, that of the Holy Trinity. At first sight, nothing could be seemingly more remote from the modern consciousness and more alien to it than the mysterious notion of One God in Three Persons. The modern consciousness is impatient of mystery and impervious to technical theology. One would expect that the danger of abstractness and technicality would make modern contemplatives turn more spontaneously to God in His unity and simplicity rather than to this mystery of God as triune. But on the contrary, the special character of Christian contemplation cannot be grasped unless due importance is given to the revelation of the Father in the Son by the Holy Spirit. We have obviously no intention of entering into a technical discussion of the theology of the Trinity, but only of pointing out why this theology is important both in itself and in special relation to our own time.

Since, as we have said above, God is, in His intimate essence, beyond all our human concepts, the revelation of God as Father, Son and Spirit is in fact a revelation of Him as totally other than any being which we can conceive of as existing. In God's revelation of Himself we nowhere find Him giving a definition of Himself. He simply reveals that He *is* (Exodus 3:14). Or rather He reveals that He is who He is: that is to say he reveals Himself not as a thing but as a presence, an active living and personal identity. And this identity, this "Who," is at once Father, Son or Logos, and Spirit or Pneuma. This revelation of God as who He is (not as what) is therefore a revelation of Him as living, personal presence, as utterance of Himself, as communication of Himself, as love, as mercy, as gift, as life. The self-revelation of God as the Father in the Son through the Spirit, is the self-revelation of infinite giving and dynamic personal communication. We say with St. John that "God is love" (I John 4:16), and we recognize with the Apostle that the God who is love is known to no one except to him who loves. God is Father who gives Himself in love as Son; He is Son who gives Himself as love in Spirit; He is Spirit who communicates to us the immense love which we believe to be Father and Son, so that we ourselves, in the Spirit, become sons and give ourselves in love to the Father. This is the self-manifestation of God as the infinite personal ground of all love and all being, of God as loving Creator of all things, not only infinitely transcendent but also present within the metaphysical depths and goodness of being itself. God thus reveals Himself not simply as the power to cause all effects, but as the Act and Living Presence of Love from whom all beings receive the loving and gratuitous gift to be real.

It is very important to grasp the significance of the fact that God is not conceived by Christian theology as numerically three. The three divine persons are not three countable things or three beings or three natures or three objects lined up, so to speak, side by side: they are (and here the inadequacy of human speech makes itself felt, since we have to use the plural) the inner communication and dynamism of love in which God is present to Himself in Being, Vision and Love, or perhaps we might say in Reality, in Realization and in Ecstatic Delight.

Christian contemplation does not of course imply a clear vision, or a rational understanding of the processions of the divine persons on a technical theological level. What we mean to emphasize here is something quite different: that Christian contemplation gives a certain intuitive appreciation or savor of the divine inner life in so far as it is a personal

participation, by grace, in that life itself. Thus the Christian
contemplative experiences in himself, in the love which is
granted to him by the gift of the Spirit, something of
the dynamism of love that the unknown God has revealed as
His actuality, His presence, His identity, His personal and
intimate self-communication. The loving knowledge of God
is then not something to be acquired by objective study but by
subjective (personal) identification (which traditional theology has called "connaturality"). St. Paul makes this clear
when he compares a man's consciousness of his own identity
to the Spirit "which looks into the depths of God" (I Cor.
2:10). Now we have received the Spirit of God, and hence
the Spirit in us gazes into the abyss of the unknown and unseen Father. We recognize the unseen Father in so far as we
are sons, in and with Christ. The Spirit utters in us the cry
of recognition that we are sons in the Son (Romans 8:15).
This cry of admiration, of love, of praise, of everlasting joy
is at once a cry of glad self-annihilation on the part of our
transient human ego, and an exultant shout of victory of
the New Man raised from the dead in Christ by the Spirit
who raised Christ himself from the dead. Christian contemplation, in one vivid blaze of love and illumination, apprehends at once the reality of God as the totally other and the
unknown, as a dynamism of reality, realization and ecstasy,
as incarnate in Jesus Christ, as given to us entirely in the
Spirit, as taking us entirely to Himself in the death and resurrection of Christ. But Christian contemplation is not merely
lost in God. It also includes in its vision an eschatological
understanding of the world redeemed in Christ. It sees the
world transformed in the divine light, it sees all things re-
capitulated in Christ (Eph. 1:10). It is aware of the victory
of Christ and the reality of his Kingdom in the world even
now, in all the confusion, the chaos and the risk of this historical and revolutionary time of crisis which we call the
atomic age.

It is by deepening this Christian consciousness and developing the capacity for mystical understanding and love that the
Christian contemplative keeps alive in the Church that pure
and immediate experience without which theology will always

lack one of its most important dimensions. The Second Vatican Council has reminded us of this:

For there is a growth in the understanding of the realities of the words which have been handed down. This happens through the contemplation and study made by believers who treasure these things in their hearts (Luke 2:19, 51) through the intimate understanding of spiritual things they experience, and through the preaching of those who have recieved through episcopal succession the pure gift of truth. (On Revelation, ii, 8)

Here the Council makes very clear the importance of contemplatives in the Church. Their special task is not merely to pray for those in the active apostolate, but much more to keep alive and to deepen the "intimate understanding" of and "experience" through which divine revelation is handed down not merely in Christian preaching but as a living and experienced reality.

XI

ECUMENISM AND RENEWAL

The highly successful Protestant monastic experiment of Taizé has in a short time come to be seen by many Catholics as a providential sign of the times and even as a paradigm for Catholic monastic renewal. Not that Taizé is the only manifestation of its kind, or that it is unique in Protestantism: it does combine a traditional form of Christian monastic life with a welcome flexibility and with a strong ecumenical emphasis. The combination of these elements is even more significant than the fact that a "Protestant monastery" should exist.

The crisis and collapse of Luther's life under religious vows (Luther was not strictly a "monk," since he was an Augustinian) marked a decisive point in the Reformation. Luther's "monastic" experience was in fact quite central to his whole view of the Church and Christian life, and his repudiation of religious vows was a critical point in his theology of *fides sola*. He challenged the whole medieval ethos, dominated by the monastic order as reformed and incorporated into the cultural and political life of Europe since Charlemagne.

The defensive reaction of the Catholic Church was to reject the challenge and to reaffirm without question the essentials of the medieval monastic structure. The Council of Trent did not consider for a moment any radical change in the traditional monastic institution. Monasticism after Trent sought only to restore discipline and to eliminate abuses, by a return not so much to original sources as to the Carolingian reform of Benedict of Aniane. It is significant that Taizé is located near the site of Cluny, the capital of medieval Benedictinism and the center of the fervent cultural, liturgical, ascetic and artistic life which set the tone for the early Middle Ages. Though Cluny was attacked and severely criticized for its wealth and power by Cistercian reformers in the twelfth century, we must not take too literally or too seriously their sometimes sweeping condemnation of Cluniac monasticism which, like that of the Cistercians, maintained an authentic life of disciplined fervor and mysticism until well beyond the thirteenth century.

Two main cycles of monastic reform have taken place since Trent, roughly in the seventeenth and in the nineteenth centuries. They did not make any fundamental changes in the traditional monasticism of western Europe though they did begin the work of "return to sources" (both theological and ascetic) which prepared the way for the new movement in monasticism after Vatican II. It must be said that the Second Vatican Council did not start this movement, which was already in existence and which had already initiated important changes in the decade before the Council. But only after the Council has the problem of monastic renewal taken on its full dimensions.

The press has given a certain amount of attention to the superficial aspects of renewal in Catholic religious life. The symbolic question of nuns' habits acquired, perhaps naturally, an exaggerated importance. Nor is it difficult to get a column or two of acceptable copy out of the fact that the sisters have been running around more and doing things that are characteristically "modern." This tends to obscure the real nature of the problem which is more than a mere matter of "updating" and getting around.

The problem of monastic renewal, at the deepest level, is theological and it is at this point that the monks are finally coming face to face with Luther's challenge. In "returning to sources" they are only doing in a more thorough and systematic way what Luther himself did by re-examining his vocation in the light of the Gospel and the Pauline Epistles. Studying the original monastic sources, seen in their historic and cultural contexts, monks begin to ask themselves more disturbing questions than those which merely bear on meaningful observance.

It is now no longer just a matter of recovering a genuine understanding of monastic enclosure, silence, worship, fasting and trying to adapt these to a modern situation. The very concept of a vowed and cloistered life, of a life devoted to prayer apart from the world, of silence and asceticism, has to be re-examined. This need is realized as yet only obscurely by the majority of monks, but its nagging, disquieting presence is felt. And some of those who are now consciously aware of it are thrown into a mild panic, with the result that they are more ready to abandon the ship than they are to examine carefully whether it is about to sink.

Catholics anxious for renewal have perhaps been too grateful for press coverage—any press coverage—which gives an impression that much is happening. And certainly much is happening. But both the happening and the coverage tend to be quite equivocal. The fundamental purpose of all monastic life is (to paraphrase a brilliant page of Claude Lévi-Strauss[1] about Indian initiations) to deliver the individual and the charismatic community from the massive automatic functioning of a social machine that leaves nothing to peculiar talent, to chance, or to grace. The monastic vocation calls a man to desert frontiers, beyond which there are no police, in order to dip into the "ocean of unexploited forces which surrounds a well-ordered society and draw from it a personal provision" of grace and vision. But the historical fate of monasticism is of course that it has become more organized and better policed than secular society itself, and while continuing to offer promises of charismatic vision and liberty it has in fact subjected its disciples to all the most banal monotonies of an unimaginative ecclesiastical bureaucracy, all the timidities of monastic businessmen intent upon the security and prestige of their institution, all the refusals of operators interested mainly in the corporate image. But it happens that now the business and institutional aspect of the monastic corporation stands to profit a great deal from a solid merger with the forces of mass society. Not all the managers are fully aware of all the implications of this, but generally speaking, the idea that the monk can recover his charismatic liberty by joining forces with "the world" (call it Madison Avenue or Secular City) is perhaps the greatest of illusions.

[1] See Claude Lévi-Strauss, *Tristes Tropiques,* Paris, 1966.

It is one thing to admit that Luther had come to grips with a real problem, and another to conclude that one cannot find any other solution than his. If a ritualistic attachment to archaic observance is, indeed, theologically futile, it does not follow that monastic life cannot be lived on a deeper and more valid level. In other words, the monastic community has other choices than perpetuating an antique formula or going out of existence. Nor is everything "old" necessarily antiquated and obsolete. One of the most hopeful things about Taizé has been, in fact, its ability to welcome and to make use of traditional forms when they are found to have a real validity in the present. But the fact remains that Luther's challenge now has a definite relevance for Catholic monks who are anxious to renew their monastic lives and to test the seriousness and authenticity of that renewal.

Before Vatican II it was still possible for monks to ignore the Reformation with its serious charge that the vowed life of the monk, lived under traditional disciplines and devoted to a complex system of pious works, was in fact an evasion of the basic call to discipleship. Instead of responding to the summons of Christ in faith, placing his entire trust in the word and promises of the Risen Savior, seeking salvation, grace and light in the community of those called to confide entirely in the all-merciful Redeemer, the monk took refuge in vows and rites which (in the context of the late Middle Ages) could seriously be seen as a system of more or less superstitious fictions. In Reformation thought, monastic obedience became an abdication of mature responsibility and an escape from freedom which could, in extreme cases, turn the monk into a blind instrument of the most nefarious kind of power politics. Poverty became a mere hypocritical formality which enabled one to enjoy the goods and comforts of the world without even having to do an honest job of work to get them. Chastity was a fruitless evasion of the duty of marriage, corrupted perhaps by the most shameful kind of failures.

Of course there had always been abuses. The monk had to admit it. But on the other hand, he knew that the Reformation polemic had distorted the true picture. He knew that his own faith and that of his community was sincere. And like all good Catholics he was intent on proving the sincerity of his faith by what he considered to be good works. The best works he could think of were those which had from time immemorial been held in highest respect by his community: the complete renunciation of one's own will in order to live in selfless service of God and man, the giving up of all possessions in order to live "poor with the poor Christ," and the renunciation of all sexual pleasure in order to answer the challenging invitation extended to the few who could "take it" (Matt. 19:11–12).

The tension thus set up between the zeal for monastic reform within traditional structures and the often tendentious attack on monasticism from outside provided plenty of energy and motivation in individuals and communities. The result was a rather inflexible but sincerely devout life. Stern emphasis on "regularity," not to say legalism, was justified by a casuistical and sometimes arbitrary theology. Monastic determination after Trent bore fruit now in a fantastically single-minded intentness on "heroic virtue," now in touching, though bizarre, manifestations of mystical stamp.

Not only among monks, but in all kinds of sectarian milieux, this state of struggle and of tension sustains an illusion of special election and of incorruptible truth. The endemic disease of monasteries and of sects is that people in them do so much to save their souls that they lose them: not in the sense that they are damned for being good, but in the sense that they concentrate on such particular, limited aspects of good that they become perverse and singular. This singularity begets blindness and deafness to Christ. The tense concentration of sect or monastery on some completely peripheral concern can give an impression of heroic faith—but so can the feat of engraving the Lord's Prayer on a pinhead. Fidelity to tedious but predictable rule can become an easy substitute for fidelity, in openness and risk, to the unpredictable word. But the whole point of monastic "desert" life is precisely to equip the monk for risk, for walking with God in the wilderness, and wrestling with Satan in vulnerable freedom. The monk should by rights be one who knows that faith is his only true protection against the power of great evil. But the monastic institution has surrounded him with so many other protections that the seed which is called to grow, in pure trust in the desert, is in fact nurtured in a greenhouse. The rationalization is that the greenhouse is really a desert in intention and that God, through kindly representatives, provides a steady supply of water. Instead of wilderness faith and the peril of death by dryness or exhaustion one accepts faith in another kind of desert: that of protective authoritarian routine.

When one experiences the sterility and unfreedom of an existence which has become self-contradicting, then one can of course completely repudiate it, get out of it, put it behind him. That is what Luther did. His repudiation of a false and formalistic monasticism struck a blow for monastic truth. In doing so he was really being faithful to the grace that had originally called him to the cloister. And it is possible, too, that one might undergo the same kind of experience as Luther and yet remain in the cloister—or rather in the community to which one was originally called—not in order to reform its rules but in order to be renewed in experiencing its common recovery of meaning and hope, its common renewal in the Spirit. However, this renewal has to be something more than a matter of legislation or of reforming expedients. It has to be a kind of miracle of water in the desert.

It is at this precise point that two important lines of development are, one hopes, going to intersect in monasticism: one, the lived theology which is the monastic experience, and, two, the expansion and opening of perspectives which lead to a lived unity, the common sharing of Christian grace in crisis, irrespective of Church divisions. I would also extend this to meet a third line: the common religious aspiration of humankind and its groping for transcendent experience, however you may want to qualify it ("mystical," "prophetic," "contemplative," "metaphysical," "shamanic" . . .).

The crucial need in monastic renewal is then something quite different from a simple recovery of pristine disciplines or a deeper penetration of their meaning. The ecumenical opening of the monastery is going to have to mean more than just admitting Baptist or Methodist seminarians to view a living diorama in Church history. Nor will it be enough for monks who still meditate (a few do) to get together and compare notes (or swap *mondo*) with a Zen *roshi*. In a word, if the monastic life is to be validly renewed, it must retain or recover a threefold relevance. First, the monastic life must have an authentic relevance in its own right as a focus of Christian experience with a monastic orientation. The monastic orientation is eschatological: "out of this world to the Father." The monastic community—like Faulkner's Dilsey at the Negro church—is convoked not merely to listen to polite religious discourse but to hear the living word and to open up to it as a flower opens to the sun. The result will be, in one way or another, "vision" or "contemplation" (admittedly a bad word), prophetic and eschatological awareness: the awareness of Dilsey who wept at Rev. Shegog's Easter sermon because it made her "see the beginning and the end." Second, the monastic life must preserve or acquire an ecumenical relevance, in the form of an openness which is not only ready and able to discuss creedal or sectarian differences with polite detachment, but which is able to share on the deepest level the risks and agonies of Christian crisis. And this, certainly, will mean something more than sharing gripes about the stupidities of one's ecclesiastical establishment. Third, the monastic life must prove itself able to be relevant even to the unbeliever who is nevertheless concerned with a self-transcending experience, the unpredictable and unexplained illumination that flashes out of the ground of one's own being.

The monk should not be concerned merely with what is transient and accidental—certainly not with what is merely fashionable—in contemporary Christianity. His renunciation, his simple life in dedicated community, is supposed to clear his view of secondary obstructions and enable him to gaze steadily at the whole truth of Christ. He sees and experiences the Kingdom of Promise as already fulfilled. The monastic life is at once a recovery of paradisal simplicity, of wilderness obedience and trust, and an anticipated completion in blessed light. Monastic "contemplation" is not merely reposeful consideration of eternal verities but a grasp of the whole content of revelation, albeit obscurely, in the deep experience of a fully lived faith. As Luther said: *Ideo habens verba per fidem habet omnia.* This is the exact root of monastic experience, and the "works" of the monk, far from meaning to justify him, should help him to celebrate and articulate the witness of faith.

There are some monks who are so diffident about their charism that they try to make their lives relevant to the rest of the world by systematically emptying them of everything monastic: that is to say, by repudiating all that is eschatological, contemplative, otherworldly, everything that has to do with the desert, with asceticism, with hope and with prayer. There is certainly every reason for an incarnational and worldly Christian witness, especially in the Christian apostolate. But just as in the past there has been a one-sided emphasis on the eschatological, so today we tend to see only the incarnational side and to forget the necessary dialectic between eschatology and incarnation. The reality with which the monk lives is not a deduction of God from the mystery of creation, still less a pure divine immanence at work in the technological world of man: the monastic life is centered on Christ as alpha and omega, as the final revelation of God the Father, in whom one day the meaning of all the rest will be made finally plain—not by man's zeal or ingenuity but by the pure grace of the Spirit. In any case, the monk not only retains the eschatological privilege and duty of smashing idols —worldly, ecclesiastical, secular and even monastic—but he also has the incarnational privilege and duty of having his feet on God's ground and his hands in the fruitful dirt.

The monk should not be too quick to repudiate his admittedly unprofitable task as a farmer (or perhaps forester —conservationist, fire guard in a national park, game warden . . .). There is both incarnation and eschatology in the monastic praying community which is daily aware of the presence of the *kyrios* in the word and the breaking of the bread, and celebrates that awareness for those who are less attuned to it. Is it too romantic still to suppose the monk can bake the bread he will eat at table and consecrate on the altar—and bake it well? His work is part of his witness, both to the goodness of God's world and to its transience.

It might be mentioned in passing that the purest kind of monastic witness in this area of work has been given, in America, not by Catholic monks but by the Shaker communities, where an extraordinary integrity of eschatological faith bore fruit in work of consummate perfection. The craftsmanship of the Shakers is the most authentic, tangible and impressive fruit of the monastic and mystical spirit in America. It is also completely *American,* and remains as a model of what the native American spirit can achieve in the monastic sphere. The Shaker spirit is entirely monastic in its celibacy, its poverty, its humility, simplicity, faith, pacifism, gentleness and in its combination of otherworldliness with a profound respect for materials and for their proper use in everyday human existence.

Whether in the city or in the mountains, the monk works for his living and his work is "worldly," not churchly: he is (at least ideally) more directly in contact with matter than other religious and clerics. His should be the least abstract of vocations. The instinct that pushes modern monastic experiments toward salaried employment in industry is sure and authentic, though it raises special problems of its own.

The wholeness that is, or should be, the hallmark of monastic experience, is able to resolve the apparent contradiction of sacred and secular not in theorizing but in the proper use of work as a means of livelihood and as a way of prayer.

Monastic work remains, however, eschatological. It resolves the apparent contradiction, sacred-secular, in terms of "the beginning and the end," of creation fulfilled in eschatology, rather than in striving for unambiguous joy over the world as such. The monk does not have to prove that technology is good—or bad—it is enough for him that God is good. Everything else has its use in the light of God's good purpose and the important thing is to recognize and apply Augustine's distinction between "use and fruition" (*uti et frui*), or his other distinction between "science" and "wisdom" (*scientia et sapientia*). A more modern approach to the same thing has been made by Heinrich Ott,[2] contrasting the *emeth* of the Bible with the *aletheia* of the Greeks and Heidegger's *Unverborgenheit*. The definitive truth is that which is unshakably secure, assured by the fidelity of God, but hidden in faith. Provisional truth is that which is "clear" and non-hidden, *unverborgen,* but attained only in the changing historical context of developing science. Wisdom embraces and includes science by attaining to the ultimate, hidden and definitive truth which is believed rather than known and which is the ground of provisional and changing certitudes. Behind all that is unveiled and "discovered," wisdom touches that which is still veiled and covered. As Heidegger (quoted by Ott) says: *In aller Entbergung wartet die Verbergung.*

It is important that the monk retain his fundamental sense of identity and vocation by affirming in his life and work this orientation to the definitive (eschatological) truth, which is God Himself. It is in this fidelity to the truth of his own vocation that he renders service to the activist and the scientist who need his witness to the hidden definitive ground of their own visible and provisional certitudes. "Faith, in so far as it is faith," says Heinrich Ott,[3] "maintains its direction to the last truth, the definitive and irrevocable truth." But the great temptation is to substitute the provisional, the penultimate (Bonhoeffer) for the ultimate, to claim that one has reached the end when one has not begun, to announce that one is going to the North Pole and then take a walk around the block (Kierkegaard).

This brings us to the crucial question. Is it possible that the whole nature of the vows needs to be theologically reexamined? Does the very idea of a vow imply the foreclosure of vital future possibilities, the selection of some provisional certitude, that seems ultimate at the moment, for the final and definitive truth? Does the vow, instead of surrendering our liberty to the unpredictable liberty of God, on the contrary

[2] Heinrich Ott, "Hermeneutique et eschatologie," in *Ermeneutica e Tradizione,* ed. by Enrico Castelli, Rome, 1963, p. 28.
[3] *Loc. cit.,* p. 109.

seek to bind God's hands and confine Him to the plans we have determined for our own lives—or, worse still, to the myopic plans that others, who are not guaranteed to be either prophetic or wise, may impose in His name? Does the very nature of a vow put one in a position where he may be forced to choose for his vow in opposition to God Himself? Or is it possible that the true concept of a vow is precisely that of a freedom committed to risk and to the unpredictable, to the refusal of all bonds to the provisional, to an open-ended newness of life that peels off the "old man" like a snakeskin which was new last year but is no longer alive and sensitive? Can it be that Luther was mistaken in thinking that the monastic vows and a legalistic existence were necessarily one and the same? Can there be a monastic life without vows? Is a monastic life with vows necessarily better and more authentic than one without vows? Is the rigid juridical structure of the dedicated life an obstacle to real renewal? Does the monastic life have to be organized as it is, in such a way that by his vows the monk is incorporated into a complex institutional machine in which his life is subject to very narrow limitations, his movements are all largely predetermined, his capacity for choice and initiative is sometimes at an absolute minimum so that, in practice, the Orders with the strictest rules and most stringent obligations, in which everything is regulated for the monk in advance, have been regarded as "the most perfect"?

In the earliest days of desert monasticism, there were no vows, no written rules, and institutional structure was kept at a minimum. The monastic commitment was taken with extreme and passionate seriousness, but this commitment was not protected by juridical sanctions or by institutional control. There was strict obedience on the part of the novice who sought to reproduce in his own life all the actions and thoughts of his spiritual master or "spiritual father." But the spiritual father had been chosen freely because of his own experience and his evident charisms of renunciation and vision. Once mature and able to live on his own, the novice became capable of living under the direct guidance of God.

Today the enormous number of professed religious seeking dispensation from their vows—and of others who leave the vowed life without any permission at all—makes the question of vows inescapable. It is certainly true that all community life demands a definite organization, an element of discipline and of rule, of administration and of control. A community cannot exist without its members being reasonably sure of what they can expect of one another from one day to the next. This supposes a certain amount of codification and a formal commitment to elementary obedience.

However, it is possible that the taking of vows might be reserved for a minority of monks, and solemn profession might become something analogous to the taking of the "great habit" in Greek monasticism. Why could there not be monasteries, with a nucleus of permanently dedicated monks, to which others come temporarily for two or three years, for periods of training or for retreat (as for instance in Zen Buddhist monasticism)? Why could not married people participate temporarily, in some way, in monastic life?

The monastic community is a covenant community whose gaze, as we have said, is fixed on the definitive eschatological truth: the *emeth* of God, the unfailing promise that is obscurely apprehended by faith as already fulfilled. The vows then are intended simply to bear witness to the monk's completely engaged faith in this fulfillment, this definitive reality made known by God in Christ. They testify that he will seek no other fulfillment, and they remind the monk himself that if he does turn aside and seek fulfillment in something less than the whole, if he abandons the whole in order to put a part in place of it, then he has fissured and severed his own identity by an act of untruth, an infidelity to what he has once experienced as definitive (cf. Heb. 6:4–8).

On the other hand, the historical development of the vowed life has more and more institutionalized this radical engagement and has transformed it into an organizational mystique, so that in effect it is the institution itself that becomes definitive. The monastic organization is then seen in practice, though not, perhaps, in theory, as the incarnation of God's definitive truth, as the practical realization of the Kingdom, complete with all kinds of built-in charisms (for instance the "grace of state" invested in superiors enabling them to act in all things as God's representatives and in fact to replace Him; every expression of their will is automatically guaranteed to be "God's will"). Thus the vows are expressions no longer of an immediate and direct engagement to the definitive truth of God's *emeth,* but of a mediate engagement, the institution itself being taken as practically definitive and as the incarnation of *emeth.*

Once the institution itself becomes a completely conservative establishment, the monastic vows become a firm social commitment to ecclesiastical conservatism. Faith in God's *emeth* is reduced in fact to faith in the *status quo,* and any criticism of the *status quo* becomes an act of unbelief, the first step toward apostasy and atheism.

The whole question of ecumenism and monastic renewal must be seen in this context. On one hand if this problem is evaded, then the monastery will be regarded and used as a point of contact in which the "separated brethren" are painlessly exposed to established Catholic orthodoxy incarnated in a well-regulated institution which incidentally knows how to update its machinery and keep its members modern and happy. It lets them be American and express themselves in dialogue, using all the latest clichés and perhaps enjoying a good laugh over the problem of relics and indulgences, now definitely laid to rest.

But on the other hand, if this problem is faced, Luther's experience and his challenge will be seen as a focus of ecumenical relevance for monastic renewal itself. The dialogue of monasticism and the Reformation will not be academic only. The Reformation experience is something badly needed if monasticism is to recover its own identity in the contemporary Church. But at the same time the depth and authenticity of the monastic experience can and should contribute something to the ongoing Reformation which now takes the form of ecumenism. The Reformation can make monasticism conscious of and faithful to its own truth. A renewed monasticism can in its turn do something of the same for the Reformation. True ecumenism enables the Catholic to find himself by discovering what the Reformation means to him and for him (not against him), and the Protestant to rediscover in and for himself the relevance that Catholicism has never ceased to have for him. This is something much more than a mere getting closer, a *rapprochement*. It is a Christian experience of identity in complementarity, a lived theological dialectic which is essential not only if we are to achieve some kind of unity, but also if we are to be faithful to ourselves. The definitive truth of God's *emeth* is not fully grasped without a complementary experience of mercy and reconciliation.

The theological direction taken by the vows since the Middle Ages has led to an affirmation of the part (the monastic institution) over the whole (Christ, Christian unity, the *emeth* of God). As long as the vowed life is seen exclusively in this distorted perspective, it will remain a cause of separation and disunity. It will simply enable the monk to affirm himself coldly as a separate kind of human being and his community as a little, exclusive, perfectly pure and illuminated Church. His fidelity to his vows will confirm him in this illusion of separateness and exclusive perfection. In so doing it will short-circuit the personal sincerity of his well-meant faith and close his Christian love in upon itself in a cloistered ghetto of pious fantasies.

In reality the vows are meant to open wide the life of faith and love, not to close it in upon itself. The original expression of the Benedictine vows, "conversion of life" (*conversatio morum*) implies a complete *metanoia*, a total conversion of all one's hopes and aspirations to the unfailing promise of God to send His Spirit and give joy and meaning to the ascetic life of the monk by unifying it in the wholeness of love. The vows then should deliver the monk from fixation upon the partial, the limited, the provisional. They should unify his life in engagement to the definitive, the "one thing necessary," God present in His word and in His promise. They orient his life entirely to a wholeness and fulfillment, realized here and now in the darkness of faith. Whether or not vows can still mean this to modern man I will not attempt to decide here. For my own part, I still think they can, or I would not keep mine. But at the same time I am convinced that a monastic life without vows is quite possible and perhaps very desirable. It might have many advantages. (There are in fact some members of monastic communities—oblates—who live like the other monks but without vows.)

A greater flexibility in the monastic structure would permit the development of ecumenical monastic communities. There is no reason why non-Catholics and even unbelievers should not be admitted to a serious participation—at least temporary—in monastic community life. Obviously the details would have to be worked out, but there is nothing in the monastic life itself which makes this impossible.

However, if this is to be really fruitful for all concerned, it would have to take place in communities that would be well on the way to a renewed sense of identity, a recovery of the authentic and I believe primitive Christian monastic outlook. In such communities the support of a strong authoritarian framework would have to be replaced by something else, less tangible and more hazardous: the authority of genuine Christian experience in a really qualified monastic leader (a charismatic guide or starets, perhaps) and in a well-tested, thoroughly formed monastic community. Monasticism cannot possibly retain any seriousness or any meaning without real discipline and spiritual depth. Monastic renewal is certainly not going to be the result of instant charisms and bright ideas in communities which have no more cohesion than a picnic—and which last until the sun clouds over or people get tired of the ants.

In conclusion: the monastic life is seeking authentic renewal. The Reformation experience, the discovery of a more immediate and radical commitment to God's unfailing promises in faith, called into question the highly institutionalized and mediate structure of monastic dedication which came down from the Middle Ages. But on the other hand, tradition has a crucial importance of its own. Return to sources, itself essential for real Christian renewal in every area, is not a mere matter of books and *monumenta*. Monasticism should recover contact with its primitive founts not only through study but through living participation in the theological and contemplative experience of hope which has come down more or less unbroken in the monastic Orders, through decadence and reform, despite all temporary aberrations and distortions of perspective. The hope of transcendent and final truth is something that is definitely not dead or dying in the modern world. On the contrary, we see on all sides evidences of an almost desperate need for spiritual depth and authentic hope. It is this very need which results in so much justified contempt for superficiality in popular religion. The monastic spirit is alive today, seeking new ways to express its eschatological hope and to become vitally aware of its own latent potentialities. That is why on one hand Protestantism itself is contributing to the monastic renewal, and why, on the other, monasteries are promising to become centers not only of ecumenical discussion but of deeply lived and participated ecumenical experience.

The unique and precious dimension that the monastic life can contribute to ecumenical experience is the deepening of unity that comes not only from talking together but from being silent together. The monastic life (when it is true to its own charism) is pervaded with the sense of the definitive that comes to those who, in silence, refrain from the futility of articulation. Yet also what must be grasped are the provisional needs to be articulated in honest and undogmatic speech. The two go together. The monastic dialectic of silence and language underlines the deeper dialectic of eschatology and incarnation.

There is today a glib tendency to treat this division quite undialectically and to dismiss it as "schizoid." This vice is common both to integralists who cling blindly to their own (institutional) brand of eschatology and to progressives who think that by putting all their eggs in one basket (secularity) and dismissing all other baskets, they can arrive easily and instantly at the unity which only the patient labor of dialectic can finally attain. Heinrich Ott[4] points out how the silences of Hemingway and the allusiveness of Antonioni are valid artistic apprehensions of a reality whose wholeness has to include the unspoken. Asian art, especially the "one-cornered" style inspired by Zen, has long known this, and the duty of the monk consists in maintaining this per-

[4] *Loc. cit.*, p. 114.

spective not only by academic clarification but by illumination and silence. Both the words and the silence which complete each other in deeply validating Christian experience, are rooted in the ultimate presence and reality of love.

XII

THE NEED FOR
A NEW EDUCATION

It is quite evident that the theological formation given to priests in the active apostolate is not entirely suitable for monks. To begin with, though all monks require some theological training, they will not all be ordained to the priesthood. The monastic life, whether in community or in solitude, is primarily a life of prayer and witness, not of teaching, administration or pastoral care. Theological formation for such a life cannot of course be superficial or merely elementary. On the contrary, the prayer life of the monk, liturgically in community and in the solitude of his own heart, implies a deep understanding of the Mystery of Christ and must indeed develop to the point of becoming a "lived theology"—a living experience of Christian truth.

The monastic community is something more than a group of pious men or women who are merely intent on meritorious works for the salvation of their own souls. Nor do they merely seek to win grace for a world which they are otherwise content to ignore. Monks are intent on exploring the inner meaning of the Mystery of Christ in the world of our time and this requires some understanding of the world and of themselves as modern people, as well as a realization of and witness to the presence of Christ in the world.

This means that monks must be prepared to share something of their own solitude and their own awareness of the Mystery of Christ with those who come to their monasteries. To say that the "world needs solitude, prayer, silence" is to say more than that worldly people need monks to pray for them: it means also that they need places where they can find a little silence and peace, and immerse themselves in the atmosphere of authentic prayer. But this means that the monastic experience needs to be communicable in terms which are not utterly foreign to modern man. The monastery must therefore have in it not only genuine men of prayer but also men who can communicate something of their understanding and experience to others.

The monastic life is not only contemplative but prophetic. That is to say, it bears witness not only to a contemplative mystique of silence, enclosure and the renunciation of active works, but it is alive with the eschatological mystery of the kingdom already shared and realized in the lives of those who have heard the Word of God and have surrendered unconditionally to its demands in a vocation that (even when communal) has a distinctly "desert" quality. This suggests that there is something of a charism in every monastic vocation and in the monastic witness itself. But this does not preclude study and theological understanding. On the contrary, it presupposes a thirst for the Word of God, a willingness to immerse oneself in meditation of the Bible, in a fruitful life of prayer and celebration which is not mechanical and punctilious, but full of spontaneity and intuitive understanding. Christian wisdom and understanding must grow and deepen from day to day in the life of the monk. The whole life of the monk is a pilgrimage to the sources of Christian truth. None of this is possible if the monk does not have the proper theological formation.

But the understanding and experience which gradually bring the monk to contemplative and prophetic maturity (which may above all be maturity in sacrifice), should also in some cases open out to communication with others. There must be some monks qualified to share their experience in dialogue with contemplatives from other religious traditions (Buddhists, Hindus, Sufis, etc.). And above all there must be some who will be able to speak to those modern intellectuals, whether religious or irreligious, who are intrigued by the mysterious personal dimensions of inner and spiritual experience—artists, philosophers, poets, psychiatrists, students of anthropology, comparative religion, etc. There are many such men who are curious about the monastic life and who would be very interested in discovering its real existential values in intelligent dialogue with trained minds. Though they might respect the sincerity of a closed, alien type of piety which could not speak their language, they might ultimately be disillusioned or repelled by it. They need to recognize in monks professionals like themselves who have deliberately chosen a different road and a different kind of experience, and can give some account of their choice and of its fruits.

Obviously we must not expect everyone in each monastic community to be a specialist in ecumenical or intercultural dialogue. But there may be some who are more qualified for this than others, and with the proper theological and humanistic training they can develop an understanding that will not only open them to others in a valid type of contemplative apostolate but will also enable them to live a more fruitful inner life themselves. Needless to say, they will have much more to share with their own monastic community. The theological training of monks should be especially oriented toward the formation of men of prayer who can give an intelligible account of contemplative experience to others either in spiritual guidance, or in teaching, or in dialogue. But on the other hand, to preserve the authentic monastic quality of this theology of prayer, the emphasis should be on prayer itself and on the mysteries of faith rather than on skills of communication. We will, however, have to remember that to understand prayer today we need to understand man, and we need to understand him in his present historical situation.

Monastic theology will be above all Biblical. The Bible should have first place in the formation and education of the monk from the earliest days of his postulancy. His liturgical and patristic studies will be also Biblical. The study of monastic history, of early monastic rules and ascetic literature should be seen in the relation of all such documents to their Biblical sources. It should never be forgotten that the monastic life is a special way of living the Gospel and that the monk's dedication to God by his vows (especially the vow to convert and transform his whole life in response to the Word of God) is to be understood in the light of God's promises, the eschatological Kingdom, and the recapitulation of all things in Christ.

In the light of this knowledge, the monk will also need to acquire by learning and by discipline a mature ability to cope with the forces that seek to stifle the seed of the word that has been planted in his heart. That is to say: the formation of the monk demands some training in the use of traditional ascetic means of perfecting the Christian life of prayer. This will enable him to respond more fully and effectively to his call to understand the Word of God, which does not reveal its meaning fully where there is no sacrifice.

However, while not neglecting traditional ascesis—understood in the light of new needs and of the new situation—the monk must seek to develop the special human capacities which will enable him to experience the deepest values of the contemplative life. These values are not accessible to merely abstract and logical investigation. They imply a certain aesthetic and intuitive awareness, a "taste" and connaturality or a capacity to savor (in an experience that cannot easily be formulated) the deepest truths of the Christian life. In other words, monastic education should, without neglecting scientific theology, open the way to a truly *sapiential* contemplation of the Christian mystery. Monastic theology is not "anti-intellectual," but it does nevertheless aspire to a kind of understanding rooted in love. *Amor ipse intellectus.* In plain words, monastic theology has a mystical orientation.

We have to recognize that today many candidates come to our monasteries without adequate training in the humanities. And we must not make the mistake of thinking that "training in the humanities" means simply a "classical education"—or a knowledge of Latin. Something has to be done for those who are deficient in a rudimentary appreciation of literature, art, and other humane studies. These have a definite relevance for the spiritual life of the monk.

The philosophical training of the monk should not only be a preparation for contemplative theology: it should also help the monk understand those non-Christian traditions of deeply metaphysical contemplation which have flourished especially in Asia. Together with technical philosophical disciplines the monk should learn something of anthropology, comparative religion, and of depth psychology in so far as it opens out on the regions of primitive mythology and archaic culture. This will be useful not only in possible dialogue with contemplatives of other traditions, but will also enable the monk to understand better the classics of non-Christian religions. Again, the philosophical training of the monk should be "sapientially" oriented, not a mere objective and apologetic catalogue of "non-Christian errors" but a judicious appreciation of the value of such traditions even for Christian monks. In his philosophical training the monk might learn, for instance, to grasp the characteristic differences between Greek, Hebrew, Indian and Chinese-Japanese modes of thought.

The monk should be thoroughly familiar with the mystical literature of Christianity, both Eastern and Western, from the patristic period down to the present day. And once again, the psychological dimension should not be ignored. The insights of modern psychiatry should be useful in helping the monk develop practical judgment in understanding problems and conflicts in the ascetic and mystical lives.

The spiritual and theological formation of the monk cannot make sense if it is unrelated to the world of our time. This means that the monk must not only know something of history, in order to understand the roots of present problems, but he should be exposed to those mystiques of history which are of decisive importance in our time (Hegel, Marx, Croce, etc.). He should clearly understand and evaluate their implications for our own Christian eschatology (which must not be allowed to degenerate into a mystique either of history or of evolution.)

The monk must be able to understand the crucial problems of our time and see his own monastic vocation in the light of these problems: race, war, genocide, starvation, injustice, revolution. Both the individual monk and the monastic community may have to face crucial decisions affecting their own future, decisions which will not be made intelligently and realistically if there is not sufficient understanding of the wider context of social conflict. In this matter great care and discrimination are necessary. Openness to the "world" must not come to mean a merely uncritical and superficial acceptance of everything that is said in the mass media of one's particular country. A monastic community can entirely lose its prophetic sense and witness when it identifies itself with some particular party or nation.

Finally, it is most important to relate the sapiential theology of the monk to the technological culture of our century. The monk cannot one-sidedly accept or reject the scientific world of the twentieth century. He must understand the problems and possibilities of that world, and, without being dominated by slogans or clichés, he should be able to contribute something of his own to a world view that is highly expert in science but perhaps deficient in wisdom. (Here let us note however that some of the truly wise—*sapientes*—of our time have been among the atomic physicists and most advanced explorers in the world of matter. Bohr, Schrödinger, *et al.* are there to back up this statement.)

A contemplative monastery should ideally be able to play a significant part in the development of scientific culture. The qualitative, experiential and personal values developed in monastic life should complement the objective, quantitative and experimental discoveries of science and their exploitation by technology and business. The monastery should by no means be merely an enclave of eccentric and apparently archaic human beings who have rebelled against the world of science and turned their backs on it with a curse.

The purpose of monastic formation is *not* primarily to produce a community of academic specialists capable of intellectual and mystical dialogue on a high level with everybody from Zen monks to nuclear physicists. That would be utopian. We need to form monks of the twentieth century who are capable of embracing in their contemplative awareness not only the theological dimensions of the Mystery of Christ but also the possibilities of new understanding offered by non-Christian traditions and by the modern world of science and revolution. There will obviously be different levels of training and understanding. Obviously we will still produce mostly the "simple monk," but of a more sophisticated type, nevertheless, than the one who used to be content with his beads (admirable though that might be). On the other hand, the monastery should be capable of being a place of dialogue, nontechnical and nonexpert, no doubt, but a place where men of our time would feel they could encounter and somehow "touch" a deep and existential experience of the Mystery of Christ as lived and revealed in a community of men who really measure up to the challenges and promises of a contemplative vocation.

In an age of easy communication, such a monastery would be frequently visited by specialists of all sorts and in all fields, who would be willing to give conferences and to have discussions with some of the monks. These opportunities would not be neglected, and the monks should be well enough trained to make such dialogue fruitful on a deep level for all concerned.

We must not fear to confront such possibilities as a limited and well-ordered use of modern media, even *educational* TV, while at the same time excluding the addiction to frothy entertainment.

We must also resolutely face the fact that the monastery is not a ghetto and will not profit by being kept as one. An interpretation of enclosure that is merely rigid and formal and which admits of no exceptions (beyond those which involve sickness or profitable business enterprises) will not help monastic renewal.

XIII

FINAL INTEGRATION
Toward a "Monastic Therapy"

A considerable amount of uneasiness and ambivalence in the monastic life today is due perhaps to the fact that though we possess clear conceptual formulas to explain what our "contemplative life" is all about, and though those formulas may well accord with what we would like to do, it seems they do not help us much with what we are actually doing. Thus we find ourselves with several different sets of problems which, however, we do not manage to distinguish. We have defined our ends in certain terms (a life of prayer and penance, apart from the world but not alien to it; seeking God alone, but in community and fraternal love; purifying our hearts by renunciation in order to pray more intently and simply, eventually attaining to contemplative experience; thus our community is a living sign of God's presence, etc.). But meanwhile, before we can get around to doing these things, we have to wrestle with a multitude of other problems: how to make our own living efficiently and yet remain "monastic"; how to keep our atmosphere of silence and yet communicate more spontaneously with one another; how to arrange the office, time for work, study, etc.; above all, how to cope with the contradictions in a system which at the same moment—but from different quarters—urges us to go forward and forbids us to move.

Thus, though we may be fairly clear about what we want to do, we are so confused about the way to do it that our ends become almost entirely theoretical, and our energies become involved in a rather different form of life from the one we claim to be living. This naturally causes a lot of anxiety, ambivalence, tension, not to say discouragement and even despair. Then we summon psychiatry to the rescue—and create still further problems: for the kind of adjustment that ordinary psychotherapy calls for is a realistic acceptance of our social situation, an acquiescence in fulfilling a moderately useful role and in being more or less the sort of person our society would like us to be. And yet the monastic role defined by the ideal to which we hold is one thing, and the role as defined by the actual situation of our community and of ourselves in it, quite another. This difficulty becomes all the greater and more confusing when sociology gets into the act, for then we are summoned to live at the same time by an unworldly ideal and by a worldly one: or to be monks according to norms and standards based on statistics which have nothing to do with our kind of life.

To put it quite simply: many people come to the monastery with a strong, if inchoate, sense that they are called to make something out of their lives. But after a few years of struggle they find that this "thing" they are supposed to do is not clarified, and though they may have become acquainted with formulas which explain the monastic life and justify it, they still do not feel that they are able to do anything about them. In addition, they begin to question the relevance of such formulas to modern man. The most difficult kind of vocation crisis is that in which a monk with genuine monastic aspirations comes to feel that such aspirations cannot be fulfilled in a monastery. Which means that they probably cannot be fulfilled anywhere.

The idea of "rebirth" and of life as a "new man in Christ, in the Spirit," of a "risen life" in the Mystery of Christ or in the Kingdom of God, is fundamental to Christian theology and practice—it is, after all, the whole meaning of baptism. All the more so is this idea central to that peculiar refinement of the theology of baptism which is the monastic *conversatio* —the vocation to a life especially dedicated to self-renewal, liberation from all sin, and the transformation of one's entire mentality "in Christ."

The notion of "rebirth" is not peculiar to Christianity. In Sufism, Zen Buddhism and in many other religious or spiritual traditions, emphasis is placed on the call to fulfill certain obscure yet urgent potentialities in the ground of one's being, to "become someone" that one already (potentially) is, the person one is truly meant to be. Zen calls this awakening a recognition of "your original face before you were born."

In Asian traditions as well as in Christian monasticism, there has been considerable stress on the need for a guide or spiritual father, an experienced elder who knows how to bring the less experienced to a decisive point of breakthrough where this "new being" is attained. Strictly speaking, Christian monasticism is less dependent on the aid of a guide than some of the other traditions. In Sufism and Zen the spiritual master is as essential as the analyst in psychoanalysis. In Christian monasticism, a fervent community, a living and "spiritual" (*pneumatikos*) celebration of the liturgical mysteries and of the office might compensate, to some extent, for the lack of an experienced and charismatic teacher. But if there is no sense at all of the urgency of inner development, no aspiration to growth and "rebirth," or if it is blandly assumed that all this is automatically taken care of by a correct and lively communal celebration, something essential is missing.

The monastic life is not justified simply by a sort of contractual fulfillment of a "work" on behalf of the Church—even if it be the spiritual work of the *opus Dei*, the official public celebration of divine praise, or, for that matter, the cultivation of meditative prayer in silence, strict enclosure, in an austere regime. The monastic community does not effectively act as a sign of God's presence and of His Kingdom merely by the fulfillment of certain symbolic functions. For instance, it is not enough to keep the monks strictly enclosed and remote from all external activity—this does not by itself constitute a sign of the eschatological kingdom. On the contrary, very often this limitation constitutes a serious impoverishment of the personalities of the monks and at the same time serves to prevent that impoverishment from becoming public! It is of course perfectly true that solitude and silence are essential to the monastic way of life, and discipline does contribute very much to the ends for which monastic communities exist. But the fact remains that people are called to the monastic life so that they may grow and be transformed, "reborn" to a new and more complete identity, and to a more profoundly fruitful existence in peace, in wisdom, in creativity, in love. When rigidity and limitation become ends in themselves they no longer favor growth, they stifle it.

Sometimes it may be very useful for us to discover new and unfamiliar ways in which the human task of maturation and self-discovery is defined. The book of a Persian psychoanalyst, Dr. Reza Arasteh, who practices and teaches in America, might prove very valuable in this respect.[1]

Dr. Arasteh has developed and deepened ideas suggested by the humanistic psychoanalysis of Erich Fromm, by existential psychotherapy and by the logotherapy of Viktor Frankl. But—and this is what is most interesting—he has also incorporated into his theories material from the mystical tradition of Persian Sufism. The *Final Integration* which is the object of his research is not just the "cure" of neurosis by adaptation to society. On the contrary, it presupposes that any psychoanalytic theory that is content merely with this is bound to be inadequate. Dr. Arasteh is interested not only in the partial and limited "health" which results from contented acceptance of a useful role in society, but in the final and complete maturing of the human psyche on a transcultural level. This requires a little clarification.

Contrary to the accepted theory and practice of most psychotherapy derived from Freud and popular in America today, Dr. Arasteh holds that adaptation to society at best helps a man "to live with his illness rather than cure it," particularly if the general atmosphere of the society is unhealthy because of its overemphasis on cerebral, competitive, acquisitive forms of ego-affirmation. Such an atmosphere may favor an apparently very active and productive mode of life but in reality it stifles true growth, leaves people lost, alienated, frustrated and bored without any way of knowing what is wrong with them. In fact, in many cases, psychoanalysis has become a technique for making people conform to a society that prevents them from growing and developing as they should. Quoting E. Knight's book *The Objective Society*, Arasteh says:

[1] Reza Arasteh, *Final Integration in the Adult Personality*, Leiden, E. J. Brill, 1965.

The Western individual, while opposing the integration of the Russian and Chinese models, not only accepts the herd values of his society but he has invented psychoanalysis to prevent him from straying from them. . . . The stresses that modern life often produce in sensitive and intelligent people are no longer considered to call for a change in society; it is the individual who is wrong and he consequently becomes a neurotic, not a revolutionary. No more remarkable device than psychoanalysis has ever been devised by a society for preventing its superior citizens from giving it pain.

This interesting passage, quoted out of context, might give undue comfort to those who assume that, because they enjoy their masochism, they are superior. Nevertheless it does show to what extent psychotherapy and other techniques have been frankly drafted into the service of a massive, affluent organization that is dedicated to "freedom" and yet tolerates less and less dissent. The masochism, the anxiety, the alienation which are almost universal in such a society are forms of organized evasion. The energies that might otherwise go into productive or even revolutionary change are driven into stagnant backwaters of frustration and self-pity. People are not only made ill, but they prefer to be ill rather than face the risk of real dissent. (Note the important distinction between real and pseudo-dissent, the latter being merely a token and a symbol expressing and justifying an underlying neurosis.) We know well enough that this pattern, so familiar in "the world," is even more familiar in "the cloister."

Nevertheless there is an important distinction between mere neurotic anxiety which comes from a commitment to defeat and existential anxiety which is the healthy pain caused by the blocking of vital energies that still remain available for radical change. This is one of the main points made by Dr. Arasteh's book: the importance of existential anxiety seen not as a symptom of something wrong, but as a summons to growth and to painful development.

Carefully distinguishing existential anxiety from the petulant self-defeating sorrows of the neurotic, Dr. Arasteh shows how this anxiety is a sign of health and generates the necessary strength for psychic rebirth into a new transcultural identity. This new being is entirely personal, original, creative, unique, and it transcends the limits imposed by social convention and prejudice. Birth on this higher level is an imperative necessity for man.

The infant who lives immersed in a symbiotic relationship with the rest of nature—immersed, that is, in his own narcissism—must be "born" out of this sensual self-centeredness and acquire an identity as a responsible member of society. Ordinary psychotherapy is fully aware of this. But once one has grown up, acquired an education, and assumed a useful role as a worker and provider, there is still another birth to be undergone. Dr. Arasteh studies this birth to final integration in three exceptional individuals: Rumi, the Persian mystic and poet; Goethe; and a young modern Turk who was one of Arasteh's patients.

In the past, final integration was generally a matter only for unusually gifted people. We shall return to this point later. Even today, though the need for final integration makes itself more and more widely felt, the majority not only do not try to attain it, but society, as we have seen, provides them with ways to evade the summons. Clearly, in many cases, that summons takes the form of a monastic, religious or priestly vocation. Clearly, too, there are many who leave the monastery because they feel that the way the monastic life is structured, or the way they themselves are fitted into the structure, makes a genuine response to the summons impossible.

All of us who have had to work through vocation problems with professed monks can, on reflection, easily distinguish obvious neurotics from men whose monastic crisis has taken the form of existential anxiety: this is a crisis of authentic growth which cannot be resolved in the situation in which they find themselves, and the situation cannot be changed. (Very often, in similar situations, it is the mildly neurotic who manage to stay and make some sort of compromise adjustment, nestling fearfully in the protection of the monastery with the obscure sense that further painful growth will not be demanded!)

Since his investigation is purely psychological, not theological, the question of "sanctity" or holiness does not really arise from Dr. Arasteh. But let us make clear that ordinarily a full spiritual development and a supernatural, even charismatic, maturity, evidenced in the "saint," normally includes the idea of complete psychological integration. Doubtless many saints have been neurotics, but they have used their neurosis in the interests of growth instead of capitulating and succumbing to its dubious comforts.

Final integration is a state of transcultural maturity far beyond mere social adjustment, which always implies partiality and compromise. The man who is "fully born" has an entirely "inner experience of life." He apprehends his life fully and wholly from an inner ground that is at once more universal than the empirical ego and yet entirely his own. He is in a certain sense "cosmic" and "universal man." He has attained a deeper, fuller identity than that of his limited ego-self which is only a fragment of his being. He is in a certain sense identified with everybody: or in the familiar language of the New Testament (which Arasteh evidently has not studied) he is "all things to all men." He is able to experience their joys and sufferings as his own, without however becoming dominated by them. He has attained to a deep inner freedom—the Freedom of the Spirit we read of in the New Testament. He is guided not just by will and reason, but by "spontaneous behavior subject to dynamic insight." Now, this calls to mind the theology of St. Thomas on the Gifts of the Holy Spirit which move a man to act "in a superhuman mode." Though Dr. Arasteh takes no account of specifically supernatural agencies, it is clear that such considerations might become relevant here. But of course they cannot be investigated by experimental science.

Again, the state of insight which is final integration implies an openness, an "emptiness," a "poverty" similar to those described in such detail not only by the Rhenish mystics, by St. John of the Cross, by the early Franciscans, but also by the Sufis, the early Taoist masters and Zen Buddhists. Final integration implies the void, poverty and nonaction which leave one entirely docile to the "Spirit" and hence a potential instrument for unusual creativity.

The man who has attained final integration is no longer limited by the culture in which he has grown up. "He has embraced *all of life*. . . . He has experienced qualities of every type of life": ordinary human existence, intellectual life, artistic creation, human love, religious life. He passes beyond all these limiting forms, while retaining all that is best and most universal in them, "finally giving birth to a fully comprehensive self." He accepts not only his own community, his own society, his own friends, his own culture, but all mankind. He does not remain bound to one limited set of values in such a way that he opposes them aggressively or defensively to others. He is fully "Catholic" in the best sense of the word. He has a unified vision and experience of the one truth shining out in all its various manifestations, some clearer than others, some more definite and more certain than others. He does not set these partial views up in opposition to each other, but unifies them in a dialectic or an insight of complementarity. With this view of life he is able to bring perspective, liberty and spontaneity into the lives of others. The finally integrated man is a peacemaker, and that is why there is such a desperate need for our leaders to become such men of insight.

It will be seen at once that this kind of maturity is exactly what the monastic life should produce. The monastic ideal is precisely this sort of freedom in the spirit, this liberation from the limits of all that is merely partial and fragmentary in a given culture. Monasticism calls for a breadth and universality of vision that sees everything in the light of the One Truth as St. Benedict beheld all creation embraced "in one ray of the sun." This too is suggested at the end of Chapter 7 of the Rule where St. Benedict speaks of the new identity, the new mode of being of the monk who no longer practices the various degrees of humility with concentrated and studied effort, but with dynamic spontaneity "in the Spirit." It is suggested also in the "Degrees of Truth" and the "Degrees of Love" in St. Bernard's tracts on humility and on the love of God.

Unfortunately, we can see at once that if too many people developed in this way, if entire communities were all at once to reach final integration, the effect on the community structure itself might be revolutionary. Hence, in fact, our community life is unconsciously organized to make sure that any such development will be subject to human control. We will not let the Holy Spirit get out of hand! And yet with all its shortcomings and deficiencies, the monastic life is charismatic and the Spirit does work in our midst. But in monastic communities as well as in the Church at large we are conscious of the obscure and difficult struggle between charism and institution, in which the overwhelming need to channel and control the energies of the Spirit (and of course to distinguish them clearly from other more destructive energies) has led to a kind of neutralization of Spirit by organization. This institutional strait-jacketing does not prevent individuals from breaking through in their own way and achieving an integration that is perhaps warped and singular but nevertheless authentic (sometimes in amusing ways). But the community itself cannot be truly charismatic, except in a very subdued and harmless way. The penalty paid for this is a prevalence of neurosis, of masochism, of obsessions and compulsions, of fanaticism, intolerance, narrow-mindedness, and various petty forms of destructive cruelty which have proved so ruinous in the past. The present changes and relaxations have been first-aid measures to relieve these tensions at any price: but merely opening the windows is not enough. We must still be ready to face anxieties, and realize the difference between those that are fruitless and those that offer a promise of fruitful development. Sometimes the latter are even more painful and seemingly more dangerous than the former. After all, the rebirth which precedes final integration involves a crisis which is extremely severe—something like the Dark Night described by St. John of the Cross. And it is evident that anyone who chanced to fall into the Dark Night of the Soul today would (if discovered) soon find himself getting shock treatments, which would effectively take care of any further disturbing developments!

Dr. Arasteh describes the breakthrough into final integration, in the language of Sufism. The consecrated term in Sufism is *Fana*, annihilation or disintegration, a loss of self, a real spiritual death. But mere annihilation and death are not enough: they must be followed by reintegration and new life on a totally different level. This reintegration is what the Sufis call *Baqa*. The process of disintegration and reintegration is one that involves a terrible interior solitude and an "existential moratorium," a crisis and an anguish which cannot be analyzed or intellectualized. It also requires a solitary fortitude far beyond the ordinary, "an act of courage related to the root of all existence." It would be utterly futile to try to "cure" this anguish by bringing the "patient" as quickly and as completely as possible into the warm bosom of togetherness. Jung, with whom Arasteh has much in common, says this:

[The development of the person to full ripeness] is at once a charisma and a curse because its first fruit is the conscious and unavoidable segregation of the individual from the undifferentiated and unconscious herd. This means isolation, and there is no more comforting word for it. Neither family nor society nor position can save him from the fate, nor yet the most successful adaptation to his environment. . . . [quoted by Arasteh]

Seen from the viewpoint of monastic tradition, the pattern of disintegration, existential moratorium and reintegration on a higher, universal level, is precisely what the monastic life is meant to provide. In the strictly limited, authoritarian, caste societies of medieval Europe, of India, of China, of Japan, the individual lived within extreme restriction in a framework that denied him social mobility. But the unusual person, from any caste, could become a monk. If he were able to live as an authentic beggar and pilgrim, accept the sacrifices, the insecurities, the risks, the challenges of the solitary adventure, he was freed from social limitations. He was on his own, on the road, in the jungle or in the desert, and he was entitled to develop in his own way, indeed to devote himself with passionate dedication to a freedom even from the limits of his contingency as a creature: he could get lost in the light of eternity, provided he found the way!

In the modern world, things have somehow become reversed. We live in an extremely mobile society in which, though we may not be nearly as free as we think we are, limits are still very flexible and sometimes do not exist at all. To enter a monastery is to enter into the most restricted form of life there is. This restriction has a purpose: it is imposed in order to liberate us from attachments and from self-will. But the big question is: Does it? Yes and no.

The ascesis of communal service and obedience cannot be dismissed as totally irrelevant, antiquated, repressive and sterile. It is necessary and salutary for people who have had little or no discipline at all. But on the other hand it does definitely operate in such a way that while it initiates a certain growth, it goes only so far. It frustrates and stifles growth beyond a median level. It makes no provision for anything but formal adaptation to a rather narrow and limited communal pattern. Within that pattern it tolerates "safe," moderate growth and blesses lack of growth. In fact, it is in practice more tolerant of those who do not grow.

The crisis, the challenge and the demands that Arasteh describes in terms of final integration would seldom be really acceptable in a monastery. They would be too disturbing, too exceptional, too "irregular." They would open up possibilities that would be regarded as altogether too hazardous. The result is that for many authentic vocations today the monastery has become merely a way station. To stay in the cloister for life would be to renounce their full development. And yet there is no guarantee that by leaving it they will develop any better.

Dr. Arasteh has nothing direct to say about the monastic life, but obviously those who have sufficient background and understanding will be able to apply his principles very fruitfully to our general predicament today. He will help us recover some sense of the real aim of that monastic *conversatio* which we have not only mentally approved but actually vowed. We have dedicated ourselves to rebirth, to growth, to final maturity and integration. Monastic renewal means a reshaping of structures so that they will not only permit such growth but favor and encourage it in everyone.

However, as Christian monks, we cannot properly understand the full meaning of "final integration" if we see it only in the terms of psychology. For a Christian, a transcultural integration is eschatological. The rebirth of man and of society on a transcultural level is a rebirth into the transformed and redeemed time, the time of the Kingdom, the time of the Spirit, the time of "the end." It means a disintegration of the social and cultural self, the product of merely human history, and the reintegration of that self in Christ, in salvation history, in the mystery of redemption, in the Pentecostal "new creation." But this means entering into the full mystery of the eschatological Church.

Now, as Dr. Arasteh points out, whereas final psychological integration was, in the past, the privilege of a few, it is now becoming a need and aspiration of mankind as a whole. The whole world is in an existential crisis to which there are various reactions, some of them negative, tragic, destructive, demonic, others proffering a human hope which is yet not fully clear.

The destructive and tragic solutions are not solutions at all: they simply marshal the immense resources of military, economic and political power to block real development and to maintain established patterns—in the interest of those who know best how to profit from them, and at the expense of everybody else.

The humanly optimistic answers foresee radical changes of a purely secular sort which will initiate a kind of hippie kingdom of love in a cybernated and peace-loving mega-city (presumably with free LSD for everybody). Many Christians feel that the Spirit is really summoning us to renounce our sense of spiritual privilege and enter into a fully turned-on solidarity with these secular hopes. Others, of course, and perhaps the majority, have lined up on the side of the armies and the "powers" under the mistaken idea that Christ is fully identified with the capitalist Western establishment which still refers to itself (when convenient) as "Christian."

At this point, the best one can do is hazard a personal guess that neither of these solutions is truly Christian, and neither offers a hope of final, eschatological integration to the individual Christian, to the Church, or to the monastic community. Both of these are reducible to identification with one form or other of culture, one form or other of "given" society. They are historical decisions that are merely historical and not eschatological. (Though of course they may contribute in a disastrous way to the ironies of eschatological judgment upon the organizational Church.)

Where are we to look for the true solutions? Precisely from the Spirit who will speak clearly at the right time through a renewed ecclesiastical and monastic community. The path to final integration for the individual, and for the community lies, in any case, beyond the dictates and programs of any culture ("Christian culture" included).

APPENDICES

1. *Notes on the Future of Monasticism*
2. *The Monk Today*

1. *Notes on the Future of Monasticism*[1]

Obviously the future of monasticism depends first of all on the monks (including "nuns") being monks and not something else. There is no point in talking of the future of an institution that becomes self-abolishing. It is assumed, then, that monks will continue to maintain their identity and their vocation as people who have consciously and deliberately adopted a mode of life which is marginal with respect to the rest of society, implicitly critical of that society, seeking a certain distance from that society and a freedom from its domination and its imperatives, but nevertheless open to its needs and in dialogue with it. The motive for all this is explicitly theological if not "religious" (ambiguities of this word need not be discussed here). In other words, the monk is a person who in traditional language "seeks God" or seeks by *metanoia* and inner revolution to deepen his consciousness and awareness in such a way that he "experiences" something of the ultimate ground of being and to the saving power of the Spirit, and witnesses to this in some way. In Christian terms this means of course a life of "death and resurrection in Christ," in the fullest sense a life "in the Spirit," a life of charismatic freedom, humility, peace, surrender, transformation and joy—a life of Love in terms of the Gospel and

[1] (*Editor's Note: An abridged version of this article appeared in* L'Osservatore Romano, *January 10, 1969, in Italian, translated from the English by Padre Filiberto Guala, a Trappist monk of Frattocchie. Also, a subsequent version of this article was published in the English edition of the same paper. This version was edited specifically for* Monastic Exchange *by Thomas Merton shortly before his death.*)

the Kingdom of God. But of course the monastic vocation does not seek to affirm itself as the *only* Christian vocation or even necessarily the *best* way to be a Christian. If a spaceman undergoes certain experimental tests and develops certain skills, he does not necessarily imply that he is a superior human being: but this happens to be his job and even his "vocation."

Assuming, then, that monks are doing something besides running a factory of some sort with a public prayer wheel attached, but also that they are not fomenting some sort of gnostic or contemplative mystique, and that they do have a necessary institutional structure, a communal identity, what is their place in the modern world? Will they continue to have a place in the modern world? Should they? Must they be anxiously concerned about their "relevance," or should they trust that a monastic life lived seriously is self-validating?

The following notes are suggestions which regard primarily the monastic consciousness. The monk's identity is not something that comes into being in a pure vacuum of solitude and solipsism, face to face with God. It is necessarily a result of his relationship with society, both negative (his "renunciation of the world") and positive (his "love for the world," which means not just "praying for" the—hopeless??—world but being in some kind of dialogue with it).

While some monks will certainly emphasize their solitude, asceticism and prayer even to the point of having a minimum of contact with the "world," we must recognize that the way in which this has been interpreted in the recent past has been disastrous. It has resulted in a kind of organized narcissism which has no future. Hence it need not be discussed here. Of such monks, to paraphrase St. Benedict, the less said the better.

The monumental feudal cloister with mysterious veiled or hooded figures slinking about and chanting their orisons in an unknown tongue was *not* in fact "out of the world," but very much part of a certain social structure. The conservative cloisters today remain very much identified with a certain class of people outside the cloisters, and thus (by implication) with a certain ideology and attitude which has decisive social consequences. To put it bluntly, such cloisters are often closely identified with rich and highly conservative benefactors and with a reactionary, archaic view of social reality. Their "world denial" and even their "contemplation" are in fact very much influenced by this economic and social background. This is more true of countries like Spain and Italy and in Latin America. But it is certainly true even in the United States. In time of revolutionary violence, such communities become prime targets for destruction. Theologically, the merit of their sacrifice is quite dubious. (Individually, those in good faith are doubtless "pleasing victims.") The archaic institution simply gets what is coming to it.

This brings us to the recognition of a fact which monastic ideology too often tends to ignore. No matter how "unworldly" monks may want to be, they are *always*, inevitably, in proportion as they are institutionalized, fitted into some kind of social structure and identified with other groups in that structure. For better or for worse, they must navigate the rivers of change along with these other groups with which they are more or less identified.

The question of the future of monasticism can then be looked at from this viewpoint: in a changing society, where other groups are more visibly future-oriented, the monk who is himself future-oriented will almost unconsciously find himself lining up with, identifying with, these other groups. The monk who is not future-oriented will have at least an unconscious and unadmitted identification with established power and with those who represent the *status quo*. What are the choices?

One can more or less consciously identify with:

(1) The established power structure and those who accept it uncritically—which means the majority of people in the U.S. This sector of the population is future-oriented in the sense that it *plans* itself a future in which its own established power continues unchanged. There will of course be great technological developments but the fundamental structure of the system remains the same. Hence the huge problems which the system cannot solve also remain the same. It is

then, in spite of technical virtuosity and mobility, essentially conservative. But it also thinks itself progressive.

(2) The underclass (term taken from G. Mydral): the poor everywhere who are imprisoned at the bottom of the present setup and must stay there. If anything, their mobility is down, not up. Their situation gets worse, not better. And they become more and more numerous, as well as more and more aware of their plight and of the fact that they constitute the majority of the world's population. They are the raw material of revolution.

(3) The unpropertied and marginal intellectual who does not have a vested interest in the establishment but roams freely in it, is in some sense privileged and respected, can get jobs in it if he likes, can use its foundations to foot the bill for his travels and research: the university people, academics, students, hippies, artists, poets, writers, etc., the intellectual community which is *not* identified with the establishment (obviously many of them are, living on government money and working for the military-industrial complex, the CIA or what have you—these are identified with the established power structure).

Because in fact the Catholics—the hierarchy, the clergy, the ordinary middle-class Catholic people—accept and identify with the conservative establishment, monks also in fact do so by and large. They don't know any better, to begin with. Such monks do have an ideology and a world view, and it is simply the one they acquired from the establishment. When they try to be "open to the world" and "progressive," all they do in fact is open up to more indoctrination. They uncritically accept the establishment view of things through the mass media. Their position remains *conservative*. Much of the apparent progressivism of monks and other Catholics is therefore completely illusory since it is nothing more than a more complete and submissive acceptance of familiar establishment slogans, attitudes and clichés. Its "progressive" aspect is only an uncritical admiration for everything achieved by technology.

Obscurely realizing this, many monks seek to identify with the underclass (the poor). This is the thrust of "inner city monasticism." Small monastic groups (like other groups of active religious) go and live in the ghettos, work like those of their neighbors who can get work (!) (Take a job from someone else?) and simply act as brothers and friends of the people around them. They seek to maintain lives of prayer and meditation in the milieu of the underclass. This is certainly a more honest and realistic solution than the previous one, which is really no solution (it is simply the acceptance of an established fact which is from many viewpoints questionable—identification with a society which is perhaps deeply guilty of injustice and exploitation). But inner city monks may, if not well informed, simply be acting as missionaries and apologists for the established power structure.

Speaking from experience in my own life and vocation, I see that at least for some of us—as individual monks and as communities—it is important, as well as quite natural, to identify with the intellectual who does not have a vested interest in the establishment and is in fact highly critical of it. Frankly, this class has taken over the position once held by the "monk," the "friar" and the "clerk" in the structure of the medieval world. The intellectual is the one who is free and moves about independently in the world. He has ideas of his own. He can be original, creative, iconoclastic, independent. He is not hung up in an avaricious system. He is aware of inner contradictions and injustices, indeed of insoluble problems in the system, and articulates his awareness without fear of the disapproval which must follow. He is also a man of world perspectives, and not hung up in narrow, parochial, limited and distorted perspectives like the "average people" who simply accept the whole package of ideas (or pseudo-ideas) put out by the establishment. Furthermore, this class or group is also aware of the problems of the underclass and is *open to* the underclass, in free dialogue with it, and able in some measure to help it. Yet he does *not* imagine himself to be a prophet or a revolutionary activist.

This non-propertied intellectual class also includes a large segment of disaffected and critical people (e.g. hippies) who are actively interested in "spiritual" and "religious" matters and are in fact the ones most involved in the project of self-

discovery on a spiritual level, while at the same time rejecting a society which they consider stifling and square. No
doubt their reaction may have a lot wrong with it, may end
in blind alleys (drugs etc.), but let us frankly admit that they
are not only close to us but very interested in us. They come
to our monasteries with a very keen and alert curiosity and
they want to know if we have something they can respect.
If they find nothing but a group of uninformed, pious,
narrow-minded, rigid, archaic squares who identify completely with a world they themselves see to be stupid . . .

Monastic life will be relevant in the future, specifically in
the next two generations, in so far as monasteries open themselves to dialogue and exchange with the intellectual community as defined in (3). But for this dialogue to be meaningful, the intellectual community must find in the monasteries
both a *monastic reality* (people of depth and simplicity who
have acquired the values of monasticism by living them) and
openness to social reality of the twentieth century. It is possible for one or the other of these to be achieved in our structures. *It is very difficult for both to be achieved together.*
The present structures must be changed if both are to be
realized. The survival of monasticism *demands* that both be
realized.

Monastic reality: this means, a real *monastic community*
sharing a lived experience of traditional values which are fully
relevant today. This is difficult and it requires real monastic
formation, deep awareness of what the monastic past really
had (instead of just formulas of words about it): experience of prayer, of contemplation, a lived and eloquent
liturgical celebration of community, but also deep awareness
of and witness to the eschatological message of the Gospels.
It means also *solitude* in a measure and a degree which will
vary from person to person. I am not defending a phony "hermit mystique," but some of us *have to be* alone to be ourselves. Call it privacy if you like. But we have thinking to do
and work to do which demands a certain silence and aloneness. We need time to do our job of meditation and creation.
Also in the community itself there has to be a certain quiet,
and not just an uncontrolled gabby togetherness which means

nothing. Monasticism does imply a certain distance, from which one can then come "near"—not just immersion in a confusing nearness in which there are no more people, only a mass of moving and talking objects.

Openness to social reality means not just information, but much more: a real personal communication with others who are recognized as *like-minded,* who are "other monks" with whom we can exchange ideas and projects fruitfully even though they may not even be believers. It means ability to learn from the exchange with men of other religious traditions, intellectuals, artists, writers, etc., in fact with all who represent what is most alive intellectually in the modern world, because these are the ones who in one way or another are somehow living a "prophetic" vocation. They are aware also of the forces of death which can sterilize those living seeds and bring about possible disaster for the human race.

Whether in the inner city or in the desert, monks must develop these two things, true monastic prayer and experience, together with openness to contemporary reality as it is embodied in people whose minds are alive and whose eyes are on authentic possibilities (not just people who read *U. S. News & World Report*). However, the monk should not cultivate airs of superiority because he thinks himself emancipated.

The new mediocrity. Monasticism has unfortunately always been plagued by mediocrity. It is a safe, secure, institutionalized life in which there are many ways of evading reality. One can just "keep rules" and "purify intentions" and still live a sort of indifferent, loveless, mediocre life. We know this. But when rules are taken away and we are left to "create" a new monasticism for ourselves, we can just waste our lives in useless and superficial pastimes without meaning or direction, we can seek outlets in spurious and adolescent forms of spontaneity, under the impression that this is "life" and "self-expression." Or, of course, we can get involved in more dignified but equally futile academic projects, petty ambitions as monastic scholars, editors, writers of voluminous footnotes to other peoples' footnotes. Or we can, unfortunately, spend our time in endless conversations with the affable, charming people of group (3) under the impression that we are thereby improving the world and furthering the monastic vocation. No matter what we try to do, we face risks and failures. The important thing is to have a very clear idea of our goals and of the obstacles we face, and to be faithful to the sometimes painful contradictions of our "charism."

Conclusion: To combine real monastic depth and experience with openness to the living intellectual and cultural forces of our time requires a special charism. A charism is a gift, but one must struggle to deserve and keep it (if one uses "deserve" in a very loose sense, to avoid self-contradiction). The most basic and important thing is the monastic calling to prayer and renunciation and inner transformation—what used to be called "the contemplative life." Each one of us must place this *first* in some way or other, without adopting foolish and unreal—or dishonest—ways of doing it. You cannot give what you don't have. If our monasteries are truly centers of deeply experienced monastic life, those who are most alive in the outside world will spontaneously come to share our silence and discuss with us their own fruitful insights. It is this exchange and participation which I believe to be of decisive importance for monasteries. But it all depends on solitude and prayer.

2. *The Monk Today*[1]

PREAMBLE:

Your questions are in appearance very simple. But from a certain viewpoint they contain presuppositions which might well impose limits, and which would make any reply ambiguous.

When you ask *what does the monk do to justify his existence in the modern world,* the monk seems to be definable

[1] These pages were originally written in answer to questions presented by a French author and editor, concerning the relevance of the monastic life today.—Editor

only in terms of what he *accomplishes* exteriorly, not by what *he is* or by the *tone and quality of his life*. He is summoned to give an account of himself in the world of quantity (indeed perhaps even of statistics) when his whole object in life is in the realm of quality. The monk seeks to deepen the clarity and truth of his inner awareness in order to become, in Christ, more fully human as well as a man "illuminated by grace and by the gifts of the Holy Spirit." Meanwhile, since the actions and works of the monk are quite commonplace and even trivial—they consist in work, meditation, praise, prayer, reading, liturgy, and communal service—to describe his ordinary life is apparently to describe nothing at all. That is why a fatal tendency to dramatize the monastic life comes into being. A special costume and decor. A unique behavior, a ceremonious "tenue," a ritual solemnity and obsequiousness. In the end this amounts to attachment to feudal anachronism, and the monk who pretends to justify himself by these masks is only convincing people that he is an object for the museum. But in reality these cultural accretions have nothing to do with the charism of the monastic vocation. I cannot then, try to justify the monk's existence in terms of the work he does or even in terms of his praying for the world.

What is my point of departure in answering these questions? I start from where I am, not in the twelfth century but in the twentieth. It happens that I have just been reading a very interesting essay of Camus, "Le Desert." From a certain viewpoint Camus, in this essay, is totally anti-Christian and absolutely anti-monastic. But strangely enough his conclusions are very close indeed to monastic conclusions: so close, indeed, that I am tempted to write a study of them from a monastic viewpoint. Camus, who was exposed to Neo-Platonism and Manichaeism in his study of St. Augustine under Jean Grenier at the University of Algiers, reacted against an excessive and dualistic "spirituality" that glorified "the soul" at the expense of the body and resulted in a kind of religious schizophrenia. Camus, in seeking to affirm the *whole man* in his organic unity, rejected any idea of the soul and of its immortality, and hence rejected the Christian teaching on redemption and salvation as he understood it. Nevertheless "Le Desert" shows him to be powerfully impressed by the Christian spirit of Italian primitive painting, by the example of Franciscan poverty, and even by the image of the Risen Christ in His stark austerity and simplicity, as seen by Piero della Francesca. From this Camus develops ideas of asceticism and contemplation which are closely akin to those of the purest monastic tradition. By poverty and simplicity one gains a true appreciation of the world. By an interior "nakedness" of images and elaborate ideas, by freedom from complicated speculative systems, one can gain a direct intuition of reality in "purity of heart." Camus uses this expression consecrated by Gregory of Nyssa and Cassian.

In other words, a monk today stands much closer to someone like Camus (who was neither Christian nor monk) than he does, for example, to someone like Billy Graham, a very sincere, very active Christian who is totally dedicated to a specific "task" and "mission" which is very clearly defined. I am not of course saying that I entirely agree with everything that Camus said, or that I disapprove the faith of Billy Graham. But I am saying that I understand perfectly why Camus said what he did say because it is easy for me to take his kind of position: that of a man who at once loves the world yet stands apart from it with a critical objectivity which refuses to become involved in its transient fashions and its more manifest absurdities.

The world needs men who are free from its demands, men who are not alienated by its servitudes in any way. The monastic vocation is traditionally regarded as a charism of liberty in which the monk does not simply turn his back on the world, but on the contrary becomes free with the perfect freedom of the sons of God by virtue of the fact that, having followed Christ into the wilderness and shared in His temptations and sufferings, he can also follow Him wherever else He may go. It would be a mistake however for the monk to become involved in the *organization* of high-pressure activities which are foreign to his life, precisely because *the monk should be the man in the Church who is not organized but is free with the freedom of the desert nomad.* Obviously this somewhat poetic description of the ideal monk must be severely measured against the strict institutional life that cenobites must lead today. There is no place here for the discussion of the monastic institution. What I intend to say refers to nothing but the charism of the monastic vocation in its inmost reality. The desert of the monk is his monastery—and his own heart. Yet in that desert he is free to encounter and love the whole world.

1. DOES THE MONK HAVE A SPECIFIC TASK IN THE WORLD?

The monastic life is in a certain sense scandalous. The monk is precisely *a man who has no specific task*. He is liberated from the routines and servitudes of organized human activity in order to *be free*. Free for what? Free to see, free to praise, free to understand, free to love. This ideal is easy to describe, much more difficult to realize. Obviously, in reality, the life of a monastic community has many tasks and even certain organized routines so that the monk, in his own little world, lives a social life like everybody else. This social life can become complicated and overactive. And he suffers the same temptations to evasion, to meaninglessness, to bad faith, to restless agitation. But the purpose of the monastic life is to enable a man to face reality in all its naked, disconcerting, possibly drab and disappointing factuality, without excuses, without useless explanations, and without subterfuges.

One may object that in fact the very opposite is what seems to happen: the monastic life can well be an evasion into artificiality, myth, illusion. I do not deny this: all I say is that it is futile to conduct an argument about monasticism versus the world based on the supposition that monastic life is unreal and the world is real, or vice versa. All social life tends to have in itself a certain amount of organized fictitiousness and shame. All social life has a superstructure of myth. The monk should be more aware of this than others because his life "in the desert" is a life in which, at least ideally, all the masks and disguises are stripped off. Of course, if he is in no sense living in the "desert" then the monk has no advantage over anyone else. But the monk is called "out of the world" in the sense that he is called to be free of its fictions, its myths, its rationalizations, its routine demands, its deceptive promises, its organized tyrannies. If the monk merely substitutes other myths, routines and tyrannies even more petty than those of the world, then he is to be pitied.

And this is precisely where the trouble comes: if instead of the existential reality of a "naked" and "solitary" heart the monk cultivates a special systematic ideology of his own and occupies himself with preferring his own myths to the myths of the world, then he is simply wasting his time. It is true that the leisurely medieval culture of monastic life as it is still organized today offers many advantages over the more chaotic and hurried life of the world outside the monastic walls. But, once again, the monastic life is not to be justified merely by the fact that it perpetuates a different kind of culture, no matter how noble and valuable that culture may be.

One of the "tyrannies" of "the world" is precisely its demand that men explain and justify their lives according to standards that may not be reasonable or even human. The monk is not concerned with justifying himself according to these standards. Today a man is required to prove his worth by demonstrating his "efficacy." In such a world the monk may simply decide that it is better to be useless—perhaps as a protest against the myth of illusory efficacy. As an American monk I am forced to view with shame and compassion the lengths to which the myths of "efficiency" and "practicality" have led American power in Viet Nam. To the machinery of an organized efficiency that produces nothing but mass murder I certainly prefer the relative "inefficiency" of my own monastic life, which produces only some milk, some cheese, some bread, some music, a few paintings, and an occasional book.

2. What Meaning Can a Monk Have in the World?

He should be a sign of freedom, a sign of truth, a witness

to that inner liberty of the sons of God with which Christ has come to endow us. The "life of the desert" should be a sign of hope to man crushed and alienated by the senselessness and injustice of a society with splendid hopes but also with agonizing problems. True, the challenges and promises of the world of technology are indeed inspiring: yet we must face the fact that for most men these promises will remain largely illusory. The monk is there to show that one can be perfectly happy without depending on any worldly success or achievement, without fulfilling any ambition, however subtle, however ecclesiastical, however apostolic. The monk, by the simplicity, the poverty, the detachment of his naked "desert life" and solitude—or by his obedience in the poor community of laborers which is the monastic family—bears witness to the fact that the happiness of the Christian *does not depend* on the promises of this world. One can certainly help, as far as one is able, to make life worth living for oneself and other people, but one's hope should not end there and if one meets hardship one should not despair. Great as the modern world may be, it is also a world in which there are wars, concentration camps, race riots, police states, slums, sickness and starvation: and it must frankly be said that while on one hand technology helps to combat these evils, on the other a misdirected use of technology makes them immeasurably worse than they ever were before. The monk—who can perfectly well use the latest technology on his monastic farm—is there to show that one can use technology without placing all his hopes in it and without depending on it for ultimate happiness. In a word, he is there to help men practice the freedom of the poor in spirit in the midst of the problems and the blessings of a material world in full development.

He does this not by preaching but simply by living, and incarnating in his daily life the full meaning of what he believes: the Gospel of Christ, which teaches him to live in direct dependence on the bounty of God and to share that bounty with his brothers in a life of simple honest work, study and prayer.

3. WHAT MISSIONARY AIM DOES A MONK HAVE?

Like every other Christian, the monk seeks the salvation and joy of the entire world, the "bringing together of all in Christ": but he does not seek to effect this by the power and wisdom of his own preaching. He does not organize his life in view of "making converts" whether directly or indirectly. I myself have written some books, and I am told that people have been "converted" by reading some of them. I solemnly affirm that I have never in my life made the slightest conscious effort to convert anyone or anything. I have sought only to speak the truth as I see it, and to bear witness to what I have discovered by living in the world of the twentieth century, both without the light of Christ and with it. There is a difference, and I have experienced the difference, and have endeavored to say so. That is all. Apart from that my writing has attempted to formulate reflections on other aspects of our modern world and its problems, with the peculiar perspective which a life "out of the world" gives a monastic observer. I have never claimed that this perspective was the only true one, or that I had better answers than anyone else. I do not think I have implicitly judged others or asserted that I, as a monk, knew better than they. I feel myself involved in the same problems, and I need to work out the problems of the world with other men because they are also my problems. A man who thinks that by taking refuge in a monastery he can shrug off the problems of the world is merely deluding himself. Such at least is my opinion.

On the other hand, I certainly do not think that I have a "task" of social commentator, or preacher, or pseudo-prophet, or what you will. My task is only to be what I am, a man seeking God in silence and solitude, with deep respect for the demands and realities of his own vocation, and fully aware that others too are seeking the truth in their own way.

4. DOES A MONK EXPECT SOMETHING FROM THE WORLD?

Obviously he must: he cannot delude himself that he is entirely "out of the world" as if the mere fact of putting on a monastic habit placed him on another planet. The notion that the monk "hates" the world is a myth, due in part to a certain monastic rhetoric, but also aggravated by the misconceptions and old wives' tales that are circulated about monks.

Chateaubriand's *Life of Rancé,* a beautifully written book of literature which Camus knew and admired, unfortunately depicts the monk as one who hates life and loves death. This is an altogether unfortunate error of perspective. But this exaggeration has clung tenaciously to the monastic image and people are still convinced that a monk is interested only in digging his own grave—or in imagining (quite selfishly) the joys he will have in heaven as a reward for being perversely unhappy on earth. No one who really knows the monastic life could agree with this distorted image.

Monks are very human indeed, very sensitive to human values, very open to other people, very capable of love and concern. In ten years of experience as novice master I have seen how remarkable a change takes place in this regard: a man may come into the monastery somewhat hard, tough, defensive, surly and unkind, and may very rapidly turn into a simple, open, friendly, happy person at peace with everyone and very open to the needs and difficulties of others. Of course it is true that some monks do close up in an almost pathological shell: but so do people in the world. Solitude teaches a man how poor and worthless he is in and by himself, and shows him that without others he cannot give any meaning or fullness to his life. On the other hand this does not mean that he abandons his monastic life in order to run about interfering in the lives of other people and telling them how to solve all their problems. He knows he has his own vocation to attend to, and he minds his own business. He knows, above all, that the Holy Spirit will bring him in contact with the people he is to help, if any, and he does not force the issue by following his own ideas and his own fancy. He knows that preaching and teaching are the work of others, and that God will bless these others in their work. By his own prayers his love, his occasional dialogue, written or spoken, with a few people who enter his life, he keeps in contact with the rest of the world and shares in its struggle to solve its momentous problems.

5. WHY DO MONKS LIVE IN SECLUSION?

That is asking why does a scientist work in a laboratory, or why does a sailor go on a ship or why does a duck swim in water. Why does a man go to his bedroom and get in bed when he wants to go to sleep? Why doesn't he lie down in the middle of the street? A monk seeks silence and solitude because there his mind and heart can relax and expand and attain to a new perspective: there too he can hear the Word of God and meditate on it more quietly, without strain, without forcing himself, without being carried away in useless abstract speculations. The monk is by definition a man who lives in seclusion, in solitude, in silence outside of the noise and the confusion of a busy worldly existence. He does this because seclusion provides certain necessary conditions for his life: an interior freedom, silence, liberation from trivial concerns that arise from the overstimulation of the appetites and the imagination. The monk finally seeks solitude and silence, let us admit it, because he knows that the real fruit of his vocation is union with God in love and contemplation. An apt saying of the Moslem Sufis comes to mind here: "The hen does not lay eggs in the market place."

It is of course quite true that the contemplative life can be lived outside a monastery, and that one can be closely united to God while leading a life of considerable activity. Nevertheless, a certain dimension of inner solitude and peace is necessary for this intimate union with God. However, we must always remember that union with God is not a matter of withdrawal and of special experiences, so much as it is a question of love, and the love of other men is necessary if we are to grow without illusions in the authentic love of God. The two loves are in fact one, and they are in no sense obstacles to each other.

6. CHRISTIANS IN THE WORLD.

This brings us to the last question. The fact of living a monastic life does not necessarily imply that all who live outside a monastery are imperfect or insincere Christians. Quite the contrary. A Christian is essentially a follower of Christ, and there is a diversity of graces and vocations in the Church. The important thing is not whether one is in a monastery or in the world, but whether or not one is living as a true disciple of Christ and in the state or work to which one has been called by Christ. The struggle for a better existence in the world is not contrary to the Christian life, but everything depends on the motives with which one struggles for a better life. If the struggle for a "better life" is in reality only a selfish yearning to acquire more money, more power, more self-satisfaction, then the Christian should realize that he is forgetting his obligation to live for others and for Christ. But if one is devoting himself with all his strength to help his fellow man better his condition in the world, then he will certainly find that in doing so he must meet many challenges and make many crucially important choices that will orient his life more and more to the love of Christ. One cannot live fruitfully in our world without great generosity, honesty and sacrifice. This law applies whether in the monastery or out of it.

TWO

THE CASE FOR EREMITISM

I

CHRISTIAN SOLITUDE

Christians are emerging from an era of individualistic piety. The new emphasis on the communal brotherly life of those who have been called to oneness in Christ is in fact a liberation from a narrow, self-preoccupied struggle for a perfection too evidently tinged with narcissism. An individualistic quest of "contemplation" has often resulted, in fact, in fanciful regression to a tepid womb of oceanic feelings. The reaction against individualism has therefore not only revived the Christian sense of solidarity in love, work, and responsibility, but has brought us a new realization of the meaning of the *person*. This in its turn has meant a new awareness of the seriousness of *solitude*, not simply as an expression of man's existential plight, but as a Christian value, a challenge, and even as a vocation.

The Christial life is to be seen dialectically, not only as a communal effort from which solitude is ostracized nor as a lonely pilgrimage without fraternal solidarity, but as a growth in one "Mystical Person," one Christ, in whom the solitude and independence of the person develop together with his capacity for love and commitment. Scholars have at the same time drawn attention to the importance of the wilderness theme, the desert pilgrimage, in the Bible and in the whole history of theological thought.[1]

So now, in the Catholic Church, in liturgy and in theology, while we are rediscovering the meaning of oneness as the People of God, we are also becoming aware of the fact that we are a pilgrim community traveling in the wilderness under the guidance of God, and that some members of the Holy People are bound to have a special consciousness of this wilderness and exiled aspect of the Christian life. Unless we

[1] Since this paper was originally published at Harvard, the author referred to the important study of G. H. Williams, *Wilderness and Paradise in Christian Thought*, in which the wilderness ideal is shown to have exercised a decisive influence on the founders of Harvard College.

are fully aware of the seriousness of solitude and the isolation and anguish of the person without love, our protestations of joy, hope, and communal fervor may ring dreadfully hollow in the ears of those who know the absurdity of shallow optimism.

This preoccupation with the person and his solitude is nothing new. The Christian existentialists have had a lot to say about it, and though they are perhaps not now as fashionable as they were in the fifties, their reflections about Man in Mass Society have not lost any of their point. The idea of alienation remains one of the keys to our social and psychological predicament. We know that we live in a society which needs large numbers of its members to be alienated, and which also needs slums into which it can dump those who, for one reason or another, cannot face up to the competition of living affluently. One function of the slum is to isolate the outcast not only from the rest of society but even from the other outcasts around him. The slum is the equivalent of the desert wilderness today—hence, the new quasi-monastic families, like the Little Brothers of Jesus, which began in the Sahara, and have gravitated to the slums of Paris or Detroit or to the *poblaciones* of South America. The slum is now the abode of utter loneliness, risk, helplessness: a true desert. Yet it is massively overcrowded—a tragic and unnatural solitude.

While there still remain solitudes—woods, mountains, and islands—the monastic charism will still summon a few men to live there alone, for one reason or another.

Monastic life is by definition solitary. True, its ordinary shape in modern times is communal, but even then the monastery is always a kind of wilderness community—as was Qumran. There is always an element of perilous ambiguity in monastic theories which glorify the common life of the monastery as if it were the ideal pattern for the Christian community. The basis of human and of Christian community is marriage, and celibate communities are something beyond the normal—and we are well aware of the harm done by attempting to impose a monastic style of spirituality on the lay Christian. The monk was originally a *layman* (priests were exceptional) who lived alone in the desert outside the framework of any institution, even of the Christian and Ecclesial institution. His state was consciously *abnormal*—therefore a state of penitent mourning. His loneliness had a prophetic and mysterious quality, something almost in the nature of a sacramental sign, because it was a particular charismatic way of participating in the death and resurrection of Christ.

What is lonelier than death? To confront the emptiness, the void, the apparent hopelessness of this desert and to encounter there the miracle of new life in Christ, the joy of eschatological hope already fulfilled in mystery—this was the monastic vocation. Hence *real* loneliness, real conditions of emptiness and deprivation were required. A mere intention of solitude could not suffice.

Kierkegaard used to illustrate the fact that "Christian values" could become very abstract by the story of a man who said he was going to the North Pole and then went for a walk around the block. Some of the unrest in contemporary monasticism is due to the fact that monastic values have too often degenerated into such walks around the block. Especially solitude. The monastery today tends to be a busy village, and life can become as organized, as noisy and as fussy as anywhere else. Provided one remains within the walls, keeps the rule of silence moderately well, and strives for a certain "recollection," he is supposed to tell himself that he is "alone" when in fact he is jostling along in a small agitated crowd. Obviously in such circumstances many will feel more honest if they abandon the pretense, and decide to talk to one another and get along as an authentic group. This is one of the directions being taken by monastic renewal at the present. But unless this is balanced by opportunities for physical solitude, it will only result in the monastic life becoming more busy and more futile than ever. (Note: Statements like these imply a lot that the reader may or may not be taking for granted. In all forms of communal life we tend to multiply *useless* activities—time-consuming obsessions which for psychological reasons we are unable to abandon. Pascal saw this so well and described it as man's insatiate need to escape himself in movement, diversion: "Hence it is that men so much love noise and stir . . . hence it is that the pleasure of solitude is a thing so incomprehensible.")

So, in the monastic Orders, provision is now made for the monks to go into solitude temporarily or even permanently, where the circumstances permit. This means that several monasteries now have monks living in the woods, near the monastery, as hermits. Such experiments are going on in the Cistercian monasteries in Kentucky, South Carolina, and Utah, and also at the Primitive Benedictine foundation at Abiquiu in New Mexico. In addition to this, there is the hermit colony founded recently in British Columbia by Dom Jacques Winandy, a retired Benedictine Abbot (from Clervaux in Luxembourg) and peopled by former Benedictine and Cistercian monks.

A place has thus been made for Christian eremitical solitude within the monastic institution. This is of course a very welcome development. On the other hand, the situation is not without its ambiguities. They must not be ignored. And yet it is very hard to clarify them. The whole question of eremitism has been kept deliberately out of sight for years, and its problems and possibilities have not yet been seriously studied. There is always a danger that those who are now experimenting with it may be tacitly expected to prove themselves perfect models: "All right, you wanted this, so presumably you know what it is all about. We are waiting for you to show us!" But show what? Models of what? These expectations may be loaded with tacit demands that cannot be and should not be met. For instance: must the modern monastic hermit prove himself to be a replica of some Egyptian or Syrian Desert Father of the 4th century? Well, hardly. To begin with, Desert Father stories fall into a special literary form which admits and indeed requires a generous element of distortion—an apparent inhumanity which, on closer examination, proves to be compensated by other distortions in the opposite sense. This balance of distortions is typical of *apothegmata* and *fioretti*. The first function of a modern hermitage would seem to be quite the opposite: to relax and to heal and to smooth out one's distortions and inhumanities.

Whereas in the fourth century monks were determined to prove their solitude charismatic by showing it to be beyond the human, the situation today is quite the reverse. The whole of man's life is now pushed to extremes pressing him almost to his biological and psychological limit. Hence the mission of the solitary is first the full recovery of man's human and natural measure. Not that the solitary merely recalls the rest of men to an impossible Eden. But he reminds them of what is theirs to use if they can manage to extricate themselves from the web of myths and fixations which a highly artificial society has imposed on them. The hermit exists today to realize and experience in himself the ordinary values of a life lived with a minimum of artificiality. Such a life will from the beginning seem itself artificial, because it is so completely unlike the lives of other people. The hermit will be accused of being the most contrived of all simply because he does not float away on the immense tide of artificiality with everybody else. And of course, if he is too conscious of a revolutionary intent, if he tries to put himself on display as utterly different, he may well be nothing but an eccentric. That would be unfortunate—but it is not unavoidable. In any event, the Christian solitary should avoid all trappings and decor of a theatrical eremitism—the hood, the costume, the retinue of devoted birds and squirrels (though they will be around anyway), the diet of bread and water, the stone pillow, the rosary of knotted string, the bed of twigs. These things are affectations, and we might as well recognize that even the classification of "hermit" has its dangers.

The Christian solitary life today should bear witness to the fact that certain basic claims about solitude and peace are in fact true. And in doing this, it will restore people's confidence, first in their own humanity and beyond that in the grace of God.

The monastic hermit has, as his first duty, to live happily and without affectation in his solitude. He owes this not only to himself, but to the monastic community that has gone so far as to give him a chance to try it out. In fact, this is one of the specifically Christian and communal aspects of the experiment. The monastic hermit realizes that he owes his solitude to his community, and owes it in more ways than one. First of all the community has bestowed it upon him, in an act of love and trust. Second, the community helps him to stay there and make a go of it, by prayers and by material aid. Finally the hermit "owes his solitude" to the community in the sense that his solitary life with its depth of prayer and awareness is his contribution to the community, something that he gives back to his "monastic Church" in return for what has been given him.

This is very important, because in this way monastic solitude retains its fully communal and Christian character and is not a mere escape from collective tasks and limitations.

To live happily and without affectation in solitude: this is the chief obligation of the monastic hermit because, as I said above, it can restore to others their faith in certain latent possibilities of nature and of grace. More especially it can, today, restore the faith of monks in one of the basic claims of the monastic vocation itself. If a monk can take literally the promise implicit in his vocation and find that by living entirely alone he can discover the values he came seeking when he first entered the monastery, then he will by his life affirm the truth that the values are there and that they are real. It would of course be most unrealistic to imagine that these values are to be found only, or mostly, in pure solitude. One who had not been able to find them in the beginning of his communal life would probably never find them in solitude either.

To be more precise, the monastic vocation, like any other, is a call to a life of constant organic growth. One of the problems of a rigidly institutional monastic life in which everything is organized on one pattern for everyone is that growth may be frustrated.

If after fifteen or twenty years in the common life a monk can go to a hermitage, he can there create a new personal pattern which will fulfill his own special needs for growth. He is no longer at the mercy of a pattern devised for another. In Greek monasticism this has always been taken for granted.

The granting of the "Great Habit" after many years established the mature monk in a fully contemplative life when he was finally ready for it—and did not assume that he became a contemplative on entering the novitiate.

Man is ever face to face with the inescapable specters of boredom, futility, and madness. A healthy and well-organized social life enables man to cope with these specters by fruitful work, love, and personal growth. The person who loves his ordinary life because his work is meaningful and because his relationship with those around him is joyful, open, and generous will never be bored. An unhealthy social system both exacerbates man's fear of boredom and exploits it. The modern American is kept in terror of boredom and unfulfillment because he is constantly being reminded of their imminence—in order that he may be induced to do something that will exorcise him for the next half hour. Then the terror will rise up again and he will have to buy something else, or turn another switch, or open another bottle, or swallow another pill, or stick himself with a needle in order to keep from collapsing.

In the monastic life these escapes do not exist—they are not necessary. Yet in time of crisis and change there is a great deal of concern about making the monastic life more interesting, more rewarding, by improving the patterns, enlivening the observances, diminishing tensions. All this is of course necessary, but unfortunately it tends to develop into the same agitated flight from boredom which, everywhere else, makes boredom all the more inevitable. The trouble lies in assuming that there must be some kind of social machinery which, once discovered and set in motion, will remove everybody's problems. The anguished effort to construct this machinery and get it moving drives everybody wild.

In reality, no such machinery exists. Society can simply remove obstacles or make them negotiable. It remains for the person to make use of the opportunities thus provided, and lead his own life in a happy and fruitful manner—helping others to do the same.

The hermit is, or should be, happy without having a happiness machine to solve his problems for him. He faces boredom squarely with *no other resources than those he has within himself*—his own capacities and God's grace. He puts these resources to work, and discovers that his life is never boring. On the contrary, renouncing care and concern about getting somewhere and having fun, he finds that to live is to be happy, once one knows what it is to *live* in simplicity.

The hermitage then provides the monk with something that a mature person needs: the chance to explore, to risk, to abandon himself sagaciously to untried possibilities. This is one of the most important aspects of the wilderness theme in the Bible and in the history of the People of God. After all, it was in the desert and hazard of Sinai that the People of God acquired its identity, its full consciousness of the covenant relationship which the prophets later described as an "espousal" with Yahweh.

The Christian solitary, in his life of prayer and silence, explores the existential depths and possibilities of his own life by entering into the mystery of Christ's prayer and temptation in the desert, Christ's nights alone on the mountain, Christ's agony in the Garden, Christ's Transfiguration and Ascension. This is a dramatic way of saying that the Christian solitary is left alone with God to fight out the question of who he really is, to get rid of the impersonation, if any, that has still followed him into the woods. He thus receives from God his "new name," his mysterious identity in Christ and His Church. The one great advantage of the woods is that one cannot—at least sanely—play a part in them. Or if one manages to defy reality and continue in some fictitious "role," the result will quickly prove disastrous. At the same time, it is not altogether easy to be perfectly honest with oneself, and solitude brings this fact out. The wood may well foment new madnesses that one did not suspect before. But it would seem that solitude is not a satisfactory setting for concerted, thoroughgoing madness. To be really mad, you need other people. When you are by yourself you soon get tired of your craziness. It is too exhausting. It does not fit in with the eminent sanity of trees, birds, water, sky. You have to shut up and go about the business of living. The silence of the woods forces you to make a decision which the tensions and artificialities of society may help you to evade forever. Do you want to be yourself or don't you? Do you insist on fighting the images of other people? Must you continue to live as a symbolic appendage to somebody else you desire or hate? Are you going to stand on your own feet before God and the world and take full responsibility for your own life?

Of course, this decision must naturally be possible everywhere. Love makes it possible and imperative in social life. For some, marriage is what normally brings the decision to a head, or it should. I would say that for a few others, the call to solitude, accepted and fulfilled in joy, is the only real guarantee of their being finally born. If they respond to it, if they get born, if they become happy and are content just to be themselves and not impose themselves and their private idiocies on anybody else, they will do a signal service to the rest of mankind.

Extending to mankind as a whole what I said a moment ago about the monastic community, the solitary who manages to live happily because he knows he is finally born, or that he soon will be, restores to the rest of men some elementary hope that this basic need is not an illusion and that it can be fulfilled. The example of its fulfillment in solitude must not, of course, imply a claim that solitude is the only way. But the example of the solitary has a special usefulness. The grace of solitude is a grace of independence: a breaking away from certain exorbitant claims of society and of institutions. Society has a way of enlarging its demands to the point where it arrogates to itself complete power over everyone and everything. It tells you, in effect, "you not only need the love of other people, but you need to be completely enslaved and dominated by other people. You need not only to be in rapport with others, you need to be swallowed up by them." One of the things most wrong about the exaggerated legalism and institutionalism in the Catholic Church today is this attempt to dominate Christians by fear—the implication that if they do not submit to complete overcontrol they will cease to exist as true human beings and as members of Christ. This is so manifestly false that some Catholics are literally driven away from the visible Church in which they cannot, in conscience, meet some exorbitant demand stupidly forced on them by incompetent officials. The man who can live happily without snuggling up at every moment to some person, institution, or vice is there as a promise of freedom for the rest of men. And that perhaps is one of the only reasons why the solitary can be so bitterly resented, especially by a certain type of Christian for whom the Church is mere institution and womb.

What is the pattern of solitary life in this monastic setting? The hermit is bound to the Rule of St. Benedict and to his monastic vows. He remains in obedience to his abbot, retains his status in his community, and lives according to a schedule which is roughly that of the other monks. But this is quite flexible. At Gethsemani the hermits (there are two) go to bed and get up about the same time as the community. They are both priests and both say Mass in a small chapel in the monastery. The two hermits live about a mile apart, in the woods. One of them still says the old Latin office, the other says his office in English. Both spend a certain amount of time in manual work, taking care of the hermitages and making their own living. One of them is more inclined to intellectual work than the other. He is also interested in Zen and Yoga. For recreation there are solitary walks in the woods and Thoreau's inspecting of snowstorms. Some contacts are maintained with the outside world. The hermit life does not necessarily demand absolute isolation: this too should be flexible and a matter of individual choice. There may be real reasons for a certain amount of limited correspondence, for a few visits and conversations. Obviously, however, there must be limits to all this, or solitude itself may once again be reduced to a mere abstraction.

How have people reacted to this experiment?

First of all, it has become a matter of routine and gossipy curiosity. This is understandable, but more or less irrelevant. It indicates a certain basis of acceptance without much understanding. The men who came to put up the electric line to one of the hermitages soon had it figured out in terms of "peace and quiet." In the books of the Rural Electric

Cooperative the hermitage is billed as a "lodge" and there is a certain readiness to concede that the hermits would logically live on rabbits and other game, which in fact they do not.

Some of the local Protestant ministers and professors from the Southern Baptist Seminary in Louisville, who formerly used to meet and converse with one of the monks who became hermits, have regarded it as a regrettable withdrawal and have not been disposed to understand what it was all about. They have of course admitted the right of the one concerned to follow his own conscience in this barely comprehensible fashion.

On the other hand, people from India, Japan, North Africa (Hindus, Buddhists, and Moslems) have thoroughly understood the hermit idea and approved of it without difficulty, taking it for granted as an obvious development of the monastic life.

What is most important is of course the reaction of the monastic community itself. The hermits have been thoroughly accepted, and everyone seems happy about them. One of the routine arguments against hermits, put forth before the experiment, was that if one or two were allowed to live in the woods there would be a mad rush into solitude. "Everyone will be asking for a hermitage." This has not turned out to be the case. It is clear that most members of the community do not want to live permanently alone. Others who are still young in monastic life are content to wait their turn. Meanwhile, however, there will be more opportunities for temporary solitude and a hermitage may be built in which monks will be permitted to spend a day or two now and again, if they wish. This seems to be about as much solitude as most monks need. Their real vocation remains in the monastic community.

Relations between the hermits and the community are very happy. But this of course is not automatic. It is a question of real charity on both sides. In other words, the hermit does not vanish into a void but moves into a new and special relationship with the community. The relationship clearly has mutual obligations that need to be understood and observed with good sense as well as love. The future of the hermit experiment in some monasteries could easily be prejudiced by failures in this regard. Once again, the hermit must not be an eccentric and make such odd demands that he becomes a pest to the community. The grace of the solitary life in a monastic setting definitely implies a willingness for the hermit to mind his own business and for the community to mind theirs. This is fortunately being realized so far at Gethsemani. The spirit of mutual understanding, tolerance, and affection is quite marked. The hermits meanwhile continue to contribute to the community life in one way or another. One of them for instance gives one conference a week to those who are interested (about one third of the community attends). The hermits show up for concelebration on Sundays and big feasts. The cenobites meanwhile have been very good about staying away from the hermitages and leaving the hermits alone.

To sum it up: one feels at Gethsemani that as long as the hermits are thought to be quietly happy, the rest of the community will be happy with them. And if the hermits start getting too nutty, too demanding, too eccentric, or if they take it into their heads to try to run the community from the hermitage, this will hardly be appreciated. The elementary obligation of the hermit is to renounce all arbitrary demands on other people. The hermit's ability to live alone is his gift to the community and his witness to the grace of Christ in his own life. It is as simple as that, and he is accepted on that basis by the community.

There will probably always remain some nagging doubts that the hermit life might be self-centered. Some will say: "Sure! Why shouldn't the hermit be happy? He lives in his own little world! He is content because he is the sole possessor of a universe of which he is himself the center." The most incredible thing about this statement is that anyone could accept it as a viable formula for happiness. The only possible answer is: "If you think you can be happy by doing that, why don't you just try it?" The fact is that this is a pure myth. Man is not made in such a way that he can live happily without love. If his life is centered on himself, he may indeed be able to function, but in order to do so his existence is necessarily complicated by his machinery for imposing his will on others. One cannot live a self-centered life *simply*. Too much cheating is involved—even if one only cheats himself. Supposing a man does live self-centeredly in solitude: he may manage to get by, but he will hardly be content. His discontent will obviously reach out and affect others in some way. He will be mean and unpleasant with them; he will act out his obsessions and inner frenzies upon them. He will project his self-hate on them. He will need them and use them for some irrational purpose, and they will be aware of the fact. Lovelessness cannot be kept hidden, because a loveless life is essentially unhappy, frustrated, and destructive.

The solitary life is then anything but "lonely"—if by loneliness is meant a loveless and abandoned state. The life of Christian solitude is before all else a life of love, a life of *special* love. And love is never abstract. It centers on a concrete, existential good, a value that is perceived and experienced as coming directly from the ground and source of all good—God's love for man in Christ. The solitary life of the Christian hermit is not simply a life in which one thinks about the good, but a life of total response to it, complete surrender to it, based on a personal and existential awareness that one is called into solitude by a special act of God's merciful love. It is a way of saying: "I have known and experienced the goodness of God to me in Christ in such a way that I have no alternative but this total response, this gift of myself to a life alone with God in the forest. And this witness is at the same time the purest act of love for other men, my gift to them, my contribution to their joy in the good news of Jesus Christ, and to their awareness that the Kingdom of Christ is in the midst of us."

The Christian solitary bears witness to his faith by his very solitude. Without faith such a life could not possibly make real sense. This is obvious to logic; for, if it is a life of love, the solitary life must have some way of remaining in contact with the good that is its object. That way is faith, and faith only. It is by faith, as the author of Hebrews said, that the witnesses to God's revelation in Judaism risked their lives and survived when they roamed the deserts in sheepskins and goatskins (Heb. 11:37–38). It is by faith that the solitary knows himself loved and called by God into the wilderness. If he cannot always give a perfectly satisfactory reason for his faith to other men, that does not matter. What matters is the liveliness of his faith as it burns in his own heart.

Certainly the fact of moving to a hermitage does not turn a man instantly into a saint. He retains his human defects, he remains capable of failure and error, and like everyone else in such a case he depends on the understanding and love of his brothers, just as he gives them his own love and understanding in their own need. But the real structure of the Christian solitary vocation remains this: it is a response to a personal call from God in Christ. It is a life of love for God based on faith, verified by the assent of the monastic community and supported by the loving care and understanding of that community. And it is in turn a contribution to the life and faith of the community and of the Church as a whole. Christian solitude is then essentially an expression of the mystery of the Church, even when in some sense it implies a certain freedom from institutional structures. But in the case of monastic eremitism, the solitary life retains a definite and approved institutional form. The hermit remains within the cadres of monastic obedience and community, while at the same time living a life of solitude and freedom "in the Spirit." His freedom is never a freedom *from* the Church but always a freedom *in* the Church and a contribution to the Church's own charismatic heritage.

II

THE CELL

"A brother asked one of the Elders saying: What shall I do, Father, for I work none of the works of a monk but here I am in torpor eating and drinking and sleeping and in bad thoughts and in plenty of trouble, going from one struggle to another and from thoughts to thoughts. Then the old man said: Just you stay in your cell and cope with all this as best you can without being disturbed by it. I would like to think that the little you are able to do is nevertheless not unlike the great things that Abba Anthony did on the mountain, and I believe that if you sit in your cell for the Name of God and if you continue to seek the knowledge of Him, you too will find yourself in the place of Abba Anthony."[1]

This variant of a classic Desert Father saying emphasizes that the most important thing for the solitary is to be a solitary, to "sit in his cell" because the cell will "teach him all things." Everything else is secondary. The relative unimportance of all other practices is suggested by this hyperbolic and somewhat outrageous statement. We must not interpret this saying to mean that asceticism is discounted. But fasting, vigils and so on are seen in their proper relation to solitude and prayer.

The right order of things in the solitary life is this: everything is centered on union with God in prayer and solitude. Therefore the most important "ascetic practice" is solitude itself, and "sitting" alone in the silence of the cell. This patient subjection to loneliness, emptiness, exile from the world of other men, and direct confrontation with the baffling mystery of God sets the tone, so to speak, for all other actions of the solitary. Without this clear acceptance of solitude in its most naked exigencies, the other practices might confuse the issue, or obscure the true end of the solitary life, or even become escapes from it. Once solitude itself is fully accepted, the other practices—fasting, work, vigils, psalmody and so

[1] An apothegm published by Nau, "Histoire des Solitaires Egyptiens," *Revue Orient Chrétien*, 13 (1908), 278.

on—gradually fall into place, their need and their efficacy being now properly understood in relation to the whole of "life in the cell." Then asceticism which at first seems difficult or even impossible, gradually comes to be more easy and even welcome. Each one in fact has his own measure, and "sitting in the cell" devoting himself to prayer and the search for God, he will, if he is patient and can accept a certain amount of trial and error in the beginning, finally discover the measure of discipline which he himself requires. The Desert Fathers were quite flexible in this regard, though in principle their asceticism was very severe.

To "sit in the cell" and to "learn from the cell" evidently means first of all learning *that one is not a monk*. That is why the elder in this story did not take the admissions of the disciple too seriously. They showed him, in fact, that the disciple was beginning to learn, and that he was actually opening up to the fruitful lessons of solitude. But in the disciple's own mind, this experience was so defeating and confusing that he could only interpret it in one way: as a sign that he was not called to this kind of life. In fact, in any vocation at all, we must distinguish the grace of the call itself and the preliminary image of ourselves which we spontaneously and almost unconsciously assume to represent the truth of our calling. Sooner or later this image must be destroyed and give place to the concrete reality of the vocation *as lived* in the actual mysterious plan of God, which necessarily contains many elements we could never have foreseen. Thus "sitting in the cell" means learning the fatuity and hollowness of this illusory image, which was nevertheless necessary from a human point of view and played a certain part in getting us into the desert.

Another apothegm in the same collection represents a disciple complaining to an Abba: "My thoughts torment me saying you cannot fast or work, at least go and visit the sick for this also is love." The Elder replies, "Go on, eat, drink, sleep, only do not leave your cell." (Note that the Greek words here are interesting: the word for visiting the sick is *episkopein*, "looking them over as if one were a bishop" we would be inclined to say. The word for leaving the cell is *apostatein,* with implications for us which we know well.) The Elder explains: "For the patient bearing of the cell sets the monk in his right place in the order of things (*taxis*)."[2]

Afflicted with boredom and hardly knowing what to do with himself, the disciple represents to himself a more fruitful and familiar way of life, in which he appears to himself to "be someone" and to have a fully recognizable and acceptable identity, a "place in the Church," but the Elder tells him that his place in the Church will never be found by following these ideas and images of a plausible identity. Rather it is found by traveling a way that is new and disconcerting because it has never been imagined by us before, or at least we have never conceived it as useful or even credible for a true Christian—a way in which we seem to lose our identity and become nothing. Patiently putting up with the incomprehensible unfulfillment of the lonely, confined, silent, obscure life of the cell, we gradually find our place, the spot where we belong as monks: that is of course solitude, the cell itself. This implies a kind of mysterious awakening to the fact *that where we actually are is where we belong,* namely in solitude, in the cell. Suddenly we see "this is *it.*"

In this particular story, the disciple, driven by sheer boredom, finds some palm leaves, and as if playing around discovers how to split them and weave them together into a basket. Then he teaches himself to wait and not eat until he has finished a certain amount of work, and he fits his "little psalms" into the framework of order that is taking shape and so "by little steps he entered into his order (*taxis*). In so doing, he also gained confidence in his struggle with his inner drives [*logismoi* or thoughts] and overcame them."

With the boredom of the disoriented life comes also *akedia,* or the discouragement, disgust and lassitude which, says one of the Elders, are the sign and the effect of a certain basic ignorance.[3] Ignorance of what? The old man told the

[2] *Ibid.,* p. 277.
[3] *Ibid.,* p. 277, n. 196.

disciple: "You do not have your eye on the *akme* (this has both a temporal and a spatial implication: it is at once the 'real point' and the 'moment of truth,' considered as the 'aim' to which we tend in our daily practice) and you do not see the rest that is the object of our hope nor the future punishment" (for failure in this great work). If the disciple only *saw* all this then even "if your cell were crawling with worms to the point that you were up to your neck in them, you would still bear it patiently without *akedia.*"

Another famous saying: "The cell of the hermit is the furnace of Babylon in which the three children found the Son of God and the Pillar of cloud in which God spoke to Moses."[4]

St. Peter Damian[5] develops this theme rhetorically. In the cell, the hermit fights down the flames of the Babylonian furnace by prayer and faith. There the flames of temptation burn away the bonds by which his limbs are tied without in the least affecting or harming him. The ropes dissolve in fire and the hermit bursts into a song of praise of the Lord who has freed him: "Dirupisti, Domine, vincula mea" (Ps. 105). For Peter Damian the cell is the fiery kiln in which precious vessels for the King are made. It is a shop in which "happy bargains" (*felix commercium*) are made—earth is traded for heaven. It is the workshop in which the lost likeness of the Creator is reformed in man's soul. The cell itself, says Damian, grants the gift of fasting and of contemplation. "Thou grantest that man may see God with a pure heart, whereas before, wrapped in his own darkness, he did not even know himself." Thus the cell is the place where man comes to know himself first of all that he may know God (Augustine's program—*Noverim me, noverim Te*). The cell is the sole witness of the divine love flaming in the heart of the monk as he seeks the face of God, says Peter Damian. It is like the Holy Sepulcher which alone witnessed the resurrection of the Savior in the night of Easter: the cell is the place of the monk's resurrection to the divine life and light

[4] *Ibid.,* p. 279, n. 206.
[5] Opusc, xi. c. 19.

for which he was created and, according to the Irish hermit tradition, the cell will be the place of the hermit's resurrection at the last day. "Whosoever perseveres in his love of thee (O solitary cell) dwells indeed in thee, but God dwells in him."

This is the classic language of contemplative experience. It takes us back to the first saying we quoted, at the beginning of this meditation. To "sit in the cell for the Name of God": this means something at once more concrete and more profound than simply remaining in solitude with the *intention of pleasing* God, or with the holiness of God as a *"sufficient reason"* for one's solitude. At least, we must understand the concept of "sufficient reason" here in great depth. The Name of God is indeed the *ratio* of solitude not only in the sense that "service of God" can be invoked as a plausible explanation for the solitary vocation, but in the sense that in solitude one comes face to face with God Himself, present, as the Bible everywhere suggests, "in His Name." The Name of God is the presence of God. The Name of God in the cell is God Himself *as present to the monk* and understood by the monk and understood by the monk as the whole meaning and goal of his vocation. Hence the Name of God is present in the solitude of the cell as the "Son of God" (angel) was present with the children in the fiery furnace and as the pillar of cloud was present to Moses. Two typical Biblical images here represent *all* the possible Biblical symbols for the inscrutable presence of Yahweh. The Name of God is present in the cell as in the burning bush, in which Yahweh reveals Himself as *He who is*. Hence the solitude of the hermit is *engulfed*, so to speak, in the awareness of QUI EST. This in fact becomes the true reality of the cell and of solitude, so that the monk who begins by invoking the Name of God to induce Him as it were to "come down" to the cell in answer to prayer, gradually comes to realize that the "Name" of God is in fact the heart of the cell, the soul of the solitary life, and that one has been called into solitude not just in order that the Name may be invoked in a certain place, but rather one has been called to meet the Name which is present and waiting in one's own place. It is as though the Name were waiting in the desert for me, and had been preparing this meeting from eternity and in this particular place, this solitude chosen for me. I am called not just to meditate on the Name of God but to encounter Him in that Name. Thus the Name becomes, as it were, a cell within a cell, an inner spiritual cell. When I am in the cell or its immediate environs, I should recognize that I am "where the Name of God dwells" and that living in the presence of this great Name I gradually become the one He wills me to be. Thus the life of the cell makes me at once a cell of the Name (which takes deeper and deeper root in my heart) and a dweller in the Name, as if the Name of God—God Himself—were my cell. But since God is infinite, He cannot become a "cell" except in so far as He seems to take on certain limits, in a Name which defines and distinguishes Him: as if He were present in His Name and absent elsewhere. (Yet at the same time He is in all, through all things. But it is from the vantage point of the particular solitude in which I meet and discover His Name for myself that I can understand His presence everywhere else. Thus the reason for stability in solitude is that the hermit goes wandering out of solitude in the world, the "presence" of God may remain as an abstraction which he *knows* but which he no longer experiences in all the concreteness that is demanded and that is possible when the Name is present in the cell. True of course the Name goes with me wherever I invoke him, and dwells in my heart everywhere, but this is thanks to the cell. Here we see the Name implies not only identity but WILL and LOVE. The name that overshadows the monk in the cloud of solitude is the creative and redemptive will of our Father, and this Name impregnates everything with a redemptive and loving significance, with promises of love and salvation, with invitations to compassion and intercession for all men. Thus through the Name of God the solitary comes to the knowledge of him who makes Himself present in solitude.

Above all, of course, He reveals his Name as that of JESUS, Savior, in whom and with whom I am one with all men. Thus my place as intercessor and brother is also my solitude and my cell where I find and love all men in the warm and human love of the presence of Christ, for it is the Word *Incarnate* (signified by the pillar of cloud and by the angel present in the furnace) who alone can give me full comfort in trials that are essentially human and bound up with my physical being. There is no peace and no reality in an abstract, disincarnate, gnostic solitude. St. Peter Damian insists that since the Christian hermit is hidden in Jesus Christ he is therefore most intimately present (*praesentissimus*) to all the rest of the Church. His isolation in solitude unites him more closely in love with all the rest of his brothers in the world. Hence there is every good reason for the hermit to say *Dominus vobiscum* in his office and Mass even though no one may be physically present. We can see here the implications of having the Blessed Sacrament reserved in the hermit's cell.

The mercy, the compassion, the human-hearted wise and ever faithful love of God (all these are Names in the Name) are represented in a new and surprising, but very tender form in one of the apothegms.[6] A brother asks one of the old men what he should do if in affliction and loneliness he should be left helpless with no one to whom he might explain his trouble. The answer is that God will send help "if you pray in truth" and this is illustrated by a story. At Scete a hermit was suffering in absolute isolation with no one to console or help him in any way. He got his things together in order to leave the desert. "Then divine grace appeared to him in the form of a virgin who encouraged him and said: Do not go away BUT STAY HERE WITH ME, for none of the evils you have imagined has ever happened to you. HE OBEYED AND STAYED THERE, and at this moment his heart was healed."

Here is a deep and moving insight into the reality of that Name which is also full of tenderness and which is revealed as Wisdom, Sophia, and in whose mysterious and beautiful form God is pleased to make Himself present to the sons of men (Prov. 8:31).

[6] Nau, *op. cit.*, p. 283, n. 215.

The Book of Wisdom speaks of this mysterious and intimate love of man for divine wisdom as his bride and friend whom he has preferred to everything else. "For all the gold in the world, compared with her, is but a little sand and next to her all silver counts as mud" (Wis. 7:9). "But with her friendship one becomes truly the friend of God" (Wis. 7:14). "She makes them friends of God and prophets, for God loves only those who dwell with wisdom" (Wis. 7:27–28).

This then is the true secret of the cell, a paradise in which he who is called meets, in silence, awareness and peace the consoling and healing presence of that wisdom whose beauty is "a reflection of the eternal light and a spotless mirror of the doings of God, the image of His excellence" (Wis. 7:26).

> For she is fairer than the sun
>   and surpasses every constellation of the stars.
> Compared to light, she takes precedence;
>   for that, indeed, night supplants,
>   but wickedness prevails not over Wisdom.
> Indeed, she reaches from end to end mightily
>   and governs all things well.
> Her I loved and sought after from my youth;
>   I sought to take her for my bride
>   and was enamored of her beauty.
>
>   (WIS. 7:298:2)

Feast of St. Benedict, 1966

III

FRANCISCAN EREMITISM

St. Francis' love of solitude, intimately related to his conception of a poor and wandering life, can easily be treated as so much romantic trimming, something to be admired but not imitated, like preaching to the birds. But the eremitical solitude is more than mere ornament in Franciscan spirituality. The spirit of solitary adoration, in the midst of nature and close to God, is closely related to the Franciscan concept of poverty, prayer and the apostolate. At the present moment, when there is a revival of eremitism in the monastic setting, it might be interesting to consider Franciscan hermits in their historical perspective. To do this, we have to understand the very important pre-Franciscan movement of itinerant and preaching hermits in the tenth to twelfth centuries.[1]

Traditionally, eremitism in the West was closely related to the monastic Orders. The *Rule of St. Benedict*[2] provided that after a long period of probation in the monastic community certain monks could retire into solitude for the sake of greater mortification, perfection and prayer. This solitude could be absolute or relative and the pattern of life was usually worked out by the monk himself under the guidance of his abbot. But in any case monastic eremitism at this time implied a further withdrawal from the society of men into a life entirely alone with God in contemplation. In a conception of the monastic life in which the community provided a mitigated solitude for the average man who could not go all the way into the desert, the step to eremitical solitude was considered higher because more perfectly and unequivocally "monastic" and world-denying. Many monks obtained permission to live as recluses, permanently enclosed in a cell in the monastery itself usually adjoining the Church, and at a certain period these monastic recluses formed a kind of

---

[1] G. G. Meersman, "Eremetismo e predicazione itinerante dei secoli XI e XII," in *L'Eremetismo in Occidente nei Secoli XI e XII*, Milan, 1965.

[2] *Rule of St. Benedict*, Ch. 1.

spiritual and contemplative elite. We seldom find a really developed conception of any obligation to share with others the fruits of contemplation. True, the recluse was often consulted in spiritual matters by his brethren. But he was normally not in a position to preach and no one would have expected him to do so.

In the tenth century a new movement began which was for the most part independent of monasticism. Lay people or secular clerics began to withdraw directly into solitude without passing through a period of monastic formation. Living in the woods and developing as best they could their own mode of life, they remained in rather close contact with the poor (that is, generally speaking, with their own class), with outlaws and outcasts and with the itinerants who were always numerous in the Middle Ages. Closely identified as the hermits were with the underprivileged, the oppressed and those for whom the official institutions of society showed little real concern, the nonmonastic hermitage quickly became a place of refuge for the desperately perplexed who sought guidance and hope—if not also a hiding place and physical safety. Thus the nonmonastic hermit by the very fact of his isolation from the world became open to the world in a new and special way. Since in fact preaching had been practically abandoned in the parish churches and the monks did not preach to the people but only to themselves, there was an urgent need for the Gospel message to be announced to the poor in simple language they could understand—the language of penance, conversion, salvation and love of the Savior. Consequently these lay hermits often became itinerant preachers and the movement of preaching hermits acquired a kind of charismatic aura in the eleventh century. The name of Peter the Hermit, preacher of the First Crusade, is there to remind us of this fact. Many of these hermits had their preaching mission confirmed by the Popes themselves. Others were approved by bishops. Still others just "got up and went" and their words were well received. Some of these itinerant hermits thought of going to preach to the Saracens and even attempted to do so in the hope of being martyred. When they failed they returned to their solitude and to the "martyrdom of contemplation." The picture is a familiar one: we can see that the movement of itinerant hermits of the tenth to twelfth centuries provided a background and a precedent for the eremitism of the first Franciscans.

It is true that by the thirteenth century the eremitical movement had died out or been absorbed back into monasticism. The Cistercian lay brothers of the twelfth century were largely recruited from among the kind of people who might otherwise have become itinerant hermits. The Cistercian lay brotherhood in the twelfth century had something of an eremitical as well as a distinctly "lay" character: the brother was destined by vocation to live outside the monastic enclosure if necessary, on distant farms and granges or in crofts where he might be entirely alone for long periods. The simple life of the brother was very close to that of the lay hermit, and the brothers of Cîteaux and other monastic reforms tended to replace the hermit movement.

St. Francis was, however, in the direct line of the earlier hermit tradition. The First Rule of the Friars Minor, approved orally in 1209, does not specifically legislate for hermitages, but it mentions them in passing as taken for granted.[3] "Let the brothers wherever they may be in hermitages or other places take heed not to make any place their own and maintain it against anybody else. And let whoever may approach them, whether friend or foe or thief or robber, be received kindly." Here we find not only the spirit we would expect from having read the lives and legends of St. Francis but also the authentic tradition of the earlier itinerant hermit movement which was nonmonastic and completely open to the world of the poor and the outcast. It is taken for granted that the hermit will meet with thieves and robbers and he must not place himself above them or separate himself from them but must show himself to be their brother. The hermit is not just the man who, like St. Arsenius, has fled entirely from men. He is not just the man of deep contemplative recollection: he is the vulnerable, open and loving

---

[3] *First Rule of St. Francis*, 7.

brother of everyone, like Charles de Foucauld in our own time. He is a "Little Brother of the Poor."

The special statute or instruction composed by St. Francis for those retiring to hermitages is well known.[4] A hermitage is in fact a small community of three or four brothers, some living entirely in silence and contemplative solitude with others who take care of their needs as their "mothers." These also see that their "children" are not disturbed by outsiders. But the contemplatives should also from time to time take over the active duties and give their "mothers" a rest. It is a charming document which, however, does not give a very detailed picture of the life these hermits led.

The importance of the document lies in the spirit which it exhales—a spirit of simplicity and charity which pervades even the life of solitary contemplation. It has been noted that the genius of sanctity is notable for the way in which it easily reconciles what seems at first sight irreconcilable. Here St. Francis has completely reconciled the life of solitary prayer with warm and open fraternal love. Instead of detailing the austerities and penances which the hermits must perform, the hours they must devote to prayer and so on, the saint simply communicates the atmosphere of love which is to form the ideal climate of prayer in the hermitage. The spirit of the eremitical life as seen by St. Francis is therefore cleansed of any taint of selfishness and individualism. Solitude is surrounded by fraternal care and is therefore solidly established in the life of the Order and of the Church. It is not an individualistic exploit in which the hermit by the power of his own asceticism gains a right to isolation from an elevation above others. On the contrary, the hermit is reminded above all that he is dependent on the charity and the good will of others. This is certainly another and very effective way of guaranteeing the sincerity of the hermit life of prayer since it shows him how much we owe it to others to become a true man of God.

Meanwhile, we shall presently see that Franciscan eremit-

---

[4] See *Mirror of Perfection*, 65, quoted in *The Words of St. Francis*, an anthology compiled and arranged by James Meyer, O.F.M., Chicago, 1952, pp. 111–113.

ism had another aspect: it was open to the world and oriented to the apostolic life.

St. Francis founded at least twenty mountain hermitages and there is no need to remind the reader what outstanding importance his own solitary retreat at Mount Alverna played in his life. He received the stigmata there in 1224. Franciscan mysticism is centered upon this solitary vision of the Crucified and the love generated in this solitude is poured out on the world in preaching.

Blessed Giles of Assisi was essentially an itinerant hermit. On his return from the Holy Land in 1215 he was assigned in obedience to a hermitage by St. Francis. In 1219 he went to Tunis vainly seeking martyrdom. From 1219 to about 1225 he lived at the Carceri in a small chapel surrounded by other caves. It is interesting that the Carceri which had once been used by Benedictine hermits became after Mount Alverna the symbol of Franciscan solitude. It is thought that St. Francis wrote part of the Rule there. The mysticism of Blessed Giles developed in the hermitage of Cetona, and he also founded other hermitages himself.[5] With Blessed Giles we also find another emphasis. The hermitage is the stronghold of the pure Franciscan spirit, the primitive ideal of the Holy Founder, threatened by others too preoccupied, as some thought, with power and prestige. In the struggle to preserve the primitive spirit of poverty and utter Franciscan simplicity, the hermitages played the part that may be imagined. It is interesting, incidentally, that when St. Bonaventure was made Cardinal he received the news while he was washing dishes in a hermitage.

It is not hard to understand that in periods of reform the ideal of solitude has had an important part to play in renewal of the Franciscan life and apostolate. This is especially clear when we study St. Leonard of Port Maurice and the Franciscan revival in Italy in the eighteenth century. St. Leonard himself got his vocation while listening to the friars chant compline in the *Ritiro* on the Palatine, and his promo-

5 For Blessed Giles see Raphael Brown, *Franciscan Mystic, Giles of Assisi*, New York, 1961.

tion of the *Ritiro* movement is both characteristic and important in his life as a reformer.

The *Ritiro* movement[6] went back perhaps to the sixteenth century. In addition to hermitages, which always existed and provided solitude for Friars desiring a life of more intense prayer, especially fervent communities were formed to serve as models of observance. A *Ritiro* must not in fact be confused with a hermitage. It was simply a community of picked volunteers who elected to live the Rule in its perfection with special emphasis on poverty, cloister, prayer and all that could enhance the contemplative and ascetic side of the Franciscan life. However, the *Ritiri* were not unconnected with the eremitical strain in the Order, and the first *Ritiro* founded by B. Bonaventure of Barcelona had developed out of a hermitage.

St. Leonard of Port Maurice began by reforming a *Ritiro* (even a *Ritiro* could eventually need to be reformed!) when he became Guardian of San Francesco al Monte in Florence. His emphasis here was not specifically on solitude and contemplation, but simply on the exact observance of the rules. The *Ritiri* were not originally centers of eremitical life: they were meant to be houses of model regularity and fervor. To promote greater solitude, St. Leonard of Port Maurice created the *Solitudine*.[7] The purpose of this more frankly eremitical type of community was the life of pure contemplation.

St. Leonard described his purpose in these words: "By complete separation from the world to become able to give oneself to pure contemplation and then after the acquisition of greater fervor to return into the communities to apply oneself more avidly to the salvation of one's neighbor."[8]

As always, in the Franciscan tradition, the idea of solitude is not self-sufficient. Solitude opens out to the world and bears fruit in preaching.

[6] Angelo Cresi, O.F.M., "S. Leonardo di Porto Maurizio ed i conventi di Ritiro," *Studi Francescani,* XLIX (1952), 154 ff.

[7] Angelo Cresi, O.F.M., "S. Leonardo di Porto Maurizio e l'Incontro," *Studi Francescani,* XLIX (1952), 176 ff.

[8] *Ibid.,* p. 168.

The character of the *Solitudine* instituted by St. Leonard is that of the reforms of that time. The strictness and austerity remind one of De Rancé and La Trappe. The cells were so small that when standing in the middle one could touch the ceiling and the two sides. The discipline was taken daily in common for half an hour. Fasting continued all the year round. Perpetual silence was observed, the Friars went barefoot. There were small hermitages attached to the convent, and to these one might retire for greater solitude and more prayer.

This rigorous and solitary life was not intended to be permanent. Most of the five retreatants in the community were men who were there for two months only. However, Friars could remain in the *Solitudine* for longer periods and even for years. Besides the retreatants, there was a Superior (*Presidente*) with a gatekeeper and a cook (the latter a Tertiary). There were also cells for religious of other Orders who might want to come there to renew their fervor.

There is an obvious resemblance between the *Solitudine* and the Carmelite "Desert." It is a place of temporary eremitical retreat to which one withdraws in order to renew the spirit of prayer and fervor and from which one returns to the work of preaching with a more perfect charity and a message of more convincing hope. The emphasis is on the fact that in solitary prayer and meditation one gets deeper into the root of things, comes to see himself more clearly as he is in the eyes of God, realizes more perfectly the real nature of his need for grace and for the Holy Spirit and comes to a more ardent love of Jesus Crucified. With all this one is normally opened to the world of other men and made ready for the more complete gift of himself to the work of saving souls.

However, both the *Ritiri* and the *Solitudine* came under very heavy criticism. First, they seemed to create a division within the Order. Second, it could be asked whether their spirit was too formal and rigorous to be called authentically Franciscan. It is certainly true that the rather forbidding austerity of the *Solitudine* might be considered a little alien to the primitive Franciscan spirit of simplicity and evangelical freedom. The severe regulations contrast with the warm and tender spirit of St. Francis' statute for hermits. But the solitary convents evidently had the effect that St. Leonard desired, and the preaching of the Saint when he emerged from his solitude was said to be characterized by a great tenderness which instead of frightening sinners, encouraged and strengthened them.

This very brief outline suggests a few conclusions. The eremitical spirit has always had a place in the Franciscan life, but it is not the spirit of monasticism or of total, definitive separation from the world. The eremitism of St. Francis and his followers is deeply evangelical and remains always open to the world, while recognizing the need to maintain a certain distance and perspective, a freedom that keeps one from being submerged in active cares and devoured by the claims of exhausting work.

In all forms of the religious life we are asking ourselves, today, whether the accepted methods of renewing our fervor are quite adequate to present-day needs. Certainly the prescribed eight-day retreat has its value. But the new generation is asking itself seriously whether this rather formalistic exercise really produces any lasting fruit. Is it simply a tightening of nuts and bolts on machinery which is obsolete? Modern religious who feel the need of silence generally seek it not merely for the purpose of self-scrutiny and ascetic castigation, but in order to recuperate spiritual powers which may have been gravely damaged by the noise and rush of a pressurized existence. This silence is not necessarily tight-lipped and absolute—the silence of men pacing the garden with puckered brows ignoring each other—but the tranquillity of necessary leisure in which religious can relax in the peace of a friendly and restful solitude and once again become themselves. Today more than ever we need to recognize that the gift of solitude is not ordered to the acquisition of strange contemplative powers, but first of all to the recovery of one's deep self, and to the renewal of an authenticity which is twisted out of shape by the pretentious routines of a disordered togetherness. What the world asks of the priest today is that he should be first of all a *person* who can give himself because he has a self to give. And indeed, we cannot give Christ if we have not found him, and we cannot find him if we cannot find ourselves.

These considerations might be useful to those whose imaginations and hopes are still able to be stirred by the thought of solitude, and of its important place in every form of the religious and apostolic life, in every age, especially our own.

THE SPIRITUAL FATHER
IN THE DESERT TRADITION

The place of the "Director of Conscience" or "Spiritual Director" in modern Catholic practice since the Council of Trent need not be treated here in detail, but it must at least be mentioned as the term of a long evolution of which we wish to discuss the beginning.[1] The "Director of Conscience" as his title suggests is usually a confessor and also by implication a "specialist" with an appropriate theological and spiritual training. If he is called a "Director of *Conscience*" this suggests that he is adept in settling *casus conscientiae*, or special cases and problems, for which he provides professional solutions. But this imposes rather unfortunate juridical limitations upon the traditional concept. The term "Spiritual Director" is broader, and suggests one who, by virtue of his learning and experience, is equipped to help others make progress in the spiritual life. Ideally speaking, the "spiritual director" will help others to reach the heights of spiritual and mystical perfection. In the lives of Saints since the Middle Ages, for instance St. Teresa of Avila,[2] the importance of the spiritual director is sufficiently underlined. His influence may be positive or negative. He may prove to be a great obstacle to progress, or he may remove obstacles and help one to attain to the liberty of spirit which is necessary in order to obey the mysterious action of the Holy Spirit and attain to union with God. But in any case the director, if not essential

[1] For an excellent survey of the whole history of spiritual direction in the Christian context see the article "Direction Spirituelle" in the *Dictionnaire de Spiritualité*, Vol. III, cols. 1002–1214.

[2] See the *Life*, St. Teresa's autobiography, where for instance in C. 28 she speaks of the great help she received from Fr. Balthasar Alvarez. In her *Interior Castle*, VI Mansion, she speaks of the injury done to mystics, during their time of purifying trial, by bad directors, and how the fears and scruples of confessors can add to the suffering of one who is already disconcerted by inexplicable experiences.

for the spiritual life, is considered in practice to have had a decisive part to play in the lives of saints and mystics, with a few notable exceptions. St. Francis de Sales may be taken as the typical saintly "director," who by his prudence, learning, experience, good sense and intuitive understanding of others, helped many to find their spiritual path, leading them safely to high contemplation and mystical union. Such directors have clearly exercised a providential function in the lives not only of individuals but also of religious congregations and of certain social milieux, indeed of the Church herself.

However, it is not of these modern directors that we are writing here. Rather we wish to return to the *archetypal* figure of the "spiritual Father" as depicted in the literature of early monasticism, that is to say, the monasticism of Egypt, Palestine and Syria in the fourth and fifth centuries. Particularly valuable as source material are the *Apophthegmata* or sayings of the Desert Fathers.[3] Even though these are "typical" stories of figures that have become quasi-legendary, we need not question the fact that they represent an authentic spirit and indeed a historical attitude, a view of life that was so profound and so real that it exercised a permanent influence on centuries of Christian spirituality.

The Abba or spiritual Father was first of all one who by long experience in the desert and in solitude had learned the secrets of desert life. He was, by reason of his holiness, endowed with charismatic gifts which enabled him to detect and dispel the illusions that would inevitably tempt the beginner—or even the experienced monk who had not yet attained to the full maturity and perfection of the monastic life. But the function implied by the name "Father" is not fully accounted for in spiritual advice and instruction. The spiritual Father exercised a genuine "paternity"—in the name of God—engendering the life of the Spirit in the disciple. Of course, this

[3] The *Apophthegmata* are to be found in Migne's Greek Patrology, Vol. 65, and many of the same stories are reproduced in the *Verba Seniorum* in the Latin Patrology, Vol. 73, col. 739 ff. For the sake of convenience the excellent English version of E. Wallis Budge, in the *Paradise of the Fathers* (from Syriac) 2 vols. (London, 1907), will be used here.

concept must not be exaggerated (as it has sometimes been in later monastic circles, for instance in Byzantine cenobitism). The only source of the spiritual life is the Holy Spirit. The spiritual life does not come from men. The Holy Spirit is given in Baptism. However, as we know too well, the seeds of the spiritual life planted in Baptism too often remain dormant or die altogether. The Abba or "spiritual Father" was one who was recognized as a charismatic and "lifegiving" influence, under whose care these mysterious seeds would truly grow and flourish. The Fathers attracted disciples who came not only for lectures and counsel, but seeking *life* and *growth* in a special relationship of filial love and devotion—indeed, in later times, of actual veneration.

The sayings of the Fathers show us in simple, often naive terms, the archetypal life-giving charismata of these quiet, humble, often very humorous, always human figures. To such experienced and spiritually gifted *seniores* or "elders," even though they might not be priests, the young would spontaneously direct themselves with their questions, asking for those "words of salvation" that would awaken new life and growth in their hearts.

In the *Apophthegmata* we are concerned chiefly with the desert hermits, rather than with the cenobites. In fact the distinction is important, for though the heads of cenobitic communities, like St. Pachomius and Theodore, were also spiritual Fathers with great experience and wisdom, the large cenobitic communities tended to receive their guidance first of all by a Rule and observances which doubtless implemented a spiritual doctrine, but which were by their nature general rather than personal. The *Apophthegmata* on the other hand represent the direct and personal answers to the question of individuals. The "word" becomes, in each case, endowed with a general validity for "everyone" in the same or in analogous circumstances. Among the hermits these individual directives tended to take the place of general written rules: or rather they were intended to help the monk discover his own rule of life, or God's will *for him* in particular.

In order to understand these directives, we must first understand the objective of the solitary in the desert. It would be an oversimplification to say that the Egyptian and Syrian hermits went into the desert "to find solitude and lead the contemplative life." It is true that many of them were Greeks, or had a Greek outlook on life (acquired in Constantinople, Rome or Alexandria) and for these the search for a primarily intellectual intuition of God was the most important thing about desert life. This particular tradition is represented in the writings of Evagrius Ponticus[4] and was doubtless prevalent at Nitria and Scete. But the term contemplation, *theoria*, is not prominent in the *Apophthegmata* or other popular stories of the Fathers, though we read of them "seeing the glory of God" or having prophetic visions. There is, then, another term which is at once simpler, more profound and more general, and which embraces all the different modes of desert spirituality—whether the intellectual or the volitional, the Platonic or the Biblical: that term is "tranquillity," in Greek *hesychia* and in Latin *quies*. This repose is essentially "contemplative" if you like, but it is more: in its deepest meaning it implies perfect sonship of God, union with God by a complete renunciation of self, and total surrender to the word and will of God in faith and love. This is exemplified in a classic anecdote about the vocation of the desert father St. Arsenius.

When Abba Arsenius was in the palace, he prayed to God and said, "O Lord, direct me how to live" and a voice came to him, saying, "Arsenius, flee from men and thou shall live." And when Arsenius was living the ascetic life in the monastery, he prayed to God the same prayer, and again he heard a voice saying to him, "Arsenius, flee, keep silence and lead a life of silent contemplation, for these are the fundamental causes which prevent a man from committing sin."[5]

The *fuge, tace, quiesce* of Arsenius became a classical trope of the contemplative life. The "flight" was of course

---

[4] The most characteristic work of Evagrius—as well as the most influential—is his treatise on prayer, *De Oratione*, long ascribed to St. Nilus, and available in a French translation by Père I. Hausherr, S.J.

[5] *Paradise of the Fathers*, II, 3. This saying is the first in the entire series and thus acquires a certain importance as a paradigm for the whole monastic ascesis.

from the monastery into complete desert solitude as a hermit. The silence is self-explanatory, and the *quies* as we have said above is the real goal of the solitary life: the rest and "purity of heart" which comes from complete liberation from worldly care, from the concerns of a life devoted to the assertion of a social ego and from the illusions consequent upon such a life. John Cassian, in his first conference, defining the whole purpose of the monastic life, brings together three things which he identifies with monastic perfection. These three are simply aspects of the same spiritual reality. Perfection does *not* consist merely in solitude, asceticism, prayer, or other practices. All these may be sought for basically selfish motives, and they may in the end be simply more subtle and more stubborn ways of affirming one's own ego. True perfection is found only when one renounces the "self" that seems to be the subject of perfection, and that "has" or "possesses" perfection. For Cassian this perfection is "charity . . . which consists in purity of heart alone" and which he identifies with *quies,* since it consists in "always offering to God a perfect and most pure heart, and in keeping that heart untouched by all perturbations."[6] Behind this formula we must recognize the doctrine of Evagrius, for whom the monastic life was a purification first from all passionate desires, then from all disturbing thoughts, then finally from all conceptualization, leading thus to the attainment of *theologia.* The highest "rest" is in direct intuition of the Trinity. If the Greek tradition gave this *quies* some sophisticated and intellectual implications which the simple Coptic hermits never knew, the fact remains that all sought this tranquillity and liberty of spirit in one form or other and all identified it with love of God. In all the different traditions—Greek, Coptic, Palestinian and Syriac—we find a common agreement in this:

---

[6] Cassian, *Collatio* I. 6. Migne P.L. 49: 488. Cf. St. Peter Damian: "As the proper office of the priest is to apply himself completely to offer sacrifice, and the doctor's function is to preach, so no less is the hermit's office to rest in fasting and silence—*in jejunio silentioque quiescere.*" Opus xv. 5. P.L. 145: 339.

Dom J. Leclercq, O.S.B., has developed the theme of *quies* in *Otia Monastica,* Studia Anselmiana, Rome, 1963.

that in the desert the monk renounces his own illusory ego-self, he "dies" to his worldly and empirical existence, in order to surrender completely to the transcendent reality which, though described in various terms, is always best expressed in the simple Biblical expression: "the will of God." In his surrender of himself and of his own will, his "death" to his worldly identity, the monk is renewed in the image and like-ness of God, and becomes like a mirror filled with the divine light.

This doctrine of man finding his true reality in his remem-brance of God in whose image he was created, is basically Biblical and was developed by the Church Fathers in con-nection with the theology of grace, the sacraments, and the indwelling of the Holy Spirit. In fact, the surrender of our own will, the "death" of our selfish ego, in order to live in pure love and liberty of spirit, is effected not by our own will (this would be a contradiction in terms!) but by the Holy Spirit. To "recover the divine likeness," to "surrender to the will of God," to "live by pure love," and thus to find peace, is summed up as "union with God in the Spirit," or "receiv-ing, possessing the Holy Spirit." This, as the 19th-century Russian hermit St. Seraphim of Sarov declared, is the whole purpose of the Christian (therefore *a fortiori* the monastic) life. St. John Chrysostom says: "As polished silver illumined by the rays of the sun radiates light not only from its own nature but also from the radiance of the sun, so a soul puri-fied by the Divine Spirit becomes more brilliant than silver; it both receives the ray of Divine Glory and from itself reflects the ray of this same glory."[7] Our true rest, love, purity, vision and *quies* is not something in ourselves, it is God the Divine Spirit. Thus we do not "possess" rest, but go out of our-selves into him who is our true rest.

In the Coptic life of St. Pachomius we read a touching episode in which Pachomius, not yet founder of his commu-nity, but living as a hermit with his brother, is praying to know the "will of God." He and his brother are living in

_____
[7] Serm. VII on II Epist. to Corinthians. Quoted by Callistus and Ignatius in *Writings from the Philokalia on Prayer of the Heart*, edited by Kadlubovsky and Palmer, London, 1951, p. 166.

an abandoned village, Tabbenese, and they are occupied in harvesting for neighboring farmers, thus earning their bread. One night, after their common prayers, Pachomius goes apart and "he was desolate and broken hearted about the will of God which he desired to learn." A luminous personage appears before him and asks, "Why are you desolate and broken hearted?" "Because I seek the will of God," Pachomius replies. The personage tells him: "It is the will of God that you serve the human race, in order to reconcile it with him." Pachomius is at first shocked: "I ask about the will of God and you tell me to serve men?" The personage repeats three times: "It is God's will that you serve men in order to bring them to him."[8]

The story is interesing from many points of view. First of all it contrasts in some respects with the *fuge, tace, quiesce* of Arsenius. The spirituality of the Pachomian communities was more active than contemplative, and in any case Pachomius is here being called to the task of being a Father and Founder of cenobitism. It is characteristic of St. Pachomius's thought that in the cenobitic life the monk is brought to perfection not so much by an isolated ascetic struggle directed by an enlightened spiritual master, as by participation in the life of the holy community, the brotherhood of those gathered together "in the spirit." Pachomius is said by his disciple Theodore to have declared: "This Congregation . . . is the model for all those who wish to gather together souls according to God, in order to help them until they become perfect."[9]

But in the Pachomian system too the goal is peace, *quies,* the spiritual security that comes from complete detachment and self-renunciation. The Abba regulates the life and work of the monks in the way that seems to him best for their spiritual advancement and they in turn, trusting completely in him as God's instrument, find peace in following his regulations.[10]

[8] L. Th. Lefort, *Les Vies Coptes de Saint Pachôme,* Louvain, 1943, pp. 60, 61.

[9] Lefort, *op. cit., Avant Propos,* p. 1.

[10] Lefort, *op. cit.,* p. 74.

Meanwhile, however, we find Pachomius himself seeking peace, tranquillity and *quies* in the clear perception of and surrender to God's will. What is important for us in the story we have quoted is the fact that in "desolation and with a broken heart" Pachomius is seeking the *ultimate meaning of his life*. This is characteristic of all the Desert monks. They have come out into the desert tormented by a need to know the inner meaning of their own existence, which to them has lost all significance and purpose in the cities of men. And though the individual answers may take different and even contradictory forms, yet they all have this one thing in common: all authentic answers come from God and are the expression of his will, manifested in his word, and when one receives and obeys this word one has peace, *quies*. These answers are not easily come by. One must seek them in repentance, suffering and patience, for no one can demand an answer as by right, and each one must be prepared to accept an answer that may be in many ways disconcerting. The suffering and solitude of the desert life are, in the eyes of the Egyptian monks, the price that has to be paid for such an ultimate solution to the question of existence. The price is not too high.

Meanwhile, though the stories may tell us that some of the pioneers like Arsenius, Pachomius, Anthony, received their answers by interior inspiration or from "luminous personages," the other Desert Fathers had to be content with a more prosaic and ultimately more secure source of information: they had to ask other monks who had found their answer. They had to approach a "spiritual Father."

Anecdotes about the Desert Fathers are more often than not direct and succinct reports of spiritual consultations; and the "sayings" (*Apophthegmata*) of the Fathers are generally solutions of problems or difficulties. These may have been presented by a disciple living in the same cell as the Master or in a neighboring cell, in order to be taught and formed by him; or they may be posed by a stranger who has travelled a long distance with the precise purpose of getting this answer from a famous Abba. Sometimes the questions are general and fundamental, involving what we would call today a vo-

cational decision, changing the entire course of the questioner's life. In the terminology of the "sayings" such questions
are formulated: "What ought I to do?" "Speak to me
a word" (i.e. "a word of salvation," manifesting the will of
God and thereby showing the way to the goal of my existence). The answer to such a question is a programme of life
in the desert, or, if you like, a "Rule" expressed in three or
four words appropriate to the needs of the one asking. In
each case, the reply of the Master is intended to meet the
personal need of the inquirer, but it is also a fundamental
statement about the monastic life.

One of the best examples of this kind of statement is found
in the Coptic life of St. Pachomius. It is the story of Pachomius's first encounter with the hermit Abba Palemon, his
request to become the old man's disciple, and Abba Palemon's
reply.[11]

Pachomius knocks at the cell door. The old man cries out
rudely, "Why are you knocking?" The youth says, "Father,
I desire you to let me be a monk with you."

The old man then launches on a sobering, if not discourag-
ing, account of the solitary vocation: "Many have come here
for that very purpose and were not able to stand it; they
turned back shamefully. . . ." Nevertheless, he briefly ex-
poses the purpose of the monastic life ("Scripture orders us
to pray and fast in order that we may be saved"), and the
actual Rule that is followed by the monks. "The Rule of monasticism, as we have been taught by our predecessors, is as
follows: at all times we spend half the night—and often from
evening to morning—in vigils, reciting the words of God, and
doing much manual work, with thread, hair or palm-fibre,
so as not to be importuned by sleep and to provide for our
bodily needs; whatever remains over and above what we
need, we give to the poor." He continues with details about
the fasting and prayers, and concludes: "Now that I have
taught you the law of monasticism, go and examine yourself
on all these points. See if you are capable of doing what I
have said. . . ." He also says, "go to your own house, stay

[11] Lefort, Les Vies Coptes, pp. 84–85.

there and hold fast to what you have received. See . . . if you are capable of enduring."

This passage is a paradigm for monastic formation and the deciding of vocations.[12]

Other simpler examples:

A cenobite comes to the hermit Abba Bessarion and asks advice about how to live in his community: "The old man said unto him, 'Keep silence and consider thyself to be nothing.' "[13]

"A brother asked Abba Muthues saying: 'Speak a word to me'; and the old man replied, 'Cut off from thee contention concerning every matter whatsoever, and weep and mourn, for the time hath come.' "[14]

This "compunction," and the eschatological perspective which saw all things in the light of their end, was sufficient to revolutionize a man's whole outlook on himself and on life.

Notice that in these two examples, chosen at random, emphasis is laid on being at peace with others, "not contending" with them, even in thought. This is a very common theme in the sayings of the Fathers. Retirement into solitude is of no use if the hermit is to live alone with aggressive and hostile fantasies. A prerequisite for this tranquillity (*quies*) of the true solitary is the renunciation of all judgements, all criticisms of others and all interior argumentation. Living in the presence of the divine judge of all was the beginner's way to reduce all these things to their true dimensions.

Sometimes the question concerns a particular problem in the ascetic life. The solution given constitutes a principle which has a certain importance in analogous cases.

A brother to Abba Poemen: "My body is weak and I am not able to perform ascetic labours; speak to me a word whereby I may live." And the old man said unto him: "Art thou able to rule thy thought and not to permit it to go to thy neighbour in guile?"[15]

[12] See *Rule of St. Benedict*, chapter 58.
[13] *Paradise*, II, 13.
[14] *Ibid.*, p. 32.
[15] *Ibid.*, p. 83.

A brother asked the same Abbot Poemen:

"What shall I do, for I am troubled when I am sitting in my cell?" The old man said unto him, "Think lightly of no man; think no evil in thy heart; condemn no man and curse no man; then shall God give thee rest, and thy habitation shall be without trouble."[16]

There are some sayings in which the Master is, so to speak, certifying that the disciple has reached a certain state of perfection and that he is now able, with spiritual freedom, to go forth and help others. Thus Theodore, himself an "old man" and therefore experienced,

asked Abba Pambo saying, "Tell me a word." And with much labour he said to him, "Theodore, get thee gone and let thy mercy be poured out on every man, for thy loving-kindness hath found freedom of speech before God."[17]

An answer of an anonymous Abba covers the whole field of monastic asceticism, according to his view of it:

In my opinion the work of the soul is as follows: to live in silence, persistent endurance, self denial, labour, humility of body, and constant prayer. And a man should not consider the shortcomings of men, but his own lapses; if now a man will persist in these things the soul will after no great time make manifest the fruits of spiritual excellence.[18]

If the Fathers answered different questioners to their needs, it followed that sometimes they solved the same problem in different ways or gave seemingly contradictory answers to identical questions. Once Abba Joseph was reproached with this. When asked how to deal with tempting thoughts, he told one monk to resist them forcefully and thrust out, and another to pay no attention to them. It was this second who complained of the contradiction. The answer of the Abba was: "I spoke to *you* as I would have spoken to myself"[19]— in other words he knew that his questioner was experienced, and that forceful resistance was not necessary as the tempt-

---

[16] *Ibid.*
[17] *Ibid.*, p. 97.
[18] *Ibid.*, p. 199.
[19] *Ibid.*, p. 198.

ing thoughts made no real appeal to his will, while direct resistance would only cause him to be unnecessarily concerned with them, devoting his attention to them when it would be better occupied elsewhere.

This purpose is well stated in a Syrian work of the 5th or 6th century, outside the context of Egyptian monasticism, and more speculative than the practical "sayings" of the Fathers. Yet the gist of it is much the same.

A disciple asks the question: "What is the beginning of the conduct of the interior man?"

Master:

Renunciation of the love of money. After renunciation of the love of money, it is necessarily required of him that he strip himself of the love of praise. Then after that it is possible for him to be in the virtue of understanding: in humility and in patience, in quietude and lucidity of spirit, in the joy of his hope, in the vigilance of noble concerns, in the perfect love of God and of men: by these things he will come to purity of soul which is the crowning of all the conduct God has enjoined upon man to attain in this life.[20]

This fact will help us to understand the various statements of principle which are made by the Fathers: all must be understood in the light of concrete situations. At one moment stern asceticism is declared essential, at another non-essential. Everything depends on the concrete case. In a word, the sayings of the Fathers are not to be taken as hard and fast rules which apply in the same way in every situation: they are applications of broad general principles, which we have already considered. The most fundamental of them is stated clearly in the first Conference of Cassian: every practice, every decision, every change in one's mode of life is to be judged in terms of the purpose of the solitary life. That purpose is purity of heart, perfect charity, and *quies,* or the tranquillity of the selfless and detached spirit.

The worth and meaning of every ascetic practice is to be estimated in terms of quietude, lucidity of spirit, love, and

[20] John the Solitary, *Dialogue sur l'Ame et les Passions,* trans. by I. Hausherr, S.J., Orientalia Christiana Analecta, 120, Rome, 1939, pp. 31–32.

purity of heart. Anything that does not lead to these is worthless, for instead of liberating us from self-preoccupation, it only reinforces our illusory and obsessive concern with our own ego and its victory over the "not-I." True quietude and purity of heart are impossible where this division of the "I" (considered as right and good) and the "not-I" (considered as threatening) governs our conduct and our decisions.

When one has been liberated from this obsession with self, says the same text, one attains to *integrity,* to the "conduct of the new man." This is the "beginning" of the true life, the life of the interior or spiritual man who lives entirely as a son of God and not as a slave.

Is there one principle above all which can be said to cover almost every case, a basic norm of the solitary life? Yes, there is one. Its observance is practically synonymous with *quies* because it is the essential condition for tranquillity. It is the key principle of the solitary life and is sometimes stated with such finality that it even seems to dispense with further advice. Here is a classic statement of it:

A certain brother went to Abba Moses in Scete, and asked him to speak a word; and the old man said, *"Get thee gone, and sit in thy cell, and thy cell shall teach thee all things."*[21]

This saying has obvious implications for the practice of spiritual direction. As stated here, it clearly implies that there is no use in the monk leaving his cell and running about asking advice, if he is not first prepared to *face his own solitude in all its naked reality*.

Though we cannot go into all the depth of this idea at present, let us at least say this much: it is in solitude that the monk most completely comes to discover the true inner dimensions of his own being, at once "real" and "unreal." The conviction of one's "self" as a static, absolute and invariable reality undergoes a profound transformation and dissolves in the burning light of an altogether new and unsuspected awareness. In this awareness we see that our "reality" is not a firmly established ego-self already attained

[21] Paradise, II, 16.

that merely has to be perfected, but rather that we are a "nothing," a "possibility" in which the gift of creative freedom can realize itself by its response to the free gift of love and grace. This response means accepting our loneliness and our "potentiality" as a gift and a commission, as a *trust* to be used—as a "talent," in the language of the parables. Our existence is then at once terrible and precious because radically it belongs not to us but to God. Yet it will not be fully "His" unless we freely make it "ours" and then offer it to Him in praise. This is what Christian tradition means by "obedience to the Word of God." The monk must learn this for himself.

Of course he needs the assistance of others but he cannot be helped by others if he is not first determined to help himself. Others will be of little use as mediators between himself and God if he does not have enough faith to give first place to prayer and solitude in his own eremitical life. In other words, it is the solitude of the cell itself that teaches one how to face illusion, how to resist temptation, how to pray. All other advice and direction is first of all contingent upon the young hermit's willingness to accept this basic principle. One might say that all other advice assumes that one is ready and willing to sustain the purifying silence and loneliness of the cell, in which one is stripped of his illusory image of himself and forced to come to terms with the nothingness, the limitation, the infidelity, the defectibility, or as we might say today the "void" of his own life.

St. Anthony, who knew better than anyone the meaning of this solitary combat with thoughts ("demons"),[22] said that life in the cell was at times like being in a fiery furnace. Yet in that furnace one came face to face with God. The saying recalls that of a modern monk of Mount Athos, Staretz Silouan, who lived "as though in hell" but did not despair.[23]

[22] In all spiritual traditions there is recognized a stage in which thoughts and desires, whether good or bad, are projected and objectified as external beings or persons. This stage has to be transcended, but the experiences that belong to it have to be taken into account even if "illusory." The question of the metaphysical reality of angels or demons is another matter.

[23] See *The Undistorted Image* by Archmandrite Sophrony, London, 1962.

Anthony left us a most important saying, with deep implications about the mystical life (of which little is said explicitly in the *Apophthegmata*): "The cell of the monk is the furnace of Babylon wherein the three children found the Son of God, and it is also the pillar of cloud wherefrom God spoke with Moses."[24]

The monk who faces this fire and darkness will not be able to continue in the cell at all unless he lives as a man of faith and prayer. A monastic saying has it that when you do not live worthily in your cell, the cell of its own accord vomits you out. This accounts, perhaps, for the fact that the Desert Fathers were not carried away with enthusiasm over the specious zeal to convert others which often presented itself as an honorable evasion from the solitude of the cell and from the *acedia* caused by the "noonday demon."[25]

A young monk, tormented by this kind of problem, confesses to Abba Arsenius:

My thoughts vex me and say: "thou canst not fast; and thou art not able to labour; therefore visit the sick which is a great commandment." Then Abba Arsenius, after the manner of one who was well acquainted with the war of devils said to him: "Eat, drink and sleep and toil not but on no account go out of thy cell," for the old man knew that dwelling constantly in the cell induceth all the habits of the solitary life.[26]

The rest of this charming story tells how the young monk, remaining in the cell, gradually found himself working and praying more and more steadily and finally won the ascetic battle—the great battle of the solitary—against all his "thoughts." (That is to say he found *quies* by resolving the division caused in himself by useless interior activity and self-projection into words and ideas which were obstacles between himself and his life.)

Another old man discussed the problem of wandering thoughts in the following terms:

[24] Paradise, II, 14, for the pillar of cloud as a mystical symbol. See St. Gregory of Nyssa, *De Vita Moysis*, French trans. by J. Daniélou, S.J., *Sources Chrétiennes,* 2nd edition, Paris, 1955.

[25] See Cassian, *De Cenobiorum Institutis*, Lib. X, P.L. 49, vol. 359 ff.

[26] Paradise, II, 4.

The matter is like unto that of a she-ass which hath a sucking foal. If she be tied up, however much the foal may gambol about or wander hither and thither, he will come back to her eventually, either because he is hungry or because of other reasons which drive him to her; but if it happen that his mother be also roaming about loose, both animals will go to destruction. And thus is it in the matter of the monk. If the body remain continually in its cell the mind thereof will certainly come back to it after all its wanderings, for many reasons which will come upon it, but if the body as well as the soul wander outside the cell both will become a prey and a thing of joy to the enemy.[27]

If the Fathers place so much emphasis on staying in the cell, this does not mean that there are no other rules to follow and that the beginner, provided he stays out of sight, can do anything he pleases. "Become not a lawgiver to thyself," said one of the elders.[28] Another saying of monastic tradition is, "those who are not under the law of the governors shall fall like leaves."[29] The reason for this is not only that the beginner is inexperienced and needs to be instructed and helped. Everywhere in the sayings of the Fathers we find men who are themselves experienced and yet follow the guidance of others, not trusting their own judgement. Though the solitary must certainly develop a certain ability to take care of himself, this does not mean that he trusts in his own strength or in his own ideas. His search in the desert is not merely for solitude in which he can simply do as he pleases and admire himself as a great contemplative. There would be no real *quies* in such an exploit, or if there were peace, it would be the false peace of self-assurance and self-complacency.

Hence we have another story which qualifies the saying: "Stay in thy cell and it shall teach thee all things." One must be in the cell for the right reasons.

[27] *Ibid.*, p. 12. Here we see that the importance of "staying in the cell" is analogous to the emphasis on *Zazen* (sitting in meditation) in Zen Buddhism. Dom J. Leclercq has an important essay, "Sedere" (sitting) in the volume *Le Millenaire du Mont Athos*, Chevetogne, 1963.

[28] *Ibid.*, p. 161.

[29] Palladius, *Historia Lausiaca* 24. Paradise, I, 136.

A certain brother had recently received the garb of a monk and he went and shut himself up in a cell and said, "I am a desert monk." And when the Fathers heard this, they came and took him out of his place and made him to go about the cells of the brethren and to make apologies to them saying, "I am not a desert monk, and I have only just begun to be a disciple."[30]

The monk does not come into the desert to reinforce his own ego-image, but to be delivered from it. After all, this worship of the self is the last and most difficult of idolatries to detect and get rid of. The monk knows this, and therefore he determines to take the proper means to destroy instead of reinforcing the image. For this purpose he renounces his own will in order to be taught and guided by another, even though he may live alone. Still he consults a spiritual Father and as we have seen above in the story of Abbot Theodore, he may be an old man himself before he is told, by the spiritual Father that he can now go out on his own because he has obtained the freedom and confidence not of the self-opinionated proud man who believes in his own ascetic prowess, but of the humble man who has perfect trust in God.

A brother confessed to an elder:

"In my cell I do all that one is counselled to do there, and I find no consolation from God." The elder said: "This happens to you because you want your own will to be fulfilled." The brother said: "What then do you order me to do, Father?" The elder said: "Go, attach yourself to a man who fears God, humble yourself before him, give up your will to him, and then you will receive consolation from God."[31]

The term "consolation from God" is not explained. In the normal context of monastic spirituality it means "compunction." Now, compunction is a sign of valid and authentic repentance, that is to say of *metanoia* or *conversatio*. This means much more than simply a "feeling" of sorrow for sin expressed in the "gift of tears." It is, more basically, a sense of *truth*, a sense of having reached the ground of one's being

---

[30] Paradise, II, 240.
[31] Paul Evergetinos. See I. Hausherr, S.J. *Direction Spirituelle en Orient autrefois,* Orientalia Christiana Analecta 144, Rome, 1955, p. 162.

(or, if you prefer, of one's "nothingness") in the crucial realization that one is completely defectible, that one is *"he who is not"* in the presence of "him who is." The heart of "consolation" lies precisely in this sense that in the center of one's nothingness one meets the infinitely real. In a word, humility and consolation go together, for humility is truth experienced in its concrete and existential factuality in our own life. One who simply "runs his own life" by putting into effect ideal projects designed to establish his own ego-image more and more firmly, cannot possibly taste "consolation from God." He is not debarred from other consolations—those which come from the image he has constructed for himself! But these consolations are laborious fabrications, ambivalent and nauseating to anyone with a sense of truth.

Merely reading books and following the written instructions of past masters is no substitute for direct contact with a living teacher.[32] The Master does not merely lecture or instruct. He has to know and to analyze the inmost thoughts of the disciple. The most important part of direction is the openness with which the disciple manifests to the spiritual Father not only all his acts but all his thoughts.

An apothegm attributed to St. Anthony declares: "The monk must make known to the elders every step he takes and every drop of water he drinks in his cell, to see if he is not doing wrong."[33]

Since the real "work of the cell" is not a matter of bodily acts and observances, but of interior struggle with "thoughts" (that is, in the last analysis, with the ego-thinking-centered passion and pride), it is most important for the disciple to be able to make known to the Spiritual Father all that is going on in his heart. The purpose of this is to learn *diacrisis,* or the discernment of spirits, which identifies these motions in their very beginning and does not mistake proud, vain, illusory or obsessive drives for "the will of God" and "inspirations of the Spirit." The stories of the Desert Fathers abound

[32] *Ibid.,* pp. 167–168 (quoting St. Gregory of Nyssa).
[33] *Apophthegmata,* Alpha Antonii, n. 8, Migne P.G. 65: col. 88.

in examples of monks who were stern ascetics but who, for lack of discernment (*diacrisis*) went to fantastic extremes or completely wrecked their lives.

Cassian, using an expression which had become current in monastic circles because it had even been attributed to Christ in a *logion,* said that monks should, "according to the commandment of the Lord become as wise money-changers,"[34] able to distinguish gold from brass, and to accept only genuine coin. Cassian applies this to the testing of thoughts.

Seemingly spiritual thoughts may indeed be only illusions or superstitions. Or they may be merely superficial. Sometimes monks are dazzled by words, or by subtle-sounding methods that promise to bring them to a new kind of illumination. Or else they are too ready to follow a train of thought that, in the end, is entirely contrary to the true purpose of the monastic life (i.e. detachment from self and *quies*).

Since the appetite for novel doctrines and for curious new methods provides an outlet for self-will, which can defeat the monk's own purpose, or at best induce him to waste his time in trivialities, the spiritual Father will not tolerate any such fantasies. He severely demands the renunciation of all these subterfuges by which the disciple is merely trying to flatter his own ego. Conversely, a monk who takes pains to avoid having a master shows by that fact that he prefers his own will and his own illusions.

Is it therefore possible to think a man leads a Divine life, in accordance with the Word of God, if he lives without a guide, pandering to himself and obeying his own self-will? Naturally not. . . . [To such monks St. John of the Ladder says] "know that you are attempting a short but hard way which has only one road, leading into error."[35]

The monk should of course be free to choose his own Spiritual Father, but he will only deceive himself if, in making the choice, he seeks out a Master who will never tell him anything except what he wants to hear, and never commands him anything against his own will. In fact the Spiritual Father

---

[34] Cassian, Conference I, c. 20. Migne P.L. 49: 514–516.
[35] Callistus and Ignatius in *Writings from the Philokalia,* p. 175.

must if necessary be uncompromisingly severe, and make extremely difficult demands upon the disciple in order to test his vocation to solitude and help him make rapid progress. It was naturally of the greatest importance for the disciple to accept these trials and face them squarely. The young monk was expected to give uncompromising and complete obedience to the demands and advice of the Spiritual Father no matter how disconcerting some might appear. In this hard school of training—and here alone—the monk would learn to "get rid of three things: self-will, self-justification and the desire to please."[36] If he can put up with rough treatment, realizing that the Spiritual Father knows what he is doing, he will rapidly come to a state of detachment from his own will and his own ego. He will then enter a state of spiritual liberty in which, instead of being guided by his own subjective fantasies and desires, he completely accepts objective reality and conforms to it with no other purpose than to "walk in truth." This implies a state of complete indifference to his own subjective preferences, to the desire to be praised and accepted by others, to have a respected place in the society of men. In the language of the Fathers, this transformation was the result of a complete substitution of God's will for the will of the individual ego.[37]

Such is the spiritual freedom without which there is no tranquillity, no *quies,* no purity of heart. In other words, the purpose of the spiritual training given by the Fathers was to bring their disciples as quickly as possible to this state of inner liberty which made them able to live as sons of God.

Nevertheless, a loose and irresponsible reading of the Fathers has sometimes led less discerning ascetics of a later age to place undue emphasis on arbitrary and unreasonable commands, systematically insulting the intelligence and the essential human dignity of the subject, as if the sole purpose of ascetic training were to break down his personal integrity by so-called blind obedience. Fr. Hausherr points out that the

---

[36] Barsanuphius, quoted in Hausherr, *op. cit.,* p. 165.
[37] Hausherr, *ibid.*

term "blind obedience" is not found in the *Vitae Patrum*, and that the Fathers in any case would certainly not have thought that one who was following a guide endowed with a charismatic gift of understanding, was obeying blindly.[38] A more accurate expression would be "uncritical" or "unquestioning" obedience. This is not blind, unreasoning and passive obedience of one who obeys merely in order to let himself be "broken," but the clear-sighted trusting obedience of one who firmly believes that his guide knows the true way to peace and purity of heart and is an interpreter of God's will for him. Such obedience is "blind" only in the sense that it puts aside its own limited and biased judgement: but it does so precisely because it sees that to follow one's own judgement in things one does not properly understand is indeed to walk in darkness.

At this point, passing from the viewpoint of the disciple to that of the Master, we see that the Master must be extraordinarily humble, discerning, kind, and in no sense a despotic character. The "hard sayings" which he administers must spring from genuine kindness and concern for the interests of the disciples and not from a secret desire to dominate and exploit them for his own egotistic ends. The Master must, in other words, be himself one who is no longer in the least attracted by "superiorship" or by the desire to rule and teach others. In fact, we find many of the Apothegms devoted to stories of monks who refused to take on the role of Abba, or who fled from those who attempted to gather around them as disciples. However, as in the case of St. Pachomius and the other great Masters, they eventually gave in and accepted, realizing that this service of others was a further step in their own self-renunciation. But they always taught first by example, and only after that by their words.

A brother said to Abba Poemen: "Some brothers are living with me: do you wish me to command them?" The old man replied: "Not at all. Act first, and if they wish to 'live,' they will put the lesson into effect themselves." The brother said: "Abba, they them-

[38] *Op. cit.*, p. 197.

selves want me to command them." The old man said: "No, become a model for them, and not a lawgiver."[39]

One remarkable characteristic of the Desert hermits as reflected in the "sayings" is their great respect for the variety
of personal vocations and "ways." They did not seek to impose hard and fast rules, reducing all to an arbitrary uniformity. Far from seeking security in a kind of servile conformism, they were able to appreciate the diversity of gifts
which manifested the One Spirit dwelling in them all (I Cor.
12:4):

Abba John used to say: "The whole company of the holy men
is like unto a garden which is full of fruit-bearing trees of various
kinds, and wherein the trees are planted in one earth and all of
them drink from one fountain; and thus it is with all the holy men,
for they have not one rule only, but several varieties, and one man
laboureth in one way and another man in another, but it is one
Spirit which operateth and worketh in them."[40]

Finally, to sum up, we can say that the Spiritual Father
must indeed be "spiritual" in the technical sense of *pneumatikos,* a man entirely guided and illuminated by the Divine
Spirit, one who has totally surrendered himself to God, and
who is therefore guided by love and not by merely external
or logical norms. John the Solitary distinguishes the "spiritual
man" (*pneumatikos*) from the merely rational and virtuous
man whom he calls *psychicos.* Actually he is simply following
the terminology of St. Paul (I Cor. 2:14) where the *psychicos* is sometimes translated the "natural man," and where
the Apostle says: "The *psychicos* does not receive what comes
from the Spirit of God, for it is folly to him." The spiritual
man is he who has received the Spirit of God and knows the
"things of the Spirit" (see I Cor. 2:6–13).

For John the Solitary, transferring the Pauline teaching
into the monastic context, the *psychicos* is the well-meaning
but literal-minded monk who seeks to gain much merit by his
good works, and estimates everything by the yardstick of

[39] *Apophthegmata,* Alph. Poemen, 174, P.G. 65: 364; see Hausherr,
op. cit., p. 190.
[40] Paradise, II, 148.

human respect. "If his good works are eclipsed (by the superior action of the Spirit) he falls into a kind of despair."[41] He is unable to give genuine spiritual guidance, for all he knows about are the externals of asceticism and cult, which are good in themselves, but which he does not know how to relate to their true end.

We can sum up the teaching of the Fathers on spiritual direction by saying that the monk who is merely a *psychicos* lacks the wisdom required to make a true spiritual Father. He cannot liberate minds and heart, he cannot open them to the secret action of the Spirit. He trusts entirely in an external and legalistic knowledge of mere rudiments, and does not "give life" or open up the way to genuine development. On the contrary, by an insistence on non-essentials and by consistent neglect of the living needs of the disciple, he tends to stifle life and to "extinguish the Spirit" (I Thess. 5:19).

John the Solitary observes very acutely that while the *psychicos* has overcome his grosser passions and lives virtuously, he does not really love God and men. He is in a kind of intermediate state in which he has ceased to be moved by passion and crude self-interest (which would make him "love" those who accorded with his own interests) and he has not attained to the spiritual freedom which loves all men perfectly in and for God. "The love of God is not acquired by bodily asceticism but by insight into the mysteries; and since he has not attained to this he fails to love all men."[42] He does indeed have love for some men, but what is the basis of this love? It is, says John, his love *for his own doctrine,* his own ascetic system, "his rule, his way." He is capable of loving *only those who acquiesce in his teaching.* Hence this charity is not authentic. He loves his disciples *for the sake of his own doctrine,* that is to say he makes use of the disciple to affirm the truth and rightness of his own system, or in the end, to show that he himself is a good director!

On the contrary, a truly spiritual Father is sought out not only by beginners but by those who are themselves advanced,

---

[41] John the Solitary, *op. cit.,* p. 34. Compare St. John of the Cross, *Living Flame of Love,* III, 29 ff.

[42] *Op. cit.,* p. 43.

because he has the "words of life," and loves men as God does. They see that he loves not a doctrine, not a method, but men. Since he loves not his ideal but them, they say to him:

We have hastened to come to you . . . because we have found in your words so many things that had never even entered our minds. For although for many years we had never gone out of our cell, the fact of coming to see you has been of much greater profit to us than our stability. We had fixed certain customs for ourselves but we have now set them aside as trivial on account of the knowledge you have shown us. We feel as St. Paul must have felt . . . who at first gained credit for himself and took satisfaction in living according to the law, thinking that there was no other way of perfection until he received the knowledge of Christ. So we also thought that what we had was perfection. . . .[43]

Since in fact one of the pitfalls of the strictly regulated ascetic life of the monks was this spirit of legalism and trust in external works, the true spiritual Father was necessary to insure that the solitaries did not forget the "freedom of the sons of God" which was so ardently preached by Paul and is at the very heart of the New Testament. It was in this freedom alone that they could find authentic purity of heart and true *quies*. This freedom and tranquillity are the "good ground" in which the seed of grace and wisdom can bring forth fruit a hundredfold. This state of purity and rest is not what one can call the "summit of perfection," whatever that may mean. It is simply the last stage of development that can be observed and discussed in logical terms. It is what John the Solitary calls "integrity," but his integrity is not the end, it is really only the *beginning* of the true spiritual (*pneumatikos*) life. "Beyond integrity is mystery which cannot be defined."[44]

They used to say that one of the old men asked God that he might see the Fathers, and he saw them all with the exception of Abba Anthony; and he said to him that showed them to him: "Where is Abba Anthony?" And he said to him, "Wheresoever God is, there is Anthony."[45]

[43] John the Solitary, *op. cit.*, p. 39.
[44] *Op. cit.*, p. 46.
[45] Paradise, II, 165.

V

THE CASE FOR A RENEWAL
OF EREMITISM IN
THE MONASTIC STATE

"Would we be yielding to an exaggerated idealism if we were to hope for a decisive renewal of the hermit life in the bosom of the Western Church? We may judge, on the contrary, that God could give the world no more persuasive sign of the persistent, untiring action of His Spirit among men."

THÉOPHILE RECLUS, in *La Vie Spirituelle*, October 1952, p. 242.

"To glorify eremitism in general seems to me to be a dangerous thing, for each vocation to solitude is a problem of spiritual direction and aspirants should not be encouraged, without distinction, to seek it."

S., in *La Vie Spirituelle*, October 1952, p. 278.

I

The time has come for a renewal of the eremitical life within the monastic state. There are monastic Orders which still strive to maintain a semi-eremitical life, as the basis of their observance. But the traditional comprehension of the purely solitary life as a normal fulfillment of the monastic vocation in certain cases, within the framework of monasticism itself, needs to be rediscovered.

There still exists a traditional distinction in the Western Church between the eremitical state and the religious state, even though there is nothing explicit in the present Code of Canon Law about hermits. Yet the distinction is affirmed implicitly in Canon 487: "Status religiosus seu stabilis *in communi* vivendi modus . . ." The Code of the Oriental Church includes the hermits in the monastic state, and does not consider them outside that state at all (see Canon 313).

It would be worth while to study in detail just how this Western distinction came into being, but such a study must be left for another occasion. The materials are abundant but there is much work to be done in organizing and interpreting the various data. It must suffice to indicate, very briefly, how the distinction arose, and this will situate our remarks on the eremitical renewal in their proper historical and canonical context, since we are here concerned not with the eremitical state as apart from the religious state, but with the possibility of a renewal of eremitism within the religious state itself. We might remark at the outset that a monk living as hermit near his monastery would not necessarily cease to participate both spiritually and materially in the "common life" in the sense of Canon 487. Indeed he would be much more of a participant in the common life of his monastery than a monk serving as pastor in a parish a thousand miles away, who barely, if ever, returns to his community.

As is well known, the present renewal of eremitism which is associated with Dom Jacques Winandy and the Hermits of St. John Baptist in British Columbia is taking the form of a *pia unio* and hence is going on outside the religious state, even though most of the hermits have come from Benedictine or Cistercian monasteries, and remain members of their Orders. The "eremitical state" in this sense is closer to the lay state than to the status of religious or of monk, since the hermit outside the religious state is not vowed to poverty. The hermits properly so called, according to this definition, are proprietors without vows. It may be mentioned that the very interesting article of Dom P. Doyère on *Ermites* in the *Dictionnaire de Droit Canonique,* is concerned chiefly with hermits in this sense, though he does devote some space to eremitism in the religious state.

Writing in the *Vie Spirituelle, Supplément,*[1] Dom Winandy pleaded for a recognition of the hermit state as canonically distinct from the religious state. Even though he admitted that hermit vocations were arising particularly in Monastic Orders (he cited the cases of five priests in the

[1] *La Vie Spirituelle, Supplement,* T. XII (1959), 343 ff.

Congregation of Solesmes who had received *Exclaustrations ad Nutum Sanctæ Sedis* to become hermits), he felt that the most satisfactory solution was *exclaustration* and therefore departure from the religious state. He took into account the serious ambiguities this would imply, since actually exclaustration has a certain note of ignominy about it—a "step down" which is disconcerting canonically, just when the hermit is presumably taking a "step up" spiritually. But unfortunately, as Dom Doyère's article shows, the hermit state as it was canonically constituted in the late Middle Ages is in fact a "step down" from the monastic state. However this "step down" could be accepted as a motive for greater poverty and humility: "L'état érémitique présente un caractère *mineur*, un caractère d'humilité et de complet effacement."[2] We shall return to Dom Winandy's article, which is the most important contemporary treatment of our question so far.

Originally the hermit life was considered to be the normal perfection of the monastic life. The hermit was then the monk par excellence. The cenobitic life, even when not actually oriented to eremitism as its fulfillment, participated to a great extent, by silence, enclosure, etc., in the solitary character of the hermit vocation.

We need not dwell here on some of the extraordinary charisms of the solitary life found in the records of Syrian and Egyptian monachism from the fourth to the seventh centuries. The spread of the monastic ideal to the West, aided as it was by the diffusion of Athanasius' *Vita Antonii* in the mid-fourth century, was marked by an emphasis on eremitism. The eremitical and cenobitic ideals developed harmoniously together in the monasticism of St. Martin in West-central Gaul and in that of Cassian and Honoratus in the South East, not to mention the monks of the Alps and Jura.

Already in the fifth century we find a council in Gaul legislating for hermits. The Council of Vannes in 463 provides as follows:

Servandum quoque de monachis ne eis ad solitarias cellulas liceat a congregatione discedere nisi forte probatis post

[2] DDC, V, 418.

emeritos labores aut propter infirmitatis necessitatem ab abbatibus regula remittatur. Quod ita demum fiet ut intra eadem monasterii septa manentes, tamen sub abbatis potestate separatas habere cellulas permittantur.[3]

This text is concerned exclusively with the passage from the cenobitic to the solitary life within the unified monastic state, while remaining a member of one's community and subject to one's own abbot. The following points may be noted:

1. In common with most of the early legislation, the point at issue is to regulate the transition from community to solitude and limit it to those who have a serious reason for making the change and who are well-prepared to do so. See also Council of Agde (506), Canon 38; Council of Orleans (543), Canon 23; Toledo (633), Canon 53; Toledo (646), Canon 5; Frankfort (794), Canon 12, etc. The Council in Trullo (692) concerns itself with requirements for reclusion: it demands three years of cenobitic life and one year of solitary life as pre-requisites for this most exacting form of solitary life.[4]

2. In particular, insistence is placed on the fact that the solitary must be one who has been proved and tested by *emeritos labores* in the cenobitic community. He must prove himself a monk, for if he is not yet a worthy monk in the cenobium, he will hardly be any better in solitude. This same question is repeatedly taken up in the Councils of the fifth to seventh centuries, and it provides the background for the familiar, one might say classic, text in Chapter One of the Benedictine Rule: *"Qui non conversionis fervore novitio sed Monasterii probatione diuturna didicerunt contra diabolum multorum solatio iam docti pugnare . . . etc."* In short, the eremitical life is considered a normal fulfillment of the monastic life, but it must not be embraced prematurely and without the control of obedience.

3. At the same time the Council of Vannes permits a monk to live in a solitary cell for another reason: bodily or perhaps mental illness, *propter infirmitatis necessitatem.*

[3] Mansi, VII, 954. Text quoted from H. Leclercq, *Reclus*, in DACL, XIV, 2149–2159.

[4] Dom Besse, in DTC, I, 1139.

4. Care is to be taken in either case that this solitary cell is within the monastic enclosure and that the solitary, whether hermit or merely invalid, remains under obedience to his abbot. The prescription that the hermit should be within the enclosure appears to have been broadly interpreted.

5. In any event, we have here what seems to be regarded as the normal situation. It is considered perfectly normal to make provision for a certain exceptional solitude within the framework of the monastic life. The hermit monk is to be protected by enclosure and obedience. But is it enough to call this "eremitism?" There is a further distinction between the hermit and the recluse. Gregory of Tours and many other early writers, especially hagiographers and chroniclers, bear witness to the frequency of *reclusion* as the perfect form of solitary life that is specifically germane to the monastic *institution*. The recluse, enclosed in a cell, is completely dependent on others for physical and spiritual care. This certainly implies "community." Hence the cell of the recluse (or "anchorage") will normally adjoin a church, perhaps a monastic church. St. Gall is an example of an abbey where reclusion was in honor. The area of Metz, Trier and Liège was rich in recluses. The Rule for Recluses (Regula Solitariorum) by Grimlaicus (ninth century) was evidently written by a priest-recluse of Metz. This Rule for Recluses had more influence than is generally supposed. A recent article has shown that it became the basis for the observance of reclusion in the Camaldolese hermitages, where reclusion is still held to be a further perfection of the eremitical-monastic life.[5] A study of Grimlaicus and the very nature of reclusion itself suggests that in the High Middle Ages reclusion was a normal form of solitude for the cenobite who, in his anchorage, continued visibly to be a special part of the community, already "entombed" in a life of eschatological contemplation, and perhaps exercising a charismatic apostolate in his "prison."

The High Middle Ages were years of formation and of

[5] J. Cacciamani, "La Réclusion dans l'Ordre Camaldule," RAM (1962), pp. 142, 151.

crisis in western monasticism. St. Benedict already speaks of the problem of the wandering monk. After the Viking invasions swept the Celtic monks and hermits from the Hebrides, Orkneys and other islands where they had gone to find "a desert in the sea," the Irish, who were already fond of pilgrimages, descended in even greater numbers upon the continent. Irish monasteries grew up on the continent, as at Corbie and Péronne. Later we see the famous Schottenkloster in Regensburg and other Bavarian cities. Reclusion was of course in favor with them. For various reasons, including the fact that many of the wandering monks were also, incidentally, bishops (*episcopi vagi*) without a diocese, the pilgrim-eremitism of the Celts may have aggravated a problem that had been regarded as very disturbing particularly since the Carolingian reform. This fact may have contributed to the sense that hermits needed to be regulated, and certainly the "crisis of cenobitism" in the twelfth century brought up once again this same aspect of the problem.[6]

Meanwhile, it might be of interest to refresh our memory on the Irish question in the High Middle Ages. It has been said of the Celtic wanderers:

The appearance of the strangers must have been striking. They had long flowing hair and tatooed certain parts of the body, especially the eyelids. Their tonsure went from ear to ear, that is to say the front part of the scalp only was shaved. . . . Thier love of wandering was proverbial. . . . The famous scholar Dungal wrote that the Franks disliked his countrymen because of their noisy clamour. . . .[7]

Dungal was himself a recluse at St. Denis.

A certain spirit of independence and the attachment to strange customs must have made the Celts seem something of a problem on the Continent. But there were also other pilgrims (the Anglo-Saxons especially) on the road. Besides that, Oriental visitors, Greek and Syrian monks, brought their

[6] See for instance G. Morin, "Rainaud l'ermite et Ives de Chartres," in RB (1928), 101 ff.

[7] J. M. Clark, *The Abbey of St. Gall as a Center of Literature and Art*, Cambridge, 1926, p. 27.

own customs and religious ways to the West, and we find references to monasteries of Greek and Irish monks living together celebrating their own liturgies side by side.

It must not be imagined that these problems of order rose exclusively from a lack of legislation and from a too-free development of "charisms" of pilgrimage, hermit-solitude or reclusion. On the contrary, it was precisely the influence of canonical and penitential measures that aggravated the problem of the wandering monk and indeed of the wandering Christian in the High Middle Ages. The common Irish practice of sending monks into exile or on pilgrimage for sins, or indeed for simple irregularities, and the equally common practice of sending sinners and criminals on pilgrimage resulted in mixed bands of monastic and lay penitents travelling about to fulfill canonical penances. The result was disastrous.

We might here briefly summarize the ways in which the problem of organizing and regulating eremitism was met in the time of the Gregorian reform and after. Most of the solutions were within the monastic state.

1. First of all the Church blessed and encouraged the formation of well-organized communities of hermits dwelling in lauras, as at Camaldoli or Fonte Avellana. This led eventually to the establishment of "Orders" such as the Camaldolese, the Carthusians, the Grandmontines (or Bons Hommes), etc. It may be mentioned here that Congregations like the "Hermits of St. Augustine" ceased to be in any sense eremitical almost as soon as they were formed.

2. Reclusion of a monk belonging to a cenobitic house (or to a laura of hermits) remained in principle the traditional solution for the member of a cenobium who wanted a more perfect solitude without leaving his monastery. This practice was more common in some areas than in others. It is found in certain English abbeys (e.g. Westminster) all through the Middle Ages. Speaking of the Westminster recluses, Dom David Knowles says:

Here at the heart of what must always have been one of the most distracted and least secluded of communities, provision was made for a recluse who had been and indeed still was a monk of the house. . . . This may have been regarded as an attempt to implement a commonly neglected passage in the Rule of St. Benedict [he refers to the passage on anchorites in Chapter One].[8]

Knowles adds that it is not clear whether the recluses at Durham, Sherborne, Worcester, etc. were monks of the community. On the whole the recluses (Ancres) tended to be women rather than men. There grew up a rather widespread practice of reclusion of women in cells adjoining parish and other Churches. Often anchorages were benefices at the disposition of the Abbot of a Monastery. St. Albans, in England, was especially active in patronizing recluses (for instance Christina of Markyate). Nevertheless these women were very frequently associated with monastic communities at least spiritually. They received the habit of the Cistercians or Benedictines, they followed modified monastic rules, etc.

St. Albans was one the big Benedictine Abbeys of the Middle Ages which, like Cluny, Monserrate, Subiaco, Lérins, Marmoutier, etc. permitted and even encouraged some of its monks to become hermits, while remaining under obedience to their Abbot. Temporary as well as permanent retirement into solitude was common. Often cenobites would obtain permission to spend Lent in a hermitage, or to make more or less long retreats apart from the community, and Dom Henri Leclercq said: "Few are the saints who have not spent more or less time in solitude."[9] These hermitages were sometimes close to the monastery, sometimes far from it, but generally on monastery property. There are numerous references which take for granted those *fratres qui solent sedere longius a monasterio*. They are treated with love and respect and the brethren are glad to see them when they occasionally visit the monastery for the synaxis and assist at the sermon in chapter. They are praised for the humility and charity they show in visiting the community, and the brethren are not to rebuke them for doing so.[10] In the twelfth century there was

[8] *Religious Orders in England*, II, 219.
[9] DACL, *Reclus*, p. 2150.
[10] See Dom J. Leclercq, *Studia Anselmiana*, 40 (1956), 105.

a group of at least six monks of St. Albans living several miles from the monastery in the hills, with one of them acting as their Spiritual Father. However, it was also possible for a monk simply to sever his bonds with his monastic community in order to embrace the hermit life, perhaps, even in a distant country.

3. Eremitism thus developed outside the juridical framework of monasticism, and once again England was especially rich in non-monastic hermits of this type, who produced an eremitical literature of high quality that permanently influenced the tradition of English spirituality. We need only mention the poet and mystic Richard Rolle. On one hand there were small loosely organized congregations of hermits, who made vows before the Bishop, and on the other there were non-monastic hermits without vows making their own living and owning their own little plot of land, or receiving a hermitage as a benefice or cure, who came to form a perfectly distinct state, and they were watched over by the Bishops. Gradually they formed a class apart, made up of simple and often illiterate or eccentric personages who nevertheless lived devout and useful lives as bridgekeepers, roadmenders, lighthouse keepers or custodians of remote chapels and places of pilgrimage.

4. Finally, under the inspiration of St. Francis, the mendicant Orders favored the solitary trend in their own milieu. There is a lively and rich Franciscan tradition of eremitism, developing into the *ritiro* movement of later centuries. The Franciscan *ritiro* is analogous to the Carmelite "desert" (instituted in the sixteenth century) as a small, solitary and poor community where eremitism or very simple and primitive cenobitism can be practiced either temporarily for a few months, for a year or two, or for life. The Dominicans, incidentally, generally seem to have sought their greater solitude as recluses, when they did not transfer to the ancient eremitical Orders. It would be interesting to keep these other solutions in mind as we proceed in our study, but unfortunately space does not permit us to consider the mendicant Orders. We will confine ourselves to *monastic* hermits.

5. Another solution was that of the Cistercians, who offi-

cially showed disfavor to eremitism, but encouraged a very simple and remote form of community life in which isolation and silence were explicitly supposed to provide an ambient of solitude in which the monastic ideal could be realized without resort to eremitism or reclusion. Twelfth-century Benedictines in northern England who wanted a more austere life would at times transfer to the Cistercians or at times repair to hermitages belonging to their own monastery—such as the hermitage on Farne Island in the North Sea, occupied by monks from Durham. From this it will be seen that the austerity and silence of the twelfth-century Cistercians made them rank with hermits in the eyes of the broader and more active cenobitic communities. The Cistercians seem to have been proud of the fact that they attracted hermits to their monasteries, as this seemed to indicate that the Cistercian life was a higher and more perfect way than that of the hermit. Hence the practice of investing hermits with the Cistercian habit and then including them in the Menology and even in the liturgical Calendar (St. Galgan, for example, was solemnly invested with the habit *after death*). In practice there were also a few Cistercian hermits, as we shall see. However it appears that the Cistercian Order preferred its members to leave the Order entirely if they intended to be hermits (see below).

II

Having thus outlined the historical background against which we must consider the question of a renewal of hermit life within the monastic state today, we might also draw attention briefly to some of the material that might be studied more thoroughly in order to discover principles and norms to help us in understanding such a renewal.

The question of vocation: Obviously the most important question of all is that of determining the vocation of a monk who claims to be called to the solitary life. Is such a vocation possible? Is it normal?

Following St. Bernard, Cistercians have so consistently answered "No" to this question that we have come to regard an exclusively cenobitic monasticism as the sole norm. The monastic life is a common life and sets a standard by which everything else, even an exceptional and modified eremitism in connection with a cenobium, is to be regarded with extreme distrust as a hazardous and perhaps delusive adventure. Dom Jean Leclercq reminds us:

We have developed the habit of regarding eremitism in reference to cenobitism considered as "normal" monasticism which provides the norm for everybody. . . . This was not the traditional attitude.[11]

As a result of this wrong attitude, with the common life regarded as the *ne plus ultra,* the plea of the hermit vocation is dismissed as a delusion prompted by a spirit of independence and instability. And in some cases it may well be so. The point is, however, that this empirical fact must not be made into a general abstract principle which admits of no exceptions whatever.

In the Cistercian golden age, St. Aelred stands out among many others as a witness to the traditional respect for solitude. A glance at his tract on the life of reclusion, written for his sister, shows that he readily admits that some people have a special need for solitude. Because of this, Aelred accepts without question the ancient tradition of eremitism or reclusion. "For some people," says Aelred, "it is actually harmful to live among many companions (*inter multos vivere perniciosum*). For others it is at least an impediment, and for some who can live with 'many others' without difficulty, it may *still be more fruitful* to dwell in greater retirement: (*secretius habitare magis æstimant fructuosum*)." Aelred is speaking in altogether general terms, and hence there is no logical exclusion of Cistercian monks from his categories. As a matter of fact we shall see that Revesby, an abbey of which Aelred was founder and first abbot, had three hermitages, at least one of which probably dated back to his time. He admits without too much difficulty that the sincere and well-

[11] J. Leclercq, "L'érémitisme en Occident jusqu'à l'an mil," in *Le Millénaire du Mont Athos,* Chevetogne, 1963, p. 178.

considered conviction of the one "called" to solitude is something that can be accepted within the bounds of ordinary prudence. The fact that such persons themselves believe (*magis æstimant*) that a more hidden life would be more fruitful for them is not, therefore, to be taken as a delusion until proved otherwise, but rather as a reasonable and good spiritual option until shown to be otherwise. However, because of the danger of a too-free and unstable form of eremitism, the strict life of reclusion is accepted by Aelred as a higher and safer way of life than that of the simple hermit.[12] In any case, Aelred is by no means blind to the dangers and abuses found in the anchorages of his time. He describes them, not without rhetorical amplification.

William of St. Thierry left us a classic eulogy of the solitary life in the opening chapter of his Golden Epistle, where he praises the rebirth of that *orientale lumen*, that *cælestis forma conversationis*, that *antiqua vitæ solitariæ gloria* in the forest of the Ardennes. He multiplies the familiar tropes on the dignity of the solitary vocation and adds: *Sileant ergo qui in tenebris de luce judicantes vos arguunt novitatis ex abundantia malæ voluntatis: ipsi potius arguendi vetustatis et vanitatis.*[13] He is speaking of Carthusians, and here even St. Bernard would agree with him. But there is no doubt that for William eremitism has an essential part in the *ordo monasticus*.

The fourth Advent Sermon of Guerric of Igny praises the desert life, consecrated by the fast of Jesus, and speaks of the Cistercians' monasteries as deserts where the monk is alone in silence, but has the support of *sancta societas* with his silent brethren.[14] Here it must be admitted that Guerric is praising the eremitical spirit rather than the actual practice of physical solitude. But the eremitical spirit cannot be kept alive without concrete examples of lives lived alone with God.

The letters of St. Peter Damian provide us with interesting material on the eremitical vocation and on particular

---

[12] *De Institutione Inclusarum*, Pt. I, n. 2. See C. Dumont, trans., *La Vie de Recluse* (Sources Chrétiennes 76) Paris, Cerf 1961, pp. 43 ff.

[13] Lib. I, C 1, PL. 184:310–311.

[14] PL. 185:22.

canonical problems that arose within his eremitical reform. St. Peter Damian is consistently opposed to the opulence and relative comfort of the big cenobitic communities of the eleventh century. He emphatically prefers the hermit life and encourages passage from the cenobium to the hermit life as a normal progress in the perfection of the monk. When one has embraced the solitary life, he must remain stable in it, and regard all thought of return to the cenobium as a temptation to be manfully resisted. He writes with strong disapproval when his nephew Damian, a hermit, is persuaded to go back to the monastery to follow a course in sacred chant (*pro discendis ecclesiasticæ cantilenæ modulis*).[15] "When I heard this," says the Saint, "it seemed to me that I had been told of a frail lamb wandering forth from the sheepfold into the bloody jaws of the ravening wolf." The young monk must therefore return to the hermitage in all haste.

Needless to say that Peter Damian joined the other reformers of his time in condemning wandering hermits, whether they were merely making pilgrimage a pretext for instability, or whether they claimed to have a charism of preaching and prophecy.[16] It can be said that St. Peter Damian disapproved of eremitism outside the monastic state as much as he approved of the monk-hermits who remained in the established or renewed monastic institutions.

Dom Leclercq has published a letter in which St. Peter Damian approves the petition of two hermits who do not want to go down to the cenobium even when they are ill (they may stay in the hermitage, he says, as long as they do not have to eat meat). They have asked to be buried in the hermitage (not in the cemetery of the cenobium), and he approves this also as a sign of stability.[17]

St. Peter Damian admits postulants directly to the hermitage without previous training in the cenobium, which, he implies, may in some cases be undesirable.[18] In any event, he foresees that newcomers can be gradually accustomed to

[15] Epist. VI. 22. PL. 144:405.
[16] See St. Peter Damian, *Opusculum* XII, C 24, PL. 145:277.
[17] *Studia Anselmiana,* 18, 1947, pp. 283–293.
[18] Opusc. XV, 29, PL. 145:361.

the rigors of the hermit life. An interesting chapter of the same Opuscule[19] gives some motives for leaving the cenobium in order to be a hermit. St. Peter Damian thinks that the cenobite who is a prospective hermit ought to give some thought to the disadvantages of the cenobium: *superstitiosas quasdam monasticæ disciplinæ censuras, supervacuos tintinnabulorum clangores, cantilenarum multiplices harmonisa, ornamentorum phaleras. . . .*[20] The complexity and in some sense the "vanity" of an observance that St. Peter Damian does not shrink from calling superstitious contrasts unfavorably in his mind with the simple austerity and freedom of spirit that should be the hallmark of the hermit life. He quotes St. Paul to this effect, and the prospective hermit is to be persuaded that he will serve God much better in the simplicity and freedom of the hermitage. Nevertheless, the advantages of the cenobium must also be remembered, and if the young hermit starts getting too complacent, emphasis must be placed on obedience and humility, cenobitic virtues which, in the hermitages of St. Peter Damian, form an essential part of the solitary life, but which would normally be best learned in the cenobium.

St. Peter Damian makes no difficulty about admitting that not all hermits are blessed with humility and a pure intention. Many have failed to take advantage of cenobitic obedience to form their spirit. Opuscule 51 gives a diverting portrait of a cenobite who, after insulting his abbot, has marched off into solitude under the prompting of his own self-will and who, when Peter and the Abbot came to visit him, thrusts them unceremoniously out, heaping them with choice insults. The trouble with this hermit, says St. Peter Damian, is that he has never been properly formed in humility. He has learned to show off his austerity in an urban monastery. He has become self-willed and singular. He is argumentative and stubborn, and accepts no authoritative statement about anything. When the example of the saints is proposed to him, including that of St. Romuald himself, this hermit dismisses

---

[19] Opusc. XV, 30, PL. 145:362.
[20] *Loc. cit.*

it with a wave of the hand: "How do I know they were saints anyway?" Even in this case, however, St. Peter does not advise him to return to the cenobium, but tries to inculcate a little humility and patience into the man, so that he may become a true hermit and live worthily in solitude.

While St. Bernard had the greatest admiration for the Carthusians and for certain hermits like the Jezelinus who was living naked in the woods of Luxembourg, and while Bernard commended himself to the prayers of holy solitaries and recluses living in the Holy Land,[21] he nevertheless emphatically and habitually discouraged passage from the cenobium to eremitical solitude. A typical letter of St. Bernard on this subject has been published by Dom Leclercq. It is addressed to a Cistercian (probably English) who has repeatedly sought St. Bernard's approval for his "hermit vocation." Bernard calls it an imprudent desire and refuses to countenance it. Though he does not attack the hermit vocation as such, he seems to think that the desire for solitude is *usually* a deception. *Solent enim hujusmodi desideria de spiritu concepi levitatis, ab hiis præsertim qui vires suas metiri nescientes, indiscrete affectant quæ eis non expedit.*[22] And he proposes a general principle: not to leave what is certain for what is uncertain. St. Bernard concludes by invoking his own apostolic authority in order to command the monk to remain where he is. It is curious that another Cistercian uses this identical principle to solve a "case" in moral theology: that of a hermit who has a vow to remain in solitude and who is asked to leave his cell and undertake apostolic work. Guy de l'Aumône, a Cistercian abbot and theologian of the thirteenth century, resolves the case by this principle: *tenendum est certum et dimittendum incertum.* The hermit therefore should remain in solitude where he belongs.[23]

There is an interesting letter attributed to St. Bernard and found in a manuscript volume in the collection of the Abbey of Gethsemani. It has recently been published by Dom Jean

[21] See letter 288, PL. 182:494 c.

[22] *Analecta S.O.C.* IX (1953), 138.

[23] *Studia Monastica*, IV, 1 (1962), p. 101.

Leclercq.[24] Far from condemning the solitary life, this letter is a traditional eulogy of "the cell" and "the desert," and contains copious quotations from St. Peter Damian's praise of the hermit life. Commenting on this letter Dom Leclercq treats it as another indication that the early Cistercians were closely related to the eremitical movement in monastic reform, and says "this letter bears witness to the favor which the eremitical idea often enjoyed in the past in Cistercian milieu."[25] Other texts of St. Bernard (authentic) have found their way into collections "on the hermit life" and the fact that this letter is attributed to him at least shows that such an attribution was looked upon as credible in the 15th century when the manuscript was written. Thus we must not insist, without further qualification, that Bernard was always and unchangingly opposed to eremitical vocation. In point of fact, the formula "O beata solitudo, o sola beatitudo" was attributed to St. Bernard. The letter in the Gethsemani manuscript contains the phrase "O solitudo beata." The letter purports to be one of advice to a new hermit who has "recently entered upon the holy warfare" (of the solitary life). The cell is praised as the paradise where Christ dwells with the monk. Peace is found in the cell, outside there is nothing but conflict. The silence of the desert is the source of wisdom, and this wisdom is developed above all by meditation in solitude upon the mysteries of Christ. It is quite likely that this letter is the product of some Cistercian milieu, probably one in which there were recluses. South Germany naturally suggests itself. While not regarding the attribution to St. Bernard as totally implausible, Dom Leclercq does not seem to take it very seriously. But this letter was very probably written by a Cistercian to another Cistercian who had just embraced the solitary life as a recluse.

However, there is one Cistercian hermit who was without question closely associated with St. Bernard and who is said to have gone to Palestine with Bernard's blessing to live there

[24] *Studia Monastica*, IV, 1 (1962), pp. 93 ff.
[25] *Loc. cit.*, p. 94.
   2 DDC V. *col.* 418
   3–2149–2159

as a solitary. This is Blessed Conrad, for whom there is a feast in the Cistercian calendar on February 14. The facts about his hermit vocation are very obscure and uncertain, but it is possible that Conrad was a monk who had passed from Clairvaux to Morimond and who had departed irregularly from Morimond in the company of Abbot Arnold, in a notorious scandal which would presumably not dispose St. Bernard too well toward projects for foundations in Palestine. Nevertheless it is still held to be certain that Conrad went to live as a hermit in the east with St. Bernard's approval.[26]

Whatever may have been St. Bernard's feelings about the hermit life, and whatever may have been the weight of his authority in the matter, we must remember the forceful statement made by "Apostolus" (i.e. M. D. Chenu), writing in the special number of *La Vie Spirituelle* on solitude: "It is for the Church to discern and to test the spirits, but she cannot bring it about that one who is truly called by the Spirit to holy solitude, is not in fact called."[27]

In practice the Cistercian Order did admit the possibility of a monk becoming a hermit on the property of his monastery, and among the saints of the Order the most outstanding example of this is St. Albert of Sestri, a lay brother of St. Andrew's monastery in Liguria (Italy) who received his abbot's permission to live a solitary, penitent life in a hut in the nearby forest. He spent thirty years there, working miracles and dying in the odor of sanctity in 1239.[28] His cult was approved by Innocent IV. The lives of the saints of the Order would reveal not a few examples of relative or temporary solitude, and the brothers dwelling in granges sometimes found that this more lonely life contributed to their sanctification. However, many "hermit saints" in the annals of the Order were men who renounced eremitical solitude to become Cistercians and afterward departed again into solitude or on pilgrimage (e.g. Blessed Famianus).

In any case the validity of vocation to the solitary life has

[26] See J. Grillon, "Saint Bernard et les ermites," in *Bernard de Clairvaux*, Paris, 1953, p. 253.

[27] *La Vie Spirituelle*, n. 377 (October 1952), p. 299.

[28] *Hagiologium Cist.*, n. 46, Vol. I, pp. 144–145.

clearly been admitted in practice within the Cistercian Order as well as anywhere else. We possess for example a letter of Stephen of Lexington, apostolic visitor of the Irish monasteries of white monks in the thirteenth century, in which he takes up the question, and permits two monks and a brother of Holy Cross Abbey to become hermits.[29] He recognizes that they have had a long-standing attraction to the solitary life "but that they did not dare to put this desire into effect because they believed that such aspirations could not be carried out by Cistercians without the counsel of the General Chapter." However, they have applied to his special apostolic authority and in virtue of this he grants their petition. It is interesting to note in what terms he does so. He frees them from their bond of obedience to the Order, and puts them under the full jurisdiction of the bishop in whose diocese they intend to settle. If they do not live worthily as hermits, then the bishop must deprive them of their Cistercian habit and punish them in other suitable ways. Here we have an instance of what may have been considered the "best solution" for Cistercians desiring to be hermits in the Middle Ages: the change of life also involves a change of state. In order to become a hermit one ceases juridically to be a monk; one passes from obedience to his abbot to obedience under a bishop. The monastic habit is still worn, but one is now in a different state of life, that of the hermit. If this was what "becoming a hermit" meant, in the Cistercian context, we can readily understand St. Bernard's objections. On the other hand, we can assume that those monks who retired to a hermitage or anchorage belonging to their own monastery or to some other monastery probably did not leave the monastic state.

Canonically the letter of Stephen of Lexington is perhaps the most interesting document on this subject that has come down to us from the early centuries of the Cistercian Order. (We reprint the text in Appendix I.) It is not clear from this letter whether or not Stephen of Lexington is assenting to

---

[29] Letter XX in *Registrum Epistolarum Stephani,* ed. B. Griesser, *Analecta S.O.C.* (1946), p. 27. (See text, Appendix I.)

the proposition that petitions to embrace the hermit life normally had to be approved by the General Chapter. This is a point that merits further study.

III

We may now briefly consider the evidence offered by monastic history to show that in actual fact hermitages and anchorages depending on Cistercian and Benedictine monasteries were quite plentiful in the Middle Ages. We have already mentioned such famous cases as Westminster, St. Albans and Durham. Another typical case is that of Cluny. Some of the monks who were venerated after their death as saints of Cluny were, in fact, hermits: for instance Blessed Adhegrinus who, in the tenth century, first made a three-year trial of the solitary life and then established himself permanently in a hermitage two miles from the monastery where he lived as a quasi-recluse (*parva spelunca subarctus*), but came down to the monastery for Sundays and big Feasts.[30]

Another monk of Cluny, Anastasius, first obtained permission from Peter the Venerable to spend his Lents in solitude. He later got permission to retire as a hermit into the Pyrenees, where he established himself on a high mountain. Later he was called back to visit his brethren, but died on the way to Cluny.[31] St. Hugh of Cluny allowed two monks to live as hermits on the Atlantic coast in the diocese of Bordeaux, where later a small community of monk-hermits acted as lighthouse keepers.[32] Peter the Venerable allowed one of his secretaries to live as a hermit for a while, but later called him back because he needed his help.[33] For the monk Gerard of Cluny, who lived apart from the monastery on a lonely wooded hill with several other like-minded companions, Peter

[30] See J. Leclercq, "Pierre le Vénérable et l'érémitisme clunisien," *Studia Anselmiana*, 40, 106–107.
[31] *Op. cit.*, pp. 107–108.
[32] *Ibid.*, p. 108.
[33] *Ibid.*, p. 109.

the Venerable wrote a letter which can be classed as a "Rule" for monastic hermits.[34]

It is interesting to note that various degrees of partial solitude were also encouraged at Cluny. There was a quiet part of the Church set aside for those who preferred solitary contemplative prayer. It was possible to withdraw for a time of retreat to hermitages near the monastery. One monk was allowed to have a cell in a high tower where he could retire to meditate and pray. Reclusion also existed within the framework of the common life at Cluny. Here again we see that the spirit of Cluny differs from that of Cîteaux. The Cistercian hermit often had to cut himself off forever from his Order. The Cluniac on the contrary, even though he might be living as a hermit hundreds of miles from his monastic home, was normally considered a member of the family and could even be summoned back for no other purpose than to visit the brethren and spend a little time with them.

There is a great deal of material about Cistercian recluses, but unfortunately it is not always clear that they were monks or nuns of the Order who had received permission to become recluses. More often they appear to have been holy men or especially holy women who were taken under the protection of some house of the Order and given an anchorage in a monastery or convent, or adjoining a church of one of our monasteries. Blessed Hazeka (d. 1261), who spent thirty-six years as a recluse in our convent of Sichem, is a case in point.[35]

These recluses observed in their own way the consuetudines of the Order. However, it is quite certain that some of the recluses were indeed professed members of the Order who had received this permission to live in solitude.[36] Friar B. Griesser, S.O.C. has examined a Rule for Recluses supposedly written by and for Cistercians.[37] The Rule was not

[34] See Epist. I, 20; analyzed by Leclercq, *op. cit.*, pp. 114 ff., PL. 189:89–100.

[35] See Acta Sanctorum, June, III, 374.

[36] Otmar Doerr, *Das Institut der Inclusen in Süddeutschland*, Münster, 1934, pp. 33, 34.

[37] *Analecta S.O.C.* (1949), pp. 81 ff.

in any sense official. It was, he thinks, probably written by a recluse (male) living in an anchorage under Cistercian auspices, and this recluse may perhaps have been himself a professed Cistercian monk. The General Chapter of 1279 (n. 28) forbade giving the habit to recluses who lived under the protection of houses of the Order, but this prohibition was never strictly observed.

That there were departures from Cistercian monasteries to the hermit life goes without saying. At least one English hermit saint, Robert of Knaresborough, first tried his vocation as a lay brother at Newminster, but after a few months decided upon solitude in Knaresborough forest. After his death in 1218 the monks of Fountains were anxious to obtain his relics but did not succeed.

There were Cistercian hermitages in France and Belgium. Dom Leclercq mentions Aiguebelle and Clairmarais as having hermitages in the Middle Ages. He adds that in the reform of the Strict Observance, in the seventeenth and eighteenth centuries, Chambons and Orval possessed hermitages and there was a hermit living an austere life in the shadow of La Trappe in the time of De Rancé.[38]

R. M. Clay in her book *The Hermits and Anchorites of England* (London, 1914) has listed many hermitages and anchorages depending on Cistercian monasteries in England and Wales. It would be useful to consider them here. First of all we find that Revesby, where St. Aelred was founder and first Abbot, had three hermitages, one of which, according to Clay, dated back to the time of Aelred's abbotship (before 1147). Aelred himself, as Abbot of Rievaulx, had to live in a cottage apart, but this was for reasons of health. It must be noted that the fact that a monastery has a hermitage or anchorage does not necessarily mean that one of the monks was a hermit, though certainly this must have been the case more often than we can clearly prove, especially in the early days. But it is quite possible that the "hermit" or "ancre" was simply one who had been taken under the protection of the house. Clay indicates that at least one Revesby hermitage

[38] See *Studia Monastica,* IV, 95.

was occupied by a monk. We also hear of a monk of New-minster occupying a hermitage there in the thirteenth century, and the three hermitages belonging to Garendon were occupied, at least sometimes, by monks from the community. Did they then sever their connection with the community as suggested above by Stephen of Lexington?

There is a curious case of an anchorage in a London churchyard (St. Giles, Cripplegate) which was given to the Cistercians of Garendon by Edward III. A monk of St. Albans who transferred to Garendon was for a time a recluse in this London anchorage, but after a year there returned to St. Albans.[39] We hear of another Cistercian of Garendon applying to live in a hermitage belonging to the Benedictines of Tewkesbury Abbey.[40] This reminds us of the fact that a monk did not necessarily need to confine his desire for solitude to a hermitage belonging to an abbey of his own Order.

Other Cistercian monasteries which had one hermitage each were Flaxley, Margam, Grace Dieu, Bruerne, Kirkstead, Meaux and Furness. The case of the Whalley anchorage in Lancashire later became rather notorious, but the ancre there was not a Cisterican. Whalley also had a hermitage, in addition to this reclusory which was in the village churchyard.

The Whalley scandal took place in the fifteenth century, which was a late and decadent period in any case. The (female) recluses, particularly one by the name of Isold of Hetton, were not living up to the ideal of the solitary life. However, the records of the case provide us with an interesting insight into the practical working of an anchorage. The foundation was given over to the monks in 1361 by Henry Duke Lancaster. It consisted of two cottages and the revenue from six hundred and seventy acres of land. In effect, the Abbot of Whalley was simply charged with administering this foundation. He provided a secular priest to take care of the spiritual needs of the two ancresses, and sent weekly provisions of food for the ancresses and their two maids (i.e. extern helpers). This included thirty-four loaves of bread and

[39] See Clay, *op. cit.*, p. 67.
[40] See Clay, *op. cit.*, p. 27.

eight gallons of beer. The monks did not even have the right to appoint the ancresses, who were appointed by the Duke. The monks paid the Duke rent for the anchorage but kept the surplus from the income after the ancresses had been provided for as agreed.

The arrangement at Whalley is probably quite typical of many anchorages and hermitages that one may find, in England and on the continent, listed as dependencies of Cistercian abbeys. In this case the recluses had nothing whatever to do with the Order. In others, they may have worn the habit of the Order, followed certain customs of the Order and been directed by monks. However, we do have records, especially in Germany, of nuns of the Order who became recluses. The necrologies of Cistercian monasteries and convents in South Germany indicate that some members of the communities died as recluses. It is curious especially to notice that in the necrologies of monasteries of men we find the record of women recluses who in some cases were certainly nuns of the order. To mention a few of these, found in Doerr:[41] Wettingen, Engelszell, Wilhering, Lilienfeld, and especially Seligenthal where thirteen recluses are on record, two or three of whom were men, one other being designated as "monialis" and still another as "sor" (sister). In the necrology of Tennenbach (a monastery of men) we find this entry: *"Beata Adelheidis virgo de Tonningen S. Ord. Cist. quæ ob amorem Christi prope Thennenbach in fratrum domuncula ad Aspen dicta, ubi adhuc visuntur rudera, inclusa multos annos ibidem sanctam et austeram ducens vitam, sancto fine quievit, sepelitur in Thennenbach."*[42]

Returning to Britain, Ford Abbey is not listed by Clay as having a hermitage or anchorage, but on the other hand there exists an official document concerning the transit of a monk of Ford to an anchorage at Crewkerne (Somerset) in the fifteenth century. The relations of Ford with the anchorage of Crewkerne were entirely spiritual, and had apparently persisted since the early days of the monastery when a recluse

[41] *Op. cit.*, pp. 97, 98, 100, 103, etc.
[42] Doerr, *op. cit.*, p. 97.

of Crewkerne, Blessed Wulfric of Haselbury (d. 1154), was a close friend of at least one of the brothers of the monastery. John of Ford wrote a life of this recluse. Thus the monks of Ford must always have had a respect for the solitary ideal, and the writings of John of Ford are there to show that this was a house where the contemplative life was especially prized and doubtless lived. It is not surprising then that a monk of the Abbey, Dom Robert Cherde, asked and received permission to live as a recluse. The document that has come down to us is a letter to the pastors of neighboring Somerset villages (including West Cokyr, evidently next door to T. S. Eliot's East Coker) concerning the steps to be taken. We give this text in an appendix (see Appendix II). It confirms our supposition that those who left Cistercian monasteries to become hermits also by that very fact departed from the Order and from the "monastic state."

Six miles from Ford was another Cistercian Abbey, Newenham, which gained possession in 1300 of the anchorage in Axminster Churchyard. We do not know if any monk of the Abbey lived there, but there is no reason against supposing that one or other of them might have tried his vocation there. A woman recluse in another village, Colyford, was actually walled in by the Abbot of Newenham, by delegation from the Bishop of Exeter. She was one of the few English ancresses actually "blocked up." There is no indication that she was a Cistercian.[43]

One of the Cistercian abbeys on the Scottish border had four hermitage chapels, distinct from its five granges. This was Holm Cultram, in Cumberland. The hermitage of St. Cuthbert had two garths containing one acre of land and was occupied by a hermit at the time of the dissolution (1574). Another, St. Christian, had one garth of a half acre and was also still occupied in the sixteenth century.[44] However, the most famous attempt at the hermit life in those parts, at least among Cistercians, was the rather unique case of Abbot Adam of Holm Cultram who had been deposed (in

---

[43] See Clay, *op. cit.,* p. 141.

[44] See G. S. Gilbranks, *Some Records of a Cistercian Abbey, Holm Cultram,* London, n.d., p. 36.

the early thirteenth century) in a special visitation by the abbots of Rievaulx and Melrose, for squandering monastery funds in an attempt to get himself elected bishop of Carlisle. He retired to one of the hermitages on his monastery property, but evidently had no solid vocation and in fact went mad. He was brought back to the monastery and imprisoned. He is not to be numbered among the authentic Cistercian recluses!

This very brief and by no means inclusive survey gives some idea of the rich variety of material on the subject that remains to be studied in greater detail. Whatever may have been the objections of a St. Bernard to the solitary life, we find not only that the Cistercians of the twelfth to fifteenth and sixteenth centuries were sometimes enthusiastic patrons of recluses and owners and administrators of anchorages and hermitages, but also that monks of the Order retired to hermitages or became recluses, not only in hermitages belonging to houses of the Order but in others belonging to the Benedictines. Thus, in addition to those who relinquished the "monastic state" entirely to become hermits, there is evidence that eremitism existed and flourished within the Cistercian Order as well as among the Benedictines in the Middle Ages.

IV

CONCLUSIONS:

In recent years an unpublished essay by Dom André Louf has once again taken up the question of eremitism in the monastic state. Viewing all the monastic families as members of a single *ordo monasticus,* Dom André came to a tentative conclusion: it should be considered normal for monks with aspirations to solitude, to try out their vocation by passing over to one of the eremitical congregations within the *ordo monasticus,* and canonical steps should be taken to make this easy. This tentative suggestion of Dom André Louf would simply accept the monastic orders and congregations as they actually are, with their familiar traditions and their current interpretations of the monastic ideal. Supposing that the Cistercian ideal is so purely cenobitic that the hermit life within the Cistercian Order would be unthinkable, then the solution for a Cistercian would be to pass over to the Camaldolese. The aim of Dom André was to win at least a favorable consideration for Cistercians who thought they ought to be solitaries, and he felt that this might be a practical and acceptable way of doing so. It so happens that at the time when the article was written, even this moderate view was not found acceptable.

Considered in itself, the view of Dom André has the advantage of fitting into the situation that existed before the Second Vatican Council without appearing to be too bold or unusual. And of course it is true that at any time the passage to a well-established eremitical institute would be an easy and practical solution for monks who would not feel themselves able to embrace a life of total solitude, without special rule and without the support of an organized community of other hermits. On the other hand, it must be frankly admitted that both the Carthusians and the Camaldolese have certain limitations and problems of their own, and it is well enough known that their own members often seek a more satisfactory form of solitary life elsewhere. Carthusians may, for instance, go over to the Camaldolese in order to become recluses there.

Dom Jacques Winandy, in the article already cited, considered two solutions for the problem of the cenobite with a call to solitude: first, exclaustration *ad nutum Sanctæ Sedis*, which would allow the monk to withdraw from obedience to his superiors while remaining under obedience directly to the Holy See, and so trying out his vocation as a hermit (under a benevolent bishop). The second solution considered by Dom Winandy was the traditional one of the monk receiving permission to live as a hermit under obedience to his own superiors on the property of his own monastery, and therefore without any rupture of the bonds uniting him to his monastic family. While recognizing the obvious simplicity and the traditional character of this solution, Dom Winandy brought up certain well-founded objections to it. The incomprehension of the monastic community, the possible ill will of a new superior revoking the decision of his predecessor, and other such factors, might make the experiment risky, uncertain and even altogether abortive. There is no question that if the community and abbot are cool toward a hermit experiment, the situation can easily be "rigged" so that its failure will be a foregone conclusion and the familiar thesis *contra eremitas* will once again be manifestly "proved."

It is clear that as long as there exists a general state of suspicion and prejudice toward eremitism in monastic communities, the safest and most practical procedure will be for the monk to leave his community and go elsewhere. He may then either:

(a) transfer to another monastery (for instance a primitive Benedictine community) where the superior is favorable to such experiments. Yet this might entail much the same risk over again. In any case this would hardly be possible unless the monk were well known to the superior in question. In any event a period of trial in the monastery *ad quem* would be necessary. In the case of a change of Order, the present legislation would still demand an indult and a new novitiate. Doubtless steps could be taken to simplify this, and in the revised Code of Canon Law such steps could be considered.

(b) obtain an exclaustration *ad nutum Sanctæ Sedis*. But Dom Winandy foresaw that the Congregation might prove unwilling to grant many such exclaustrations and very definite refusals are in fact on record in recent years.

I am not sure whether all those cenobites who have joined Dom Winandy have obtained exclaustrations *ad nutum*. In any event, it would not be necessary for them to do so, as an ordinary exclaustration would be quite sufficient in this case: the bishop is well disposed to the hermits and even made a (written) intervention in the Third Session of the Council, in favor of juridically recognizing the hermit state. The problem that arises here, in terms of our present consideration of changes in the new Code, is that recognition of a separate hermit state might possibly complicate the generally admitted need for recognition of the *monastic state* as such in the law of the Church. Hence it would seem that instead of pushing to obtain the recognition of two separate states, the eremitical and the monastic, it might be advisable once more to bring the hermits back into the monastic state where they belong in any case, at least traditionally. There must be technical difficulties involved in this, and there is obviously a good practical reason why not only the hermits but also other primitive monastic experiments like that of Dom Minard in North Carolina, U.S.A., are getting themselves in the *pia unio* class. Thus, paradoxically, the avant garde of the monastic *life* now finds it necessary to get out of the monastic *state* in order to develop in a satisfactory manner.

But we still face the question whether or not it is both desirable and possible to revive the hermit life within the monastic state, and under the protection of well-established cenobitic monasteries.

Although in Dom Winandy's article and in the special number of *La Vie Spirituelle* of October 1952, it was taken completely for granted that Abbots and Abbots General would remain uniformly hostile to all experiments in the solitary life, especially within the Cistercian Order, we are now witnessing a change that can only be accounted for as providential. What the explanation of it may be, one cannot say. It is quite possible that because many American communities have lost as many as three or four members each to Dom Winandy, the Camaldolese or the Carthusians, this has finally brought home the serious need of reconsidering the hermit question within our own Order. Cistercians cannot help but be impressed by the fact that new primitive Benedictine foundations now assume, as a matter of course, that monks who have a real solitary vocation will be permitted, in due time, to live as hermits in the shadow of the monastery. This is taken for granted as a normal, if rare, development of the monastic vocation.

In any case, not only is the hermit question now open for serious and objective discussion even in the Cistercian Order, but practical proposals are already being made "for a life of complete solitude to be lived on the property of our (Cistercian) monasteries." This would make it possible for well-tested vocations to solitude to find their fulfillment without leaving the religious state, the Order, or the monastery of the monk's profession. It is understood that such vocations would always be quite rare, and the solution to the hermit problem would have to be worked out in a prudent manner, so authentic cenobites would not be disturbed in their own monastic life. It should always remain clear to such cenobites that the hermit life is an unusual way and is *not required for monastic perfection.* The chief "danger" of a hermit life near the monastery might possibly be the implication that each and every cenobite is thereby challenged to go beyond the common life, by the very presence of a hermit on the property. This is of course not the case. The hermit vocation is always exceptional. However, to be realistic about it, if the hermit really remains a member of the monastic family, which would imply that he might have some continued contact with his community, the others will be able to see that he is no angel and will be able to preserve an objective view of the question, thus avoiding "temptation."

The proposals now being made for the recognition of eremitical solitude as compatible with the Cistercian life, are not to be confused with other proposals which are not strictly speaking "eremitical" but which do open up the way to a relative solitude, considered as a necessary element in the common life of the monastery. This relative solitude would consist, for example, in opportunities for a day or so of silence and solitude, apart from the community, in a cabin or chapel somewhere on the monastic property. These days of retreat would be available first of all to officers of the monastery, but doubtless also to other monks who might be considered able to make good use of them.

We are not concerned here with the concrete plans that are now under consideration to restore eremitism within the monastic state. The important thing is the new attitude which must necessarily accompany any such renewal in the life of the *ordo monasticus.* There will certainly not be many hermits living in the shadow of our monasteries. Nevertheless a certain respect for solitude and a mature evaluation of the special needs of certain individuals can be a sign of strength and ripeness in a monastic community. Our monks should learn to treat solitude realistically, not as a delusion of the devil nor yet as a miraculous panacea for all one's troubles, but as a special development which grace demands occasionally in the lives of certain ones. When such a demand really proceeds from grace, then not only the one concerned but also his Abbot and his community have certain obligations to see that the demand is met. When the monk-hermit has to work out his vocation on the property of his own monastery, it becomes clear that his struggle and his venture are in some way the concern of all the community. He is called to develop in a way that is somehow relevant to them all, because it is the prolongation not only of *his* cenobitic life but of theirs. This development will always be difficult, even hazardous. The one who embarks on it does so at considerable risk, and the fact of his doing so should not constitute a boast that he is somehow superior to the rest of the community. On the contrary, he will be brought face to face with his own weakness and his own poverty in ways that would perhaps be quite unbearable without special grace and the help of the community's prayers and understanding.

The problem and paradox of these hermit vocations, which will always tend to make them seem disturbing and sometimes even scandalous, is that though they are a normal fruit of the monastic life they are also *unusual,* even in the sense of implying a *break in continuity* in the life of the one who is called to be a hermit. Obviously, the normal monastic life does not simply and continuously grow into a hermit's solitude. He who is called to this solitude is called, perhaps abruptly, to start on a new path. He receives a new vocation, which is certainly a perfection of his former calling, but is nonetheless a new breakthrough of grace, demanding that he now abandon a certain security and familiar pattern that he has created for himself out of years of faithful monastic observance. In a very real sense he has to begin all over again at the beginning and this time without the help of a novice master, a wise guide, and encouraging companions. If he feels himself to be regarded as a kind of apostate, or as an eccentric or as a deluded fool, it will not make things any easier for him. But this lack of understanding may itself be an element willed by God to confirm his solitary vocation.[45] Needless to say, the argument that the hermit is sitting around "doing nothing" and that his solitary existence has ceased to have any meaning or justification is in itself no more valid than the same superficial arguments proposed against the cenobitic life by people in the world.

The purpose of these pages has been to show that there has been a constant tradition, in Western monasticism, and even within the Cistercian Order, which has not only recognized the rights of the solitary vocation in theory, but has even permitted certain simple, concrete solutions within the juridical and institutional framework of the monastic state. It has never been unusual, it has never been an aberration, for monks to seek and find solitude in the shadow of their own monastery, without having recourse to indults, and without giving up their monastic vows. This remains in itself the simplest, the most practical and the most traditional monastic solution. But of course it cannot be worked out in practice without a great deal of prudence, tact, charity and understanding.

Let us hope that with a more frank and objective view of the situation, it may now become easier both for subjects and superiors to discuss this matter in a spirit of openness and sincerity, completely disposed to bow to God's will in whatever way it may manifest itself. We can only regret that this problem has too often been fought out, in the past, between minds completely closed on both sides, in a *dialogue de sourds* that has naturally been without issue.

If the question is now, we hope, to be discussed more openly and with less passion, monks will have to recognize clearly that no one can ever claim as *a strict right* that his demand to live as a hermit on the monastery property *must* be heard by superiors, in spite of all their objections. One of the most telling indications of a false "vocation" to solitude

[45] Cf. Dom P. Doyère in *La Vie Spirituelle*, October 1952, pp. 253–254.

will perhaps be the unreasonableness, the arrogance and the impatience with which the candidate might presume to assert his claims without brooking any contradiction. Obviously, in order to meet this eventuality, those concerned with establishing norms by which to judge solitary vocations, will want to make these norms fairly strict in order that unreasonable demands may be eliminated right away. Of course there remains a possibility of erroneous judgement, but the candidate in that case could always have recourse to a transitus. Thus it remains altogether likely that even admitting the possibility of a monk becoming a hermit on the property of his monastery, there will still be some who, for one reason or another, will have to seek their solution by transferring to the Carthusians, the Camaldolese or other communities, or else even by leaving the monastic state. But much will have been gained if at least one or two genuine solitary vocations are seen to develop and grow out of our common monastic life and flourish with the protection and love of the monastic community. We must conclude by remembering that this will always be God's work and not man's.

Having begun with a quotation from a writer who signed himself "Théophile Reclus" and who sounds remarkably like Dom Winandy, let us end with another quotation from the same writer in the same article.

The hermit is a sign of God, destined to remind men of the transitoriness of this world and to present to their gaze an image of the world to come. More than in any other vocation, perhaps, is the initiative in this one entirely from God. . . . And does not God have the right to act thus? Who then will be presumptuous enough to demand an account from Him? It is more fitting to adore in awe the mystery of His designs.[46]

Appendix I[47]

Letter of Stephen of Lexington granting permission to three Cistercians to embrace the hermit life.

[46] *La Vie Spirituelle*, October 1952, p. 241.
[47] Analecta S.O.C., January–December 1946, p. 27.

"Registrum Epistolarum Stephani de Lexinton"
XX.

OMNIBUS CHRISTI FIDELIBUS SALUTEM IN DOMINO

Licet dilecti nobis fratres Ysaac et Jacobus quondam monachi de Sancta Cruce et Flan conuersus eiusdem domus ad uitam solitariam et heremiticam se transferre multo tempore ardenter anhelauerint, tale tamen desiderium effectui mancipare nullatenus ausi sunt, eo quod certo haberent monachis Cisterciensis ordinis absque consilio capituli generalis huiusmodi non licere. Auctoritatem igitur capituli memorati nobis in potestate plenaria traditam per Hiberniam audientes tam per se quam per viros auctenticos et Deum timentes omni qua potuerunt instantia supplicarunt, ut ad propositi sui consummationem de nostra licentia possent conuolare.

Nos igitur cum uiris deuotis atque prudentibus habita deliberatione et tractatu diligenti de ipsorum consilio prefatorum monachoruum atque conuersi petitionibus benigne annuimus eos ab obedientia ordinis tantum absoluentes, ita tamen quod uitam heremiticam ducere omni deuotione religiose de cetero studeant. Insuper tres predictos uiros iurisdictioni archiepiscoporum seu episcoporum, in quorum diocesi conuersabuntur, plene subicimus, ut si forte ipsos agnouerint in scandalum religionis suadente diabolo a preconcepti propositi sanctitate exorbitare, ipsis habitum nostrum auferant aliisque modis castigent, prout animarum suarum saluti et honori ecclesie et ordinis magis expedire decreuerint. In cuius rei et cet.

Appendix II[48]

Letter from the Diocesan Curia of Wells, concerning a Cistercian Anchorite.

Richard Pates—Canon of the Church of Wells, Vicar General in Spirituals of the Venerable Father in Christ the Lord Henry [Bowett], by Divine Grace Bishop of Bath and Wells, engaged in distant parts—to the discreet men Masters William Sture of Whitstanton, John Battyn of West Cokyr—rectors of churches—and

[48] F. D. S. Darwin, *The English Mediaeval Recluse*, London, 1943, pp. 48–49.

John Wall, proctor: greeting conjointly and severally in the Saviour of all! Considering the laudable purpose of Dom Cherde—monk of Ford Abbey of the Cistercian Order, in the diocese of Exeter, who appeared personally before Us on the twenty-seventh of the month of October in the year 1402, in the chapel of St. Mary the Virgin near the cloister of the cathedral church of Wells, exhibited letters of discharge from his Abbot of Ford, and in our presence made choice humbly of a solitary and anchoretic life in a certain house constructed for such a person near the parish church of Crukern [Crewkerne] within the cemetery at the western portion of the same church, and made instant supplication for admittance by Us to live perpetually the solitary life in the said house—We, desiring to be certified as to the life, character and conversation of the said Robert after diligent inquiry into the truth of the aforesaid, have admitted and examined carefully the witnesses produced herein by the same Dom Robert under the form of oath for witnesses to be sworn; through whom and other proofs We have found Dom Robert of laudable life and honest conversation—constant, fit, and suitable for admission to the solitary life. And accordingly—after previous reception, from the same Dom Robert, of a bodily oath touching the faithful maintenance of chastity and other observances due—We have admitted his supplication aforesaid as consonant with reason; and we decree that Dom Robert be introduced into the said house—according to the manner, form, and custom usually practised in such cases—and that he be shut up in the same perpetually, without any egress whatever, as justice counsels. To you therefore conjointly and severally—touching whose fidelity and industry We have full trust in the Lord—We commit Our powers to introduce and enclose Dom Robert Cherde canonically into the said solitary house of Crukern, to tarry or abide perpetually in the same *without egress* from that time—this with the usual solemnities, together with power of any sort of canonical coercion. And of what you have done in the aforesaid—after expediting the business in question—take heed to inform Us, when requested on the part of the said Dom Robert. . . . Given under the Seal of Our Office, &c.

THREE

CONTEMPLATIVE LIFE

IS THE CONTEMPLATIVE
LIFE FINISHED?[1]

"Contemplative" is a bad word. When we talk about ourselves, monks, as contemplatives, we come face to face with the problem that we are not more than contemplatives. We are not prophets. We are failing in the prophetic aspect of our vocation. Why? Perhaps because we belong to a Christianity so deeply implicated in a society which has outlived its spiritual vitality and yet is groping for a new expression of life in crisis. Our monasteries are not fulfilling any kind of prophetic vocation in the modern world. Whether we should be able to do that or not is another matter. The prophetic charism is a gift of God, not a duty of man.

But on the other hand, if the gift has not been given perhaps we who had the call have not prepared ourselves. It seems to me that contemplatives should be able to say to modern man something about God that answers the profoundly important and significant accusation of Marx against religion. Marx said religion inevitably leads to the alienation of man. It is not fulfillment but opium. Man in his worship of God divests himself of his own powers and of his own dignity and attributes these to an invisible and remote God and then begs God to grant them, give them back to him bit by bit, in retail packages. But that is not the case. We are learning more and more that the denial of God is really the denial of man. Yet, on the other hand, the affirmation of God is the true affirmation of man. Barth somewhere said: "Merely to talk about man in a loud voice is not to talk about God." Unless we really affirm God, we do not affirm man. Unless we affirm God as He who calls man into existence and to freedom and to love which is the fulfillment of that freedom—unless we affirm this God, we fail to affirm that without which man's life has no meaning.

[1] Notes from taped conferences.

Monks ought to be able to reassure the modern world that in the struggle between thought and existence we are on the side of existence, not on the side of abstraction. But can we honestly affirm this? I don't know.

A great deal of monastic life and "contemplative spirituality" is not necessarily abstract in a philosophical sense, but it is an artificial behavior in which thought, embodied in ritual forms, opposes itself to the concrete facts of existence. Do we make a fetish out of subjecting the realities of human existence to ritual forms and legalisms, to convince ourselves that in so doing we are leading spiritual and contemplative lives?

We monks should be able to reassure modern man that God is the source and the guarantee of our freedom and not simply a force standing over us to limit our freedom.

In the conflict between law and freedom, God is on the side of freedom. That is a scandalous statement! But it is the New Testament! How are we going to affirm to the modern world the scandal of the New Testament? It is here that we confront the seriousness of our *prophetic* as distinct from our *contemplative* calling.

Surely this is the "message" the monk should give the world. But to what extent can monks express this? We are, so it would seem, as committed to law as anybody. More than others! We multiply laws. We live a highly mediated existence in which at any moment rule and rite can substitute for authentic experience and encounter.

Our encounter with God should be, at the same time, the discovery of our own deepest freedom. If we never encounter Him, our freedom never fully develops. It develops only in the existential encounter between the Christian and God, or between *man* and God—because not only Christians encounter God. Every man at some point in his life encounters God, and many who are not Christians have responded to God better than Christians. Our encounter with Him, our response to His Word is the drawing forth and calling out of our deepest freedom, our true identity.

Prayer

To properly understand prayer, we have to see in it this encounter of our freedom emerging from the depths of nothingness and undevelopment, at the call of God. Prayer is freedom and affirmation growing out of nothingness into love. Prayer is the flowering of our inmost freedom, in response to the Word of God. Prayer is not only dialogue with God: it is the communion of our freedom with His ultimate freedom, His infinite spirit. It is the elevation of our limited freedom into the infinite freedom of the divine spirit, and of the divine love. Prayer is the encounter of our freedom with the all-embracing charity which knows no limit and knows no obstacle. Prayer is an emergence into this area of infinite freedom. Prayer then is not an abject procedure although sometimes it may spring from our abjection.

Of course, we have to face the existential reality of our wretchedness, nothingness and abjection because it is there that our prayer begins. It is out of this nothingness that we are called into freedom. It is out of this darkness that we are called into light. Therefore, we need to recognize this as our true starting point. Otherwise our prayer is not authentic. But we are called *out* of this nothingness, darkness and alienation and frustration, into communion and intimacy with God, in His freedom. That is the meaning of prayer. Prayer therefore is not just simply a matter of thrusting ourselves down into a position of abjection, and grovelling in servile submission asking God for things which are already our own. That is the picture that Marx in his idea of religious alienation gives us. Prayer is not something that is meant to maintain us in servility and helplessness. We take stock of our own wretchedness at the beginning of prayer in order to rise beyond it and above it to infinite freedom and infinite creative love in God.

Prayer infallibly does this if we believe it and if we understand its true dimensions. The great problem of prayer arises from the fact that if we take the alienated view we remain fixed in our own ego and we are no longer able to go out from ourselves into freedom. If we remain in our ego, clenched upon ourselves, trying to draw down to ourselves gifts which we then incorporate in our own limited selfish life, then prayer does remain servile. Servility has its root in self-serving. Servility, in a strange way, really consists in trying to make God serve our own needs. We have to try to say to modern man something about the fact that authentic prayer enables us to emerge from our servility into freedom in God, because it no longer strives to manipulate him by superstitious "deals."

Good Souls

Suppose, for a moment, that the term "contemplative" has a value and can be retained: in what sense are we contemplatives? In what sense are there real contemplatives in our monasteries? Obviously there are, especially among the older generation, a lot of people who have been and are authentic men of prayer. Yet so few, so very few seem really to be deeply *contemplative*. They are more what you would call "good souls." They are worthy products of the religious system that has prevailed up to now, good regular people who have been faithful to their obligations. They have put their obligations before everything else and come to choir on time. They have been rewarded with satisfaction and peace. They have a kind of solid interior life going. Over the years they have acquired a certain experience and a deep love of God—no question about that. What they have apparently failed to develop is real depth of insight and a real fullness of *life*. Few have a real depth of spiritual consciousness and a real depth of interior experience. If they have, it is something that they are absolutely unable to articulate, something they are not even aware of. And of course, that is as it should be. But are they *contemplatives*? Or *should* they be?

You expect to find simple and deep people in the contemplative life. The true contemplative should not necessarily have much to say about his contemplative life. The business of articulating it can be a charism or it can be a delusion. But the fact remains that there is something to the articulation of this deep experience. One should be able to teach it to others, to make others understand what it is, and help them to attain it. That is the question that is raised by this message of contemplatives of the modern world. Do we have any depth of experience that we can communicate to the modern world in its own terms? Or should we just assume that the modern world is so far out that it does not deserve any message from us?

Is the contemplative merely there to create a sense of stability, devoutness, piety and peace? Is his the message of confidence that what has been is still going on and will continue to go on? He may indeed comfort you with such a message, but when he stops talking and when you start reflecting on all he has said, you realize that what has been is *not* going to go on. What has been has ended. We hope certainly that some of the qualities of that kind of interior life will continue. We would hate to lose the qualities of simplicity and devotion and piety and all that. But the message of our venerable and ancient system is not good enough. Its emphasis is almost always on something secondary. The emphasis is not on the deep realities of life. You may say our contemplative speaks of the cross and so forth—well, the cross is certainly not secondary. But it is too often seen from the point of view of the secondary. So much is taken for granted, so much is assumed. When the cross is spoken of in the context of what one might call milieu Catholicism (that is to say in which a Catholic milieu is taken for granted), then we assume that all the big things are taken care of by the milieu, and we are only responsible for minor details. The basic problems of life are taken for granted as having been solved years ago and nobody even raises them any more. In that context the cross, instead of being a deep mystery which shakes the very depths of man's being in death and resurrection, becomes a matter of not blowing your top when somebody is late. The cross is a matter of being patient when you have to wait outside the abbot's office.

The "contemplative life" is then reduced to little things like: learning to become a man of interior prayer by making good use of the moments when you just have to kick your heels waiting for something to happen—or for someone to provide something you need (and will maybe never get)—or for someone in authority to notice you are there and pat you on the head and say you are a good boy. The cross is emptied of all seriousness by this kind of fiddling around, even though from a certain point of view it's not fiddling around. It can only appear serious within the context of a well-established, stable society, a Christian bourgeois society which is firmly built on its foundation which shall never be shaken. But that has ended. The foundations are thoroughly shaken. That kind of society no longer exists. We're living in a world in revolution. The foundations of everything familiar are menaced, and if in the midst of this the mystery of the cross means practicing patience and offering it up and so forth when you're sitting in front of a man's office in order to get permission to do something that you ought to have sense enough to do for yourself, it becomes ludicrous in the eyes of the modern world. Therefore if the message of contemplatives to the modern world springs from something as trivial as this—even though it may be using big words like cross, death, resurrection, prayer, contemplation, vision—it's going to be ridiculous! It's not going to touch anybody. They don't want any part of it. If this is contemplation, then we might as well pick up our marbles and go home.

The Sacrifice of Security

Let us now face the question of how badly we need renewal and how little the renewal is really taking place. We don't even know where to begin this renewal. It has to be *our* renewal, not just simply a renewal which introduces the active life into the cloister. We cannot seek the same kind of renewal as is sought in the active orders because we have a different job to do in the Church. True, we're all going back to the gospel; but nowhere in the gospel are we told that the mystery of the cross and the mystery of the Resurrection and so forth are reduced to the little formalities to which we have reduced them. Nor is renewal simply a question of broadening out within the enclosure wall and just fitting a more liberal and more relaxed spirituality into the framework of offices and duties. Nor is it a matter of unending dialogue about those same offices and duties. Renewal means much more than that. You who are interested enough in this matter to be reading and I who am trying to develop these ideas are all involved together in a very crucial search for the realities of renewal. We are trying to see what demands are really going to be made on us. We want to estimate those demands properly and objectively. We want to be ready to pay the price—and the price here is not going to be just a matter of gritting our teeth and following orders that we instinctively realize to be beside the point!

It may be the price of sacrificing our security, *sacrificing the psychological stability we have built on foundations that we do not dare to examine.* We have to examine those foundations even though it will mean unrest, even though it will mean loss of peace, even though it will mean disturbance and anguish, even though it may mean the radical shaking of structures.

Certain structures need to be shaken, certain structures have to fall. We need not be revolutionaries within our institutions. Nowadays one sees too much of the neurotic rebel in the cloister, the neurotic who is interminably complaining about everything and has absolutely no intention of substituting anything positive for all this negation, the person who is always discontented and automatically throwing the blame for everything on somebody else—we don't need that. But on the other hand we don't want to go to the other extreme and just simply be ostriches, refusing to see that these institutions are in many respects outdated, and that perhaps renewal may mean the collapse of some institutional structures and starting over again with a whole new form.

There have perhaps been some unwise attempts at experimental foundations. In a few months they have proved to be pathetic: but that does not mean that we must not continue searching for new ways. On the other hand (now I really am rambling), we have to remember that there is an order in these things and that you do not sit down and start writing a new rule first thing of all. The writing of new rules should be the *last* thing of all. What one needs to do is to start a conversion and a new life oneself, in so far as one can. Thus, my new life and my contribution to a renewal in monasticism begin within myself and in my own daily life. My work for renewal takes place strictly in my own situation here, not as a struggle with the institution but in an effort to renew my life of prayer in a whole new context, with a whole new understanding of what the contemplative life means and demands. Creativity has to begin with me and I can't sit here wasting time urging the monastic institution to become creative and prophetic. To begin with there is really not much change to be expected within the framework of the institution. It can change so much and no more. After that the structure won't take any more change. So it is useless lamenting over the fact that it can't be more creative. It's useless lamenting over the fact that the best people continue to leave and it's useless building hopes on illusory token changes which are after all a little petty. What each one of us has to do, what I have to do, is to buckle down and really start investigating new possibilities in our own lives; and if the new possibilities mean radical changes, all right. Maybe we need radical changes for which we may have to struggle and sweat some blood. Above all we must be more attentive to God's way and God's time, and give everything when it is really demanded.

We, the supposedly "contemplative" monks, need renewal as much as everybody else and we've got to do it ourselves. We have to find out for ourselves what we're supposed to be doing. We cannot sit around waiting for somebody else to tell us. You who read this are yourselves studying possibilities of renewal. Let me encourage you as a brother to forget about other people who are supposed to help you do it. Do it yourself with the help of the Holy Spirit. Find out what you are really looking for in the spiritual life. What did you really come to the cloister for? Why do you want to be a Carmelite, a Trappist, a contemplative? What are you seeking? Are you seeking security or are you seeking God? Are you seeking pleasant experiences or are you seeking the truth?

Are we seeking the truth that is to make us free? Are we

seeking the truth of Christ? Are we responding to the Word of God which breaks through all structures of human life and institutions? These are the things which we have to ask ourselves. We can hardly expect others to answer these things for us!

The important thing for us is to clarify our aims and to rethink not only the accidentals but even the essentials of the contemplative life—in the sense of re-thinking our aims, our motives and ends. What do we come to the contemplative life for? Each of us may have a different answer. And let us not make the mistake of imagining ourselves re-thinking the life in order to *re-legislate* it. In other words let us not kid ourselves by talking now and living later. If our re-thinking is valid it is also a re-living. Don't let's get lost in words. Let's live now. Let us not project ourselves too far ahead. Let us live in the present. Our re-thinking of the contemplative life is part of our present contemplation. Our new life will emerge from authenticity *now*. This is not merely an empty moment of transition. We are not in an interval of dynamic reconstruction in which we are simply going to put back together again a static life in which we will rest. Our rest is in the reconstruction itself. Transition is also fullness. We can have a certain personal fullness even when the changing institution is provisional, and we have to learn to be able to be contemplatives in the midst of the dynamic, in the midst of movement.

We can do this without being obsessed by the movement, without being too conscious of ourselves in movement. We can live happily in change, not worrying about change. Change is one of the big facts of all life. It we're not able to be contemplatives in the midst of change, if we insist on being contemplatives in some completely stable situation which we imagine we are going to construct in the future, then we're never going to be contemplatives.

So let's move on in a quiet, confident way and be content. Let us not try to be too conscious of ourselves moving and not demand that everything be secure. Let us first live in Christ, fully open to his Spirit, unconcerned about institutional security, free from all care for ideal structures that will never be built, and content with the Dark Night of faith in which alone we are truly secure because truly free!

Contemplative Life

What do we think the contemplative life is? How do we conceive it? As a life of withdrawal, tranquillity, retirement, silence? Do we keep ourselves apart from action and change in order to learn techniques for entering into a kind of static present reality which is there and which we have to learn how to penetrate? Is contemplation an objective static "thing," like a building, for which there is a key? Do you hunt for this key, find it, then unlock the door and enter? Well, that is a valid image from a certain point of view, but it isn't the only image.

The contemplative life isn't something objective that is "there" and to which, after fumbling around, you finally gain access. The contemplative life is a dimension of our subjective existence. Discovering the contemplative life is a new self-discovery. One might say it is the flowering of a deeper identity on an entirely different plane from a mere psychological discovery, a paradoxical new identity that is found only in loss of self. To find one's self by losing one's self: that is part of "contemplation." Remember the Gospel, "He who would save his life must lose it."

The contemplative experience originates from this totally new kind of awareness of the fact that we are most truly ourselves when we lose ourselves. We become ourselves when we find ourselves in Christ. Our contemplative vocation can become perverse and selfish if we are surreptitiously using tricks and bad faith. Bad faith for us consists in trying to play around with this concept of finding ourselves by losing ourselves. Bad faith wants to learn some trick way of losing ourselves so that we find ourselves and we come out on top in the end. This is one source of the self-deception and frustration that are so frequent in the contemplative life. Consequently, one of the basic rules is that it is always a gift of God. It is always something for which we must learn how to wait.

But it is also something which we must learn to *expect actively*. The secret of the contemplative life is in this *ability for active awareness,* an active and expectant awareness where the activity is a deep personal response on a level which is, so to speak, beyond the faculties of the soul.

Contemplative prayer is a deep interior activity in the very roots of our being in response to God who has the initiative and yet draws us into certain very subtle forms of obedient initiative on our own side. This combination of initiative and expectant passivity is different in different people. So many things enter into it. In the renewal of the contemplative life we must not narrow down the possibilities for individual development as we have done in the past.

In the past, the contemplative life was proposed in a rather rigid formal sort of way. You entered the contemplative life by making a list of things which you were going to drop, so to speak. You took the world and all its possibilities and you just crossed everything off the list. You crossed off the joys of human love, you crossed off the joys of art, music, secular literature, enjoyment of beauties of nature, enjoyment of natural recreation, sports, swimming. All these things, you just discarded: and when you had crossed everything off the list then the one great thing was left, the *unum necessarium,* the one thing necessary!

I think we have to radically re-evaluate our whole view of this "one thing necessary." The one thing necessary is not that which is left when everything is crossed off, but it is perhaps that which includes and embraces everything else, that which is arrived at when you've added up everything and gone far beyond. I don't want to put it in a quantitative way however. Of course you understand, in reality the crossing-off process was supposed to be an elimination of a quantitative view, in order to get down to a strictly qualitative approach. You were supposed to end up, not with what was *most* but with what was *best.* I think we should aim for the most as well as the best but not the most and the best *outside* ourselves. The most and the best *in* ourselves. Here I think we need a great deal of subtlety and flexibility in recognizing the real vital possibilities of each individual in the contemplative life. Contemplative discipline is both hard and flexible. The contemplative life should be a life in which there is austerity. There has to be a real challenge. It's got to be a tough life. This business of just softening up the contemplative life is foolish. In fact it means the end of all contemplation. But the contemplative life has to be tough in such a way that it's also livable. The toughness of the contemplative life should not be that restricting toughness which arbitrarily rules out good possibilities. It should be a toughness that tones us up to meet new possibilities, the unexpected, that for which we have not been previously capable, for which we have not been previously ready.

In other words, the toughness of the contemplative life was to lift us above ourselves, above our capacities. A life of self-transcendence must be hard—hard and rewarding, not hard and frustrating.

This should give us some insight into the new way of asceticism, a rewarding hardness, a hardness that brings you out. The kind of hardness you get in football when you have to really *play*. So a re-evaluation of our aims in the contemplative life should, I think, take this new form of not simply assuming to begin with that we have crossed off all kinds of possibilities.

Art comes to mind here. By "art" I don't mean fiddling around, please! There is always a temptation to diddle around in the contemplative life, making itsy-bitsy statues. If this is wanted as a legitimate recreation, as a relaxation, or as occupational therapy, let's be honest and call it occupational therapy.

Yet art in the contemplative life can really open up new capacities and new areas in the person of the contemplative. Everything depends on how it is used. The real key is guidance and direction and selectivity. The contemplative life is extremely selective. One of the things that has ruined the contemplative life has been the leveling process which has eliminated this selective quality, this capacity for creative personal judgment in special cases. The contemplative life has become a kind of assembly line on which everybody is put together according to one pattern. This is utterly deadly, and of course it kills selective judgment.

The lack of qualitative judgment, of taste, of personal discrimination, of openness to new possibilities, is bound up with one great defect—a failure of imagination. Our prayer itself is poor in imagination. The pragmatic and legalistic approach to the religious life in general, and to the contemplative life in particular, has resulted in a dreadful banality. Creativity has not been desired, imagination has been discouraged, and emphasis has been on submission of will, accepting the incomprehensible stupidity of a mechanical existence instead of thinking of a realistic way of improving things. But the solution is not in changing observances and practices, or in changing laws. The solution lies deeper, in the life of prayer. If what goes on inside our minds and hearts is banal, trivial, petty and unimaginative, we cannot be creative in our outer works. So much that is new and experimental is proving to be a frightful letdown because it is so second-rate, so superficial, so imitative. And so much of it is in the worst possible taste—as many of our old pieties were also in the worst taste.

The Imagination

Let us consider now whether the imagination has a place in the contemplative life. The imagination is one of the things we have tended to rule out of the contemplative life, largely in reaction against its formalized use in systematic meditation. Most of us, I suppose, ran into a period of revolt against the formalized use of the imagination in systematic "composition of place" and that sort of thing.

Here we must distinguish. I would say that a deliberate use of imagination in prayer might perhaps be a good thing for people who have weak imaginations, whose imagination has never been developed in any way at all. They might profitably be encouraged to exercise their imagination a little. But they must exercise it, not just follow a book written by someone whose imagination has gone dead.

I spoke a moment ago about ruling out everything in order

to arrive at contemplation. Those of us who have read St. John of the Cross remember the chapters of the Ascent of Mt. Carmel where he strongly emphasizes the fact that anything that can be imagined or apprehended by the inner or outer senses has nothing to do with God. Whatever can be "seen" cannot be God. Therefore it is better to withdraw from imaginative activity in contemplative prayer, and of course that's true.

On the other hand, imagination has an important part to play in our lives. We all know that when imagination is not constructively used, is not creatively used, it uses itself destructively. It works whether we want it to or not, and one of the places where we all run into imagination is in distractions. Because of the constant struggle with distractions we tend to take an excessively negative view of the imagination.

Some people cannot abide to have distractions. Their imagination works automatically, creating distractions, and then they hate themselves for it. Their whole life is reduced to a despairing struggle with distractions which, of course, makes distractions worse.

Distractions are produced by the imagination, and in many people distractions are worse because their imagination has nothing constructive, nothing creative to work on. For some people the great cross of distraction and imagination is the fact that imagination, when not constructively used, has a tendency to fix itself on what we call "impure" images. Now, perhaps I might mention in passing that this should just be ignored. To begin with, no image is impure. It is neither pure nor impure. There is nothing "wrong" or "dirty" about images. The wrong lies in a disordered affection of the will. A mere image is never impure, it's neutral. The thought of a part of a body is not impure, it just *is,* that's all.

I am speaking about imagination that doesn't have any constructive outlet. It is important for us to find creative outlets and work for the imagination. Imagination has to be sublimated, not necessarily in prayer but certainly elsewhere. Where are some of the fields where we can find work for the imagination? Well, obviously the first thing that suggests itself is in reading the Bible. There is plenty in the Bible that appeals to the imagination, and the psalms are full of imagination. Anything poetic, anything literary, anything creative, in that sense, is full of imagination.

Imagination has the creative task of making symbols, joining things together in such a way that they throw new light on each other and on everything around them. The imagination is a discovering faculty, a faculty for seeing relationships, for seeing meanings that are special and even quite new. The imagination is something which enables us to discover unique present meaning in a given moment of our life. Without imagination the contemplative life can be extremely dull and fruitless.

Remember also that imagination doesn't just create fictions. These are *real* meanings that the imagination discovers, not just delusions. Yet of course they can be delusory and this is another problem. You see, with imagination you also need judgment. Imagination needs to be corrected with a certain intellectual estimate first of all on a prudential level, and then also even on an artistic level.

We have to consider the artistic truth of things that are brought together by imagination. This, in fact, is what is wrong very often with a crazy imagination. There can be a beauty in a deliberate grotesque and bizarre effect, but then one must be able to be conscious of this. But when imagination goes haywire in the contemplative life people get slightly nutty. They come to you with grotesque illusions, idiotic and often extremely complicated hang-ups—visions, voices, pseudo-prophecies, and take them very seriously in the wrong way. This is work of the imagination, and from a certain point of view you can regard it as creative in a nutty sort of way. But they are drawing wrong conclusions from it. They are rationalizing and verbalizing.

The contemplative life should not lead us just to suppress the imagination in order to get more pure messages from God. We must allow both for a contemplative prayer in which the imagination has little or no part, and for a creative, imaginative, genuinely poetic side in our life. Our imagination must be able to click and find correspondences, symbols and meanings. It should point up new meanings. It should create nuclei of meaning around which everything can collect significantly.

So when we talk about using the imagination in this particular way we imply a certain training or discipline of the imagination. This training should not be a matter of exterior compulsion, the domination of imagination by intellect and will. There are times of course when that is necessary. But the imagination should be allowed a certain freedom to browse around, find its own spontaneous material and work with that material. The intelligence and will should go along with it meanwhile—permissively, so to speak.

The training of the imagination implies a certain freedom and this freedom implies a certain capacity to choose and to find its own appropriate nourishment. Thus in the interior life there should be moments of relaxation, freedom and "browsing." Perhaps the best way to do this is in the midst of nature, but also in literature. Perhaps also a certain amount of art is necessary, and music. Of course we have to remember our time is limited and first things have to come first. We can't spend too much time just listening to music.

You also need a good garden, and you need access to the woods, or to the sea. Get out in those hills and really be in the midst of nature a little bit! That is not only legitimate, it is in a certain way necessary. Don't take your cloister concept too materially. Of course now I may be running into all kinds of problems with constitutions. But the woods and nature should be part of your solitude, and if it's not periodically part of your solitude I think the law should be changed.

Liberating the Imagination

The contemplative life should liberate and purify the imagination which passively absorbs all kinds of things without our realizing it; liberate and purify it from the influence of so much violence done by the bombardment of social images. There is a kind of contagion that affects the imagination unconsciously much more than we realize. It emanates from things like advertisements and from all the spurious fantasies that are thrown at us by our commercial society.

These fantasies are deliberately intended to exercise a powerful effect on our conscious and subconscious minds. They are
directed right at our instincts and appetites, and there is no
question but that they exercise a real transforming power on
our whole psychic structure. The contemplative life should
liberate us from that kind of pressure, which is really a form
of tyranny. It should subject our imagination passively to
natural influences. There has been in the past a certain danger of unnatural influences and sick fantasies in the cloister
itself. So often in cloistered life we have seen people simply
imprisoned in an atmosphere of total ugliness, the pious ugliness of sick statuary and sentimental holy cards. There has
been a great deal of house cleaning in various religious orders, and in the Church in general, in regard to bad art and
bad influences on the imagination. In training the imagination we should work with the inexhaustible supply of images
in the Bible, for example. Take a certain passage of the Bible
and simply be fully conscious, completely aware of what is
addressed to the imagination. *See* it and *grasp* it and *experience* it with the inner senses. Liturgy, too, is a favored means
(at least ideally) for this education of all the senses and of
the whole man.

Our imagination should be spontaneous but it should not
always be completely unconscious or instinctive. Certainly a
contemplative has to be liberated from a completely mechanical imagination. The imagination needs a certain critical reflection, a certain conscious awareness, a certain, let us say,
conscious freedom of judgment in its exercise. The healthy
imagination is one which can spontaneously move itself to
what it likes *better*—consciously aware, not *self*-consciously.
The imagination moves in a state of conscious awareness but
not in *self*-conscious examination of itself; not watching itself
act but simply acting in full and joyous consciousness of the
fact that it acts.

When reading the Bible your imagination should be distinctly aware of the images, the pictures presented to it. Besides taking account of these separate elements, it should also
see how they are fused together in a symbolic unity, in what
the Germans call a *Gestalt,* a form made by things converging

in a new living unity. Train yourself to see those things when you are reading the Bible.

Don't think that every time you read the Bible you must always be getting the loftiest possible theological sense! In the Bible, theology is embedded in material images and if you don't see the images you don't get the theological sense completely. The theological sense is not only an intellectual message addressed purely to the mind, a purely speculative meaning. There are meanings in the Bible which are communicated in concrete, living, material imagery, in material elements, fire, water, etc. One has to be sensible, sensitive, sensitized to the material qualities of these things in order to get the divine message.

Catholic Pessimism

The English Benedictine, Dom Sebastian Moore, in a book called *God Is a New Language,* frankly discusses what he calls "a Catholic neurosis." He hits some nails pretty squarely on the head. He is talking (among other things) about life in Catholic institutions. He talks about how a layman teaching in a Catholic school may complain quite justly of the fact that he is dealt with in a very dishonest and devious sort of way by the religious who are running the school. They won't meet things squarely. Instead of telling him directly and frankly about something, they try to get it to him through a lot of other people. Then, they think, there won't be any argument!

That happens in monasteries, too. Superiors, not wanting to run into open conflict with subjects, don't tell them directly what they want to tell them. They avoid confrontation and try to get it to the subject indirectly or by hints. You get rumors about what the superior thinks rather than hearing from him personally. And you are somehow expected to act on the rumor. An "obedience" based on this kind of thing is pretty equivocal! But that is not the point. The point that he brings up is of great value for contemplatives because it is one of the curses of our cloistered life.

Sebastian Moore talks about a kind of Catholic pessimism. It is related to the disgust and despair and discouragement we get in the contemplative life. This sense of frustration and hopelessness is due to the conditions of the life. This is something that we've really got to learn how to deal with. He says:

The effect of being continually exposed to the truth which is doing one no good is distressing to the soul. There can even result a kind of unbelief, an exhaustion of the spirit which is all the worse for being partly unconscious.

He relates this to the medieval concept of *acedia,* a kind of spiritual lassitude approaching despair. This is one of the curses of the contemplative life and we have not even begun to know how to deal with it. "The effect of being continually exposed to the truth which is doing one no good!"

Now let's make a distinction here. Does he mean continually exposed to an *ideal* which is held up before us and which, we feel, is doing us no good? An occupational disease of contemplatives consists in this unconscious conviction that we are in the presence of wonderful spiritual values which aren't reaching us. Somehow we are failing them, we are never quite measuring up.

One of the ways of reacting is to deny that this is happening at all or to get around it in some equivocal way—by verbalizing or rationalizing. The classic example of this is the old Latin choir and the classic "solution" is to make an act of pure intention. The will to mean it is equivalent to meaning it even though you do not understand. Thus it becomes a sacrifice of praise, the prayer of the Church, etc. There is of course some truth in this: but not enough truth to serve as a solid foundation for one's *whole contemplative life!* Now, the key word here is *alienation.* To be alienated is to be a prisoner in something of which you cannot possibly take an active personal part. This accounts for the kind of choir neurosis that people get into. There is a deep resistance that gradually develops against a thing in which one is participating and yet *not* participating.

This is aggravated by an over-emphasis on the ideal and on the wonderful values that are present—that we are missing.

The ideal is extolled and magnified until it gets to be so great, so superhuman, that we *can't* participate in it. Besides, it is all presented in a completely abstract sort of way. We see with our mind that these values are there. We're told that these values are there and we believe it. We're constantly reproached for not measuring up, and we believe that too. We become obsessed by it. This is all done in an abstract sort of way so that you have to have a peculiar kind of intellect and a peculiar kind of will to be able to measure up to this inhuman challenge. You have to be able to believe in pure, disembodied, mathematical willpower (helped by an abstract kind of grace!). Hence the sense of awful futility, of being confronted with something that we're not measuring up to. Here is this immense truth and it is not getting through to us!

And yet, on the other hand, there *is* a great deal of this truth around that *could* get through to us. But we are not paying attention because we've not been trained to pay attention. We would even feel guilty for paying attention to it. We think it is not supernatural enough! Here again we neglect the imaginative content of some of the things that we live with all the time, the Bible for example. The imaginative and human appeal of the Bible and the liturgy is something that we completely bypass. We do not pay attention to it because we suppose that it is something inferior and we "want only the best." So we bypass a value which we *could* participate in and could experience. Take the joy of singing in choir. Of course that gets knocked out of us because when we sing we are apt to ruin the whole choir! Still, that is what the choir is for. People should be able to enjoy the singing and enjoy what's going on! But perhaps when they enjoy it, they make it intolerable for other people, so there is a problem. We have to face the fact; but we would be able to get to a lot of these values quite easily and quite simply if we would just be natural about them.

But we are told *not* to be natural. If you are taking a *natural* pleasure in something, it is not *supernatural* and that's wrong. I think we should be able to take these natural pleasures and realize that they're not opposed to the supernatural at all. They are a means of entering into contact with the real spiritual values which are given to us. We should not be afraid to make use of them. Then we might better face this situation of frustrating alienation in the religious life, this feeling that we're constantly exposed to an immense truth which is not coming through and is not getting to us. We're not responding to it on levels on which we could respond. We are attempting to respond on impossible levels. This is a highly destructive situation, and when a person lives under this day after day the whole thing gets to be incomparably sick. People saying over and over again what these great values are, etc., and nobody experiencing them at all. For you realize that the person who is giving you this enthusiastic pep talk doesn't experience them either. Better just to smell a flower in the garden or something like that than to have an unauthentic experience of a much higher value. Better to honestly enjoy the sunshine or some light reading than to claim to be in contact with something that one is not in contact with at all.

So, therefore, I would say that it is very important in the contemplative life *not to overemphasize the contemplation.* If we constantly overemphasize those things to which access is inevitably quite rare, we overlook the ordinary authentic real experiences of everyday life as real things to enjoy, things to be happy about, things to praise God for. But the ordinary realities of everyday life, the faith and love with which we live our normal human lives, provide the foundation on which we build those higher things. If there is no foundation, then we have nothing at all! How can we relish the higher things of God if we cannot enjoy some simple little thing that comes along as a gift from Him! We should enjoy these things and then we will be able to go on to more rare experiences. Take the enjoyment of our daily bread. Bread is true, isn't it? Well, I don't know. Maybe one of the troubles with modern life is that bread is no longer true bread. But around here, in this monastery, we have pretty good bread. Things that are good are good, and if one is responding to that goodness one is in contact with a truth from which one is getting something. The truth is doing us good. The truth of the sunshine, the truth of the rain, the truth of the fresh air, the truth of the wind in the trees, these are *truths*. And they are always accessible! Let us be exposed to these in such a way that they do us good because these are very accessible forms of truth, and if we allow ourselves to be benefited by the forms of truth that are really accessible to us instead of rejecting and disparaging and despising them as "merely natural" we will be in a better position to profit by higher forms of truth when they come our way.

Natural Problems

Another point raised by Sebastian Moore: sometimes our ordinary personal and human problems are treated in terms of the highest kind of ethical or religious crisis. Dom Sebastian points out that if all ordinary difficulties are always faced on the highest religious level as crucial problems, matters of life and death in the realm of faith and morals, we are never able to get to grips with them on our own personal level.

Suppose a person has difficulty coming to terms with some truth of faith. If this is immediately treated as a religious crisis of the highest order instead of as a personal and even psychological problem, it may be impossible to solve it. Perhaps it is not a problem at all on that religious level. It may not be a problem of sin, for example. If every problem that comes up is immediately treated in terms of sin and betrayal, our grasp of it may be totally unreal. Of course it *may* be a matter of sin. But let us not confuse a feeling of anxiety or insecurity with a sense of moral guilt. If we automatically assume that every little anxiety is the sign of a moral problem and then try to deal with it as a moral problem we may end up in the most awful confusion—and completely without reason. There is usually no need at all for the moral anguish we create over certain problems.

We ignore an important, psychological, natural element, which may really be the thing at issue in this particular case of this particular person. The solution of the problem may well not be in the confessional, not on a moral level, not on a religious level. It may not be a matter of faith and it may not involve one's friendship with God at all. It is quite possibly a psychological, natural, emotional problem, something that could be more easily solved on a simple, human level. Some people just can't stand to have their problems on this lower level—they prefer a full-scale crisis because it makes them feel more "Christian!"

The confessor very often does not realize this. Or he may grasp it intuitively, without knowing how to tell the penitent. We have a penitent who is bothered by this kind of problem which is not really a moral problem and yet is an acutely anguishing problem nevertheless. He or she goes to confession with the problem and the confessor realizes that this is neither a moral nor a religious problem. So he simply dismisses it. Then the person gets extremely worried about this because for him or for her it really *is* a problem. That is to say, it causes an experience of real insecurity and anxiety. Now, what the priest is saying is, not that this is no problem, but that it is nothing to worry about in confession. But he may brush it off as completely absurd, so that the penitent now feels guilty about having a problem. What he should really be saying is, "Look, this is not a *religious* problem, this is not a moral problem, and this is not a matter of sin. Your friendship with God is not involved here, and even though you may feel that it is, it isn't. This has nothing to do with your friendship with God."

What we really need to learn is how to face and handle this sort of thing on a *natural* level. This is a *natural* problem, and we have to get in touch with the natural values in ourselves that are the resources with which to meet problems like this—for instance, the resources of growing up. Problems of this kind are often problems of maturity and problems of human experience. The real trouble with many religious is that authentic human experience is side-tracked or short-circuited in the convent. One is not allowed to be an ordinary human being because one is always supposed to be living on the superhuman level. One must always be on an intense level of religious crisis or about to lose one's vocation or one's faith. As a result, some people are driven in sheer desperation to "lose their vocation" and get it over with!

But we always have to remember that all problems are illusory without some basis of natural maturity and a natural human growth. It is very important to stress these natural values. We must constantly emphasize the importance of *growing up*. Needless to say, we must not go to the other extreme and make everything an intense psychological problem. There are real religious problems which are not just psychological problems but they may be more rare than we realize. Many religious are just not mature enough to have an authentic religious crisis!

To sum up, I would say that it is essential for us contemplatives to really hang on to the essentials of our vocation. We must face the fact that we are called to be contemplatives. If there is a real threat to our contemplative life, we must resist that threat. We must refuse to be involved in useless and foolish substitutes for the contemplative life. At the same time, we cannot possibly hang on to a dead formalistic set of pseudo-contemplative routines. The contemplative life has to be renewed and it has to be renewed *from within*. It has to be renewed by us with the help of the Holy Spirit. This is no time for fooling around, and it is no time for being unduly influenced by the slogans of people who don't know our problems. It is possible that a great deal of the conflict that is going on in the Church today is marked by neurosis. Between the obsessive compulsive formalisms of some conservatives and the adolescent autistic thinking of some progressives! It's for us to keep our sanity if we possibly can, and to keep a certain amount of lucidity and a genuine fidelity to God's call. Let us keep alive especially the awareness of what is really authentic within our own experience, because we know, we have experienced in moments of prayer, in moments of truth and realization, what God really asks of us and what He really wishes to give us. Let us remain faithful to that truth and to that experience.

What Is Monastic?

Let us now try to clear the ground for a better approach to our problems as contemplatives. The main problem is of course the renewal of the contemplative life. Our first question concerns, precisely, the term "contemplative." Should the term "contemplative religious" be used at all? There seems to be some protest about the term "monastic." I find this in a letter which I am taking as my starting point. Reference is made to a sister who protested against the word "monastic." The sister is quoted as saying: "I think that what I am objecting most to is the monasticism that has been imposed upon us and has become part of our structure."

Since I do not know this sister and do not know exactly in what situation the statement was made, I cannot quite comment on it. This letter comes from a Franciscan milieu and the complaint against monasticism being "imposed" upon others, which is very common and in many cases a justified complaint today, usually arises in the active life and in priestly life, and even in lay life where a monastic form of spirituality has historically tended to prevail since the Middle Ages. As if sanctity for a lay person or for a secular priest consisted in living somewhat like a monk. I think perhaps it would be worth while to discuss a little what we mean by the monastic life and also, by implication, the contemplative life.

What is the best way to approach this whole question? There is no point in just giving a definition of the essence of a monk and the essence of a contemplative and so forth. Let us rather approach it from a kind of phenomenological viewpoint. This is a more modern way of looking at it. Let us consider the different kinds of aspiration and vocation which draw people to the particular life that we are leading. What induces them to seek among us something that they particularly want? What brings them here to do, together with us, something that they particularly need to do? What is it that they feel will give their life its true meaning as their personal response to God's call? In other words, let us consider the *kind of thing people have traditionally wanted to do in a cloistered life,* a life apart from the world, separated from the world.

In all religious life the postulant gets into a special relationship with civil society: a kind of relationship of *opposition* in some way or other with the rest of the world. This is central in all traditional forms of "dedicated life" but it's most central in the so-called contemplative and cloistered orders. After all, when you talk about "cloistered life" you are defining a life (perhaps very unsatisfactorily) in terms of "separation from the world." And of course, this whole idea of separation from the world is a big problem of our time. We have to be not only separated *from* the world but also *open to* it. Let us take for granted that when we talk about separation from the world we are not talking about a fanatical hatred of the world or anything like that.

The whole question of defining our precise relation to the world is another problem which will have to be treated somewhere else. But no matter how we look at it, when we talk about the kind of life that we have in fact embraced we are talking about a life which involves leaving the ordinary life that we knew before in order to do something else which we consider to be better because it is free from certain obstacles and hindrances. We have left our homes and families and civil life and our jobs (if we had them). We have left the university or wherever else we were. We have left our former kind of life and taken on the kind of life that we have now. Doubtless every single one of us has at one time or other stopped to consider whether this was really worth while. Certainly one of the great problems in the religious life today is this question: Has it been worth while in terms of authenticity, reality, integrity, and so forth, for me to leave that other kind of life and embrace *this* kind of life? Is this really more real? Is this more authentic?

Very often you find people solving this question, or trying to solve it, by going from a more active kind of religious life to what we provisionally call a more contemplative life, a more cloistered and hidden kind of religious life. This assumes that one can create certain conditions which are "better" because the experience of generations has shown them to work in a certain way. We assume we can create this set of conditions and get into this new situation ourselves and thereby arrive at something very special to which we are called by God. And so in our cloistered life we try to set up conditions which make it easier and more effective to do something quite special. And what is this that we want to do? Why do we set up these conditions and do these things and what is it that we are after?

To begin with, I think that you can't say that everybody in the cloister is simply trying to do the same thing. The monastic vocation really allows quite a lot of scope for individual differences; at least it *should* allow quite a lot of scope for the individual to follow a personal call, to follow something that he feels is especially relevant to him.

Historically, in the beginning of the monastic life, you find people called to a kind of special individual union with God which they are supposed to find out about and work out for themselves after an initial period of training. The earliest model for the monastic life is that of the ascetics and virgins who lived apart from their fellow citizens in the towns of the Roman Empire, or outside the towns. These more experienced ascetics would follow their own manner of life, praying and denying themselves, and following a hidden quiet way of prayer and worship. They would receive young people who thought they were called to the same kind of thing, give them a rudimentary and individual training, and then turn them loose to carry on for themselves.

Monastic communities came only later. And these early monastic vocations were people who felt that they had an individual call to a particular kind of life. They would go off in the desert to live in a cave or somewhere, or they would take to the road and live as pilgrims and beggars.

The Franciscan way came into the Middle Ages as a salutary revolt against the highly institutionalized monastic system. St. Francis made possible once again an open-ended kind of existence in which there wasn't very much predetermined for you. You were pretty free to do this or that or anything.

You could be a pilgrim, you could be a hermit, and you could be a pilgrim for a while and a hermit for a while and then a scholar for a while. Then you could go to the Muslims in North Africa and get yourself martyred if you had the grace! And so forth.

The Franciscan ideal could really be regarded as a return to the authentic freedom of early monasticism. I would venture as a kind of personal guess at this point that actually the ideal of St. Francis was more purely *monastic* in the true original primitive sense than the life lived by the big Benedictine and Cistercian communities of the thirteenth century where everything was so highly organized behind walls.

A Life of Charismatic Freedom

One of the essential elements of the monastic life is a kind of charismatic freedom. This seems to me to be right at the heart of this monastic vocation; and this creates a problem, of course, precisely because the monastic life as we have it is so highly organized. To what extent does this organized and disciplined and systematic life enable a person to attain a certain level of freedom interiorly in order to do what God has called him to do? To say "a life of charismatic freedom" is to speak of a life in which a person is free from certain routine cares and responsibilities and claims and demands which are regarded as less fruitful, as somewhat deadening. The monastic charism seeks to be free from these in order to be more constantly awake, alert, alive, sensitive to areas of experience which are not easily opened up in the midst of the routines which we shall call "worldly routines." On the other hand, of course, we must not develop a sort of magic idea of the contemplative life and say that when a person puts on a certain kind of habit and goes into a certain kind of cloister and lives a certain kind of rule automatically a deep inner kind of contemplative life follows. This is not necessarily so and the problem of substituting cloister routines for worldly routines can really be an evasion and a falsification of this call to authentic inner freedom. But the point is that the contemplative or monastic life is supposed to liberate a man or a woman from certain routines which are fruitless for them, although perhaps fruitful for other people, in order to let them do something else that they feel they are called to do.

I suppose here we had better say something about freedom. Here we realize that we are in trouble! We cannot possibly take these big words for granted. They call for a great deal of study, a great deal of reflection from all of us collectively and individually. It is definitely not enough to pick up some of the echoes and resonances and emotional implications of a word like freedom as it is bandied around in the religious life. These are loaded words, and they are being used in a way that can be very fruitful and very helpful, but can also be very destructive.

Freedom is also a fighting word, and we have to reflect on the reasons why. Freedom is a fighting word in the religious life today, just as it is in civil life, simply because it has been denied people so consistently and with so many fraudulent excuses. Religious have been abused in this matter like everyone else. Authority has not always been honest in its exercise. "Obedience" has been used to justify almost anything. The time has come to rectify that abuse. But as I say, we have to consider and study what freedom means, especially for us in the contemplative life.

Asceticism

Freedom for what? Obviously the traditional idea, although this has to be examined too, still holds. Traditionally in the monastic life, in the contemplative life and in the ascetic life as a whole, there's a question of asceticism. It is understood that the freedom we seek is a freedom which is purchased at the price of renouncing another kind of freedom. The freedom that we are talking about in the contemplative life and in the monastic life is the freedom which is bought by the renunciation of license or the simple capacity to follow any legitimate desire in any legitimate direction. Besides renouncing illegitimate freedom we also give up a certain lawful autonomy. So that we come face to face right away with the fact that the freedom we look for is bound up with restrictions. Of course, if we're going to consider contemplative freedom intelligently we must go back to the real sources in the New Testament and especially in St. Paul and St. John. I am not going to do that here. The freedom we seek in the contemplative life is to be understood in the light of St. John's statement that the truth shall make you free and St. Paul's statement that we have the freedom of the children of God and the freedom of the Spirit. It is also the freedom which is not under the law. Monastic freedom does not place its hope in the fulfillment of legal routine observances. Therefore it is very important indeed to understand the contemplative life or the monastic life or whatever form of life you want to call it in such a way that it does not become a life dominated by law or a life defined by the hope of salvation through good works. We have to take into account the fact that Luther was a religious. They speak of him as a "monk." He was not a monk—the Augustinians are not monks. But Luther was a religious reacting against a decadent religious system and returning to St. Paul. Luther wanted to "return to sources."

Whether we agree with Luther or not is another matter, but Luther is historically important for the religious life of the Catholic Church and for our monastic renewal. Obviously the reforms of the Council of Trent were aimed against Luther. But now we clearly understand also that one of the main points of Vatican II has been an implicit recognition that we are now beyond the Council of Trent. The need for the defensive measures taken at Trent no longer exists. We are in a totally different situation. Without abandoning the historic continuity which links us with the medieval past through Trent, we have to remember that the defensive attitude taken by Trent cannot be what governs and guides us in our religious renewal today.

To return to my point: in the contemplative and monastic life we have sought out a certain kind of solitude and separation from the world for the sake of *freedom*.

Martha and Mary

One of the ways in which the freedom of the contemplative life is expressed is perhaps not very popular today. Still, let us consider this example. We find it in the gospel of Martha and Mary. Martha working to provide the meal which our Lord is to eat and Mary sitting at the feet of the Lord listening to what he has to say. Martha complains that Mary does not help her, and Jesus defends Mary, saying: "Martha, you are solicitous, you are disturbed with many things! Mary has chosen the best part and it shall not be taken from her."

Traditionally this has been explained by the fathers of the Church, in a way that we all well know, to justify a certain renunciation of good, productive, healthy social activity in order simply to listen to the words of Christ, to be silent and listen to God. Of course this really doesn't solve any problems, yet the use of this text as a justification of the contemplative life does rest on a solid psychological basis, on a basis of real experience which can be verified in the lives of those who have tried to put it into practice and know what it means.

When someone has an authentic call to the contemplative life or to the monastic life, that call can be understood in terms of this gospel text and experienced in the way that is suggested by it. Our vocation can be understood as the resolution of a conflict which is expressed in this story, a conflict in ourselves. Now the important thing is that the conflict is *in ourselves* rather than projected outward into *institutions*. It is one thing to experience in our own lives the difference between the action of Martha and the listening of Mary—but quite another to "prove" that Trappists are "better" than Dominicans!

The fact that this conflict between Martha and Mary became an institutional matter in the thirteenth century does not concern us here, it simply obscures the issue. Ever since that time, there has been a great deal of argument about the respective value of active orders and contemplative orders. This is no longer to the point. Where the conflict resolves itself is in our own hearts as individual persons or small groups, called to this particular life of quiet, of *freedom to listen* to the Word of God in our hearts. We experience in ourselves a new and special kind of truth when we imitate Mary. We who have this particular call recognize that when we are agitated by all kinds of external concerns which do not touch us deeply at all we are less authentic, less real, less ourselves, less what we are supposed to be. We feel less faithful to the will of God than when we remain simply in an attitude of freedom and attentiveness to His word, His love and His will. This gospel text illustrates our experience that we are summoned by the Holy Spirit to make *an act of preference*. We are called to prefer the apparent uselessness, the apparent unproductiveness, the apparent inactivity of simply sitting at the feet of Jesus and listening to him. We are called to prefer this over an apparently more productive, more active, more busy life. We quietly affirm that there is something more important than "getting things done."

Together with this is another implied assumption: that this preference goes against the ideas of the majority of our fellow human beings at any given moment and especially today in the twentieth century. Our act of preference for "quiet" is at the same time an implicit protest and defiance, a protest against and a defiance of the counter opinion of those who are absolutely convinced that our life is useless and who reproach us for it.

Here we find another piece in the jigsaw puzzle that we are putting together. A very important piece is this element of preferring to be at the feet of Jesus and to listen to him in secret, even though we can't fully explain it to other people. Other people are not going to understand it. Other *good* people are not going to understand it, other Christians and other Catholics. We realize all this and we make our choice anyhow. In this contemplative life of ours, in our monastic existence, we are going against the stream.

The Discipline of Listening

This puts us in a very uncomfortable position. We realize
that if we get excited about those who criticize us and devote
too much effort to answering them, we become solicitous
and troubled about many things and get into a kind of useless
activity which conflicts with a deep inner silence and peace
which we are called to cultivate as a special kind of discipline. This brings us to another point in this Martha-Mary
picture that we are considering. It is an obscure realization
which is never emphasized enough. Just remaining quietly
in the presence of God, listening to Him, being attentive to
Him, requires a lot of courage and know-how. This discipline of listening and of attention is a very high form of
ascetic discipline, a rather difficult one to maintain. In fact,
there are lots of people who do not have the strength nor the
grace to maintain this kind of discipline for very long. Doubtless when a person is clearly not able to do this, maybe he
shouldn't try. Our asceticism will consist in discovering to
what extent each one of us can simply remain quiet in passive attention to God, and to what extent we do need some
activity, some work that does not completely interfere with
this but which relaxes us and takes us away from mere concentration. We all need a certain amount of activity which
enables us to participate healthily in the life of our community. We need work that keeps us in tune physically and psychologically so that we are able to listen fruitfully instead
of just going stale and turning off completely. There is such
a thing as over-doing interior prayer and over-doing concentration and over-doing recollection. This can be harmful. It
only deadens our capacity to listen and to attend to God.

This we all know. But let us emphasize the fact that our
attention to Jesus alone, our listening to his word, our attitude
of interior conviction is something we come to experience as
the highest value in our life. Contemplatives are people who
experience this. This is in itself a most effective discipline and
a most purifying form of ascetic training and formation. In
this tranquil, empty, peaceful solitude a person receives

quietly, hiddenly and secretly from God a great deal of benefit, simply by listening and quiet attention.

In this connection let me refer to a passage by St. John of the Cross. Speaking of solitude and the benefits of solitude on the soul, and the tranquil listening to God which he calls the "tranquillity of solitude in which the soul is moved and guided to find things by the spirit of God," he says that in this solitude, in this listening, in this tranquil attention to God, God acts directly upon the one who prays, doing it by Himself, communicating Himself to the soul, without other means, without passing through angels, men, images or forms. He adds that in this solitude, God and the beloved are together in great intimacy.

The solitude wherein the soul lives before time was the desire to be without all the blessings of the world for the sake of love.

Now, that is a good definition, or a good indication of something of that choice that I was speaking of—a desire, an active desire to forgo the benefits, privileges, blessings, advantages which are characteristic of a worldly life or an active life. Characteristic, incidentally, of a good worldly life. We do not deny the goodness of all these things but we renounce their goodness for something else which we see to be better for us, but which does not appear at all to anybody else.

Even at the very beginning of a contemplative life, when a person has received this call from God, he does realize obscurely that for him the supreme value of life is going to consist in a surrender directly to God, in the hope and confidence and belief that God will act directly upon him without the intermediary of ordinary active human ideas or agencies. Of course it may be normal and may be fruitful and sanctifying for most people to reach God through the medium of married love and by bringing up children in an active life, and many may find God better in an active apostolic life fully mixed up with the things of time and of the world. This may be a perfectly normal and perhaps in some respects a better way. Certainly it is a way that the rest of the human race appreciates more. Nevertheless, there is for us this mysterious call to a life of direct communion with and dependence upon and guidance by and formation by and purification by God in silence, in prayer, in solitude, in detachment, in freedom.

It is here that we have to seek the real meaning of freedom in the contemplative life. We renounce other forms of freedom in order to have *this* kind of freedom. Therefore it becomes necessary to accept restrictions, restraints, self-denial, sacrifice and so forth, as we have always heard and always known. But it is much deeper than we have always heard. Restriction and sacrifice have to be accepted in order that this inner freedom may grow. Therefore in the contemplative life, in the monastic life, there is necessarily an element of renouncing advantages, renouncing even certain fruitful activities which sanctify people in other vocations, in order to find our expansion and development and rest and peace in a totally different dimension. For a great deal of the time this solitude and listening are painful, difficult, full of hardship and very demanding. The contemplative life is especially demanding because we are alone and unable to explain ourselves to other people. Admittedly this is very hazardous. So many people are not able to handle this isolation, as we know from experience. They crack up! Perhaps we can say that in our life there are many people who do have an authentic appreciation of what this *might be* for them and yet they are not able to attain to it. We must not blame them. We must not say that it is their fault. We must not say that they have not been generous enough. It is just a fact that few people are able to live in this solitary "desert" for a lifetime. Those of us who recognize ourselves really called to this should be very happy—much more happy than we usually are about it. We should be very grateful to God that He called us to this life and that He has called us to this particular kind of peace in this particular kind of fulfillment, which in so many respects is an unfulfillment and which is almost scandalous to people of our time, so intent upon human fulfillment. Yet even they, when they come in contact with people who have lived in a solitary or cloistered life, recognize that there is a special kind of happiness in this life.

Contemplative and Mystic

Let us finally consider the question of using the word "contemplative" for all this. This word, contemplative, is another one that calls for a great deal of reflection and study on our part. There are many problems. First of all, the term "contemplative" is ambiguous. In the debates that were carried on rather hotly in the nineteen-twenties between the Jesuits and the Dominicans in France about the mystical life, mystical graces and contemplative life, the term "contemplative" tended to be used as it had been used for several centuries before with overtones of *mysticism*. Indeed, very often you find that the word "contemplative" is a safer, vaguer, broader and more discreet word for "mystic." Mystic seems to be a more scary word than contemplative. People hesitate to use it. Also mystic tends to suggest women with stigmata and people having visions, or people who have manifestly attained to mystical union in an extraordinary way. As I understand it from having read a lot of the literature on the subject, the word "contemplative" has been rather widely used as a discreet term for persons enjoying a certain low grade of mystical grace which has nothing to do with visions and has nothing to do with anything very special, but corresponds to a kind of quiet, unitive and passive absorption in God. This is definitely a special grace of God which is much more widespread than is usually realized. It is really accessible to lots of people. Doubtless many who receive it cannot stay with it for very long but nevertheless it is a sort of borderline mystical state.

Now, this use of "contemplation" can be very misleading because if you say we are a "contemplative order," we are a "contemplative community," This is a "contemplative cloister," are you intimating that everybody in the cloister is a mystic of this particular kind? Or that everybody in the cloister *should be* a mystic of this particular kind? The answer is obviously "No!" Nor is anyone asserting that contemplatives in this sense are found only in cloisters. They are found rather widely outside cloisters. There are plenty of housewives with noisy children and all kinds of duties who are leading a contemplative life in this sense. And there are plenty of people teaching in universities or engaged in intellectual life in one form or other who are or can be contemplatives in this sense without very much difficulty.

It is not even necessarily true that life in a contemplative cloister is more propitious to this unitive way of prayer than any other kind of life. It should be, it's designed for that. We have to admit this when we speak of Carmelite cloisters. Obviously St. Teresa meant Carmel to be a place where this kind of contemplative prayer, quasi-mystical prayer, near-mystical prayer, should be not unusual. But nevertheless, we all know from experience that there are lots of people in monasteries and cloisters who do not respond to this kind of thing at all, who are mystified by it or scared by it or upset by it or disturbed by it, and who nevertheless can do very well indeed in a life of service, charity and devotion. This brings us to the important point that the essential of our life is not precisely or chiefly that it disposes us for contemplation in the sense that I have just described but that it produces *a community in which the Spirit can speak to us all in different ways*. The longing for a real evangelical community life is certainly as strong today, above all in the young people who are coming to religious life.

Christian Community

There's nothing wrong whatever in dropping the use of this word "contemplation" completely if we want to look at the whole thing from a different point of view and use a different language—the language of the last chapters of St. John's Gospel, for example. Here the mystical theology, so to speak, of the New Testament is fully exposed in the context of the Last Supper; that is to say, in the ideal, perfect expression of Christian community. And so suppose that the term "contemplation" is unsatisfactory—suppose there are lots of people who are mystified and put off when we express the idea of union with God and direct communion with him in the language of "contemplation." If this insistence on "contemplation" becomes scandalous and difficult for them let us re-formulate it in terms of the New Testament. Let us think of it in terms of knowing Jesus, being one of his disciples, being a member of the loving community which is called together in his merciful love, called to share his body and his blood together around the table of the Eucharistic banquet, called to realize in our love for one another and in our love for Jesus his presence in us. Let us consider the fourteenth chapter of St. John, for example, as an expression of the experience of Jesus present to us in our communal life, in the quiet of that cenacle which we have chosen and which is our cloister.

Do not let your hearts be troubled. Trust in God still and trust in me. There are many rooms in my Father's house. If there were not, I should have told you. I am going now to prepare a place for you and after I have gone and prepared you a place, I shall return to take you with me. So that where I am, you may be too. You know the way and the place where I am going. Thomas said, Lord, we do not know where you are going so how can we know the way. Jesus said, I am the way, the truth, and the light. No one can come to the Father except through me. If you know me, you know my Father too. From this moment, you know him and have seen him.

Our life in our cloistered community is a life in which we should have access to many mansions. Let us always remember that. That should be a kind of *magna carta* of the monastic life. "There are many mansions in my Father's house." Here is a place where we are gathered together, called out of the world in the sense that the disciples were called there to the cenacle with Jesus. Like the disciples we are waiting for him to come and bring us to the place that he has prepared for us. This is the language of the New Testament. This may appeal more to some than the language of "contemplation" but it comes basically down to the same thing, the same experience, Mary's love and total trust in the Lord who promises to manifest His glory to us and in us through the Church.

In this life of waiting and of trusting, of attending entirely to Jesus' will for us and to his love for us living in simplicity with the brothers and the sisters, in the breaking of bread and in mutual love, we learn gradually to experience a new dimension of our Christian life. We come to see not only that we are going somewhere but that we have already arrived, and that Jesus is both the way and the truth and the life. He is the beginning and the end; to live in him is to be not only on the way but at the end, to have arrived.

Our life in Christ is all-sufficient. What we have been calling the "contemplative life" is a life of awareness that one thing is necessary, that Jesus is alone necessary and that to live for him and in him is all-sufficient. To live in him pacifies everything. To live in him takes care of everything. To live in him answers all questions even though we don't quite understand or hear the answers.

So when Philip says to him, as we do, "Show us the Father," Jesus replies (and this is our life), "To have seen me is to have seen the Father, so how can you say, let us see the Father? Do you not believe that I am in the Father and that the Father is in me? It is the Father living in me who is doing this work."

This we have to believe in our own life. If we are living in Christ, we are, so to speak, face to face with the Father but we do not know it and we cannot see Him. We have to be content to be face to face with Him in a way that we cannot understand or see. But we must realize that Jesus working in us is carrying out the Father's work and manifesting the Father to us. "It is to the glory of my Father that you should bear much fruit and then you will be my disciples. As the Father has loved me, so I have loved you. Remain in my love. If you keep my commandments you will remain in my love, just as I have kept my Father's commandments and remained in his love. I have told you this so that my joy may be in you and your joy may be complete. This is my commandment, love one another as I have loved you. A man can have no greater love than to lay down his life for his friend. I call you friends because I have made known to you everything I have learned from my Father. You did not choose me. No, I chose you and I commissioned you to go out and bear fruit, fruit that will last; and then the Father will give you anything that you ask him in my name. What I command you is to love one another."

Built into all this passage of St. John is the basic idea that if we live by Christ's love in the Christian community, we will experience, obscurely, in some way, what it means that Christ is sent to us from the Father and dwells in us by His Spirit, fulfilling in us the will of the Father, so that what we experience in our communal Christian life is what it means to be united to God in Christ and to be children of God in His Spirit.

We have now considered two aspects of our life, one the more personal solitary one, and the other more communal one. We have emphasized the fact that these are two aspects of the same thing. We do not need to know which one of these is right because they are both right. What we really have to discover for ourselves and for our communities is how to reach the right kind of combination of these two elements so that each one of us will be able to live fully the kind of vocation to which he or she has been called.

Active Service

The word "contemplative" is used both juridically and mystically, and this creates confusion. The term "contemplative life" has become a kind of juridical term synonymous with "cloistered life" and yet it also has mystical overtones. Now, you cannot really have such a thing as a *contemplative institution*. Contemplation simply cannot be institutionalized. In fact you can create a cloistered life with certain laws and regulations, and inside this cloistered life there may be some people who are really called to be contemplatives in the sense of mystics of a very simple kind. There may be other people, perhaps the majority, whose whole life is centered on a kind of simple active service and worship within the cloister, without a thought of mystical prayer. And this is a very special, very real kind of vocation. It emphatically does not want to become involved in active outside external concerns, and does want simply to lead a quiet, well-ordered life in the cloister, centered principally on liturgical worship, on manual work, simply service, and communal life and fraternal charity.

What we have to do at this present point in our study is to realize that when the law talks of the contemplative life it is really thinking of this second class of people, interested more in active service in the cloister than in simple contemplative prayer. Now, it would be a great mistake to oppose these two to each other, because in fact a person who is called to be a contemplative in the cloister is going to be greatly helped toward that end by living the simple life of service we have been talking about. Also those who live a life of cloistered service and liturgical prayer, with a certain amount of meditation with reading, will come very close to a kind of simple contemplative peace in their hearts which, however, they will experience in a slightly different way. It may be a sense of peace from having done their duty—the peace that comes from living an ordered life, a quiet industrious life of devotion and consecration. Perhaps this simple and active, dutiful and devout peace is what most cloistered religious seek.

The opposition between the two kinds of approach can be exaggerated, and cause an unfortunate split in the community. To some extent this is due, I think, to the fact that the active service people lack imagination. They seem to feel that we who have emphasized solitude and contemplation are somehow running them down. There is a kind of "chip on the shoulder" attitude on the part of the active service types—they resent the claims of the more contemplative members of the community, as if on the one hand we claim superiority, and on the other are trying to get out of work. So we notice a kind of defensive attitude on the part of some in our monasteries, who are good people and work hard. They get a lot of satisfaction out of work, which is fine; but they feel that the "Marys" are shirking their responsibility and are not realistic. They seem to think the "contemplatives" are deceiving themselves and just sitting around twiddling their thumbs in a state of quietism and inertia. There has been a certain amount of tension between the two groups on this account.

And so contemplation, even in the so-called contemplative monasteries, tends always to be in disrepute. Even so-called contemplatives can look upon contemplation as something unrealistic, as if the real point of monastic life were only active cloistered service. Perhaps it is—I'm not coming to any conclusions on this now. I am just sorting out the different manifestations of these two tendencies. Many so-called contemplatives are simply called to a kind of cloistered service, and it is therefore unfortunate that the life should be officially called contemplative, because the use of the term is ambiguous for these people and causes a lot of doubt and confusion. In practice they solve it by saying that liturgy is contemplation, and he who is zealous about going to choir on time is a "true contemplative."

Attentiveness to God

I am now talking more particularly to those who really seek a deeper experience of God, a deeper expansion of the religious consciousness, a deeper understanding and knowledge of the things of God through love. A moment ago we described two approaches to the life of Mary, the life of sitting at the feet of Christ. The life of Mary can be seen as a life of solitary listening, solitary attentiveness, interior purification, interior disposability, openness, readiness to be spoken to, an interior sensitivity, an interior awareness, all of which we cultivate in prayer. A person called to this kind of contemplation will quite spontaneously seek more time to be alone, quiet, simply listening to God.

Of course where people go wrong is that they fail to realize that this simple prayer can go on even though one may be at work. This state of attention to God certainly can co-exist with a simple kind of action, and the fact that one is not aware of attending to God is perhaps better. It is not necessarily the best and most healthy thing for a person to be sitting quietly, intensely aware of himself as passive. It is better for a person to be somewhat active and not to be aware that anything special is going on, provided that there is no absorption in anything else.

Take the activity of sweeping the floor or washing dishes or chopping wood or cutting grass or something like that. These activities are not distracting. We do not become absorbed in them and it is quite possible to engage in them without any sense that we are praying or that we are doing anything other than simply doing what we do in such a way that we remain quietly close to God. Now, the point I am trying to get to is this: what this attentiveness to God really means is not just a particular psychological state or a peculiar kind of recollection, but it is part and parcel of the experience of love in everyday life. Consequently love is the thing that really creates unity in the apparent division between the Marthas and the Marys of the cloister. It also creates unity in ourselves—and unites us with *reality*. Maybe the Marthas obscurely realize that when they are giving their bodies and their senses something neutral to do they are at peace and somehow or another united with God, without realizing it or experiencing anything special. They may find that when they sit down and do nothing and simply try to attend to God in a recollected state they become tense and confused, too aware of themselves. The other people, the contemplatives and the Marys, so to speak, are able to do this and enjoy listening to God and they think perhaps they are better off that way. In actual fact, what happens is that the Marys also enter into great dryness and do not necessarily enjoy or get much sweetness out of this attentiveness to God. But they have to go on with it anyway because they cannot help themselves.

They are called and drawn to this in such a way that they realize that the greatest benefit in their life is going to come from this simple peaceful attentiveness to God even though it is arid and quiet and dry. And they too will learn, as I said, to combine it with simple tasks and manual work. It is also a good thing to be involved in some work that takes your mind off prayer completely, that rests the mind and gives it a change. The mind is not rested by falling into complete inactivity but by varying its activity. This variety is important.

The essential thing in our life is this fact that it be centered on love as sufficient unto itself. Love alone is enough, regardless of whether it produces anything. It is better for love not to be especially oriented to results, to a work to be done, a class to be taught, people to be taken care of in the hospital, or anything like that. In the active life love is channeled into something that gets results. In the so-called contemplative life love is sufficient unto itself. It does of course work, it does do things, but in our life the emphasis is on love above everything else, on faith above everything else. Especially on faith above works! The characteristic of our life is that it makes us realize more deeply how much we depend directly on God by faith, how much we depend directly on the mercy of God, how much we depend upon receiving everything directly from him and not through the mediation of our own activity. While we continue to act, we act in such a way that this consciousness of dependence on God is greater, more continual, more all-embracing and more satisfactory than it is in the active life. It is in this that we find our peace. It is in this that we find our whole meaning for existence. What is called the contemplative life is really a life arranged in such a way that a person can more easily and more simply and more naturally live in an awareness of direct dependence on God—almost with the sense of realizing consciously, at every moment, how much we depend on Him; and receive from Him directly everything that comes to us as a pure gift; and experience, taste in our hearts, the love of God in this gift, the delicacy and the personal attention of God to us in His merciful love, whch St. Thérèse de Lisieux brought out so beautifully.

This is of course true to some extent of all religious life. But in other forms of religious life the emphasis tends to be outgoing, centered on what we are doing and on the results we are getting and on the relationships we are setting up with other people; whereas in our life, the so-called contemplative life, the emphasis is on our direct relationship to God and our experience with that relationship, that experience of spiritual childhood, sonship in the spirit. We cultivate a sense of direct dependence on God and look to God in order to receive all from Him at every moment.

And this life takes two forms, as I say. Some see it more in terms of a simple service in the cloister, liturgical prayer, and active work around the house. Others see it more in terms of solitary meditation and direct listening. But the contrast between these two should not be exaggerated; they're really doing pretty much the same thing and they should feel that they are sisters to one another like Martha and Mary. For the medieval writers always ended up by saying that Martha and Mary complete each other and that no community would be a full monastic community if there were not Marthas and Marys together. They are both needed, and the real community is a synthesis of these two aspects of the one monastic life.

Deviations

At this point it might be well to pause and consider the fact that in both these approaches to the hidden life of prayer, the cloistered life, there can be and often are, as we know by experience, deviations and wrong directions. Many people misunderstand both these ways of approaching our life with God, the way of cloistered service and the way of solitary meditative absorption and prayer and listening. Now, the problem is in each case to insure a genuine, living, healthy occupation with God which is based on faith, on real living faith and also on common sense. We must cultivate a realistic and healthy view of human life. It is easy to live *inhumanly* in a cloister, to cultivate a sort of fanatical and compulsive addiction to the practices of cloistered life. Instead of living our lives in a healthy, productive, normal, humble, quiet, matter-of-fact sort of way, on a basis of deep faith, one may get tense and overpreoccupied, over-anxious, almost superstitious and fanatical about the things that he or she is doing. The more active people whose life is centered on cloistered service tend to develop a kind of scrupulosity, a kind of obsession with doing everything the right way—they become obsessed with the idea that there is only *one* right way to do it and that's the way it's going to be done by everybody! They are obsessed with what they are doing and in seeing that it is recognized as right by others. In other words, they develop an excessive preoccupation with themselves.

The same thing happens in a different way with the person who tends to prefer a silent, solitary, meditative approach. By way of brief and shorthand identification, I would say that what we are concerned with is people who become unconsciously centered on themselves rather than on God. We find that they develop a kind of cult of themselves, a cult of their own works, their own personality and their own activities. They are engrossed in their own prayers and their own feelings and their own experiences, instead of the cult of God. They're not worshipping God, really. They become, as it were, hypnotized by themselves. And they can do this sometimes with the best will in the world. They can rationalize all this very cleverly as service of God and it can become really a complicated business, this sort of fanatical involvement in oneself, justified by rationalization in which everything is theoretically ordered to God.

So there are people who are intensely involved in themselves, all tied up in themselves, and rather unpleasant to live with because of this. They take it out in various subtle ways on other people. They justify all this by appealing to God, to faith and to religion. Sometimes passive meditating people are extremely aware of every little thing that disturbs them, and become extremely critical of anything that interferes with their absorption in the experience of sweetness that they are having. This is, generally speaking, a sign that there is something wrong somewhere, that the contemplative thing isn't quite as authentic as it appears to be. It is more centered on one's own self than it is on God.

In all cases, we have to remember the basic importance of a good, common-sense, realistic, human view of life; and where this common-sense, human realism is not found it must be cultivated. If it cannot be cultivated, then there is something definitely wrong with that person's vocation. But of course there will always be people who have been to some extent wounded, twisted, and injured by the inhumanity of an abstract kind of life. They will be semi-neurotics, who nevertheless get along in the cloister. They can remain in the cloister. They can be lived with and helped. They can even be of real positive value to the community in spite of their shortcomings. I suppose we could say that in a certain way we are all slightly nuts. We are all a little bit crazy and we all have to get along with one another in spite of our little eccentricities and quirks of character. There is evidently a little bit of the neurotic in almost everybody today. This has to be understood and accepted. Anyway the great thing is to maintain a healthy atmosphere.

The basic requirement of the contemplative and cloistered life today is this: before all else, before we indulge in asceticism or go on to quiet contemplative absorption in God, we must recognize the need to maintain a healthy human atmosphere and a normal human relationship to one another and to reality in our communities.

This, of course, goes without saying, but it cannot be overemphasized; it's so easily forgotten. People become so tied up in abstract ascetic or contemplative projects, things that they think they ought to do, that they forget the basic reality of living as human beings first of all. We have to be, first of all, healthy, mature, honest, objective, humble men and women before we can go on to be ascetics and mystics and contemplatives. This must never be forgotten and it has to be continually returned to because it is the foundation on which all the rest is built.

Penance

Now let us take up another very important aspect of the contemplative life. In so far as it is a life of freedom it has to be a life of penance. This may sound contradictory to those who only take a superficial view of freedom, but when we realize the true depth of the Christian idea of freedom we realize that it is essentially bound up with penance. What our life is supposed to do for us is to guarantee us a certain freedom of spirit. The true freedom of spirit that St. Paul and St. John speak of is the *truth* that makes us free. The monastic life seeks to provide a certain kind of truth by a really authentic penance. One of the things necessary today in the renewal of our religious life and our contemplative life is the renewal of the spirit of penance. But it has to be a *renewal*, not a return to a concept of strictness which has prevailed for the last two or three hundred years. True penance is more than legalistic strictness, a fanatical, obsessive and compulsive sort of strictness about keeping small and rather arbitrary rules, just for their own sake. Let us face the fact right away, that this unsatisfactory concept of penance, while it had a value at a certain time, is much too limited and much too rigid. It has to a great extent lost all meaning to people in our time, whether for better or for worse. I won't go into the discussion of whether this shows that the people of our time are better or worse than people of other times. But the fact remains, that the kind of penitential discipline presupposed by a series of formal and rigid little observances has ceased to have any meaning to modern people.

A person who had bought this concept of life felt that in doing all these things he was being a real "penitent" and "denying himself." And yet they were comparatively easy to do. It was to some extent simply an act, playing a penitential role. Of course it was not all that easy. Some of the penitential things were really a hardship. For example, the old rules about clothing when you had to sleep in all your habit even in the hottest nights of summer. There was all the paraphernalia of the old habit with the rather complicated and heavy underwear we used to have. You really were hot in that dormitory cell, sleeping in all those clothes! You knew that it was summer! That was a trying and exacting and difficult thing to do and it required a lot of resolution and a lot of prayer! It meant a certain amount of anguish—the business of having prickly heat all summer long with no relief possible from it. You just couldn't get away from prickly heat because you just never stopped sweating and there was no way to be dry for more than ten seconds. You just never dried out.

Well, without going on with this, you can see that this refinement of discipline in matters of petty regulations is no longer adequate as a Christian idea of penance even though it may be difficult, even though it may be demanding. This is not the right approach. Experience has taught us that this simply no longer really works. We still have in our communities many excellent people who have been formed by this kind of practice and we admire these people very much; but we also have people who have been broken and twisted and distorted by this kind of practice. We instinctively feel that they did not come to the cloister just to be deformed in this particular kind of way, and therefore this dehumanizing concept of penance is insufficient. It does not come near the demand of the New Testament idea of penance. The distinction is this: the old idea of penance that I've been talking about is a limited one, very demanding within a small area but not really going very deep. It is external, and, in a certain sense, it's easier—it's kind of an evasion of the real penance of giving up ourselves. Is it real self-sacrifice or is it only will-training? It may be purifying up to a point but it leaves intact the inmost ego, and a person can be really strict in this kind of penance and remain very proud and harsh and extremely uncharitable. A cruel, aggressive and vindictive kind of person can flourish on this kind of penance. Real penance is aimed at the deep root of pride and the deep root of uncharitableness. Real penance aims at that vindictiveness and that persecuting mentality which so many of these strict people developed in the past.

But we must not go to the other extreme. That we now in the monastic life or the cloistered life or the contemplative life are simply throwing away all these practices and living in a kind of freedom of spirit without any real discipline is fatal. There is no hope of any good coming out of this. It will only destroy monasticism. The freedom that we are looking for must never be considered a kind of mere spontaneous following of natural tendencies, innocent natural feelings, and so forth. This idea of mere personal fulfillment, a more or less natural fulfillment of spontaneous good instincts and desires, is not good enough. If there is real charity present, if you have real honest-to-goodness community relationships in which there is real love, certainly this will do an enormous amount—but you can't have this without real self-denial, and the problem is, of course, to what extent real love is found in these relationships which are sought for and pointed to as the solution. To what extent are they really love, and to what extent are they mere gregariousness, vapid togetherness? We cannot be content with a superficial chumminess and euphoria, the kind of cheerfulness which depends on having a good time. We have been at this kind of thing for a couple of years and I think we are beginning to see the insufficiency of a community life in which there is a great deal of chumminess and a certain amount of openness and also a lot of confusion. Community means more than people propping each other up in a desperate kind of way. It means more than interminable talking and interminable wandering around looking for something that brings joy. This is not going to do the trick.

Basically there is only one Christian freedom, which is the freedom of the cross. It is the freedom that comes for one who has completely given himself with Christ on the cross, has risen with Christ and has his freedom—not simply in ordinary human spontaneity but in the spontaneity of the Spirit of God, who is given to us in exchange for our own spirit when and if we die on the cross with Christ. The pattern of the monastic life is a real death and resurrection, and for us especially there is this element of a real death to the world, to the ordinary life that we would otherwise be living as Christians or as active apostles. Whatever we call our life, cloistered or contemplative or monastic, it does imply a real break and therefore a real liberation, by a kind of death, from the claims and demands of a highly distracted and confused life in the world; although this, of course, may have a few Christian dimensions of its own. It might even be more Christian than our life. In certain circumstances it might be, but the fact remains that in response to the call of God we have made this real break and sought this real liberation from the whole network of needs, servitudes and demands which secular life imposes on people. There is no real freedom in our life without this death and resurrection—without this clean break.

Our freedom is by no means simply a removal of obstacles which permits us to fulfill our best natural aspirations. That has to be perfectly clear. We do not come to the cloister simply to become artists or to become musicians or to make friends with other people. We do not come to the cloister for the expansion of a merely human existence, because that can be done much better somewhere else. The real expansion of human existence in that kind of dimension is to be sought in married life. We do not come to the cloister to find the same kind of fulfillment and expansion of our human character and personality as we would find in marriage or in a creative secular existence, a professional career in the world. We come here for a specific and precise aim, which is a special kind of transformation in Christ and a special kind of transformation in the Spirit. The root of our penance is not at all just the embracing of ascetical routine. We come here for transformation, to be transformed not by simple convent discipline or by monastic ascetic practices. We come here to be transformed by the Spirit. We do not bring to the cloister or to the solitude of the monastery or the woods simply our own personality and our own aspirations plus a set of ascetic tools that we're going to work with to make ourselves more perfect. The idea that one remains essentially oneself and in command of oneself, and simply uses ascetic techniques to become more perfect, is essentially misleading. It leads to a wrong concept of penance, which is really no penance at all. It is mere willful rigidity without any transformation.

We come to the cloister to surrender ourselves to Christ and to his Spirit in a kind of death, in order to live again in a life which he gives us. The freedom that we seek in the cloister is the freedom to be open to the new life which comes from Christ, the freedom to follow his Spirit. We seek a virginal freedom to follow the bridegroom wherever he goes, to be attentive to his every inspiration and to listen to the personal message that he has for us. This can come to us from no other source except from him speaking in our hearts. The institution of a certain kind of strict cloistered and solitary life is aimed precisely to protect this inner atmosphere of silence, listening and freedom in which Christ can do in us the work he wishes to do.

The root of our penance is faith. The root of our life of *metanoia* is a real faith in Christ, a real faith in our vocation, a real faith in the transforming power of the cross, a faith in God's promises, a faith that if we give up ourselves and our ambitions, even our spiritual ambitions, if we deliver ourselves utterly and totally into the hands of Christ and to his love, we will indeed be transformed in his time, in his way, by his Spirit. Not in our time, not in our way, and not by our own spirit.

We do not come here to be transformed by our own will and our own spirit. We come here to make this complete surrender in faith. Whether we go by the old way or by the new way, this faith is radically and urgently and critically the most important thing. This is what we have to cultivate and this is what we have, above all, to pray for.

Prayer for Faith

So I would say, the root of renewal for our life implies renewal in the spheres of prayer and of penance. We do not yet know exactly in what this renewal will consist. These are the things that we have to discover collectively and individually by a real cooperative search under the guidance of the Holy Spirit. But the root of it all for all of us is prayer for faith. We must pray to the Lord at every moment to increase our faith because the root of renewal is faith. In proportion as we grow in faith, we keep closer and closer to him who has called us. In proportion as our faith develops it gives us the vision by which we can see our errors, and we can see the wrong road, instinctively. By our faith we will come to a closer union with Christ, a deeper dependence on him so that he will be able to guide us through the difficulties, the obstacles, the confusions and the errors that we are likely to meet in this way of renewal. So prayer for faith is absolutely the most fundamental thing and we must not forget how great is the power of God to give us what we need and in the most surprising ways. For example, I just had a letter from a person who claimed that she had been an atheist for quite some time. She is a young married woman, evidently baptized a Catholic in childhood and brought up perhaps as a Catholic. She could see no logical reason for the existence of God. People had been trying to prove to her the existence of God and it made no impression on her whatever. All this had no meaning whatever to her and she simply could not believe in God. Until all of a sudden one day, instead of arguing with her, some priest said, "Look, God wants your heart, not your mind: God loves you!" All of a sudden this whole thing collapsed and there broke through into her heart the sense of who God really is and what He really meant to her. She saw how desperately she needed this God who loved her, who was calling her to accept His love and to love Him in return. The whole reality of the thing just simply burst through, whereas arguments about the existence of God and intellectual discussion of God and so forth had meant nothing. So it is with us. We get so involved in all these intellectual and abstract discussions that we forget the basic—this call of God's love to us, urging us to love Him in return and to open our hearts to Him and to give Him our hearts so that He may fill them with love and faith. So let us then do this. Let us pray for faith, let us pray for an increase of faith and give ourselves, totally, completely, and with perfect confidence to the God who loves us and calls us to His love.

In closing, let me quote a sentence from Clement of Alexandria which I just happened to turn up in some notes here. Comparing the Christian to Ulysses on his ship as he travelled in his journey homeward, he speaks of how Ulysses escaped the lure of the sirens by being tied to the mast of his vessel. This has traditionally been a kind of image of the soul resisting the allurements of what does not really concern it. Clement of Alexandria compares the Christian to Ulysses bound to the mast. It is a good image of our life and its restrictions. He says:

Bound to the wood of a cross, thou art free from all danger of destruction. God's Logos will steer thy ship and the Holy Pneuma or the Holy Spirit will give thee a safe return to heaven's harbor.

So let us consider our own lives in the light of this image, and, trusting God, remain bound to the wood of the cross; so that dying with Christ and rising with him we may be brought to union with him forever in heaven by his Holy Spirit.

OTHER IMAGE BOOKS

OTHER IMAGE BOOKS

A WOMAN CLOTHED WITH THE SUN – Edited by John J. Delaney (D118) – $1.25

INTERIOR CASTLE – St. Teresa of Avila (Translated by E. Allison Peers) – (D120) – $1.45

THE GREATEST STORY EVER TOLD – Fulton Oursler (D121) – $1.45

WE AND OUR CHILDREN – Mary Reed Newland. Counsels for molding the child in Christian virtues (D123) – 95¢

LIVING FLAME OF LOVE – St. John of the Cross (Translated by E. Allison Peers) – (D129) – $1.45

A HISTORY OF PHILOSOPHY: VOLUME 1 – GREECE AND ROME (2 Parts) – Frederick Copleston, S.J. (D134a, D134b) – $1.75 ea.

A HISTORY OF PHILOSOPHY: VOLUME 2 – MEDIAEVAL PHILOSOPHY (2 Parts) – Frederick Copleston, S.J. Part I – Augustine to Bonaventure. Part II – Albert the Great to Duns Scotus (D135a, D135b) – $1.45 ea.

A HISTORY OF PHILOSOPHY: VOLUME 3 – LATE MEDIAEVAL AND RENAISSANCE PHILOSOPHY (2 Parts) – Frederick Copleston, S.J. Part I – Ockham to the Speculative Mystics. Part II – The Revival of Platonism to Suárez (D136a, D136b) – $1.45 ea.

A HISTORY OF PHILOSOPHY: VOLUME 4 – MODERN PHILOSOPHY: Descartes to Leibniz – Frederick Copleston, S.J. (D137) – $1.75

A HISTORY OF PHILOSOPHY: VOLUME 5 – MODERN PHILOSOPHY: The British Philosophers, Hobbes to Hume (2 Parts) – Frederick Copleston, S.J. Part I – Hobbes to Paley. Part II – Berkeley to Hume (D138a) – $1.45; (D138b) – $1.75

A HISTORY OF PHILOSOPHY: VOLUME 6 – MODERN PHILOSOPHY (2 Parts) – Frederick Copleston, S.J. Part I – The French Enlightenment to Kant (D139a, D139b) – $1.45 ea.

A HISTORY OF PHILOSOPHY: VOLUME 7 – MODERN PHILOSOPHY (2 Parts) – Frederick Copleston, S.J. Part I – Fichte to Hegel. Part II – Schopenhauer to Nietzsche (D140a, D140b) – $1.75 ea.

A HISTORY OF PHILOSOPHY: VOLUME 8 – MODERN PHILOSOPHY: Bentham to Russell (2 Parts) – Frederick Copleston, S.J. Part I – British Empiricism and the Idealist Movement in Great Britain. Part II – Idealism in America, the Pragmatist Movement, the Revolt against Idealism (D141a, D141b) – $1.45 ea.

OTHER IMAGE BOOKS

RELIGIONS OF THE WORLD (2 Volumes) – John A. Hardon, S.J.

THE R

MOME

CHRIST

CHRIST

THOUG

WE NE

McAfee Brown (D267) – $1.45

A 72 – 4